REDCASTLE

A Place in Scotland's History

To: Cathy and Brian

Enjoy!

REDCASTLE

A Place in Scotland's History

GRAHAM CLARK

Graham

ATHENA PRESS
LONDON

REDCASTLE
A Place in Scotland's History
Copyright © Graham Clark 2009

ISBN 978 1 84748 563 2

First published 2009
ATHENA PRESS
Queen's House, 2 Holly Road
Twickenham TW1 4EG
United Kingdom

Every effort has been made to trace the copyright holders of works
quoted within this book and obtain permission. The publisher apologises for any
omission and is happy to make necessary changes in subsequent print runs.

Printed for Athena Press

Acknowledgement

The author wishes to place on record his thanks to the North Kessock and District Local History Society, who successfully applied to 'Awards for All' for a grant to support the publication of this book.

'Awards for All' provides grants to local organisations to assist community development. The author has assigned all royalties from the sale of this book to the North Kessock and District Local History Society, so that the funds generated can be used to encourage the local community to investigate and learn about the heritage of this part of the Black Isle.

Preface

I set out to research the history of our house, and soon discovered the obvious. Quarry Cottage did not exist in isolation but was an integral part of the 'micro-village' of Quarry of Redcastle. My research, therefore, was extended to include the other houses, as well as the ruins of the old school, Redcastle pier and Redcastle quarry – these collectively comprising the micro-village. It was supposed to end there, but some members of the North Kessock and District Local History Society, knowing that the extensive and fascinating history of Redcastle needed to be written, persuaded me to expand my research yet further to encompass the whole of Redcastle.

This was a problem, because unfortunately I am neither a historian nor a native of Redcastle. This means that I possess neither the historical expertise nor the intimate local knowledge to write a 'true' history of Redcastle – one in which the information gleaned from archival and documentary evidence would be interwoven with an understanding of the underlying historical, political and economic contexts. In consequence, I would describe this book as a narrative based on the primary source documents and other records that I have discovered relating to Redcastle.

The documents and records that I have consulted were located in numerous archives. Those in which I spent most time were the Highland Council Archives and reference libraries in Inverness and Dingwall, the National Library of Scotland in Edinburgh and the National Archives of Scotland (at both Register House and West Register House) in Edinburgh. I also visited the National Archives at Kew in London and the Royal Commission for the Ancient and Historic Monuments of Scotland (RCAHMS) in Edinburgh on several occasions. Others that I visited were the British Library, the London Metropolitan Archives, the libraries of the universities of Aberdeen and Edinburgh, the National Gallery of Scotland, the Headquarters of the Free Church of Scotland, the Archives of Fettes College in Edinburgh and the archives of the Regimental Museum of the Highlanders at Fort George. I am enormously indebted to the staffs of these organisations for the assistance, advice and encouragement that I always received. I have discovered that librarians and archivists rank amongst the most helpful and willing of professionals, and, although it is an overworked cliché, it is true to say that this book could never have been compiled without them.

I also spoke to many local people, most with roots in Redcastle much deeper than mine. They were generous with their time, their memories and (often) their personal belongings. I thank them for allowing me to intrude into their private lives and for all their contributions. Finally, it is important to recognise the importance of the internet. In the comfort of my own home, I was able to explore the local history of Redcastle through the searchable catalogues of many of the organisations mentioned above and the multitude of articles and images posted on the pages of the World Wide Web. Also of particular help were the websites of Access to Archives (A2A), COPAC, the Scottish Archives Network (SCAN) and the online archives available through 'Am Baile' and 'ScotlandsPeople'.

I should emphasise that I have not undertaken any 'original' research – at least, not in the strictest sense. Whenever possible, I have consulted original documentary sources in local and national archives, and have extracted relevant information from them. However, I do not regard such investigations as original, because they neither expand the body of known historical information nor give enhanced insight into any historical events. My studies have only collated what was already documented. In consequence, this text is neither an academic monograph nor a popular history. Nevertheless, by gathering information about Redcastle into a single volume, I hope that I have produced a source document that might, sometime in the future, form the basis of a true social history of Redcastle. Even if I have not achieved that aim, perhaps the many references to the documents that I have encountered will ease that task for some future local historian.

Because I have always attempted to access the original documents, I regularly quote from them in the text. Unless there has been good reason, I have quoted verbatim in both the language and spelling of the original text. In many Scottish historical documents, the text can be tortuous and the spelling can be quaint (and variable) by modern standards. There are also many words that have fallen out of use or are specialist to the context. Where I have deemed a word or phrase unlikely to be understood by the average reader, I have placed in square brackets the modern equivalent of its meaning. Nevertheless, it may be worth keeping a Scots dictionary to hand!

I also place on record the huge contribution made by my wife, Linda. Her unwavering support and encouragement throughout the years of research have been invaluable. She also made numerous helpful suggestions about avenues of research, visited archives on my behalf, drew the sketch map in the Introduction, and discovered many errors when proofreading the manuscript several times. Despite our attempts to be as accurate as possible, in a volume such as this there will inevitably be errors of fact and interpretation. These are entirely my fault and I apologise if a mistake or misinterpretation causes offence. I am also acutely aware that I may have missed important documents that I should have found and incorporated into the text. Please inform me (or the North Kessock and District Local History Society) of any such errors and omissions so that they can be corrected and recorded for the future. I hope you enjoy reading the fascinating and, at times, extraordinary history of this remarkable part of Scotland.

Graham Clark
Quarry Cottage
Redcastle

References

The following abbreviations have been used throughout:

AUSLA   Aberdeen University Special Libraries and Archives, Aberdeen.
BL   British Library, London.
HCRL   Highland Council Reference Library, Inverness.
HCA   Highland Council Archives, Inverness.
LMA   London Metropolitan Archives, London.
NAS   National Archives of Scotland, Edinburgh.
NLS   National Library of Scotland, Edinburgh.
RCAHMS   Royal Commission for the Ancient and Historical Monuments of Scotland, Edinburgh.
TNA   The National Archives, Kew, London.

Contents

Introduction

There have been at least four stately houses in Scotland known as Redcastle: one at Haugh of Urr near Castle Douglas in Kirkcudbrightshire (now part of Dumfries and Galloway); one at Lunan in Angus; and two in Ross-shire (now part of Highland). Of the Ross-shire castles, very little seems to be known of the Redcastle that was located east of Tain near Portmahomack, of which there has been no visible trace since the last remains of its walls were removed in 1870. The subject of this book is the Ross-shire Redcastle that is located on the Black Isle, approximately midway along the northern shore of the Beauly Firth between Spital Shore (in the west) and Corgrain Point (in the east). In the days when parishes were administratively important, Redcastle was the dominant focal point of the parish of Killearnan. Indeed, the terms Redcastle and Killearnan were commonly used synonymously, an error that is still to be found today at the gate of the Killearnan parish church graveyard, on which there is a sign stating 'Redcastle Parish Churchyard'.

Figure A: Aerial view (2008) of the postcode area IV6 7SQ, within which Redcastle is located (reproduced from an original by permission of Mr Jim Bone)

Nowadays, Redcastle scarcely warrants the title of 'village', being little more than a scattered hamlet of twenty-one houses with a resident population of barely forty; its bounds correspond approximately to those of the modern postcode IV6 7SQ (Figure A).

However, in the past, Redcastle was an important centre of local and regional power that sustained a far greater population. In consequence, it can now boast a significant social history as well as a distinctive industrial heritage. These are based around its three major geographical features:

(i)   The medieval royal castle of Redcastle, now in ruins (Figure B) but whose estate lands still sustain major farming and forestry operations.

(ii) Killearnan parish church, built on Pictish foundations and still actively serving as the community centre.

(iii) The now unworked Redcastle quarry, with its distinctive stone pier projecting 150 m into the Beauly Firth.

Figure B: The Redcastle (2008)

These three features form the loci of the three principal groups of houses (or micro-villages) that comprise Redcastle: 'Milton of Redcastle'; 'Killearnan' and 'Quarry of Redcastle'. (It should be noted that the term 'Killearnan' is here

14

used specifically to describe the immediate area around the parish church, rather than generically to refer to the whole parish.) Although each micro-village was undoubtedly a community in its own right, the residents of Killearnan and Quarry of Redcastle have always relied on Milton of Redcastle for the facilities provided by a shop, an inn, a mill and a smithy, as well as the services of local shoemakers, carpenters and tailors.

Arguably, other nearby locations do not strictly form part of Redcastle, but they are nevertheless integral to the area. These include Greenhill and Chapelton (both of which fall within the IV6 7SQ postcode area). A little further distant are Garguston, Garguston Shore, Blairdhu, Fettes, Newton and the now vacant Parkton and Corgrain. Yet further distant (but within a two-mile radius) are other locations that from time to time have impinged on the history of Redcastle, including Spital Shore, Shore Road, Whitewells, Wellhouse, Redcastle Station, Linnie, Tore, Coulmore and Lettoch. Several older communities (best referred to as 'fermetouns' or 'farmtowns') no longer exist but feature significantly in the early records of Redcastle. Examples are 'Croftmore', 'Hilltown', 'Spital Wood' (or 'Braes of Garguston'), 'Pecks' and 'Burntown'. They are occasionally named on early maps, but otherwise there is little evidence to determine exactly where they were. Pecks was north of Blairdhu, about halfway to Wellhouse; Hilltown was above Corgrain Point and may have taken its name from Gallow Hill, on whose southern flanks it was located; Burntown (sometimes written as Barntown) was between Chapelton and Parkton and may have taken its name from the Redcastle burn; Spital Wood was a significant collection of crofts (often referred to as 'maillers') to the north-west of Garguston Farm; and Croftmore (which may also have been called Smiths Crofts) seems to have been between the Killearnan parish church and Blairdhu, and may have taken its name from crofts (or maillers) that are now farmland.

The whole of the IV6 7SQ postcode area falls within the western reaches of the ancient Redcastle estate. Until the twentieth century, the estate extended beyond Kessock Ferry, six miles to the east of Redcastle itself. The main estate farm is Redcastle Mains, but several others are significant in the context of the history of the area, particularly Garguston, Fettes, Blairdhu and Parkton, but also Coulmore and Lettoch in the eastern reaches of the estate. Through expansion into larger working units, Garguston and Redcastle Mains are nowadays the only two working farms in the immediate Redcastle area. The buildings that formed the steadings of Fettes Farm are now the administrative offices of Fettes sawmill.

The accompanying sketch map provides a visual aid to the relative geo-graphic locations and contiguities of the three principal micro-villages, and includes their distinctive features. It also marks many of the neighbouring locations noted above.

There are four adjoining estates (Tarradale, Kilcoy, Allangrange and Drynie) whose histories from time to time became intertwined with Redcastle. Kilcoy and Allangrange are especially important, because their proprietors were the only other significant 'heritors' of Killearnan parish, together contributing about one-third of the financial burden. Drynie, to the east, lies in the parish of Knockbain, and Tarradale, to the west, lies in the parish of Urray. The first of the Baillie family to own the Redcastle estate was also the owner of Tarradale, and the Baillies (of Dochfour) retain ownership of Redcastle to this day.

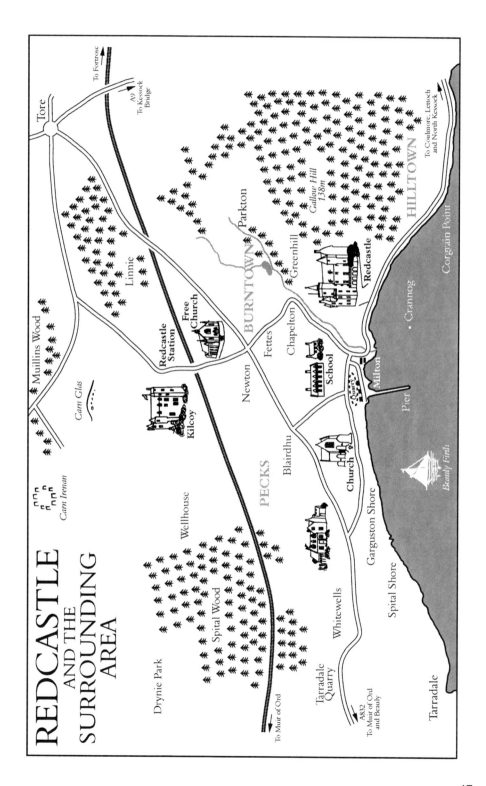

REDCASTLE
AND THE
SURROUNDING
AREA

To Fortrose

Tore

A9
To Kessock
Bridge

Muillins Wood

Carn Glas

Carn Irenan

Linnie

Drynie Park

Wellhouse

Kileoy

Redcastle
Station

Free
Church

Newton

Fettes

Chapelton

BURNTOWN

Parkton

Greenhill

Gallow Hill
138m

Redcastle

HILLTOWN

To Coulmore, Lettoch
and North Kessock

Corgràin Point

PECKS

Blairdhu

School

Spital Wood

Whitewells

Garguston Shore

Church

Milton

Crannog

Pier

Beauly Firth

Tarradale
Quarry

A832
To Muir of Ord
and Beauly

To Muir of Ord

Spital Shore

Tarradale

Chapter 1

THE REDCASTLE

1.1 Etherdouer, Eddirdule and the Reidcastell

The last ice age receded from northern Scotland around 10,000 BC, and it is likely that man began to enter the area as soon as vegetation became established. If human settlements existed around the shores of the Beauly Firth before 5000 BC, evidence of their existence may have been lost in the tsunami caused by a geological slip under the North Sea which is thought to have flooded the east coast of Scotland during the Mesolithic period (8500–4000 BC).[1] The earliest evidence yet discovered of human activity in the vicinity of Redcastle is from samples of burnt timber that appear to be associated with woodland clearance by hunter-gatherers at a site near Tarradale.[2] These have been radiocarbon dated to *circa* 5000 BC. A Bronze Age (2500–500 BC) roundhouse and an enclosed settlement from the middle centuries of the first millennium AD are also thought to have stood on this site.

Several texts describe the archaeological history of the area,[3] and many of the ancient sites have been documented by both the Royal Commission on the Ancient and Historical Monuments of Scotland (RCAHMS) and the Highland Council Historic Environment Record (HER).[4] The oldest surviving man-made structures in the area are two communal chambered cairns, known as Kilcoy South and Kilcoy North. They are over twenty metres in diameter and are of the 'Orkney-Cromarty type' dating from *circa* 3000 BC in the Neolithic period (4000–2500 BC). The South cairn has three chambers and was originally thought to be 'short-horned', but an excavation in 1997 suggested it was round. Skeletal remains, a saddle quern and pottery shards have been recovered from the central circular chamber, which is one and a half metres in diameter. The North cairn contains two chambers, each about three metres long and about two metres wide. The burial cist was reported to be about one metre long and about half a metre wide. Another nearby cairn, known as Carn Glas, is over twenty-five metres in diameter but has been ruined in the past and is now overgrown with gorse. It dates from the early Bronze Age and seems not to be chambered. During an excavation by Capt O H North in 1908, a single cist, 1.1 m long and 0.6 m wide, was discovered to contain bone fragments and a food urn (which is now in the Bowes museum at Barnard

Castle). The urn is about 13 cm tall and about 16 cm wide at the top, reducing to about 8 cm at its base. The external surface is patterned, probably by wrapping braided string around the clay before it was fired. It is thought that there may be other cists in the cairn, as it seems very large for a single burial cist. Photographs of an excavation in 1965 are held by RCAHMS. In September 1881, a stone coffin was discovered about 400 m south of Carn Glas. It was about one metre long, about one metre deep and about half a metre in breadth, and contained a skull, fifteen teeth and some arm and leg bones. There is also a stone cairn near the top of Gallow Hill. It measures about twelve metres in diameter, but its historical provenance is unknown.

Figure 1: The Bronze Age Carn Irenan

The only 'Clava-type' chambered cairn that has been discovered in the Black Isle is the Bronze Age Carn Irenan (or Urnan) near Kilcoy (Figure 1). It dates from *circa* 2000 BC. The cairn stones have been removed, but the central ring of large kerb stones (twelve metres in diameter) is almost complete and four stones of the outer circle of monoliths (twenty-two metres in diameter) remain standing, the tallest being almost two metres high. The cairn housed an oval passage grave (about three and half metres by four and a half metres), but its contents seem to have been removed before any recorded excavations were carried out. In 1881, eight of the outer stones were in place and three of the chamber lintel stones were lying in proximity to the passage.[5]

Figure 2: The Iron Age Redcastle crannog

In the immediate Redcastle area, the earliest indication of human settlement comes from the Redcastle crannog (Figure 2), one of four intertidal Iron Age (500 BC to AD 400) structures in the Beauly Firth.[6] It is named Carn Dubh (Black Cairn) on some early maps, but this name properly refers to the largest structure in the centre of the Firth. A letter written in 1699 by Rev. James Fraser, the minister of Kirkhill Church, records that:

> There are three great heaps of stones in this lake [the Beauly Firth], at considerable distance one from the other, these we call 'cairns' in the Irish [Gaelic]. One of a huge bigness [Carn Dubh] (in the middle of the Frith) at low water is accessible; and we find it has been a burial place by the urns which are sometimes discovered. As the sea encroaches and wears the banks upward, there are long oaken beams of 20 or 30 foot long found; some of these 8, some 12 or 14 foot underground. I see one of them 14 foot long, that carried the mark of the ax on it, and had several wimble-bores [holes made with a hand borer] in it.

In the early twentieth century, Rev. Odo Blundell, who carried out early underwater excavations of many Scottish crannogs, also describes a visit to Carn Dubh and confirms that it is built of round boulders (of around fifty kilograms) and oak beams (of about half a metre diameter) from which burial urns of unknown age are said to have been recovered. Several other recorded visits – for example, by the Inverness Scientific Society and Field Club in 1936 – verify the descriptions given by earlier studies.

In 1882, a lady named Christian Maclagan visited the Redcastle crannog and wrote:

> We visited it at low water … and believe it to be a crannog greatly resembling one in the neighbouring Loch of the Clans, but resting on stronger piles. Our boatmen declared they had often drawn out of it beams 9 or 10 feet long and 3 feet broad, fresh and fit for use. They had great difficulty in pulling them out, which they did by fixing their anchors in a log or pile.

Despite this desecration, some of the piles and crossbeams are still in place. The structure, which is covered for four to six hours at high tides, is located about 300 m from the shoreline and is about two metres high and approximately oval (*circa* forty metres long, and twenty-five metres in breadth). It has been suggested that it was not a true crannog but was a mooring place for ships, a beacon-stance (to warn boats of the sand banks) or the site of a slaughterhouse or tannery that was originally built on a promontory, now submerged by a rise in sea level. However, recent excavations[7] of its structure and mode of construction have confirmed it to be a true marine crannog and, in consequence, it is now catalogued as a protected ancient monument.

During the recent excavations, its construction was shown to be based on a foundation of wattle-sided pits lined with clay and packing stones, supporting a horizontal rectangular framework of worked alder timbers. This framework was held in place with oak piles driven through square cut slots. Above the framework, the surface covering consisted of boulders, beneath which were cobbles, pebbles, sedimentary deposits of sand and clay, timbers and other well-preserved organic remains. Amongst the sediments were found seeds, cherry pips, shells, beech nuts, brushwood, leather fragments, and animal and fish bones. Some of the leather, bone and timber fragments were radiocarbon dated to the latter half of the first millennium BC (later Bronze/early Iron Age).

It is said that an urn recovered from one of the 'island structures' in the Beauly Firth was of Roman origin. This could have been traded further south, and does not necessarily provide evidence of Roman settlement in the Redcastle area. However, it has been suggested that some of the Roman army led by Agricola, which defeated the Picts at Mons Graupius (probably in modern Aberdeenshire), wintered in AD 84 at an encampment at Wester Lovat, near Beauly. Several possible flanking support sites have also been identified, including one at Tarradale that aerial photographs suggest might have been a square fort.[8] Most historians are doubtful that the Romans reached as far north as the Beauly Firth but, if they did, this would be the most northerly point on the British mainland that they reached, because in AD 85 their army withdrew south to defend the Antonine wall.

The earliest written record of human occupation on the Black Isle seems to be given by the Roman geographer Claudius Ptolemy, who – on his *Geographica* map of the British Isles, produced *circa* AD 150 – wrote that the area around 'Varer Aest' (now Beauly Firth) on the eastern shores of Ross was occupied by the Cantae (sometimes Decantae) tribe of Picts.[9] It is thought that the threat of further Roman invasion from the south was a factor in encouraging co-operation between the previously fragmented Pictish tribes and in creating the embryonic Pictish kingdom, which, by the time of the Roman withdrawal from Britain in AD 410, had become dominant in northern Scotland.

Just as the northern shore of the Beauly Firth may have been the limit of Roman infiltration from the south, so too does it appear to have been the limit of Viking infiltration from the north (during the eighth century onwards). No direct evidence for Viking occupation around Redcastle has been discovered, although Bain[10] suggests that Tarradale and Garguston are names derived from a Norse origin and that the Black Isle is the land of the Dubh Ghuile [Black Danes], which became anglicised to 'Black Isle'. An alternative explanation is that the Black Isle is a corruption of Eilean Duth or Eilean Dubhaich [the Isle of St Duthac], which had to be crossed by pilgrims to reach St Duthac's shrine at Tain.[11] A further suggestion is that the term Eilean is a corruption of Allan [a grassy meadow], and that the Black Isle was originally Allan Duth.

The earliest record of the castle that would become known as Redcastle is medieval.[12] In 1179, King William I of Scotland (who was known as William the Lion because he adopted the lion rampant on his shield) marched into Ross-shire with a large army to subdue an insurrection led by Harald Maddadson of Orkney and Caithness. Harald's wife was the sister of Malcolm MacHeth (the 1st Earl of Ross, who had died in 1168, and whose earldom had been suppressed by William). On defeating Harald, and to 'bring Ross and Moray firmly under royal control', William ordered two royal castles to be established, one of which was at Dunscaith on the north Sutor overlooking the Cromarty Firth and the other at Etherdouer (now Redcastle) on the north shore of the Beauly Firth.

There may already have been a castle at Etherdouer by 1179, although there is no evidence of this. If so, it would have been a motte that William ordered to be strengthened. [A motte was built on top of an earth or natural mound, sometimes with a defensive wall (a bailey) around the base.[13] They were mostly constructed from wood with an encircling palisade enclosing a major residence, such as a tower or keep. There are over 100 motte sites known in the north-east of Scotland. Like Etherdouer, most are sited close to a deep-cut stream and near good agricultural land close to the coast, guarding routeways including ferries. Three mottes (Redcastle, Tarradale and Ord) overlooking the northern coast of the Beauly Firth and two (Erchless and Kilmorack) on the northern banks of the Beauly River formed a defensive line protecting Inverness from attack from the north.] The building works at Etherdouer were overseen by William's brother, David, the Earl of Huntingdon. Various sons and grandsons of MacHeth and Maddadson, particularly Donald Bane MacWilliam (a grandson of MacHeth), led further rebellions during which the castle appears to have been briefly captured in 1211 by Godfrey MacWilliam. An act of 1211 pronounced by King William at Nairn refers to 'vassals of Dunfermline Abbey … along with the King's other responsible men … who worked at Etherdouer', probably making repairs.

Several accounts suggest that Etherdouer castle was originally sited further west than the present Redcastle, perhaps at Spital Shore near Tarradale.[14] However, there is no real evidence to support this contention, other than scanty traces of some possible earthworks in a location that has never been specified. One account suggests that Etherdouer was originally located north of the present Redcastle near Chapelton,[15] but most architectural scholars seem to be of the opinion that the present sixteenth-century L-plan tower house probably incorporates the foundations of the twelfth-century motte.[16] Whatever its original location, the castle became known as Eddyrdor (numerous other spellings, such as Edradour, are found), translating from the old Gaelic *Eadar Dha Dhobhar* [between two waters] and thought to be referring to the Beauly and Cromarty Firths. Later, the term Eddirdule (or variants, such as Eddirdail) became more common, and this is thought to translate as 'between the dales'.

During the twelfth and thirteenth centuries, Scottish kings imposed a feudal social and land ownership system by granting charters to supplicant Scoto-Normans as they gradually conquered the old Pictish *mormaers* [provinces, comparable to earldoms]. Their mottes acted as centres of royal administration and local justice, and as garrisons for their militia. *Circa* 1212, towards the end of King William the Lion's reign, Eddyrdor Castle was granted to Sir John Bisset (or Byset). Of Anglo-Norman descent, he was married to the King's sister, Agnes, and his lordship of the Aird already stretched across the Beauly River into Ross. [It is worthy of note that Sir John Bisset's predecessors as Lords of the Aird were almost certainly descendants of 'Gilleoin of the Aird', who lived around AD 830–890 and who is thought to have been the progenitor of the Mackenzie clan, one branch of which were destined to become the owners of Redcastle.] In all probability, Sir John Bisset became the keeper of Eddyrdor Castle for his part in quelling the MacWilliam rebellion of 1211–12. He is also known to have been the founding patron (*circa* 1230) of Beauly Priory, one of three Valliscaulian monasteries (effectively, centres of royal control) founded in Scotland by William the Lion. [The Valliscaulians were a minor French order who, unusually, wore white robes.] The founding of the Priory was subsequently confirmed in the First Beauly Charter by means of a Papal Bull issued by Pope Gregory IX in 1231.[17] Sir John Bisset was later exiled for his part in the murder of the Earl of Athol in 1242, but it is generally thought that he was granted a royal pardon. He died *circa* 1259 and was buried in the Priory, leaving his lands of the Aird equally to his three daughters: Marie, Cecilia and Elizabeth. In September 1278, a Beauly Charter,[18] witnessed by William, Vicar of Eddyrdor, granted occupation of the castle to Elizabeth and her second husband, Andro de Bosco (also known as de Boscho or Besco). [The de Bosco family had also been Scoto-Norman implants into the Black Isle.] In medieval times, nobles who were granted land (or fiefs) were required to pay homage and provide services or pay taxes to the reigning monarch. They generated the funds either by working the land themselves or, more usually, by leasing their land and collecting rent from their tenants. The fiefs were hereditary, but heirs who rebelled or disaffected forfeited their land and rights. It is recorded that Andro de Bosco was charged two merks per annum, payable to the monks of Beauly Priory, for his tenure of Redcastle. In 1294, their daughter Mary (who had been born in Eddyrdor in 1250) and her husband, Hugh of Kilravock, inherited the 'tenement [the permanent tenancy] of Edirdowyr' and adopted the title 'de la Ard' for their descendants. They also granted Elizabeth's brother-in-law, Sir David de Graham, a *davach* of land at Culcowy (nowadays known as Kilcoy).[19] To this day, the two estates of Redcastle and Kilcoy comprise the greater part of Killearnan parish.

[The Scots system of money was roughly equivalent to that of England until the fifteenth century when it began to depreciate. By the Act of Union of the Scottish and English Parliaments in 1707, the relative value of £1 Scots was 20 English pence (1/8d) and 1 merk (two-thirds of £1 Scots) was worth 13½ English pence (1/1½d). Although it was officially abolished in 1707, Scots money continued to be used for many years thereafter. Until decimalisation in 1971 in both England and Scotland, 12 pence (d) = 1 shilling (s), 20 shillings = £1, and £1-1s-0d = 1 guinea. A *davach* (or *ounceland*) was a measure of land for tax assessment purposes and represented the amount of land that could produce tax to the value of one ounce of silver per year. It was therefore of variable area, but was generally considered to be about 416 acres or four ploughgates. A ploughgate (or *pleuch*) was defined as the amount of land that a team of eight oxen could plough in a year. An oxgate was a plot of land measuring one-eighth of a ploughgate. A pennyland was the area of land that could generate tax to the value of one silver penny.]

It appears, therefore, that the castle of Eddyrdor in the thirteenth century formed part of the provincial lordship of the Aird. For how long it remained in the ownership of the de la Ard family does not seem to be recorded, although it is known[20] to have been in the hands of Andrew de Bois in 1278 and probably remained so until at least 1296. During his 'pacification' of Scotland, Edward I reached Elgin in 1296 before turning south to Scone. However, his armies proceeded beyond Elgin and are known to have captured Urquhart Castle (Loch Ness), so they must have been in the Inverness area. Edward's forces also reached Inverness and the Black Isle in 1303 where, according to the Wardlaw Manuscript,[21] they 'destroyed all our forts… Inverness, Beufort, Dinguall, all demolished'. Tarradale is also known to have been captured at that time, although not destroyed, as it was given to Edward's ally Alexander Comyn, brother of John Comyn, Earl of Buchan.

It is not unlikely that Edward's troops may also have been to Eddyrdor, but there seems to be no record of this. However, several medieval and late-medieval finds have been retrieved from the fields around Redcastle, the earliest of which is a shield-shaped heraldic horse pendant measuring about three centimetres high and two centimetres wide, with three white lions (the arms of England) on a red enamelled background[22] (Figure 3).

Figure 3: Edward I horse brass, discovered by Colin MacLeod in 2002 and dated to the thirteenth or fourteenth century (© Crown Office)

It has been dated to the thirteenth or fourteenth century and is currently in Inverness Museum, claimed for the Crown by Treasure Trove Scotland. Close by was also found an Edward I (1272–1307) long-cross hammered penny, minted in London in 1281–82. These finds suggest that Edward I or senior members of his entourage might have visited (or camped at) Eddyrdor during the pacification and may even have captured it in 1296 or 1303. Thereafter, it is known that in March 1308 Robert the Bruce, after his defeat of the Earl of Buchan at Inverurie, recaptured (and destroyed) Tarradale castle, but once again there seems to be no record of them at Eddyrdor.[23] This is probably because Redcastle was in the hands of the Earl of Ross, who had made a truce with Bruce. As a reward for his part in the liberation of the area, Robert subsequently granted the earldom of Ross to his brother-in-law, Hugh of Ross. This probably included Eddyrdor. By 1367, Eddyrdor had passed into the possession of the Frasers of Lovat. A local tradition, based on the saying *'Frisealich am boll a mine'* [Frasers of the boll of meal], suggests that the Bissets changed their name to Fraser in return for protection and this is the reason why the Frasers appear in Redcastle. [It was common for supporters of the clans to adopt the clan name. Those that retained their own identity but still showed allegiance to the clan chief became known as 'septs'.]

The earliest reference to Eddyrdor in the Register of the Great Seal of Scotland[24] is in 1426, when James I confirmed to James Douglas the 'land and barony of Eddirdule'. Thus, by the early fifteenth century, Eddyrdor (now generally known as Eddirdule) had fallen into the hands of the Douglases and had become established as an estate held in *'liberam baroniam'* [free barony] within the earldom of Ross and the lordship of the 'Ardmeanach'. [This translates as the 'height between' and there are several spelling variants; it was the medieval name for the Black Isle.] This gave Eddyrdor powers to hold a baron court at which disputes could be settled and criminal cases such as assault, theft and accidental manslaughter could be heard. Eddyrdor had therefore become a significant local administrative centre and the name 'Eddirdule' (and its variants) probably referred to the district or parish, whilst the castle itself gradually became known as the 'Reidcastell' (or 'Redcastell').

The proprietorship of the Douglases came to an abrupt end in 1455, when Hugh Douglas, the Earl of Ormond, who then owned 'Reid Castle and its lands of Ederdail and Ardmannock', was executed by James II (1437–60) along with the Black Douglases and their allies, many of whom had become too powerful and had fallen out of favour with the Royal House of Stewart. In consequence, the castle and its lands were forfeited to the Crown and formally annexed in perpetuity by an act of annexation[25] dated 4 August 1455. The castle is named in the act both as 'Eddirdaill, callyt Ardmanach' and 'the Redcastell with the lordschippis in Ross pertenying tharto'. After the annexation, James II gave custodianship of the Ardmeanach to his ally Sir Andrew Moray, the Earl of Moray. Andrew appointed his half-brother, Celestine (otherwise known as 'Gillespie of the Isles'), as the keeper of the castle of Eddirdule. Thereafter it is recorded that the castle and lands of Redcastle briefly passed into the hands of the Bishop of Caithness, but in 1481 James III (1460–88) granted the 'fortalice of the *Rubeum Castrum* [Red Castle] … in the King's land of Ardmannach … for singular favours' to his second son, James Stewart, Marquis of Ormand. Thus commenced a period of eighty-seven years in which the title of Duke or Earl of Ross, together with the custodianship of Redcastle, was mainly in the hands of members of the Royal House of Stewart. It is said that in 1488 Redcastle was briefly taken by Hector Mackenzie (1st of Gairloch) to garrison his troops on his retreat from defeat at the Battle of Sauchieburn, during which James III was killed. If the castle was moved to its present site, it would probably have been during this period of royal possession – perhaps originally as a royal shooting lodge and later as the sixteenth-century L-plan tower house that is still evident today. [Many of the wooden mottes in north-east Scotland were rebuilt in stone during the fourteenth and fifteenth centuries, commonly on the original site but sometimes close by.[26]] Notably, it is only in 1516 that the Exchequer Rolls[27] first name the castle as 'Reidcastell' (although this name was in use prior to 1455 – for example, in the Registers of the Great Seal,[28] suggesting that a rebuild in local red sandstone was undertaken in the fifteenth century). James Stewart died in 1504 and Eddirdule briefly came into the hands of Hutcheon de Ross. However, in 1511, James IV (1488–1513) granted it back to the Stewarts (actually to Henry Stewart) for two merks per year. James V (1513–42) granted the custodianship (for £30 Scots per year) in 1523 to James, Earl of Moray, who sublet it to Henry Stewart for £12-18/-. In 1526, it is recorded that the Reidcastell was in the custodianship of Henry Kempt of Thomastoun, who resigned the let in 1535, when 'the keeping of the Reid-castell … with the mill and alehouse' was granted to Robert Innes of Innermarky for nineteen years, in recognition of good service in the army.

At the end of the custodianship of Robert Innes, a royal charter[29] from Mary Queen of Scots (1542–67), written in Latin and dated 8 July 1554, assigned 'to Johanne Stewart, son and heir apparent of Robert Stewart … the lands of Culcowy [Kilcoy], Drumnamark, Muren and the Mill of the Reid Castle'. Later, in 1564, Mary granted the title of Earl of Ross and Ardmannach to her second husband, Lord Henry Darnley. This included 'the lands of Easter Kessock with the ferrie of Kessokkis … Kilcowye, Drumnamark, Murane, with the mill of Newtoun of Reidcastell … lands of Gargustoun … Hiltoun … and the fortalice of Reidcastell'. Mary visited Redcastle during her progress to the northern Highlands in the summer of 1564. It does not seem to be recorded who was in actual occupation of the castle at that time, but it is said that Mary, on viewing the southern panorama from the castle, declared it to be a '*beau lieu*'. From that day, the name of the Firth changed from 'Varar' (or 'Varrar') to 'Beauly'.

Henry Darnley was murdered in February 1567, and Mary Queen of Scots was forced to abdicate in July 1567 after she was imprisoned in Loch Leven Castle. Her infant son, James VI, fell heir to the Scottish crown with the Earl of Moray as his regent (or protector). Far-reaching changes in the ownership of Reidcastell were imminent.

1.2 The Mackenzies of Redcastle

The modern estate of Redcastle originated in 1568, when the fortalice of Redcastle was granted by James VI to Kenneth Mackenzie and his wife, Lady Elizabeth Stewart (the daughter of the Earl of Athol), as a reward for his 'valiant actions' during the arrest of Mackay of Farr, who had been pillaging and plundering parts of Sutherland. Kenneth was the 10th Baron of Kintail (known as Coinneach 'Na Cuirc' or Kenneth of the Whittle, a name apparently gained for his expertise in carving wood). Kenneth died that same year and was buried in Beauly Priory. His eldest son, Murdoch, had died in childhood, hence his second son, Colin 'Cam', fell heir to the Barony of Kintail and his third son, Rorie (known as 'Ruairidh Mor', the great or big Rorie), inherited Redcastle.

Ruairidh Mor already held lands in the diocese of Ross at Ardafallie (in the parish of Kilmuir Wester) through a charter given on 28 July 1560. He then successively acquired charters of the 'Lands of Killearnan' in 1578, the 'Milns of Redcastle' in 1584, and of 'Gargiestown, Newton of Redcastle and Easter Kessock' in 1589. All three are recorded in the 'Inventory of the Writs of Redcastle', although there is not a detailed description of the earliest record.[30] The charter of 1584, witnessed by his brother, Colin Mackenzie of Kintail, is 'to Roderick Mackenzie of Ardafalzie of the Milns of Redcastle with astricted multures [proportion of grain to which the mill owner was legally entitled] thereof, tofts [homesteads], crofts and pertinents, pertaining thereto, lying in the lordship of Ardmeanoch and Shire of Inverness proceeding upon a Charter granted by John Stewart of Muirens [nowadays, Lettoch], dated at Edinburgh, 1 January 1584'. It also refers to 'the yearly payment to his Majesty of the sum of three merks upon the ground of the miln lands at two terms in the year', and to the Charter of Confirmation[31] by James VI 'in favour of the said Rorry Mackenzie of Ardafallie of the mill, mill lands, multures and pertinents of Redcastle, dated 15 June 1584'.

Ruairidh Mor of Redcastle and his brother, Colin 'Cam' of Kintail, successfully commanded the Mackenzies in many of their clan skirmishes, but seem at times to have acted somewhat lawlessly against the post-reformation church. For example, in 1572 Ruairidh Mor seems to have enlarged his landholding around Ardafallie by annexing property in Wester Kilmuir that had belonged to Rev. Donald Fraser (I), the 'reformist' Archdeacon of Ross (and minister of

Killearnan church) who was murdered in 1572. Ruairidh Mor is also recorded as having ejected the Bishop of the Cathedral at Fortrose and having taken up residence in the west tower in 1573. A few years later, the brothers appear in the first record of Redcastle in the Register of the Privy Council of Scotland,[32] in which Christiane Scrymgeour, the wife of Alexander, Bishop of Ross, claimed that 'Coline M'Kainzie of Kintail and others', with force and violence, in December 1577 had taken the Bishop's house in Chanonry and had apprehended all the servants, 'specialie Williame Irvin, messenger, Thomas Merschell and Johnne Robertsoun; quhilkis [upon which], being taiken, were careit immediatlie to the said Colinis hous of the Reidcastle'. Colin 'Cam' and Ruairidh Mor failed to appear at the court hearing and were 'denounced rebels and put to the horn and to escheat' [ie proclaimed as bankrupts and made to forfeit their property to the Crown]. Technically, this judgement ended the Mackenzies' ownership of Redcastle, but the court's decision was never implemented.

Several years later, in 1586, the brothers were detained in Edinburgh to answer charges laid by Macdonald of Glengarry accusing them of 'being art and part in the cruel murder' of several of his clansmen. They are named as: Rodoric M'Allester; Gorie M'Allester, his brother; Ronnald M'Gorie, the son of the latter; John Roy M'Allane v'Allester; John Dow M'Allane v'Allester; Alexander M'Allanroy, servitor [servant] of Rodoric; Sir John Monro; John Monro, his son; John Monro Hucheoun; and the rest of their accomplices who were allegedly murdered in various locations, including the 'Ardmanich', 'Lochcarroun', 'Lochbrume' and 'Ross in the Sheriffdom of Inverness'. These murders had allegedly been committed during various ambushes, but on 5 October 1586 the brothers were given a royal pardon[33] for these and 'all other past crimes'. Thus the legal ownership of Redcastle by Ruairidh Mor Mackenzie was retrieved.

The charter of 1589 is described in the Redcastle Writs[34] as a:

...charter by Sir William Keith of Delny, Knight and Baron, in favour of Roderick Mackenzie of Ardafallie and heirs male of his body carrying the name and arms of Mackenzie of all and whole the lands of Gargiestown and Newton of Redcastle with Alehouse Croft thereof, commonly called the Smiddy Croft thereof, with the manor house, castle and fortalice of Redcastle and all and sundry the parts and pendicles thereof lying in the Barony of Delny, Lordship of Ardmeanoch and Shire of Inverness. As also of all and whole the lands and village of Easter Kessock with the ferry of Kessock as also with the fishings commonly called the Stell of Kessock, alehouse of Kessock and all and sundry parts, priviledges, commodities and pendicles thereof, lying in the said Barony of Delny newly erected into the Lordship of Ross and Shire of Inverness, dated at Edinburgh, 30 May 1589.

[Sir William Keith was the Master of the King's Wardrobe and had been rewarded with the Barony of Delny in August 1587. The charter under the Great Seal of James VI allowed for the Barony to be passed to Sir William's heirs or his assignees.[35] His assignment of part of the Barony to Ruairidh Mor Mackenzie was ratified in the records of the Parliaments of Scotland,[36] dated 5 June 1592.]

As further evidence of the existence of the Redcastle estate by the end of the sixteenth century, there is a record in the Exchequer Rolls of Scotland[37] for 1595 that the lands of Gargastoun and Reidcastell within the Lordship of Ardmannoch had been set in 'few-ferme to Rorie Makenze' for £100 (Scots money) per year. [A feu-ferme was a heritable grant of land conferred on a family in return for an annual payment.]

There is a story recounted by MacLean[38] that one of Kenneth 'Na Cuirc' Mackenzie's sons (who is unnamed) fell in love with the daughter of Cameron of Lochiel during a hunting trip in Lochaber and that they married at Lochiel in 1598 and thereafter lived in Redcastle. There seems to be no record of Kenneth and Lady Elizabeth having any other sons (although they had six daughters in addition to their three sons). The story certainly does not refer to Ruairidh Mor, because his wife was not a Cameron, but was Fionnaghal (also recorded as Florence, Flora or Finguela), the daughter of Robert Munro (15th Laird of Fowlis). Their marriage took place *circa* 1569 and their eldest son, Murdoch, was born *circa* 1575.

On 2 December 1608, James VI of Scotland (who had also become James I of England under the Union of the Crowns in 1603) gifted under his Great Seal the charter of Redcastle and its lands to Ruairidh Mor and Murdoch.[39] The original charter is in Latin and provides for the male succession of '*Roderico MacKenzie, et Murdaco suo filio et heredi apparenti, villa et terrarium de Gargastoun, Redcastle*, etc.' [ie Roderick Mackenzie, and his son and heir apparent, the town and lands of Garguston, Redcastle, etc.]. It also refers to 'the power of holding a fair yearly in the town of Newtown of Redcastle on the 7th day of July called St Andrew's Day, the said town being the Principal Village of the Lordship of Ardmeanoch'. As a consequence of the hereditary charter of 1608, a dynasty of nine generations of Mackenzies was destined to own Redcastle for almost another two hundred years.[40] Ruairidh Mor (1st of Redcastle) and his wife, Fionnaghal, had two sons and seven daughters. There is one record of a second wife, Margaret MacLeod, but this seems unlikely as Ruairidh Mor died in June 1615 and Fionnaghal is known to have remarried.

As provided for in the 1608 charter, the Redcastle estate was inherited in June 1615 by their son, Murdoch (2nd of Redcastle). Murdoch had married Margaret, the daughter of William Rose, Baron of Kilravock, in June 1599. They had five sons and six daughters, but the eldest son, Kenneth, died as a young man *circa* 1627 and Redcastle was inherited on Murdoch's death in 1638 by his second son, Roderick or Rorie (3rd of Redcastle). Rorie, who had been born in 1608, married Isobel, the eldest daughter of Alexander Mackenzie (1st of Kilcoy), in 1629, and they had four sons and a daughter. In common with his ancestors, Rorie was a staunch royalist. On 10 July 1645, he was appointed by Charles I to the Committee of War for the Sheriffdom of Inverness to oversee preparations to defend the town against Cromwellian covenanting forces. As a member of that committee, he was listed in 1646 by the anti-royalist Committee of Process and Moneys and offered protection in return for a 'loan' (sometimes described as a 'fine') of £2,000 Scots. However, he was not prepared to be blackmailed and refused to make the payment, a decision that was to have far-reaching consequences.

Charles I was executed by Cromwell on 30 January 1649, and Charles II was proclaimed King of Scotland on 5 February 1649. However, Inverness Burgh declared loyalty to the Parliamentarians on 9 February 1649 and this precipitated an attack by the royalist Mackenzie and Mackay clans (many of which came from Easter Ross and the Black Isle, including Rorie Mackenzie of Redcastle). The clans took control of the town and destroyed the fort on Castle Hill. Rorie Mackenzie is recorded as a signatory to a letter sent to the new King by the 'Committee of War' held in Inverness on 26 February 1649, in which they advise of the need for an additional garrison to protect crown lands around Inverness. Parliamentary Covenanters under Col David Leslie soon retaliated and recaptured the town.

The clans fled back to Ross-shire, pursued by the Covenanters, and in May 1649 Rorie was captured near Fortrose and taken to the 'Bog of Gight' (now Gordon Castle, Fochabers), where he was imprisoned. In his absence, Redcastle held out as the last castle in Scotland loyal to the Crown. However, it was laid siege and ultimately captured, looted and set on fire by the troops of Col Gilbert Kerr (or Carr). During the skirmish, Rorie's second son, Kenneth, (whom Rorie considered to be 'the flower of all offspring') was shot and died after falling from the ramparts.[41] Rorie was later released on payment of 7,000 merks Scots (paid by Ross of Bridly, his maternal uncle) but, after seeing the ruins of his castle, soon afterwards in 1650 'with grief and melancholy died of a malignant fever, lying in a kiln barn, having no other lodging left him'.

Colin Mackenzie (4th of Redcastle), Rorie's eldest son, was born in 1630. He was known as Colin 'Niag' [Colin the Brave] and was a Collector of Customs in Inverness when he inherited the remains of Redcastle in 1650. A year later, he received a charter from the 'Lord Protector of the Common-wealth of England, Scotland and Ireland' [the title used by Oliver Cromwell], giving him authority to re-enter the castle. In December 1656, he received a further charter (sealed in 1657) allowing him to collect rents from the lands attached to the castle[42] (Figure 4).

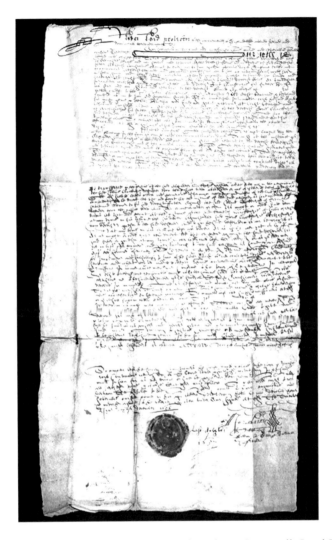

Figure 4: The 1651 and 1656 charters issued by Oliver Cromwell, Lord Protector, to Colin Mackenzie, 4th of Redcastle (© The British Library Board. All Rights Reserved, Add Mss 61570)

In March 1661, Colin was awarded decrees for £11,266-13-4d Scots to repair the castle and for £10,214-16/- Scots in compensation for the value of the contents and farm produce that were pilfered prior to the burning, allegedly by Lieuts Laurence Dundas and William Govan under the command of Col Kerr.[43]

Figure 5: Redcastle after its rebuild circa *1670*
(from Tranter, The Fortified House in Scotland*)*

The rebuilt castle was in the form of a Scottish L-shaped tower (Figure 5). It is said that the stone used for the new building came from a deposit of red sandstone which was quarried nearby, hence was likely to have been taken from the Redcastle quarry. An engraved stone that is still set into the northern elevation of the castle displays the initials 'R. MK' and is dated 1641. The significance of the date is not clear, but the initials probably refer to Rorie Mackenzie (3rd of Redcastle), Colin's father. The stone had perhaps survived the burning of the old castle and may have been incorporated into the rebuilt castle either in memory of his father or as a mark of allegiance after the restoration of the monarchy in 1660. [A subsequent appeal in 1690 by Elizabeth Kerr, Col Gilbert Kerr's daughter, declared that although her father had been 'the commanding officer of the troops then in the north', he had never given an order relating to the burning of Redcastle, so there should not have been a decree against him. He had paid £1,000 sterling, the entire value of his estate of Nether Ancrum (near Roxburgh), which Elizabeth petitioned to be paid back by Colin Mackenzie. The Committee for Fines and Forfeitures was appointed to call Colin to answer the petition, but no record of the outcome seems to exist.]

Charles II ratified the Great Charter of Inverness (originally granted by James VI on 1 January 1591) on 3 April 1661. The ratification[44] states that the burgh could hold an annual fair on each 7 July 'called St Andrew the boy's fair, which was held at the Redcastle now demolished and cast down'. However, Colin Mackenzie (4th of Redcastle), having won damages to restore his castle, protested 'that the ratification passed in favour of the town of Inverness shall be in no way prejudicial or derogatory to … [his] right of the public fair held yearly upon 7 July at Newton of Redcastle … [and] shall stand in full force and be valid in time coming, not withstanding of the said ratification as if the same had never been passed nor granted'. The protest was successful and on 3 July 1662 Colin was 'served heir' to his father, thus legally regaining the estate and restoring the right to hold St Andrew's fairs at Redcastle. Various artefacts that have recently been found in the fields around Redcastle indicate that these fairs and markets had been held in the area from at least the fourteenth century.[45] These include: a fourteenth-century annular ring brooch; an Edward III (1327–77) silver groat; and a James VI (1567–1625) silver sixpence, dated 1624.

In 1678, Colin Mackenzie (4th of Redcastle) purchased Coulmore for 17,000 merks, and on 11 August 1679 he and his eldest son, Roderick, 'resettled' the Redcastle estate back to the Crown. This allowed Charles II to issue a 'Charter of Resignation, Confirmation and Novodamus and New Erection' on 2 January 1680. This was one of the key events in Redcastle history, because on this date Redcastle became 'erected' as a Scottish Burgh of Barony. Strangely, the barony had initially been created in 1676 but Colin had failed to register it, a fact only discovered after his death. The Redcastle Writs[46] record the creation of the barony as follows:

By this Charter the said whole estate is erected into a Barony, called the Barony of Redcastle, and the village of Milntown of Redcastle is erected into a Burgh of Barony, called the Burgh of Barony of Redcastle with all the usual privileges, a weekly market to be held every Wednesday in the said Burgh. Another free fair to be held on 24 February yearly, besides that formerly granted to be held the 7 July yearly. With tolls and customs of said weekly market and two yearly free fairs with favour to the Proprietor, to elect and chuse baillies of said Burgh of Barony, deputes, clerks, dempsters [officers who pronounced court judgements and sentences], officers and other members of court and to change the same yearly. To erect and build a market cross, a tolbooth and prison, with liberty to build a sea port or harbour at said Burgh for the reception of ships and vessels and to impose and exact anchorage, shore dues and others at said port and harbour which is declared to be a free sea port or harbour in all time coming.

The arms of the Burgh[47] are described as 'azure, a hart's head cabossed and attired with ten tynes or, within a bordure indented chequy, of the second and first'. The crest is described as 'a man's heart in flames, within two palm branches disposed orle-ways, all proper' with a motto *'Ferendum et sperandum'* [we must endure and hope]. The existence of a market cross is recorded by the RCAHMS, but unfortunately the supporting bibliographic documentation, as well as the cross itself, appears to have been lost.

Colin Mackenzie (4th of Redcastle) amassed a substantial fortune from his business interests and was described as 'a very opulent man' who in 1661–68 was the elected MP for Inverness-shire.[48] He was married twice; firstly to Isobel, the eldest daughter of Sir Kenneth Mackenzie (1st of Coul), by whom he had three sons and four daughters, and secondly to Marjory, the daughter of John Robertson of Inches, who was a widow. To ensure that the succession of Redcastle followed the children of his first marriage, Colin made an entail of the Redcastle estate [a deed by which the legal descent of land can be secured to a specified succession of heirs and substitutes, also known as a 'tailzie']. It is recorded in 'The Families of Redcastle and Kincraig from Kenneth "Na Cuirc", 10th Baron of Kintail' [known as the Findon Tables] that he wrote a manuscript history of Redcastle[49] but it does not appear to have survived. At least two records state that Colin was killed at Killearnan in 1704, although neither the circumstances of his death nor any corroborating evidence is given. He is said to be buried in Killearnan parish church.

Colin 'Niag' Mackenzie's eldest son, Roderick (5th of Redcastle), was known as 'Ruairi Dearg' [red Rory]. He married Margaret, the daughter of James Grant of Freuchie, 16th of that ilk, and had four sons and three daughters. The eldest was Roderick, 6th of Redcastle, known as 'Ruairi Mor' [big Rory]. In February 1718, prior to his death in 1725, Ruairi Dearg 'disponed' [made a property conveyance of] the estate to himself in 'liferent' and to Ruairi Mor in 'fee'. One of the terms of the transfer was that Ruairi Dearg could not undertake borrowings in excess of £20,000 – presumably the estate's valuation at that time, but perhaps also an early indication that the family's finances were becoming insecure.[50] [A liferent enabled the owner of a property to continue to receive its rental revenue without the right to dispose of its capital. A disposition in fee transferred the heritable rights to the property.]

There are different accounts of Ruairi Mor's marital history.[51] He was first married in October 1707 to Margaret, the daughter of Sir James Calder of Muirtoun. In one version, Margaret is said to have been a widow who already had seven sons and a daughter and who, with Ruairi Mor, had a further fourteen sons and two daughters, thus having twenty-four children in total. The alternative version that they had only two sons (Roderick and Colin) is more probable. After Margaret's death, Ruairi Mor married his second wife, Katherine, daughter of Charles Mackenzie of Cullen, in 1727. One account suggests that they had a further twelve sons and two daughters, but the more probable version is that there was one daughter (Florence). [Colin Mackenzie, Ruairi Mor's second son, married Mary Cochrane, daughter of Sir John Cochrane of Waterside. They had a son, Kenneth Francis Mackenzie, born in 1748, who became a barrister in the West Indies and purchased the large cotton estate of Lusignan in Demerara, thus peripherally involving the Mackenzies of Redcastle in the slave trade.[52]]

The disposition of Redcastle in 1718 to Ruairi Mor (6th of Redcastle) was to prove the turning point in the fortunes of the Mackenzies of Redcastle. Ruairi Mor immediately began to sell off some portions of Wester Kessock, for example, in 1718 to John Matheson of Bennetsfield. Then he agreed to sell further portions of Easter and Wester Kessock to Capt Hugh Fraser of the 3rd Regiment of Foot Guards. The proceeds of these sales were probably intended to pay off the estate's debts, but the latter proved to be disastrous and commenced a long-standing legal dispute that continued for over twenty years and precipitated the eventual bankruptcy of the Mackenzies of Redcastle.[53] In May 1729, Capt Fraser protested over the ownership of the land that he had purchased and sued Ruairi Mor for 17,000 merks 'for clearing and disburdening the said lands of the debts and incumbrances therein … and if not sufficient … [Ruairi Mor] should be necessitate to wadset [provide a written pledge transferring land as security for a redeemable debt] or make sale of any part of his other lands and estate by Whitsunday next … or wadset right of town and lands of Killearnan and Spittle and pertinents extending to four chalders or thereby yearly at 2,000 merks per chalder for the space of nine years'.

[In Scotland at that time, 4 lippies = 1 peck; 4 pecks = 1 firlot; 4 firlots = 1 boll; and 16 bolls = 1 chalder. Unfortunately, these measures of volume were variable according to district; for example, a chalder could be any size between twenty and sixty-four Imperial bushels (1 bushel = 8 gallons). To avoid any confusion due to local variations, some contracts specified that a chalder meant the measure used at Leith.]

It seems that Ruairi Mor was unable to produce any legal documentation proving his title to the disputed land and therefore his right to sell. Whilst it is possible that the title deeds may have been destroyed during the sacking of Redcastle in 1649, it seems more probable that the land in question was the land that had been seized by Ruairi Mor's great-great-great-grandfather (Ruairidh Mor, 1st of Redcastle) after the murder of Rev. Donald Fraser (I) in 1572. Capt Hugh Fraser was the great-grandson of Rev. Donald Fraser (I), so he may have been aware that Ruairi Mor would not have had legal title to the land, and there may have been an element of revenge in his actions. Whatever his motives, Capt Fraser sued successfully and Ruairi Mor was liable for the decreed penalties. However, these do not seem to have been fully paid and further instruments of protest were issued by Capt Fraser in November 1730, October 1733 and April 1736. In the latter, Capt Fraser petitioned the High Court in Edinburgh for £2,000 Scots of penalty and for the grant of a wadset of 2,000 merks per chalder, plus the remainder of sums due (500 merks) and 'a valid and ample wadset of the right of said lands in terms of the decreet against him with horning ... and upon Rory Mackenzie's refusal and neglecting to do ... be liable to Capt Hugh Fraser for all past damages, interest and expenses'. [A horning was a court warrant enforcing a person to act as ordered or be proclaimed an 'outlaw'.] Unfortunately, Ruairi Mor's response was a less than sensible act of desperation. He arranged, in collaboration with his son Roderick, for a set of counterfeit title deeds to be drawn up. They are first recorded in 1739, but it was not until 1745 that Ruairi Mor finally admitted the fraud and provided a 'condescendence' [a legal admission of guilt] for a 'reduction' [an action whereby illegal deeds are rendered null and void]. Ruairi Mor admits in his condescendence that he was 'universally repute and known to be by the whole country a weak and facile man easily imposed upon' and that he was impecunious due to being influenced to grant bonds without securities and take out 'groundless law suits before inferior courts' and borrow (against bonds) 'such sums as £250 ... when no person in the country would credit Redcastle a shilling'. One such groundless law suit had been in 1739 over land ownership against his brother-in-law, Sir Thomas Calder of Muirtown, and the Grahams of Drynie.[54]

Furthermore, it was stated in his condescendence that he was 'a man of no expense tho' possest of an estate of about five hundred pounds of yearly rent ... [yet] did involve himself in upwards of forty thousand merks of debts which brought a sequestration of the estate [in 1735]'. The condescendence and reduction was granted in 1745 by George II on payment of 'damages that the Lords shall set'. This was recorded as £350 in February 1747, when Ruairi Mor issued a Bond of Corroboration [a confirmation by a debtor of his original debt] to the Sheriff Clerk of Ross in which 'dates and contents of the same be one or other of them are all false, forged, feigned, counterfeited, used and devised by the defender or some other person or persons in his name ... and therefore should be ... reduced, retreated, rescinded, also annulled, decerned and declared to have been from the beginning to be now and in all time coming void, null and of none avail, force, strength or effect'. In consequence, the Sheriff Court decreed that Ruairi Mor should 'make payment to the pursuers of such sum or sums as the Lords shall please'.

It is not clear whether the case ever reached the High Court, as Hugh Fraser, who had become a Lieut-Colonel in 1741, was killed at the Battle of Fontenoy in 1745. Ruairi Mor subsequently issued a 'memorial' to the Fraser heirs, stating that he was due no expenses in consequence of the original decree of April 1736, as it had been 'most surreptitiously and unwarrantably extracted'. Furthermore, the lands he had sold to Col Fraser 'consisting of 25 pieces of charters etc., all of which are no ways noticed in the extract as they ought to have been … so it is hoped the Colonel's heirs will not further push for the penalty or expenses'. It seems that this tactic worked, as there appear to be no records to suggest that Ruairi Mor was pursued any further.

Ruairi Mor Mackenzie died at Redcastle in April 1751 and was succeeded by his eldest son, Roderick (7th of Redcastle), known as 'Ruairi Ban' [fair-haired Rory]. Ruairi Ban had married Hannah (or Anna), daughter of Thomas Murdoch of Cambodden, in 1730 and they had four sons and five daughters. Their eldest son, Murdoch, was born in December 1744 and his baptism is recorded in the Killearnan Old Parish Registers. However, he died in infancy in 1746. The second daughter was Miss Mary Mackenzie, who had been Ruairi Mor's housekeeper and had retired to live in Lettoch. Two years before her death in 1828, aged ninety-six, she is said to have styled herself as '86 years and upwards' and to have regularly remarked when her food was not to her liking that it would be 'very good for servants, but don't like it for myself'.

Hannah died at the age of thirty-nine in April 1755. Despite Ruairi Ban's financial plight, he seemed determined to make 'Lady Redcastle's' funeral a lavish event. A detailed statement of account[55] from William Mackintosh, a merchant in Inverness, itemises a total of £21-16-8¼d for clothing, including 'a full suit of mourning for your self, 4½ yds black cloth … £4-14-6d'. The drinks bill amounted to £24, of which £16-16/- was for sixteen dozen bottles of claret. Amongst the other miscellaneous items itemised on the bill were rice, flour, cinnamon, grey pepper, vinegar, mustard, nutmeg, a mort cloth, coffin nails (but not the coffin itself) and four chamber pots and basins, presumably for guests staying at the castle. The total bill amounted to £64-11-2¼d.

Whilst Ruairi Mor's management of the estate's financial affairs had been little short of disastrous, Ruairi Ban's seems to have been little better. In the period 1756–61, he became embroiled in a complex legal case involving the purchase of 'bear' [barley] through numerous intermediaries.[56] The bear was part of a cargo of 'flour and victual' that was on a ship berthed at Inverness. The cargo belonged to Alexander Gray, who had employed his brother, Robert Gray, to dispose of it. However, Robert had sent another brother, John Gray, to Inverness to sell the cargo at the quayside. On 18 May 1756, Ruairi Ban wrote a letter to John Gray:

> Give Alexander Mortimer, my servant, what bear or flour he calls for; as also give Donald Macgrigor in Kessock three bolls bear, and Alexander Mortimer's receipt will oblige me to pay the price of what he receives against Martinmas next to Mr Robert Gray.

Some time later, Alexander Gray raised an invoice for twenty-nine bolls of bear and three bags of flour, requesting that Ruairi Ban pay Daniel Shaw and Mr Macgillivray of Dallcrombie. However, Ruairi Ban refused to settle the invoice because the price (£28-6-6d sterling) was too high. On 2 May 1757, Alexander Gray wrote to Ruairi Ban, pressing him to settle his account and explaining that he owed money to Daniel Shaw and Mr Macgillivray, and that he had asked many of the other purchasers of the cargo to settle their accounts in this way. Ruairi Ban still refused to pay.

It then transpired that Alexander Gray was also in considerable debt to others. One of his debts was to William Mackintosh of Balnespick, which his brother Robert had promised to honour using the money due from Ruairi Ban. As Ruairi Ban had not paid his account, Robert used the invoice as part of the debt settlement with Mackintosh of Balnespick on 15 March 1758. Five days later, the invoice was presented to Ruairi Ban by Colquhoun Grant, Mackintosh of Balnespick's agent. However, Ruairi Ban refused to accept it and on 28 March 1758 an action for non-payment was issued to Ruairi Ban's agent in Edinburgh, John Dingwall WS [Writer to the Signet – a solicitor with powers to write documents stamped with royal, or Session Court, seals]. Ruairi Ban's response was extraordinary. He raised an action of 'multiple poinding' on the grounds that he was not indebted to Robert Gray because the bear had belonged to Alexander Gray. He also claimed that his money had been 'arrested' by John Dingwall and William Fraser (also a WS in Edinburgh) and therefore they, as well as Mackintosh of Balnespick, were subject to the multiple poinding.

The case was heard by Lord Coalston, who, on 2 August 1758, ordained that Robert Gray was required to declare whether or not he was the trustee of his brother Alexander's cargo. Robert duly produced his written statement that the cargo had been the property of his brother, Alexander, and because of the various debts he had transferred the invoice for Ruairi Ban's account to Mackintosh of Balnespick. One year later, on 2 August 1759, Lord Coalston requested evidence to support Robert's claims against his brother, Alexander, so that he might determine how far these claims might be transferred to Mackintosh of Balnespick. Robert responded on 29 August 1759 and produced vouchers showing that he had agreed to relieve Alexander's debts to Lady Strathnavar (£200 borrowed in 1751), Messrs Coutts Brothers (£430), William Hogg (£310), Col Scott (£500), George Ross (£200) and various others, amounting to a total of £2,100. Lord Coalston made a judgement on 17 June 1760, in which he:

> …having again considered the above debate, with the declaration of Robert
> Gray, the oath of Redcastle and other writings produced, finds it proven by the

said declaration that the meal and bear for which the receipt libeled on was granted, was the property of Alexander Gray and that Robert, in whose name the receipt was taken, had no further interest therein than as Factor employed by his brother Alexander, for disposing of the cargo: but in respect it is instructed by the writings now produced, that Robert was creditor to Alexander in large sums, partly due to himself and partly in which he stood bound for Alexander, and that no evidence is offered that these debts are cleared; finds that Robert was entitled to retain the receipt libeled on, and sums therein contained, as a security for the claims due to him by Alexander; finds that the sums contained in the said receipt were effectually conveyed to Balnespick the pursuer, by Robert's draught on Redcastle; and that his right in virtue of said draught is preferable to the arrestment used by Mr Dingwall as creditor to Alexander.

Thus it was made clear that Ruairi Ban could not refuse to pay Robert Gray on the basis that the bear was the property of Alexander Gray, and neither could his agent (John Dingwall WS) arrest the payment. Furthermore, as advised in a paper of 1 March 1761 entitled 'Information for William Mackintosh of Balnespick, pursuer, against Roderick Mackenzie of Redcastle and John Dingwall WS in Edinburgh', Robert had transferred his right of payment to Mackintosh of Balnespick; therefore the latter had legal claim against Ruairi Ban for the invoiced amount. It has to be assumed that Ruairi Ban eventually settled his dues.

Another complex case in which Ruairi Ban became engrossed involved a trust fund that had been set up by Sir Robert Munro of Fowlis in 1738, assigning a merchant named John Gordon as sole trustee.[57] The trust held £2,000 'for the use of Mr Andrew Drummond, and others named' in a heritable bond that had been granted to Andrew Drummond. One of the persons named in the bond was Ruairi Ban, who owed money to Andrew Drummond. However, John Gordon had died and Andrew Drummond petitioned the Court of Session in June 1758 for payment. Ruairi Ban objected, refusing to pay on the grounds that the debt was due to John Gordon and that only his heirs could petition the court.

On this occasion, Ruairi Ban was successful, the court deciding that the trust was not heritable and that only the trustee could act on behalf of the trust, not the person for whom the trust was created. However, the court also determined that Andrew Drummond could, with the agreement of Sir Robert Munro and John Gordon's heirs, raise a 'declaratory adjudication' transferring the trust fund to him, thus ensuring that Ruairi Ban would become liable to settle his debt. In the meantime, the court 'found it necessary to sustain Ruairi Ban's objection'.

By 1761, Ruairi Ban must have been struggling to maintain the fabric of

Redcastle, although he seemed to keep up the outward signs of affluence. For example, the gardens still seemed to be well maintained. The Right Rev. Robert Forbes, an episcopalian bishop undertaking a tour of the dioceses of Ross and Caithness, visited Redcastle on 20 August 1762 and provides a vivid description of the estate at that time:[58]

> Reidcastle is an ancient strong-hold, the iron gate still entire. I went upon the top of the house, five stories high, and had a most beautiful prospect of a fine corn country up and down the Frith of Kessock or Bewly, which is the head of Inverness Frith, Reidcastle being close upon it, and thereby having the advantage of salmon and white fish. Here are fine gardens declining to the sun, and abounding with fruits, apricocks, peaches, nectarines, bonum-magnums [plums], etc., diversified with a den of barren wood, a rivulet running down the bottom, upon which are two corn-milns. The kirk and manse of Reidcastle are near to the seat, which is also beautiful with two birch woods.

Notably, the bishop's account is silent about the condition of the castle itself.

In 1768, Ruairi Ban was forced to take paid employment in a valiant attempt to keep the estate solvent. He was appointed Collector of Customs at Inverness harbour, which necessitated the vacation of Redcastle and relocation to Inverness. Although the consequencies of the land sale between Ruairi Ban's father (Ruairi Mor Mackenzie) and Lieut-Col Hugh Fraser of Wester Kessock had been quiescent since 1745, various boundary disputes between the adjoining estates in the Wester Kessock area re-emerged. For example, in December 1784, Dame Henrietta Fraser, Hugh Fraser's only child, lodged an action in the Court of Session claiming 'encroachment' of her Wester Kessock estate jointly by Col Graham of Drynie and the Mackenzies of Kilcoy, Allangrange, Pitlundie and Redcastle. (Henrietta was the widow of Sir Charles Erskine and had remarried to Thomas Davies, a surgeon in Bristol.) The action was inconclusive on the basis of it being unspecific about the nature of the encroachments and when, where and by whom they had been carried out. However, the five defenders were required to produce proof of ownership (or commonty) and any agreements over the boundaries between the estates. Their respective proofs are laid out in a 'memorial' presented to the court in June 1785, which makes reference to various charts and plans that delineated the respective boundaries.[59]

The boundary between the Redcastle and Allangrange estates had been surveyed in detail and agreed in September 1776, the document describing the exact locations of each of the fifteen march stones along the boundary.[60] Two of the stones near the Auldieg burn were marked 'A' (Allangrange) on the north side and 'R' (Redcastle) on the south side. However, the boundary between Redcastle and Wester Kessock was less well defined. The memorial of 1884 admits that the marches were not particularly described in any of the title deeds, but claimed that possession had been made clear in previous depositions to the court and were well known to run 'from the Moray Frith in the South … [in an] irregular direction north by Coldwells or Gailvillers, and along the Ferry Road leading from Bogallan and Allangrange', and that 'Redcastle's tenants have been in constant use of pasturing their cattle, casting fuel, feal and divot agreeable to the march ascertained by the Court [in 1784]'. Thus, the land ownership dispute between the Frasers and the Mackenzies, which had commenced in 1729, was at last settled. During the course of the boundary disputes, Ruairi Ban Mackenzie had become blind and was unable to continue in his employment as Collector of Customs. He died, heavily in debt, in May 1785 and was succeeded by his second son, Kenneth (the eldest son, Murdoch, having died in childhood in 1746).

1.3   Kenneth Mackenzie, 8th of Redcastle

Kenneth, 8th of Redcastle, was born in Redcastle on 21 February 1748 and was baptised by Rev. Donald Fraser (II) on 29 January 1748. Little is known of his early years, other than that his youth was described[61] as 'opprobrious' and it was said that he was 'the terror of Inverness mothers and the aversion of Inverness tradesmen' and that 'it was the general belief that he would come to a bad end'. Kenneth married Jean (known as Jeany) Thomson, the daughter of the Accountant-General of Excise in Scotland, James Thomson. The marriage is recorded twice in the Old Parish Register of St Cuthbert's in Edinburgh, firstly on 11 (or 17) August 1767 and, secondly, on 24 August 1767. The second entry is a correction of the first, which records Redcastle as being in Angus-shire.

On the day before the wedding, Ruairi Ban Mackenzie, 7th of Redcastle, had disponed the estate to himself in liferent and Kenneth in fee, thus ensuring as a clause in the marriage contract that Kenneth was the legitimate heir to the Redcastle estate. Immediately afterwards, on 26 August, Kenneth joined the Armed Forces, being commissioned as an Ensign (2nd Lieutenant) in the 33rd Regiment of Foot.[62] The regiment was initially stationed at Ciudadella (Minorca) but returned to England in 1768, during which time Kenneth was assigned to act for the Marquis of Lothian during his election in November 1768 to the House of Peers (Lords).[63] This entailed attending the Lord Chancellor's office in Westminster Halls to arrange dates for the formal qualification, paying the various fees, obtaining the Certificate of Qualification and delivering it to the Secretary of State for transmission to Scotland. Kenneth's bill for the expenses he incurred amounted to £38-15/-, which he received from the Lords Commissioners of His Majesty's Treasury in October 1769.

Few of Kenneth's army records have survived but, according to the Notifications of Army Commissions and the Regimental Muster and Pay Books,[64] during 1769–71 the regiment was stationed at Derby and Chatham Barracks and he was assigned to recruiting duties. (It is recorded[65] that Kenneth was once cursed by a witch for 'kidnapping' her only child; possibly as a consequence of the recruiting activities to which he appears to have been regularly assigned.) On 27 February 1771, he was promoted to Lieutenant and until 1775 was variously posted to Portsmouth, Gloucester, Cirencester, Tewkesbury and Plymouth, but with extensive periods of leave, particularly during 1774. The regiment was stationed at Cork and Dublin (Ireland) during 1775, and on 26 October 1775 Kenneth was promoted to Captain (although his army commission remained as a Lieutenant). Shortly afterwards, he transferred to the 1st Battalion of the 37th Foot and served during 1776 with this regiment in New York during the American War of Independence, and would probably have been in active service in the Battle of Long Island in August 1776.

It is not clear what happened in America, but it seems possible that Kenneth was taken prisoner during the battle or subsequent actions. There is a record[66] in 'American Archives' of a Capt McKenzie being a prisoner in Philadelphia jail and being released on parole on 18 September 1776 due to 'the state of his health requiring air and exercise'. After his release, he appears to have returned home and in 1777 to have been assigned to the 'Old Regiment' of the Scots Brigade in Holland, probably to recruit for the regiments fighting in America. In the 'Papers illustrating the history of the Scots Brigade in the Service of the United Netherlands', it is recorded[67] that 'Capt Mackenzie and his Lady' (notably, not his wife) attended a communion service with Col Gordon's Company in Nijmegen on 31 August 1777.

On 15 January 1778, Kenneth joined the 78th Regiment of (Highland) Foot[68] 'from the Dutch Service'. [This regiment was raised in 1778 by Lieut-Col Kenneth Mackenzie, Earl of Seaforth, and subsequently became known as the 72nd Foot and then the Seaforth Highlanders. The first inspection of the men and the equipment that had been issued to them was held at Elgin in May 1778.] Initially, the regiment was stationed partly at Ayr and partly at Edinburgh Castle. Kenneth Mackenzie of Redcastle is recorded in the regimental history as the sixth in seniority of the original seven captains, but – in view of his Scots Brigade Dutch service – he considered that his seniority should have been higher and wrote from Ayr to Lord Barrington, the Secretary at War, who responded on 15 August 1778 as follows:

To Captain Kenneth Mackenzie of Lord Seaforth's Regiment, Ayr, North Britain – Sir, I have received the favour of your letter of 30th past. In arranging the officers of Lord Seaforth's Corps, attention was had to the respective claims of persons proposed. Preference has also been given to the King's Service. After this explanation, I hope you will not think any injustice has been done to your pretensions. I have the honour to be, etc., Barrington.

In August 1778, the 78th Regiment was ordered to muster at Edinburgh Castle and prepare to be transported to Jersey/Guernsey en route to India. Whilst in Edinburgh, Kenneth was in command at the Tolbooth in Edinburgh when a mutiny, known as the 'Revolt of the Wild Macraes', took place. The Macraes were a sept of the Mackenzies of Kintail, and around 400 of them had enlisted as 'fencible infantry' [infantry who serve only within the British Isles]. However, it was rumoured that they had been 'sold' to the East India Company and were to sail to India, a rumour that turned out to be true. When ordered to march to Leith to board ship, the Macraes revolted and set up a camp on Arthur's Seat. A number of Macraes were held in the Tolbooth, and a party of the mutineers went there to demand the release of their comrades. Capt Kenneth Mackenzie is said to have 'bared his breast and told the mutineers to strike if they dared, but he would not release a man', and thereby gained a reputation for bravery.

Kenneth may have been brave, but he was also a 'touchy, ill-tempered, unreasonable man' who was not popular. Whilst stationed in Guernsey, he was excluded from entering the mess by his fellow officers, a ban that was only overturned after a formal warning from his (acting) Commanding Officer, Major James Stuart. He was also in the habit of engaging in duels, and is recorded as having 'in little more than one week quarrelled with, and fought no less than three duels with, different Gentlemen of the Corps'. During another altercation, on 24 May 1779 in the officers' mess, Kenneth was involved in a brawl with Lieuts McKenzie and Marshall and hit Capt-Lieut Fraser with a bottle of wine. He was immediately placed under arrest by Major Stuart, and next day wrote a letter of apology. However, he received a response from Major Stuart stating that his 'conduct and behaviour yesterday afternoon in the scandalous affair with Capt Fraser was such as cannot be overlooked … and now have it in your option, either immediately to send a resignation of your commission as Lieutenant or prepare to stand a General Court Martial'. Kenneth subsequently sent his letter of resignation and was given three months on leave whilst permission to sell his commission was obtained. However, he returned to Guernsey in August 1779 requesting that a court martial be convened.

The Court Martial was carried out under a warrant issued by the

Hon Paulus Amilius Irving, Lieut-Governor of the Island of Guernsey, appointing Lieut-Col Alexander Fotheringham Ogilvy of the 83rd Foot as its President.[69] It commenced on 20 September 1779, the charge being 'insulting Capt-Lieut Fraser and behaving in an improper manner unbecoming the character of an Officer and a Gentleman'. After several adjournments, the verdict was announced on 2 October 1779. Kenneth was found not guilty of any infamous or scandalous behaviour or of any such misbehaviour as is intended by the 23rd Article of War 15th Section, but 'guilty of a breach of the 3rd Article of War 20th Section to the prejudice of good order and military discipline in insulting Capt-Lieut Fraser and using improper language to Lieuts McKenzie and Marshall and for the indecent and irreligous expression made use of by him in his affair with Capt-Lieut Fraser unbecoming the character of an Officer and a Gentleman'. In consequence, Kenneth was sentenced to be 'reprimanded by the Commanding Officer of the garrison in the presence of the Corps of Officers of the 78th Regiment and that he shall ask pardon, in their presence, of Capt-Lieut Fraser and Lieuts McKenzie and Marshall', thus escaping a custodial sentence or a dishonourable discharge.

Kenneth's unfortunate behavioural traits also carried over into his marriage with Jean Thomson. They had six children: three sons (Roderick, born *circa* 1770; James, born in Redcastle in August 1772 but who died in childhood; and Hector, born *circa* 1775) and three daughters (Boyd, born in Inverness in August 1768; an unnamed daughter, born *circa* 1773; and Hannah, born in Redcastle in January 1777). However, in 1780, Jean brought a successful divorce action against Kenneth.[70] The grounds were that he 'casting off the fear of God and disregarding his matrimonial vows and engagements, has for several years past totally alienated his affections from his legal wife and given up himself to adulterous practices, fellowship and correspondence with lewd and wicked women … and to having carnal and adulterous conversation, intercourse and dealings with them'. It transpired that in Inverness, Aberdeen, Edinburgh and Leith he had been 'frequenting houses of bad fame known or reputed to be bawdy houses … one of which women brought forth a child in adultery … by which carnal intercourse he became infected with the venereal disease'. Many witnesses testified against him during the consistorial hearing held in Edinburgh on 12–13 September 1780. For example, a landlady, Ann Forrester, described how she had arranged for him to sleep with 'a girl of pleasure' named Jean Davidson. The fee had been half a guinea (10/6d), from which Ann had retained 2/6d for his lodgings and 1/- for a barber, the remainder (7/-) being given to Jean.

At the conclusion of the hearing, the Court decreed that they:

...hereby find and declare that the said Kenneth Mackenzie has forfeited, annulled and lost all the rights and privileges of a lawful husband and hereby find and declare that the said Jean Thomson is free of the said marriage and that she is at liberty to marry any free man as if she had never been married to the defender and that she was entitled to all the rights and privileges competent to her by law and otherways as if the defender were naturally dead.

In consequence, Jean was eventually awarded a liferent annuity of £160 and the sum of £200 in lieu of her share of furniture.

After the divorce, in what could be interpreted as an attempt to earn his fortune and pay off the Redcastle debts, Kenneth offered to raise an Independent Company of Foot. By 1 February 1781, he had enlisted the required 100 men and wrote[71] from Chatham Barracks to Lord Amherst, Commander-in-Chief of HM Forces, to:

...request that your Lordship would be pleased to order an inspection of them. When they are inspected I hope your Lordship will have the goodness to recommend me to his Majesty that my commission may bear as early date as possible. I have not yet been able to find proper persons to recommend for my subaltern commissions but I hope to be indulged to keep them open some little time. And as the raising of the Company has been attended with great expense I beg your Lordship will notify to the Commanding Officer of 78th Regiment his Majesty's permission to sell my Lieutenancy in that Regiment. I beg leave to note that the sooner directions are given at the War Office for the necessary warrants, subsistence, arms, accoutrements and clothing the sooner my Company will be fit to go on service.

The Inspector General, Col Samuel Townsend, carried out the inspection of Kenneth's Company and presented his 'Return of the Age and Size of the Men of Captain Mackenzie's Independent Company' on 7 February 1781 to Lord Amherst. In the covering letter, he reports that:

The non-commissioned officers, drummers, and privates of an Independent Company raised by Capt Mackenzie of Lord Seaforth's Regiment, consist of 1 captain, 5 sergeants, 5 corporals, 2 drummers and 98 private men, exclusive of 2 deserters now on their way from the Savoy [the London prison for deserters]. They have been minutely examined by the staff surgeon here, who reports the whole perfectly sound in health and fit for services. I have inspected them with great care and have found it necessary to reject 13 as very unfit to serve for the reasons assigned opposite to their names [ten were under size, being 5'2" or less; one was too old, being forty; one was too young, being fifteen; and one had an ulcerated leg]. The front and rear ranks are really good, the centre indifferent, several of them being young, well-read and likely to grow. I have been induced to pass them, tho' rather under size. The 11 wanting to complete will be produced without delay.

One week later, on 16 February 1781, the staff surgeon (Dr Gloster) forwarded a list of a further nine men whom he had examined and found fit for His Majesty's service. Together with the two deserters, this completed the 100 men necessary to form the Company, in practice most being convicted criminals awaiting transportation. Kenneth immediately wrote to Lord Amherst to confirm the completion of his Company of '96 privates, 5 sergeants, 5 corporals and 2 drummers, men approved of by Col Townsend. I therefore flatter myself that your Lordship will be pleased to let me have my commission as soon as possible.' There remained the problem of finding a suitable Ensign and Lieutenant. Kenneth initially wrote[72] to Lord Amherst on 9 February 1781, recommending Thomas Hawkshaw as his Ensign and attaching a character reference which agreed a fee of 180 guineas and described him as 'about twenty years of age, good figure, well educated … and in every respect properly qualified for a commission in any Corps'. [The fee referred to the payment that had to be made to Kenneth's agents, Gray and Ogilvie, to secure an army commission.] This appointment appears to have been agreed, as the Army Lists[73] confirm Thomas Hawkshaw as holding the Ensigncy in 1781.

The 78th Regiment of Foot, to which Kenneth was still formally attached, served in Jersey/Guernsey until June 1781, when they set sail for India. They fought against the French in the Battle of Jersey in January 1781, but it seems probable that Kenneth was by then forming his Independent Company. One monthly staffing return from Guernsey survives.[74] This records Kenneth Mackenzie on 1 May 1781 as 'on duty – recruiting' and is transcribed in War Office records as 'on Lord Amherst's leave'. Kenneth subsequently took it upon himself to write on 10 July 1781 to Lord Amherst about the vacant Lieutenancy[75] in his Independent Company. He explains that the formation of his Company had been financially assisted by George Ross of Gray and Ogilvie, and requested that Alexander Fraser, described as a 'near relation' of George Ross, be appointed. Alexander had served for three years in the Marines:

…but the effects of youth entangled him with some wench who diverted him from his duty till at last by loytring his time too long he was suspended. He has now come to his senses and I know him to be gallant enough. He has not a shilling to give me, Mr Ross having been so displeased with his former conduct that he will not do anything for him. As I have felt a little of the weight of misfortune myself I must feel for my countryman a wish to regain him from misery and try by attending to his future conduct to restore him to society and the favor of his friends. I therefore beg earnestly your Lordship will grant the favor of recommending him as my Lieutenant, if your Lordship wishes to fee the young man a line directed to him care of Messrs Gray and Ogilvie, Spring Gardens, will find him.

Perhaps not surprisingly, Kenneth's proposal was turned down by the Commander-in-Chief, who annotated the letter: 'I have received his letter and approve very much of the contents, til it comes to the recommendation of Mr Alexander Fraser for Lieutenancy on which subject I cannot say anything sincerely.' The Army Lists name two Lieutenants who subsequently served with Kenneth: George Mawby and James Williamson.

Kenneth's letter of 10 July 1781 was written on board the *Mackarel* transport ship at Spithead, Portsmouth. His Company had been assigned a somewhat unattractive mission, attached to the HM *Leander* to sail to the west coast of Africa to attack and capture Dutch trading settlements.[76] Survival rates in West Africa were low due to illness, and there were few opportunities for officers to make money. Kenneth's disappointment is clearly inferred in his letter to Lord Amherst:

> Pardon me my Lord, for letting a syllable escape from my lips or pen, that has the least appearance of reluctance to the service I am going on. Assure yourself my Lord, of the contrary. I have youth, inclination and a good Highland stamina that I firmly believe equal to any climate or fatigue. Tho Africa does not promise so many diamonds as Asia, yet the former may afford as many laurels. Your Lordship has been pleased to intrust me with a field to operate on, and I trust in God I shall be enabled to do my duty to the satisfaction of my gracious Master. It does not become a soldier to promise much. I shall only beg leave to add, my Lord, that Mackenzie shall never shrink from any service or his duty, but with a cheerful heart lose the last drop of his blood when the cause of his good and gracious King demands it.

HM *Leander*, in convoy with the transport ship *Mackarel* and HM sloops *Alligator* and *Zepher*, sailed via Cork and Madeira to reach Sierra Leone in January 1782. Although there were criticisms of Kenneth's leadership and tactics, successful assaults on Dutch forts were carried out, and on 2 March 1782 the Captain of the *Leander* recorded in his log[77] that they anchored off Fort Mouree, a fort that had been built in 1598 as the first permanent Dutch trading station in West Africa. At 2 p.m., they sent 'a lieutenant, 1st lieutenant of marines, 1 sergeant, 2 corporals, 20 seamen, 39 marines from the *Leander* with scaling ladders and ammunition, etc. on shore to attack the Dutch fort [Mouree] … [and at 4 p.m. they sent] the 1st lieutenant to the fort with a flag of truce to demand the surrender of the fort'. Initially, the Dutch refused to surrender but, after reinforcements were called up from HM *Alligator*, the ship's log records that the Dutch 'sent a flag of truce that the fort would surrender to the English' and that the Captain had 'sent an officer [unnamed, but likely to have been Kenneth] on shore who took possession of the same'. The following two days were spent taking on board the Dutch prisoners and unloading '112 kegs of gunpowder and various kinds of stores' before the flotilla set sail to attack another fort.

Kenneth remained at Fort Mouree (in the Gold Coast, now Ghana) to command the garrison attached to the fort. With little else to do, he seems to have turned his attention to enriching himself. His activities included pirating two neutral trading ships – one Belgian (at that time part of the Austrian Netherlands) and one Portuguese – and employing his soldiers on a plantation which he claimed as his own. He also quarrelled with his officers, some of whom resigned their commissions, and gained a reputation as a cruel leader who had his men savagely flogged for trivial offences. Subsequent to one of his officer's resignations, he appointed Kenith Murray Mackenzie, alias Jefferson (said to be his cousin), as his Adjutant, but they quarrelled and Kenith hid in the neighbouring 'Black Town' to escape a flogging. However, Kenneth threatened to fire his cannons on the town, so next day (4 August 1782) Kenith was returned to the fort. Kenith was tied to a handspike and placed in front of a nine-pound cannon. A soldier by the name of John Plunkett was then ordered at pistol point to light the fuse of the cannon. Kenith was fired into the air and 'the body was found in a very mangled state at some distance from the fort'.

The extent of Capt Kenneth Mackenzie's nefarious activities was discovered some months later when Commander John Wickey of HMS *Rotterdam* set sail with a 'Victualler and annual Store Ship' in January 1783 with orders from the Admiralty to 'visit and examine the state and condition of the forts and garrisons on the Gold Coast of Africa and to afford them such assistance as they might be in want of'. He arrived at Fort Mouree on 8 May 1783, and next day Kenneth made a formal complaint to him about 'the bad disposition of the natives' and the failure of the Commissioners to supply his troops, stating that 'the garrison had narrowly escaped being starved'. However, the Commander heard other versions from the local population, the soldiers and the Governor's staff. The African chiefs informed him that Kenneth had 'treated them with the greatest cruelty by taking away the best and greatest part of their fish which is their daily food, by cutting their canoes because they would not fish, by suffering the soldiers to plunder their houses and markets of goats, fowls, sheep and cankey [bread], by having fired upon their town and other enormities'. In retaliation, they had surrounded the fort and cut off its supplies, whereupon Kenneth had seized one of the chiefs, stripped him naked, beaten him and threatened to cut him to pieces should he ever return to Mouree.

Commander Wickey also inquired into a complaint made by Capt Hagueron, the Master of a Belgian merchant ship, the *Compte de Flandres*, owned by Romberg and Partners, who described how Kenneth had seized his ship and cargo on 21 March 1782 at Fort Commenda. The ship was carrying brandy which Capt Hagueron was offering to sell for gold dust or ivory. Kenneth had boarded, ostensibly to purchase brandy, but had pirated the ship and set sail for Mouree. On the way, they had met a Portuguese ship, the *Nostra Seigniora do Asuncas*, whose Master was Emanuel Peroni do Fonsoca, carrying tobacco and other goods from the West Indies. Kenneth cut its cables and also took it to Mouree, where he sold the cargos and allowed his soldiers to rob the crews of their clothes, books, charts and other possessions. The Commander also heard complaints from the soldiers that Kenneth had not provided them with clothes or subsistence, although he had received supplies from the Commissary, and that he had cruelly punished them for small offences, including one (Kenith Mackenzie) put to death by a shot from a cannon.

At the conclusion of his inquiries, Commander Wickey put Kenneth under arrest and seized what remained of the cargos. He also took possession of a canister, a bottle, a parcel and a case-bottle, each said to contain gold dust, and two boxes containing some papers and other small matters sealed up. He then set sail for England, having left orders to a Mr Fountaine, a Commissary appointed to supply HM troops, to collect any other items that had been taken from the ships and 'dispose thereof for gold dust and to render an account thereof to the Court of Admiralty'. On arrival, the containers of gold dust and the two sealed boxes were delivered to Lord Sydney, the Secretary of State at the Home Office, and Kenneth was imprisoned in Newgate.

A preliminary hearing was held on 23 October 1783, the outcome of which was to commit Kenneth to trial for the murder of Kenith Murray Mackenzie. During the hearing, Kenneth raised the matter of the lack of witnesses and claimed that his possessions had not been returned to him by Commander Wickey. To progress these matters, on 13 December 1783 Kenneth made a sworn statement[78] that there were 'material witnesses' and that he could not 'safely proceed to trial without their evidence'. He further indicated that at the time of his arrest he had 'delivered or caused to be delivered unto the said John Wickey a list of persons whose evidence would be material and necessary for him to produce upon his trial for any charges that might be brought against him for any part of his conduct while he was stationed in that country [the Gold Coast]'. Included in this list of the persons from whom he needed evidence were: Pindar Crawford (a free trader on the Coast of Africa); Capt Morton (Commander of the *Active* store ship); Sgt Thomas Maples and Corporal William Copeland (both of his Independent Company). Furthermore, Kenneth asserted that HMS *Hyena* had been sent to the Gold Coast to collect these men but had returned without them but, if the Secretary of State so ordered, they could still be transported to England in time for the trial. He also stated that he and his friends had made several applications to Commander John Wickey to have his property returned and had now 'caused an action to be commenced against the said John Wickey for the recovery of the said effects ... some of which are necessary and material in order to enable a proper defence'.

The action taken to the King's Bench in 1784 by Kenneth against Commander Wickey[79] was for the return of '5,000 ounces of gold dust, 6,000 pounds weight of ivory, 1,000 gallons of brandy, 1,000 gallons of wine and 1,000 gallons of rum of the value of £10,000', which he claimed to be the 'lawful prize of furnishing stores to the Dutch ports'. Commander Wickey had recently died, but his sworn affidavit was presented, in which he stated that he 'never received or took into his possession any ivory, brandy, wine or rum or any other things except said ... [four containers of] gold dust and what may be contained in the aforesaid ... [two sealed] boxes'. It was also revealed that Mr Fountaine had sold the remaining plundered cargo for 127 ounces of gold dust and had deposited this in the hands of Mr Miles, the Governor of the Cape Coast Castle. An affidavit from the Belgian envoy, Evan Napeau, was also presented, which claimed that the seizure of the *Compte de Flandres* was made 'in a violent and arbitrary manner and in violation of the Law of Nations at Fort Commenda' and that the *Notrodamo do Assumption* and its cargo had been 'plundered and confiscated and sold without the least form of process'. Letters of complaint, written in French, from the *Ministre Plenipotentiaire* (Belgian Ambassador) and from Capt Hagueron requesting compensation had also been had been sent to Lord Carmarthen, the Foreign Secretary. The outcome of Kenneth's court action was indecisive. The King's Bench ruled that, unless cause be shown to the contrary, further consideration of the proceedings should be postponed until the murder charge against Kenneth had been heard. Thus the disputed gold dust and the sealed containers of papers would continue to be held by Lord Sydney, 'ready to be delivered as the Court shall see fit'. In the meantime, Kenneth languished in Newgate prison. His Independent Company had been disbanded in 1783, and he is recorded from 1784 in the Army Lists[80] as having been entered into the Half-Pay Ledgers[81] at a salary of £44 per half year.

On 12 October 1784, Kenneth received a letter from the Admiralty Office stating that on 17 May 1784 HMS *Termagant* had been 'ordered to proceed to Africa in order to bring to Spithead the persons you desired as witnesses to attend your trial'. As the alleged murder had been committed outwith the territorial jurisdiction of the English courts, and the preliminary hearing of October 1783 had 'vehemently suspected ... the said Capt Kenneth Mackenzie ... to be guilty of the aforesaid murder ... and have certified to us their suspicion', on 6 November 1784 George III requested his Commission of Oyer and Terminer[82] [the commission empowering judges to hear cases] to 'inquire more fully the truth'. This prompted Kenneth to submit a petition to HM Justices of Oyer and Terminer, requesting that they 'take his case into consideration and admit him to bail until the trial of the said indictment and until his evidences shall arrive or to afford him such other relief as the justice and humanity of his case requires'. His justification was that his property had 'been in a most violent manner seized and sequestered, his person imprisoned closely in Newgate upwards of twelve months, his witnesses who are material to prove his innocence withheld by negligence or design' and that 'thro' his sufferings and confinement together with an ill state of health and violent scorbutic [scurvy] and other disorders occasioned thereby your petitioner hath been very near losing and is now in danger of his life'. His application for bail was refused, and a Special Commission of the Old Bailey was finally convened on 10 December 1784 to conduct the trial.[83] Amongst the witnesses was William Copeland, who had been brought back to England by HMS *Termagant*. In his defence, Kenneth asserted that his garrison was mostly composed of mutinous convicts and that Kenith Murray Mackenzie had been their ringleader. However, the jury found Kenneth guilty of wilful murder, but 'in consideration of the desperate crew the Captain had to command' they recommended him to His Majesty's mercy. The judge, nevertheless, sentenced him to be 'hanged by the neck until you are dead, and afterwards your body be dissected and anatomized, according to the statute, and the Lord have mercy upon your soul'.

Accounts of the trial appeared in several newspapers, including the *Edinburgh Evening Courant* of 15 December 1784, which described Kenneth as 'dressed in a full suit of black, his hair powdered and "a la grenadier" ... a well-made tall man, much pitted with the smallpox and about 30 years of age [he was actually thirty-six]' and his character as 'that of a "martinet" [a rigid disciplinarian] too obstinate in his determinations: but vigilant, active and undaunted'.

Despite the judgement, Kenneth did not hang. His execution was postponed and his case was sympathetically taken up by several interested parties, including *The Times*[84] which, on 11 January 1785, published the following article:

The case of Captain Mackenzie, now under sentence of death, when properly considered, is really very interesting to the Army in general. It may be the fate of the best Officers to be appointed to foreign commands, with garrisons in which seditious practices may be exerted, and where the Commander, for his own personal protection, as well as to preserve the fort or settlement which he rules, may be under the necessity of using the same means as Mr Mackenzie. The notion is a very mistaken one indeed, which supposes the interests of that gentleman only affected the question upon which he was tried.

This article seems to have sparked off a legal argument of some substance. Two lengthy letters, one from 'A Constitutional Crown Lawyer' were published in *The Times* on 19 and 24 January 1785, and a booklet[85] was published privately and anonymously by 'An Officer'. Laboriously entitled 'Address to the Officers of the British Army containing a sketch of the case of Captain Kenneth Mackenzie, who was lately tried by a Special Commission at Justice Hall in the Old Bailey, for the murder of Kenith Mackenzie at Fort Morea, on the coast of Africa, with observations which put the case in a view extremely interesting to the Army in general but particularly to Governors, Commanders, and all persons in foreign Military Employments', it is a remarkable essay which vehemently argues that Capt Kenneth Mackenzie acted in self-defence against a mutinous band of men whose leader was Kenith Murray Mackenzie and who are described as 'the most profligate banditti that ever disgraced a society of human beings'. Kenith is revealed as having been a former drummer in the Guards who had been convicted four times for capital offences at the Old Bailey and had 'artfully claimed relationship with Capt Mackenzie', and who was 'as unfit to live as he was to die'. Furthermore, it is claimed that making an example of Kenith 'had the happy effect of putting an end to the mutiny'.

The final paragraph of the address is an extraordinary piece of rhetoric:

But is the life of a British Officer to be put in competition with that of a felon whom he conducts to transportation? Is he to withhold his defence till the savage who has slipped his neck from the toils of justice, shall present the dagger to his heart? Shall the country, for whose sake he becomes a voluntary exile into climates scarcely tolerative of human existence, persecute a man whose patriotic hand has destroyed the viper preying upon her tormented bowels? Heaven forbid it! But if it must be so, farewell to that ardour of British Officers, whose active spirits establish settlements for their country wherever they head! Though the force of enterprise may conquer the combined dangers of a destructive climate – a savage country – a murderous crew – yet can the discipline, which such service there demands, guilt – expose the honour – the life of an Officer, on his return, to the perverted calls of justice – and, for British Officers, convict garrisons may command themselves.

The issue of enlisting convicted prisoners as soldiers was also raised in the Report of a Parliamentary Committee appointed to enquire into the operation of the 'Act for the effectual Transportation of Felons and other Offenders, and to authorize the Removal of Prisoners in certain Cases; and for other Purposes therein mentioned'. In their report[86] published in May 1785, the Committee members refer to the convoy that sailed to the Cape Coast of Africa in 1782. The 350 convicts are reported to have behaved very well during the voyage, but it said that twenty or thirty of them had died. After landing, however, they had become so riotous that their officers had become afraid for their lives. Also, several had deserted to the Dutch, whilst some had escaped into the country and others had died. Only a few had remained with their commander, Capt Mackenzie.

Throughout the debate, Kenneth was granted respites during His Majesty's pleasure – several of which were reported in *The Times*[87] – and was promised a royal pardon. However, by May 1785 he had fallen ill from a 'paralytic stroke' and a 'bilious fever', and on 30 May 1785 it is reported that the continuation of his confinement in Newgate 'is stated to be owing to his own misconduct. His pardon has been sometime made out, but he has peremptorily refused to pay the usual fees of office, and is said to have written a letter to the Secretary of State in a stile of disrespect becoming a man in his situation'. Then, on 9 June 1785, it was reported that 'Captain Mackenzie, confined in Newgate under sentence of death, has had a paryletic stroke within these few days under which he languishes in a most miserable situation, his mouth being drawn quite aside, and his whole person being miserably emaciated'.

It is not clear whether Kenneth had actually written disrespectfully to Lord Sydney as suggested in *The Times* in May 1785, but he did write[88] on 23 August 1785. The letter reads:

Thro' the medium of your Lordship's goodness, I presume to address your Lordship in a matter which concerns my life and I beg leave to inform your Lordship since my confinement my health has been attended with so visible a decrease that a short period must inevitably prove the total ruin of that constitution which I would more willingly lose in my country's cause. My Lord, if I do not intrude too much upon your Lordship's favour, I must humbly beg to know the ultimatum of my fate. To your Lordship's breast, I throw my cause intreating your Lordship to consider one as unfortunate. If it is my Sovereign's command my feeble efforts shall be employed in any service your Lordship's pleasure is. Or what ever may be my lot, I humbly beg to be freed from the horrors of a prison.

I ever am with the most profound respect, my Lord, your Lordship's most obedient servant.

This letter seems to have had little, if any, immediate effect. However, on 1 November 1785, the probable reason for the delay in issuing Kenneth's royal pardon became clear. *The Times* reported that:

Captain Mackenzie has received His Majesty's pardon for the murder of the soldier at Fort Moree, by shooting him from a cannon, but is now detained in Newgate and is expected will be tried at the next Admiralty Sessions for piracy in cutting out (with a detachment of his men) from under the guns of a Dutch fort, on the coast of Africa, a Portuguese ship, with Dutch colours, in consequence of which a complaint has been laid against him by the Portuguese Ambassador. Government detains £11,000 worth of his gold dust till he gives an account of the King's stores which were entrusted to his care. His father has died since his confinement, and left him an estate of near £500 a year, but it is thought he will not be able to make anything of it, it being mortgaged for a considerable sum. He is in a very poor state of health.

Presumably it was eventually decided not to proceed with a piracy trial, and Kenneth finally received the notification of his free pardon[89] from George III on 6 December 1785 (Figure 6).

It states that:

…whereas some circumstances have been humbly represented unto us on his behalf, inducing us to extend our grace and mercy unto him and to grant him our free pardon for his said crime, our will and pleasure therefore is that our cause him, the said Kenneth Mackenzie, to be forthwith discharged out of custody, and that he be inserted for his said crime in our first and next General Pardon that shall come out for the poor convicts in Newgate without any condition whatsoever.

The 'circumstances' referred to in the pardon are not stated, but presumably refer to the legal issue of whether decisions of military officers taken under martial law situations are adequately judged under common law.

On his release, Kenneth returned to Edinburgh, and in 1786 featured as one of four 'Bucks of the City' in a caricature by John Kay, the famous Edinburgh portrait artist (Figure 7). According to Paton,[90] it is an excellent likeness.

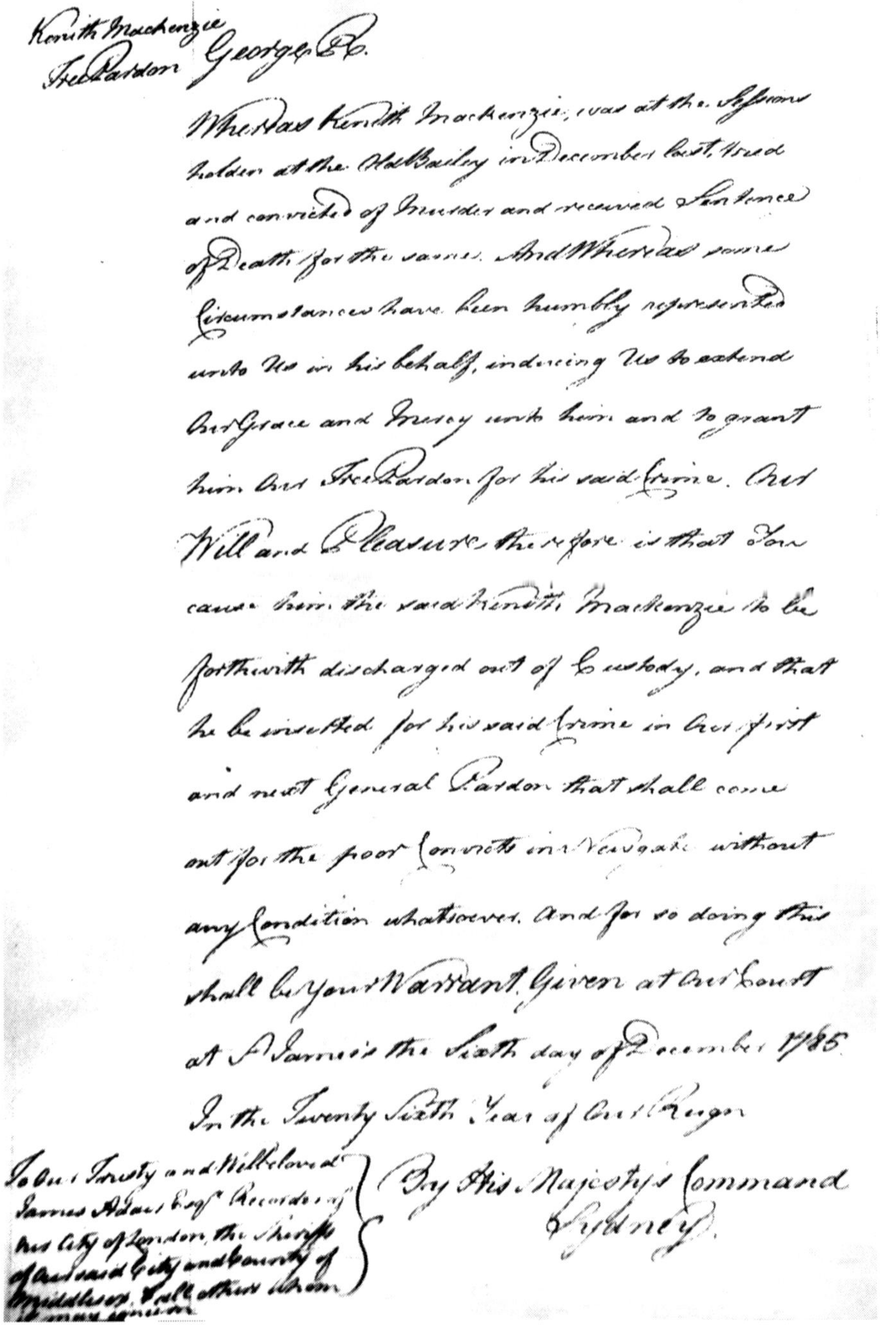

Kenith Mackenzie
Free Pardon

George R.

Whereas Kenith Mackenzie, was at the Sessions holden at the Old Bailey in December last, tried and convicted of Murder and received Sentence of Death for the same. And Whereas some Circumstances have been humbly represented unto Us in his behalf, inducing Us to extend Our Grace and Mercy unto him and to grant him Our Free Pardon for his said Crime. Our Will and Pleasure therefore is that You cause him the said Kenith Mackenzie to be forthwith discharged out of Custody, and that he be inserted for his said Crime in Our first and next General Pardon that shall come out for the poor Convicts in Newgate without any Condition whatsoever. And for so doing this shall be Your Warrant. Given at Our Court at St James's the Sixth day of December 1785 In the Twenty Sixth Year of Our Reign

By His Majesty's Command
Sydney

To Our Trusty and Wellbeloved James Adair Esqr Recorder of Our City of London, the Sheriffs of Our said City and County of Middlesex & all others whom it may concern

Figure 6: The 1785 royal pardon from George III to Kenneth Mackenzie, 8th of Redcastle (© The National Archives)

Figure 7: A caricature of Kenneth Mackenzie, 8th of Redcastle (from Paton, A Series of
Original Portraits and Caricature Etchings by the late John Kay*)*

From that point onward, Kenneth's life is shrouded in some mystery. It is said
that he fled Edinburgh as the result of another duel and, whilst still drawing
half-pay in the British Army, joined the Russian army in the war against the
Turks. By March 1789, he was living in Constantinople, where he is said to
have become an Assistant Consul, and it was on the twenty-eighth of that
month that he died in an extraordinary way.[91]

The event was first announced in the *Edinburgh Advertiser* on 30 June 1789:

The fatal duel, in which Capt Mackenzie was lately engaged, was with a Captain
Lee. The quarrel originated in a tavern in Naples, where Captain Mackenzie,
from that impetuosity of temper which ever characterised him, made use of
much unwarrantable language, and at length struck Captain Lee; this being
returned, and Captain Mackenzie, considerably worsted, he applied to the
British Ambassador for his interference. The Ambassador declined interfering;
and Captain Mackenzie meeting Captain Lee next day, presented a pistol, and
insisted on his instantly attending him to a proper place, to give him satis-

faction; this the latter objected to, as he conceived the dispute to have been settled at the time, and bore no animosity to Captain Mackenzie, whose menaces, however, induced him to consult with his friends, and they advised him to give him the meeting, which, from the character of his adversary, he acquiesced in.

This resolution being communicated to Captain Mackenzie, the parties met next day, attended by their seconds. It was agreed, that they should fire together, at twelve paces distance. Captain Mackenzie's ball grazed the side of Captain Lee's face; and he, receiving his, in return, in his right breast, and instantly fell. Captain Lee then went up to his unfortunate antagonist, who had barely time to exchange forgiveness with him, and who now candidly acknowledged himself the aggressor, and that his situation was owing to his own imprudence. He expired in a few minutes after, and the survivor thought it prudent to withdraw himself from the Neopolitan dominions.

The source of the article is unattributed, but it was erroneous in describing the event as having taken place in Naples. The next issue of the paper, on 3 July 1789, published a letter from Constantinople, dated 15 April 1789, containing further description of the event from an eyewitness, Thomas Barthold. It reads:

Sir, It is with infinite concern, I find myself under a necessity of announcing to you the melancholy decease of our mutual friend, Kenneth Mackenzie, Esq; which happened the 28th March, in a dispute of honour with Captain Robert Lee, for the circumstances of which I refer you to the inclosed copies of three acts taken by me on the occasion, the originals whereof are deposited in this office.

In begging the favour of your communicating the event to his relations in the manner you will think most prudent, I have to mention for your and their satisfaction, that the unfortunate Captain has been interred with every mark of decency and honour, in the Frank burying-place, alongside of some other English graves.

The following is one of the acts referred to:

Kenneth Mackenzie, Esq; late Captain of the first Independent Company of foot in his Britannic Majesty's service, and Robert Lee, late master of the ship Sybil of London, quarrelled over a bottle, at a French tavern in Pera, where the former was very ill used. Upon the 28th March, Captain Mackenzie, having met with Captain Lee in the public street of Pera, spit twice in his face, shaking his cane over his head, and using some harsh epithets. The same evening, between four and five o'clock, being employed in making inquiries concerning this disagreeable event, I saw the said Robert Lee, accompanied by Francis Wherry, late master of the ship *Couer de Nord*, walking towards the Armenian burying-ground, situated at the extremity of the street of Pera. Upon this, I called at Captain Mackenzie's lodgings, to learn whether he was at home; but finding he was abroad, and suspecting the parties intended to decide their dispute by a duel, I communicated my suspicions to the British Ambassador. His orders were, to repair instantly with four janissaries [Turkish soldiers], arrest the parties, and conduct them to the British Palace; and I accordingly set out, accompanied by the Rev. Dr Nicolson, Mr Warbrone, and the four janissaries, having appointed Mr Barthole meo Pifani, his Excellency's Secretary, to meet me at the place.

After gaining a plain adjacent to the burying-ground, from whence having seen nothing, we were hastening towards the tombs, when we heard the report of a pistol, at some distance, and immediately thereafter Captain Francis Wherry appeared ascending the height. Upon joining us, he said, that Captain Mackenzie was wounded and that he was going for a surgeon. I detached one of the janissaries along with him, and hastened with my company to the place of action. There I saw Captain Mackenzie mortally wounded in the right breast, extended on the ground, speechless, and breathing his last. Captain John Smith, late master of the ship *Camilla*, was standing by him; and Captain Lee, who was at some distance, appeared much affected. Immediately thereafter, Captain Smith and Captain Lee left us, and having directed Dr Nicolson and the janissaries, with the servants who attended us, to remain on the ground, I returned to relate the melancholy scene to his Excellency the Ambassador, who ordered the corpse to the British palace, where it was conducted accordingly.

Witness my hand in Pera of Constantinople, the 28th March, 1789.

(Signed) Tho Barthold, Cancillier.

What was contained in Thomas Barthold's other two 'acts' remains unknown, as they seem not to have been published. One may have referred to the cause of the dispute. According to Mackenzie's genealogy,[92] Captain Kenneth had entrusted Captain John Smith with all his possessions six years earlier, when he had been arrested at Fort Mouree.

1.4   Bankruptcy of the Mackenzies

The Redcastle estate was already in sequestration when Ruairi Ban Mackenzie, 7th of Redcastle, died in 1785. By 1782, he had been 'indebted in considerable sums … [having] allowed the interest to run on unpaid' and his son and heir, Kenneth, had also 'contracted several additional debts', mainly through the costs of forming and maintaining his Independent Company of Foot. Ruairi Ban and Kenneth, with the consent of his ex-wife, had therefore agreed to place the estate in trust, granting a trust deed to Sir Hector Mackenzie of Gairloch and John Tait WS 'with a view to put their affairs into a settled plan of management, that the rents and proceeds of the estate might be duly levied and applied regularly in payment of the interest due upon the debts, and the surplus divided in a certain proportion betwixt the father and son for maintenance of their respective families'. The terms of the trust had also allowed for the (named) creditors of the estate to be paid, or else the whole estate was to be sold. After Ruairi Ban's death, the trustees decided to sell the estate, but Kenneth refused to concur. The trustees therefore resolved to dissolve the trust and execute a reconveyance of the estate in favour of Kenneth 'under the express burden of the debts as specified in the original deed'. As this would have given preference to the estate's creditors, Kenneth refused to accept the reconveyance under these terms, thus trying to ensure that the title to the estate remained with his children as specified in the contract of his marriage to Jean Thomson in 1767.

The consequence of Kenneth's refusal to accept the terms of the reconveyance precipitated the creditors in 1788 to bring an action in the Court of Session to enforce a judicial sale of the estate and appoint a 'Common Agent' to rank the creditors. The action was successful, and advertisements placed in the *Edinburgh Advertiser* on 2 March, 6 April and 15 June 1790 indicated that the estate would be sold in three lots: lot 1 (named as Mains of Redcastle in the advertisements) included the lands of Spittal and Ward, Gargieston, Killearnan, Rencharn and Redcastle, for which the upset price was £12,779 ['Rencharn' does not seem to appear in any other document, and its location is not recorded]; lot 2 (The Culmores) included Culmore, Ardaphallie and Lettoch, for which the upset price was £4,536; and lot 3 (Wester Kessack) included Easter Kessock, the ferry and the salmon fishings at Kessock and Craigtrick [Craigton], for which the upset price was £5,086. Although the valuation of the estate in the Ross and Cromarty cess books was £1,491, the upset prices were set at twenty-five times the annual gross rent actually paid by the tenants. This amounted to £1,199, less £258 of adjustments for teinds, feu duties and other public burdens (such as the minister's stipend).

All three lots were purchased on 3 July 1790 by James Grant of Shewglie for £13,650, £6,450 and £5,350 respectively (£25,450 in total). It has been suggested that the Mackenzies were cheated out of the real value of the estate – but whether that is true or not, the purchase turned out either to be an inspired act of entrepreneurship or a case of insider knowledge on the part of James Grant. Redcastle would earn its new owner (and his heirs) a very substantial return on his investment. Throughout the period 1788–92, large numbers of Redcastle's creditors used the Session Court to win warrants in favour of their claims.[93] Others obtained inhibitions and adjudications against Kenneth (and his son Roderick) to establish the ranking of their respective claims and prevent any disposals of assets.[94] The situation was further exacerbated by the fact that Kenneth never truly inherited Redcastle. This is because he had failed after his father's death to obtain a charter of confirmation of his accession to the 'superiority' from the Crown. Thus the superiority remained vested in Ruairi Ban, whilst the assets of the estate were vested in Kenneth, and then Roderick, as the heirs.

The creditors included:

- Kenneth's surviving sons (Roderick and Hector) and daughters (Boyd and Hannah), who each claimed aliment of £30 per year, together with a settlement of £2,000 plus interest for the younger children.

- Other family members, several of whom were bondholders, for example: Mrs Elizabeth Mackenzie of Achmore, Florence Mackenzie, Abigail Mackenzie, Rev. Colin Mackenzie of Fodderty, Lieut-Col Colin Mackenzie, Catherine Mackenzie, George and John Mackenzie of Jamaica.

- Employees, for example: the tutors and curators of Kenneth Mackenzie's children; and John Mackenzie, the estate factor, for settlement of salmon fishing dues.

- Merchants, for example: David Sheppard and Sons, Nicol Summerville and James Dewar, all of Edinburgh; and Phineas and William MacIntosh of Inverness, who were owed £3,120 (Phineas MacIntosh also held a bond for 20,000 merks Scots).

- Solicitors, for example: John Dingwall WS, who had also acted for Ruairi Ban in the 1756–61 legal case; Kenneth Mackenzie WS and William Lockhart WS, who had represented several creditors; and John Tait WS, who had been a trustee of the estate.

- Bondholders, for example: George Ross and John Ogilvie of London, who held a bond of £800; Robert Mackenzie of Kilcoy (£262) and John Grant (£800); and John Peter du Roveray of London for the financing of Kenneth Mackenzie's Independent Company of Foot (£3,600).

- Trustees of deceased bondholders who had loaned money, for example: George Gillanders of Highfield and Sir James Douglas.

- Jean Thomson, Kenneth Mackenzie's divorced and remarried wife, who claimed £1,790 unpaid alimony and £316 liquidate penalty. [Her second husband was John McKenzie, an Inverness merchant, whom she had married in St Cuthbert's in Edinburgh on 18 December 1781.]

- The kirk session of Killearnan parish church, which was paid an interim dividend of £190 in March 1796 for unpaid contributions to the Killearnan Poor Fund.

- The new owner of Redcastle (James Grant), who obtained a warrant allowing him to withhold £2,311-2-2d from the purchase price to prepare a Bond of

Caution enabling him to stand surety for various estate creditors and 'for answering certain eventual annuities' from members of the Mackenzie family.

The specific provision for the younger children arose from a clause in the marriage contract between Kenneth Mackenzie and his wife, Jean Thomson, in 1767, that had bound Kenneth:

...to make payment to the younger children to be procreated of the marriage, the sum of £2,000, to be divided amongst them as he should direct by a writing under his hand; the said provisions to be payable only at the father's death, and to bear interest from the majority or marriage of the said children, whichever of these events should first happen; and they to be maintained at bed and board ay and until the period at which the interest upon their provisions should fall due and be payable.

After Kenneth's death, the other creditors collectively pleaded in the Court of Session in February 1792 that the provision to the children, if not payable during Kenneth's lifetime, did not take precedence over their claims.[95] The Court's decision was that the principal sum of £2,000 would take preference, but that the interest would not. However, this decision was subsequently overturned by an appeal made by John Peter du Roveray to the House of Lords in December 1792 and March 1793.

The basis on which the 'Common Agent' proposed to rank the creditors was threefold: firstly, those with heritable bonds and mortgages (amounting to £16,000); secondly, according to Scottish law, those who had obtained adjudications within one year and a day of the first to obtain adjudications, these being George Gillanders of Highfield (against the property of the estate in June 1788) and Catherine Mackenzie of Brahan (against the superiority of the estate in March 1789); thirdly, those with subsequent adjudications. The appeal of John Peter du Roveray[96] was lodged on the basis that, as he lived in London, he was unaware of the adjudication being sought by George Gillanders and would have conjoined with him had intimation been made in London. Objections were raised by the younger children, but the Lords sustained du Roveray's appeal and promoted him to the second rank of creditors. Furthermore, the claims of the younger children were rejected on the basis that a marriage contract could not supersede the claims of the 'onerous' creditors; otherwise a father would have powers to fraudulently 'provide for his children tho' he should spend his estate'.

One of the family creditors who obtained an inhibition[97] against Kenneth Mackenzie's son Roderick (9th of Redcastle) in June 1791 was his paternal uncle, John Mackenzie (6th of Kincraig). The Kincraig estate had originally been granted in 1615 to Colin Mackenzie, the second son of Rorie Mor (1st of Redcastle). Three generations later, Colin's great-grandson, Colin (4th of Kincraig), died without issue and the estate passed to his younger brother, John Mackenzie (5th of Kincraig). In June 1758, John made a disposition of the Kincraig estate to Rorie Ban Mackenzie (7th of Redcastle). On Rorie Ban's death in 1785, the Kincraig estate passed to Kenneth's younger brother, John Mackenzie (6th of Kincraig). After Kenneth's death in 1789, his son Roderick, under the terms of the disposition of 1758, had become 'heir of provision to the deceast Capt John Mackenzie [5th of Kincraig]' and the inhibition brought by John Mackenzie (6th of Kincraig) 'lawfully inhibited and discharged the said Roderick Mackenzie to discharge or sell any of his lands, heritages, rents, liferents and others, nor issue wadsets, securities, nor lend, nor receive bonds … [nor undertake] any other act or deed directly or indirectly in defraud and to the hurt or prejudice of the said complainant'. The judge then stated that he had signed nine copies of the inhibition, and that it was to be posted on the merket cross of Edinburgh and openly proclaimed at a public reading.

Another creditor was Alexander Mackenzie, the younger brother of Ruairi Mor, 6th of Redcastle.[98] Alexander, who had become the tidewaiter [customs official] at Strontian, held a bond for 4,000 Scots merks issued in 1710 by his father, Ruairi Dearg (5th of Redcastle). This bond had been corroborated by Ruairi Mor in 1721, but in 1728 – when he was about to leave Scotland to go to the West Indies – Alexander had agreed to allow a discharge of this bond in exchange for the issue of two new bonds, one for 2,000 Scots merks to Alexander's children and the other for 1,000 Scots merks to Alexander himself. When Alexander left Scotland, he deposited the 2,000-merk bond in the hands of Alexander Baillie (the Clerk of Ross) and the 1,000-merk bond with Ruairi Mor's wife, Margaret. When Margaret died, the bond fell into the hands of her sister, who was married to Alexander Monro, the tacksman of Dunvoronie in Ferintosh. [A tacksman was the chief tenant of an estate, frequently a younger brother or cousin of the proprietor, who sublet to lesser tenants and acted as rent collector.] Twenty years later, on his return to Scotland in 1749, Alexander discovered that the bonds had not been registered and, in consequence, Ruairi Mor refused to honour them. The complex legal position was explained in a paper of 1761, but it has to be assumed that Alexander was never recompensed, because he was listed as one of the creditors of the sequestered estate.

Given the complexity, it is not surprising that it took eight years for the Common Agent to assess all the creditors' claims and finalise his proposals for a scheme of division of the residual assets. The purchase price of the estate (£25,450) plus a small sum due for rentals from the 'superiority' comprised the entire assets of the estate, amounting to £27,468-1-6d. The total debt of the estate was assessed as £31,154-13-1d, and creditors were paid according to the scheme of division[99] approved by Robert Queen, Justice Clerk, on 7 March 1798.

Kenneth Mackenzie's eldest son, Roderick (9th of Redcastle), had lived in Redcastle until it was sold in 1790. In an adjudication hearing[100] held on 3 February 1790, it is stated that he had 'renounced to be heir in general to his deceased father and grandfather'. His younger brother, Hector, lived in New York, although he returned to Edinburgh to marry Diana Davidson on 29 March 1800. Roderick subsequently emigrated to Jamaica (where he joined in business with his cousin, George, a younger son of the Demerara cotton plantation owner, Kenneth Francis Mackenzie), and died there, unmarried, in 1798. The Mackenzie of Redcastle dynasty died with him.

At Fortrose Cathedral, there is an unusual carved stone mural above the entrance to the Mackenzie and Seaforth memorial vault in the South Isle.[101] It is thought to have been commissioned in about 1800 by Sir Alexander Mackenzie of Coul and to represent a member of the Mackenzie family as 'Death holding on to his castle of Redcastle'.

A book entitled *The Last Mackenzie of Redcastle* was written in 1888 by Rosa Mackenzie Kettle, who was Kenneth Mackenzie's granddaughter.[102] [Rosa, the daughter of Hannah Mackenzie, was born in England *circa* 1818 as Mary Rosa Stuart Kettle, and adopted her mother's maiden name as her *nom de plume*. She was a spinster who died in March 1895 in Callander, where she lived with her sister, Clara.] Although loosely based on the life of her grandfather, the book is a romantic novel, in which the hero, George Mackenzie, the son of 'Muckle Colin', joins the army and fights in the American War of Independence (1775–83), during which he meets and eventually marries Rozay Morais, the niece of a Portuguese chevalier [knight] who had left Portugal for the New World after the earthquake and tsunami that laid waste to Lisbon in 1755. They lived in a house named *Casa Bianca* [White Castle] in Georgia. After his marriage, George visits Redcastle expecting to inherit the estate, but finds that his father has died and Redcastle, overburdened by debts incurred by George's step-mother, has been sold.

There is also a reference to the MacKenzies of Redcastle in the Third Statistical Account of Scotland, written by Rev. George Ballingall in September 1954. He states that 'the last laird of the name of MacKenzie [Roderick or "Ruairi Ban", 7th of Redcastle] was Collector of Customs at Inverness. His elder son was a smuggler, and when later he joined the army was charged with fraud in India. He was called home and spent the remainder of his life in the Tower'. This version of the story of Kenneth (8th of Redcastle) is also told by MacLean,[103] and this is probably the source used by Rev. Ballingall. It may have been fabricated to protect the family from the truth (and embellished by 'Chinese whispers'), or perhaps it was a case of mistaken identity. After

Capt Kenneth (8th of Redcastle) left the 78th (Seaforths) to form his Independent Company in early 1781, the regiment was sent to India. At that time, there was a Lieut Kenneth Mackenzie who was subsequently promoted to Captain.[104] The passage to India was disastrous and many men died during the journey. Capt Kenneth Mackenzie fell seriously ill and on arrival in India was allowed to return home, after which he retired from active service. It is possible that the two Kenneth Mackenzies have been confused in the accounts of MacLean and Rev. Ballingall.

1.5   The Old (First) Statistical Account of Scotland

In May 1790, Sir John Sinclair, MP for Caithness, wrote to all 938 parish ministers in Scotland, requesting them to provide answers to a set of 160 questions that comprised what he called a 'Statistical Inquiry'. The late eighteenth century was the period of the 'Scottish Enlightenment', and the object of the inquiry was to collect social data on geography, population, religion, agricultural practices, roads, rents and wages, housing, etc., that would assist Parliament in making better political economic decisions. The last responses from the parishes were not received until 1798 (by which time Sir John had added another six questions), and the original publication of the accounts was presented to the General Assembly of the Church of Scotland in June 1799.

The Killearnan parish chapter of what became entitled the Old (First) Statistical Account[105] was written in 1794 by the Rev. David Denoon (II). In many respects, it is a disappointing chapter – not deeply researched, providing few answers to Sir John's questions and leaving many unanswered. However, it does give an insight into the history and the economy of the ill-managed and run-down estate that James Grant purchased in 1790 in the judicial sale that ended 222 years of the Mackenzie ownership of Redcastle. Of the parish's antiquities, Cairn Irenan is described as a 'Druidical temple … probably the most complete in this country', whilst the Redcastle crannog (Figure 2, page 20) 'still bears the marks of art, and indicates the existence of a considerable building of some very remote period' and the other cairns in the Beauly Firth are said to be 'temporary asylums from the predatory incursions of rude and barbarous tribes'. With regard to the names of the local settlements, it suggests that 'Chappletown' and 'Spittal [Hospital]' corroborate confused traditions and 'indicate the existence of two religious houses at some remote period, one dedicated to a Popish Saint, the other belonging to the Knights of Malta'.

Redcastle itself is described as 'annexed to the Crown, with the lordship of Ross, anno 1455' and as having 'the rights of a burgh of barony, with those of a free port, holding weekly markets, levying tolls and anchorage dues'. It also describes 'the facility with which coals, lime, wood and other necessities are conveyed'. This probably referred to the wooden pier close to Corgrain Point, rather than any facility at Redcastle itself, where the sandbanks of the Redcastle Bay are an impediment to shipping. The remains of the three rows of wooden piles of this old pier are still visible today. There was also a coal depot at Corgrain which is marked on some early maps, although there is no visible trace of it today.

The decades leading up to 1790 saw a great agricultural revolution in Scotland. Innovators and improvers brought a transformation in farming practices that had far-reaching effects on efficiency and productivity. The changes included: the enclosure of fields with dykes, ditches and hedges; the building of new steadings; the breaking up of the runrigs into consolidated fields; the draining of wetlands; the introduction of new crops (such as turnips); and the introduction of crop rotation. In reality, the Industrial Revolution could not have been sustained without improved agriculture to provide food for the fast-expanding towns and cities. Rev. David Denoon (II) would have been aware of the improvements that had taken place throughout the country when he wrote his chapter of the Old (First) Statistical Account, and was obviously much concerned about the unimproved farming economy of the parish at the time, not least because he was greatly dependent on the proceeds of his glebe to maintain his own standard of living. In consequence, he devotes much of the Killearnan chapter to a detailed analysis of the poor financial returns experienced by the tenant farmers, together with much passion on why high rents and short tenancies prevented them from making sufficient profit and mitigated against reinvestment and improvement of local farming practices. The following extracts give a flavour of this aspect of the chapter:

- Agricultural improvement is backward in the extreme.
- The farmers have no inclosures ... so that their fields from autumn until the briar appears in April are undistinguished common, through which horses, oxen and sheep range promiscuously.
- The farms are almost entirely under a constant succession of corn crops ... and an inconsiderable proportion, which exhausts a large share of the manure of the year, appropriated for potatoes.
- It may be affirmed, that on a farm of 30 acres, £2 per annum has not been cleared, at an average, by any one farmer, for 20 years, by farming alone.
- In a national view, the consolidation of farms is still more seriously objectionable. Its effect is immediate depopulation. It compels the poor aborigines ... to emigrate, friendless and unprotected, to other countries; or to crowd into towns, with a view of grasping at the casual sources of earning their pittance.

- There are 7 licensed stills in this parish ... it will be asked, why then so many distilleries? Distilling is almost the only method of converting our victual into cash for the payment of rent and servants; and whisky may, in fact, be called our staple commodity.

- The proximity of the sea is of very considerable utility to this and neighbouring parishes ... it furnishes a variety of fish, and particularly herrings in their season, which have been sometimes sold 100 for 1d. Sprats, sandals, shrimps, flounders and other small fishes are taken during summer and harvested in what we call yares [fish traps].

Many of these comments reflect the description of the Redcastle estate that accompanied the advertisement published in the *Edinburgh Advertiser* for the sale of the property in 1790. It stated:

The lands are of great extent, and being still in their natural state, are capable of much improvement ... the soil is of an exceeding good quality, and owing to the south exposure, the crops are known to be more early than in the most southerly parts of Scotland ... the mansion house could be repaired at a small expense ... there are mussel banks upon which no value is put, but which, if properly managed, would produce a considerable rent.

Sadly, the focus on the poor state of agriculture in Redcastle in the Old (First) Statistical Account means that little reference is made to the lifestyles, education, health, living standards or housing conditions of the general population of the parish. The houses occupied by the ordinary country working people were commonly built of turfs, floored with field stones and roofed with heather thatch. In a reference to Killearnan farmers, Mowat[106] reveals that:

In 1796 it was claimed that the 30-acre farmers of Killearnan had not cleared £2 per annum on average in the previous 20 years, and although the income from farms was often supplemented by the profit from spinning and distilling, by the end of the century the native tenant farmers were often in a worse position than not only cottars but even some servants. Their housing was appalling, consisting, even as late as 1806, of single roomed hovels made up (not built) of stone and feal [turf] with entry by a common door to the space shared by the family and their animals.

As the houses were heated with peat fires and the smoke was allowed to permeate through the heather roof thatch, an English visitor to the Highlands is said to have referred to them as 'smoking dunghills'!

1.6   The Grants of Shewglie and Redcastle

The purchase of Redcastle by James Grant of Shewglie was completed by the issue of a Crown charter[107] of the Barony of Redcastle, written in Latin, on 5 July 1790. [Shewglie, which is in Glen Urquhart between Drumnadrochit and Cannich, has various spellings, including Shugley, Sheuglie and Shewgley. The Grants had been awarded the Lordship of Glenurquhart by James IV in 1509, and Shewglie was the principal residence.] This charter, along with the sasine of the purchase, was presented in a lengthy petition to the Commissioners of Supply[108] in October 1790. [A sasine is a legal document establishing possession of a piece of heritable property.] The essence of the petition was that the Killearnan part of Redcastle estate was valued at £822-15/- Scots in the Commissioners' cess books, but that the 'real rent' had been judicially valued for the purposes of the sale at only £701-13-3d. However, the Commissioners were not to be denied and, whilst agreeing that the real rent was as stated, the 'valued rent' would stand as assessed in the 'cess books'. For the purposes of the assessment, the estate was divided into thirteen 'parcels' named as: Mains of Redcastle; Spital and Ward; Gargistown and Braes; Peckmore; Milltown and Croftmore (with the Markets of Redcastle); mill lands of Redcastle; Hilltown; Parktown; Chapeltown and Burntown; Blair-dow; Newtown and Ward; Corgrain; Damm Park, Pecknakyle and Smiddyfield.

James Grant also had the 'Inventory of the Title Deeds of the Barony of Redcastle' drawn up, presumably to satisfy himself that he had good and proper title over the Redcastle estate.[109] Commonly known as the 'Redcastle Writs', this remarkable manuscript lists and details the writs, charters, confirmations, dispositions, resignations and sasines relating to Redcastle and the associated lands from 1584 to 1790. He also obtained a certified copy of the agreed boundary between Redcastle and Allangrange,[110] although there is no evidence that he was able to obtain a similar agreement for his more contentious boundary with Wester Kilmuir.

One of James Grant's early priorities seems to have been to improve the estate and renovate the castle to make it habitable again after years of neglect during the latter years of the Mackenzies' tenure. To oversee the work person-ally, he moved into the castle and arranged to have his Shewglie estate leased. Several of his various business letters and papers have survived.[111] They describe many aspects of his diverse affairs – for example, the installation of a marble mantelpiece, a Rumford stove grate, curtains and carpet for the library at Redcastle and the purchase of fruit bushes, shrubs and trees for the gardens and the woodlands. In 1802, he paid £34-10/- to George Brown of Inverness for 300,000 Scots firs (1/6d per dozen) and 30,000 two-year-old larch trees (8d per 1,000). The papers also include an indenture for Donald Mackay as an apprentice and servant for 'learning the art and business of a Writer'. The indenture was for seven years, during which James Grant promised not to withhold any of his knowledge and Donald 'binds and obliges himself to serve his said Master faithfully and honestly both by day and by night and not at any time absent himself ... without liberty ... abstaining from debauchery and immorality'.

A further letter, dated 20 June 1794 and addressed to his factor (James Grant of Bught), gives an interesting insight into the character of one of the occupants of estate property. William Young had renounced his tack [tenancy] at Barntown but was still occupying the house, much to the inconvenience of Alexander MacKay and William Noble (who were presumably to take over the tack). James Grant requested his factor to intervene.

> This you cannot perhaps do so well on Sunday but you may remonstrate his case of obstinacy by taking the legal means of removing him to be executed on a future day. The truth is that the good wife of Barntown is considered a formidable personage of supernatural powers in this place of ignorant belief and both Noble and MacKay are afraid of exasperating her by direct measures for clearing the house, at the same time the poor man Young himself owns implicitly in conduct the influence of her spell.

Although the reason why William Young wished to give up the tack at Barntown is not recorded, the factor seems eventually to have overcome the matter of the reluctant wife and her witchcraft, because ten years later the Youngs are recorded at Croftmore whilst William Noble and Alexander MacKay are recorded in Barntown.

Three surviving handwritten documents are of particular interest, because they provide details of the rental income[112] of the Redcastle estate in 1790 and 1803–04. The first tabulates the rental raised from the tenant farmers of the estate for each of their hens, chickens and capons, and for the eggs they produced. The total collected was £9-11-11½d sterling, hens being assessed at 4d each, chickens at 2d each, capons at 6⅓d each and eggs at 2d per dozen. The farms are not individually named, but their locations include Spittall, Gargustown, Braes, Burntown, Blairdow, Newtown, Chappeltown, Pecks, Killearnan parish glebe, Redcastle Mill and Smiths Crofts. This is one of the few references to Smiths Crofts, which may have been an alternative name for the area sometimes known as Croftmore. [It is interesting to compare these assessments with those quoted (in Scots money) in the tack of the parish glebe[113] given to Rev. David Denoon (I) in 1764; for example, ½ merk (equivalent to 9d sterling) for hens and 4/- (equivalent to 4d sterling) for a dozen eggs.

Either Rev. Denoon (I) was overassessed in the value of his poultry or Scots money depreciated by about fifty per cent relative to sterling between 1764 and 1790.]

The second document is a list of the rent received by James Grant on 16–17 March 1803 from each farm and business; for example: Donald MacFarquhar of Chappelltown (£20), Alexander Noble of Spittal (£15), Andrew Bisset of Spittal (13/4d), Donald MacLennan of Newtown (£3), John MacFarquhar of Burntown (£8-15/-) and Donald Noble, merchant, of Milntown (£8-15/-). The sum of the annual rental income from the farms of the estate was £613-17-10d.

The third document provides a complete rental income and expenditure account for the crop year 1804, presented to James Grant of Redcastle by the estate factor. It shows that the total gross income was £2,256-4-10d, some examples being Alexander MacFarquhar of Gargustown (£43-6-3d), James Tulloch of Blairdow (£65-19/-), Colin McKenzie of Drummore (£59), Donald Noble and William Young of Croftmore (£16-6-8d), Angus Urquhart of Milntown (£56), Rev. David Denoon (II) of Killearnan (£35-4-8d) and Milntown Maillers (£17-17-6d). James Grant himself also had to pay nominal rental for the farms that were occupied on his behalf; for example, Redcastle Mains (£50), Lands of Hilltown (£41) and even the garden at Redcastle (£21). The document also gives an insight into the rentals paid by Redcastle businesses; for example: Alexander Fraser, blacksmith (£16); Donald MacLennan, tailor (£7); Donald Noble, merchant (£18-13-4d) and David Munro, miller (£135). The gross total of rents due to James Grant was reduced by payments made by the factor – for example, the salary (£12-8-3d) of the schoolmaster, Donald Leitch, and the factor's own salary as a baillie of the barony (£50).

Another source of substantial income for James Grant came from the Redcastle quarry. In 1803, Thomas Telford was appointed by Parliament to oversee the construction of the Caledonian Canal. He chose Redcastle quarry to supply the high-quality free-stone necessary to line the walls of the locks and hang the lock gates. To transport the stone to Inverness by boat, Telford built the pier that still extends 350 metres from the quarry into the Beauly Firth. James Grant was paid 1/7d per cubic foot for the best quality 'principal cut Ashlar', of which almost 95,000 cubic feet was extracted and shipped to Inverness.

James Grant had worked for many years in India, in consequence of which his health had suffered. Dr William Kennedy of Inverness dispensed regular medication for stomach ailments, including ionic powders, castor oil, magnesia, lax pills, infusions and elixirs.[114] Between July 1796 and December 1806, the bill amounted to £37-9-8d. James died single and intestate at his

London residence (Ruxley Lodge, Surrey) on 22 October 1808. It transpired that there was 'no settlement or disposition of his effects heritable or moveable found in his repositories', a situation that prompted his cousin (and heir) Alexander Grant of Lochletter, along with Hugh Grant of Moy, to petition on 2 November 1808 for permission to examine his private papers.[115] They subsequently reported that they had 'forced the mahogany secretaire in his bedroom at Redcastle ... [but had found] no deed of settlement'.

However, various papers have subsequently emerged, including the Redcastle Writs (dated 1800) and a bond of provision (dated 3 September 1808)[116] 'for the love, favour and affection which I bear to the family of my worthy friend Charles Grant, Deputy Chairman of the Honorable Directors of the East India Company ... to each of the three eldest daughters ... £3,000 sterling'. Why James Grant should have died intestate yet, only ten days previously, should have left provision for Maria, Charity and Sibylla – the three elder daughters of Charles Grant (a third cousin and himself a very rich man) – is a mystery. Charles Grant's fourth daughter, Catherine, had married Patrick, the eldest son of James' cousin, Alexander Grant, who would ultimately inherit Redcastle,[117] so perhaps James thought that she was well enough endowed. However, it is tempting to surmise that James may have been thanking Charles for his role – as a Caledonian Canal commissioner – in directing Thomas Telford to use stone from the Redcastle quarry in the construction of the canal, thus providing James with a very substantial profit.

On James Grant's death, the ownership of Redcastle estate passed to his cousin, Lieut-Col Alexander Grant. He drew up a set of regulations which were signed by forty farmers on the Redcastle estate.[118] 'We the tenants and mailers [cottars] of the estate of Redcastle whose subscriptions and whose marks of such of us cannot write are hereto adhibited having agreed with the proprietor Col Grant for a five years lease of the different possessions set to us from Whitsunday first in the current year 1811 do acknowledge that the following regulations were proposed and agreed.' Five regulations are listed:

(i)   Not to sublet without consent.

(ii) Not to injure trees, or allow others to injure them, by digging around their roots.

(iii) Not to cut any divot, feal or green ground.

(iv) To plough an end rigg of at least twelve feet parallel to any public road.

(v)   To grind all grain at Redcastle mill.

The document is witnessed by Angus Urquhart and Colin McFarquhar, and many of the farmers' surnames are those commonly found in the area – for example, Noble, Mackenzie, Bisset, MacIntosh, Thomson, Ross and MacRae.

Like James, Alexander did not keep in good health, and he issued a testament in 1814 in favour of 'the children procreated or to be procreated betwixt me and Mrs Jane Hannay, otherways Grant, my spouse', nominating their tutors and curators as his executors.[119] He died in July 1816 and for the 'love, favour and affection which I have and bear to my children' left the Redcastle estate to his eldest son, Patrick, and £3,000 to each of his daughters, Catherine (who died in 1814) and Jane Elizabeth. A third daughter, Maria, was born after Alexander's death but, although he anticipated children 'to be procreated' after the writing of his will, Maria does not seem to have been specifically endowed like her sisters. Perhaps Alexander was unaware that his wife was pregnant when he died.

As well as benefiting from the sale of stone from the Redcastle quarry to build the Caledonian Canal, the Grants also sold off quantities of the estate wood. For example, the *Inverness Journal*[120] of 23 March 1811 carried an advertisement entitled 'Wood For Sale', in which eighty-nine elm and ash trees measuring from seven to twelve inches in girth and 400 alder trees 'fit for boats, staves and carts' were for sale by private bargain. The wood, which was 'conveniently situate, being within half a mile of the sea, must be cut down by the purchasers. For further particulars, apply to the Overseer at Redcastle; if by letter, post paid'. Another example is recorded in the *Inverness Journal* of 31 October 1818. The advertisement reads: 'Roup Of Hard Wood. On Friday the 3rd of April next, there will be exposed to public roup [auction], at Redcastle, in such lots as purchasers may incline, a quantity of ash and elm. Credit will be given on good security. The sale will commence at 11 o'clock.'

Alexander Nasmyth (1758–1840), the well-known Scottish landscape artist, made a pencil drawing of Redcastle which is housed in the National Gallery of Scotland.[121] As is normal with this artist's drawings, it is distinctively signed with a monogram of the initials 'A.N.' but, unfortunately, it is undated. It was originally catalogued as 'A Castle, Inverness-shire', but is entitled 'Redcastle' in the artist's handwriting. Whether Nasmyth was commissioned by one of the Grants to make the drawing is not known, and there is no record of it having been the sketch for a painting. It was probably drawn around 1810, when Nasmyth was known to be taking commissions from wealthy landowners. The view is unusual, showing the rear of the castle from a point close to the West Lodge looking over the Redcastle burn, a view that is completely obliterated by large trees today.

A large-scale shinty match, known as a 'camach', 'caman' or 'carmack', was an ancient custom to celebrate New Year in the eighteenth and early nineteenth centuries. For example, an article in the *Celtic Monthly* of 1896 refers to teams from the Glasgow Cowal, Edinburgh Sutherland and Edinburgh Camanachd clubs participating in New Year's Day shinty matches in which there were no limits to the number of contestants. The games were usually played on a sandy beach or a large field on which 'young men enter into the fray with a dash and energy that threaten danger to head and limb'. Similarly, a report in the *Inverness Courier* of 18 January 1826 describes the 'usual camach' of 150-a-side between the Chisholms and other natives of Strathglass.[122]

An even larger 'carmack' between a team representing Redcastle and a team from the clan Grant took place during Patrick Grant's ownership of Redcastle. The *Inverness Journal* of 14 January 1820 reported that it was held over two days, Old Christmas Day (6 January) and New Year's Day (13 January). [The reason for these dates stems from Pope Gregory XIII, who decreed in 1582 that the first day of the year would change from 25 March to 1 January and that the (Roman) calendar would be re-aligned with the solar calendar by following the 4 October 1582 with the 15 October 1582, thus losing ten days. Most of Europe followed the papal decree, but both Scotland and England – being Protestant – did not. It is often stated that Scotland made the switch to the Gregorian calendar in 1600, but this is only partially true. Scotland changed its New Year's Day to 1 January in 1600 but, as in England, did not make the solar re-alignment until September 1752. By that year, the Julian and Gregorian calendars had become eleven days out of line, and 2 September 1752 had to be followed by 14 September 1752. For many years thereafter in some parts of Scotland, the celebration of New Year's Day was switched to 13 January.]

There appear to have been about 400 men on each side of the carmack, with the Grants dressed 'cap-a-pee [hat and jacket] in the Grant tartan'. [This probably refers to the version of the Grant tartan, now registered as WR 1385, which was created by Patrick Grant.[123]] The report continues:

> It was contested with some obstinacy on both sides, till the darkness of night, and the victory seeming in favour of the kilted detachment, terminated this healthy amusement amidst the loud sounds of the playing of *Cogadh na sith* ['Peace or War' – the motto of the famous MacCrimmon pipers]. Whisky and ale in abundance was given by the Laird on this occasion, and a dance, which continued till four in the morning when all repaired peaceably to their respective homes, well pleased with the liberality of *Ceann Tigh Shouglie* [the Chief of the House of Shewglie, Patrick Grant].

A second article reported that:

> ...the carmack was again resumed here yesterday [New Year's Day] when a very spirited contest took place between a party of young men in the Highland garb, headed by the Laird, and an equal number in the low country dress, led by Mr Johnson of the Artillery. The day was long doubtful; but at length declared for *Bodich a'Bhriguis* [the Lowlanders] who had the best of seven hails [halves]. A ball, and copious libations of the purest mountain dew, finished this Celtic festivity.

They certainly knew how to celebrate New Year in those days!

When Patrick Grant inherited Redcastle in 1816, he had no need to live there because he lived at Lakefield in Glen Moriston. He therefore sought to let the castle, and on 26 January 1821 an advertisement appeared in the *Inverness Journal*. It reads:

> To let furnished, the residence of Redcastle in Ross-shire. The beauty of this location is generally known and acknowledged – and the accommodations of the Castle are extensive, comfortable and fit for immediate reception of a large family. The place may be had with or without the garden, which is large and one of the most productive in the country – or with or without the Mains which contain about 200 arable acres in excellent order and several hundred acres of wood and other pasture. Lime, etc. may be landed and produce shipped in the immediate neighbourhood of the farm, where there is an excellent beach and a good road to Inverness, Dingwall and Beauly. There is a very complete square of offices, thrashing mills, etc. If the Mansion is let without the farm, there will be added a coach house and ample stabling. Apply to Patrick Grant Esq., the Proprietor.

No tenant was forthcoming, and in 1823 Patrick Grant placed the affairs of the Redcastle estate in the hands of trustees, one of whom was his brother William. In 1824, the trustees prepared to issue a bond in order to raise £120,000 needed to clear Patrick's heritable debt, complete the purchases of his houses at Lakefield and Strathconon, build a new pier at North Kessock and put a steam boat into service at Kessock Ferry (an application to the Commissioners of Supply in October 1823 to substitute a steam boat for the sailing boats had been approved). As security for the bond, they estimated that the value of Redcastle, including the woods and the quarry, was £105,000 and this was projected[124] to rise to £138,000 by Whitsunday 1828. However, Patrick Grant's financial affairs were not in good order and, instead of issuing the bond, the trustees decided that capital had to be raised by selling Redcastle.

Prior to the sale, the trustees had the Redcastle estate surveyed by Edward Sang and Sons of Kirkcaldy.[125] The resultant map of 1825 provides an extraordinarily detailed (approximately 1:5,000) overview of the estate as it had developed during thirty-five years of intense investment by the Grants (Figure 8). As well as all the major features of the area, such as the castle, the school, the church, the quarry and the pier, it shows the locations of all the estate houses and every field. Furthermore, there is also a tabulation of the tenants of each field.

In December 1825, an agreement[126] was made by the trustees to sell the Redcastle estate to Sir William Fettes, although the sale was not completed until 1828 and the sasine was not registered until April 1829. The Grants had prospered from the sale of estate-grown wood and of quarry stone. Wisely, they

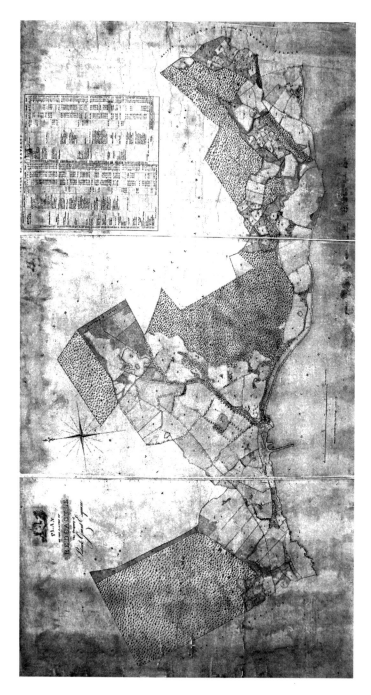

Figure 8: The 1825 Redcastle estate map commissioned by Patrick Grant, owner of Redcastle 1816–25 (reproduced from the original by permission of Mr Michael Martin)

had also undertaken many improvements to the castle and the estate grounds and, in consequence, Patrick Grant's trustees reaped a huge return on their investment. The price paid by Sir William Fettes was £135,000, five times the amount James Grant had paid in 1790.

1.7 Sir William Fettes

It is not clear why Sir William Fettes (Figure 9) purchased Redcastle. He had grown wealthy shipping tea and wine during the Napoleonic wars and had served two terms as Provost of Edinburgh in 1800–02 and 1804–06. Through his business interests in shipping, he held contracts to supply Fort George with provisions, so it is probable that he was looking for cargo for his ships on their return to England. The Industrial Revolution was in full swing, fuelled by coal-generated steam, and the woodlands of the Redcastle estate, which had been well stocked by the Grants, offered the opportunity to export wood as pit props. As the Kessock Ferry was part of the Redcastle estate, the necessary piers were also available. Sir William Fettes continued the development of the estate that had been commenced by the Grants, undertaking much drainage work, planting shelter belts, bringing wasteland into cultivation and rebuilding houses and farms.[127] He also continued to develop the estate woodlands, and engaged Mr Monteath of Stirling, a well-known forester who had written texts on forestry, to value the woodlands at Redcastle and design a plan for developing them.

Figure 9: Sir William Fettes, owner of Redcastle 1825–36
(from Whitson, The Lord Provosts of Edinburgh*)*

The summer of 1826 was unusually hot and dry, which prompted the *Inverness Journal* on 25 August to publish an article written by Mr Monteath offering 'judicious hints on the best means of remedy'. It is prefaced:

> In this year of unprecedented drought, I am well aware that your young plantations must be suffering very severely ... this I am more convinced of, not only from what I have seen personally on different estates, and in various parts of the country – but also from the numerous applications, being nearly 900, already come to my hand from different Noblemen and Gentlemen in England, Scotland and Ireland, inquiring advice what course they should take, as much as possible to recover and save their plantations, some of which being of very great extent, and which appear at present to be a total failure, which must occasion an immense expence in plants and replanting. Being well aware that many who have not as yet applied to me for advice, whose plantations may be in a similar situation, I thought of printing this circular, containing the following hints, and sending it to those Noblemen and Gentlemen who have honoured me with their employment – and should these hints be the means (of which I have no doubt from former experience) of saving all or any part of their young plantations, I will feel myself most amply rewarded.

Although he had retired in 1806 to manage his estates, Sir William was a rare annual visitor to Redcastle, preferring to send his factor, John Mackenzie, from Edinburgh to carry out his business. For example, according to the *Inverness Courier* of 15 February 1832, he sent John Mackenzie to issue instructions to the superintendent of the Kessock ferry 'to prevent vagrants and suspicious persons crossing the ferry ... [thus] preventing the introduction of rags' and, in 1836, to mediate with the local factor, Mr Suter, after Sir William had been heavily criticised by a school inspector for allowing the schoolhouse at Croft-nacreich to deteriorate so badly that it had become barely habitable. Sir William also made improvements to the Kessock ferry and its piers. For example, he introduced a steam boat in 1825, but this turned out to be an unsuccessful venture, as the increased fares were not popular and the boat could not sail in adverse weather conditions and was prone to mechanical failure. He also built a new inn at North Kessock, which opened in December 1828, enlarged the piers at the ferry and had plans to build a large storehouse. These improvements, together with those initiated by his predecessors, had – according to the *Inverness Courier* of 25 January 1837 – increased the rental of the ferry from £150 per annum in 1806 to £800 by 1837.

Sir William Fettes also sought to let Redcastle. For a brief period, it was rented by James Fraser of Belladrum, but he seems to have met with financial difficulties which led to his eviction and the sale of his furniture. In consequence, a large advertisement was placed in the *Inverness Journal* on 9 June 1831, which described the property as the beautiful 'Baronial residence of Redcastle', containing drawing room, salooon [sic], dining room, billiard room, library, eight good bedrooms, servants' accommodation, kitchen, water closets, etc., etc. Also included was the 'very productive, early, and beautiful garden (with vinery and orchard)' and the 5,000 Imperial acres of estate which 'is one of the best stocked with game in the North – besides roe deer there is no better shooting ground in this quarter for partridge, hare, black game and woodcock; and pheasants would thrive well if turned out on the grounds'. There does not appear to have been any initial uptake, but in February 1835 it was leased to Major General Sir Hugh Fraser.

In 1832, Sir William commissioned Campbell Smith from Banff to produce a chart[128] of the 'Moray Frith from the East boundary of the Lands of Sir William Fettes, Baronet, to the River Beauly'. Although its purpose was for the development of his shipping interests, this chart also shows land-based features. Of particular note is the row of four houses that comprise Quarry of Redcastle, as this was the first map to show these. Only one house is shown on the earlier (1825) map of Redcastle estate drawn up by Patrick Grant (Figure 8, page 75), thus it can be deduced that the hamlet of Quarry of Redcastle was built in the period of Sir William Fettes, between 1824 and 1832.

This chart of 1832 also shows another building about 200 metres to the west of the hamlet of Quarry of Redcastle. Today at this site, there are a few scattered stones around a flat area, suggesting that a small building may have been there. The site lies closer to the shore than any of the other houses and is just above the level of the highest spring tides. Possibly, it may have been the site of an old croft (there were several crofts along the shore between Redcastle, Garguston Shore and Spital Shore) or have been associated with the catching, processing or storing of fish (or shellfish), which were an important source of food for the working population of the time. Two local yairs [tidal fish traps] are marked on the chart, one at Milton of Redcastle and the other at Spital Shore. Another possibility is that it was associated with the manse glebe, as it is located close to a stone wall that marked the southern perimeter of the orchard. A fourth possibility is that it was a gatehouse. It is said that cattle were driven along the shore to the Redcastle, Corgrain, Lettoch and North Kessock piers from where they were shipped across the Beauly Firth to cattle trysts at Inverness and beyond.

By virtue of its Burgh of Barony status, Redcastle was able to hold fairs and markets. Enshrined in the title deeds[129] of the castle was 'the power and liberty of holding a fair or common market once a year, on the seventh day of July, commonly called St Andrew's Day, within the said town of Newton of Redcastle, at the Chapel commonly called St Palmer's Chapel, with the customs and toll pennies thereof'. It is not recorded exactly where these fairs took place, but evidence has been found by metal detection to suggest that they were held in the area between the parochial school and the parish church. Finds have included eighteenth- and nineteenth-century buttons, lead weights, brass thimbles, spoons (one being a silver spoon handle with the mark of Alexander Stuart, an Inverness silversmith who was in business in 1800–12), an eighteenth-century dagger chape [sheath], a Victorian wire brooch, a padlock inscribed 'W 1773' and numerous Georgian and Victorian coins.[130] These include half-pennies and farthings of George II, a bullhead shilling, pennies and half-pennies of George III, a penny and a farthing of George IV, and various coins (shillings, six-, four- and three-penny pieces, pennies and half-pennies) of Queen Victoria. The largest numbers of coin finds are from the reigns of George II (1727–60) and George III (1760–1820), suggesting that the Redcastle markets had reached their peak during Sir William Fettes' proprietorship.

Various sales and roups were also held on the estate at this time. For example, the *Inverness Journal* of 31 October 1823 (just before Patrick Grant's trustees decided to sell the Redcastle estate) advertised a 'Roup at Redcastle' of 'three pairs of excellent working horses … several young horses, rising three and four years … a number of cows and young cattle of various ages … some farming utensils … a field of turnips, divided into small lots. Credit will be given on approved bills, for six months, on all sales over £2'. Redcastle's horse markets were also well known. They were held each spring and summer in the early nineteenth century, and people appeared to travel considerable distances to attend them – not always without danger. It is recorded in the *Inverness Journal* of 27 March 1818 that Duncan MacLean perished on the hills on his way to the market, and on 8 March 1822 that John Fraser fell from his cart and died on returning from the market. A report published in the *Inverness Journal* on 12 March 1830 indicates the prices paid for horses during the spring sale of that year. The market was:

> …very well attended; the show of horses was pretty good but the majority of the animals were of an inferior description. The backward state of spring induced the sellers to hold out for high prices, but towards evening both sellers and purchasers gave in, and a number of horses changed owners at fair prices. Good draught horses, fit for harness, below 7 years old, fetched from £18 to £25; small horses and ponies, for which the demand was greater, brought from £6 to £14 according to size and age.

An advertisement in the *Inverness Journal* details some of the horses for sale at the market on 27 July 1836. They included, for example, a cream-coloured horse and mare which are described as 'a fair match, with full manes and tails, almost black – both strong and fit for harness'. There were also a 'beautiful dark brown mare, 15 hands high, got out of a mare on third bred by Sir Malachi Malagrowther – promises to have fine action and would suit admirably for a Lady's pony'; a 'strong bay horse, 15 hands high rising 4 years – got out of the same mare, by Don Juan – promises to have a fine action for either saddle or harness'; and a 'strong black Highland mare, 5 years old, 14 hands high, with foal at her foot, by Diamond'.

Predictably, the markets at Redcastle were accompanied by much drinking and fighting, especially in the years after the Battle of Culloden when rivalries were still simmering and Jacobite sympathisers were still being rounded up. Two incidents are recounted by Hugh Miller of Cromarty in his *Scenes and Legends of the North of Scotland*.[131] In the first incident, he describes a fight at Redcastle market in which two loyalist brothers 'of the name of Duff – gigantic fellows of six feet and a half – had stood back to back for an entire hour in the throng of Redcastle market, defending themselves against half the cudgels of Strathglass'. In the second, he describes how the fiercely loyalist Cromarty salmon-fisherman, George Hossack, had made a sale to two English drovers at Redcastle market and, to seal the bargain, had invited them to a drink in a local hostelry. The two Englishmen were already in the inn when George Hossack entered and filled their glasses. He then proposed a toast of 'health and prosperity to George the Third', but was somewhat surprised when the Englishmen responded with toasts to 'George the herd' and 'George the —'. George Hossack, who was a very large man, was outraged and set about the Englishmen until they were unable to rise from the floor!

[It is worthy of note that Hugh Miller's wife, Lydia Mackenzie Falconer Fraser, was a great-granddaughter of Rev. Murdoch Mackenzie, the younger son of Roderick Mackenzie (Ruairi Dearg, 5th of Redcastle). She was proud of her Mackenzie of Redcastle ancestry and expressed a desire in her will, written in 1875, for one of her Mackenzie descendents to repurchase 'the old Barony of Redcastle'. Her wish was never fulfilled.]

Sir William Fettes (of Wamphray) died in 1836, his only son having died of typhoid in 1815. Passionately interested in education and unable to pass on his wealth, Sir William left £166,000 in an endowment for the education of children 'whose parents have either died without leaving sufficient funds … or who, from innocent misfortune during their own lives, are unable to give suitable education to their children'. That endowment resulted in the foundation of Fettes College in Edinburgh. His trustees sold Redcastle in March 1839 to Col Hugh Duncan Baillie, owner of the adjacent Tarradale estate. To this day, Redcastle is still in the ownership of the Baillie family. The purchase price was only £120,000, £15,000 less than Sir William Fettes had paid in 1825. The reason was that Sir William had felled large quantities of the woodlands, much of which had been shipped to Newcastle for sale to coal mining companies as pit props.

1.8   The New (Second) Statistical Account of Scotland

The geography and economy of the Redcastle estate that Col Hugh Baillie purchased in 1839 is described in the New (Second) Statistical Account of Scotland. The preparation of the Second Account was initially proposed to the General Assembly of the Church of Scotland by the Committee of the Society of Sons and Daughters of the Clergy in 1832. It is broadly similar in format to the Old (First) Account, except that there are more contributions by non-clergy such as schoolteachers and doctors. It was published in fifty-two quarterly parts between 1834 and 1845. The Killearnan chapter[132] was not published until 1845, although it had been written by Rev. John Kennedy in 1837–38, before he died in January 1841.

Surprisingly, the account makes no mention of the Redcastle quarry and pier, which had been built by James Grant and Thomas Telford in 1803 to ship stone from Redcastle quarry to Inverness during the construction of the Caledonian Canal, and which had been (and still was) a major source of local employment in the early nineteenth century. However, it does state that 'vessels of a considerable tonnage can safely load and unload on the shore of the east end of the parish'. This was a reference to ownership by the tacksman of Lettoch of a schooner and a sloop with which timber (for pit props) had been exported and coal had been imported from Newcastle by Sir William Fettes. The cargos were mostly loaded and unloaded at North Kessock (where Sir William had improved the pier) or at the wooden pier close to the eastern entrance to Redcastle estate at Corgrain Point (Figure 10).

The schooner and the sloop, as well as other ships landing cargo at North Kessock or Corgrain, are also referred to in Lewis' *Topographical Dictionary of Scotland*[133] published in 1846. This early gazetteer, like the New Statistical Account, provides an insight into the geography and economy of the parish in the mid-nineteenth century. For example, it describes Redcastle as 'a large pile, surrounded with beautiful plantations, which occupy many hundreds of acres, and consist of oak, ash, birch, Scotch fir and larch'. It further states that the Redcastle estate comprised 3,796 acres, of which 577 were pasture, 1,653 were woodlands and 1,566 were arable, the crops being wheat, barley, oats, rye, clover, turnips and potatoes.

Figure 10: The old wooden pier at Corgrain Point

Some of the common land of the Millbuie was previously planted with forestry by Patrick Grant when he owned Redcastle in 1816–25. [The Millbuie is the spine of higher ground in the centre of the Black Isle, reaching 250 metres at Mount Eagle. It is now mostly afforested, but in the early nineteenth century was covered in broom, gorse and heather, from which Bain[134] attributes the name Millbuie to the Gaelic *'mhoal buie'* meaning 'yellow ridge'.] According to an advertisement in the *Inverness Journal* of 10 April 1829, this land had subsequently been re-allocated to the Drynie estate. It is headed 'Growing fir timber for sale' and notifies that there would be a public roup on Tuesday 14 April of:

> …the growing fir timber and trees of every description, on that part of the Commonty of Milbuy, formerly possessed and planted by Patrick Grant Esq. late of Redcastle, and which part of said Commonty has been allocated to Mr Graham of Drynie. The wood, consisting of about 90 acres, is situated about three miles from the pier erected by the Commissioners of the Caledonian canal, adjacent to the Quarry of Redcastle, and is accessible by means of very good country roads.

The Lewis gazetteer describes both Milton of Redcastle and Quarry of Redcastle in glowing terms:

> Milton … is chiefly remarkable for its delightful situation, and its miniature likeness to a town; and Quarry, deriving its name from the rock immediately behind it, consists of a neat line of cottages, extending along the base of a sandstone rock, which rises to the height of a hundred feet above the village, giving it a very singular appearance. There is a corn-mill on each of the two estates, for the use of the parish. Two fairs, the staple horse-markets of the country, are held, the one in February, and the other in July. Facility of communication is afforded by a good road from the ferry at Kessock to Dingwall, the repairs of which are supported by a regular toll.

Considerable depopulation of the Redcastle estate had occurred after 1820. The New Statistical Account vividly describes the improvements in agricultural methods that reduced the number of tenant farmers in Redcastle to only six when previously 'some twelve or fourteen small tenants occupied among them what is now the occupancy of one individual'. The account also states that 'new steadings of the most complete description, with comfortable dwelling houses, have been built, are building, or are about to be built, on these farms on the Redcastle property. Substantial stone dykes have been built'. The Lewis gazetteer confirms the agricultural improvements made at this time in stating that 'the lands within the last 20 years have assumed an entirely different appearance. The native heath and broom are gradually yielding to valuable crops of grain'.

An article published in the *John o'Groats Journal* in 1850 also describes[135] the improvements since 1814, when:

> …there were only three farms on the estate that might be considered in any degree well conducted, and one pair of horses would be sufficient for the working of each. What was otherwise cultivated was nothing else than scattered and unproductive patches, the occupiers of which making no exertion whatever to improve, and many of them preferring to depend upon what might be realised from the 'black pot' [illegal distillation]. However, since these days the barony of Redcastle has undergone a great and mighty change to the better for all concerned, and the hitherto rugged and sterile appearance it was wont to exhibit is now converted into a smooth, sweet and heart-cheering sight. Along the Beauly Firth for nearly six miles nothing is now to be seen but rich and fertile fields, portioned out in large farms, each of which is suitably enclosed and subdivided with stone dykes and other fences, and their annual yield cannot be surpassed in the north.

The creation of larger farms and the introduction of new agricultural methods also seem to have attracted a new class of professional farmer into the area. These farmers spoke English rather than the native Gaelic. One account[136] states:

> The language of the natives is Gaelic, and the greatest portion of the inhabitants can receive religious instruction through no other medium. The Gaelic, however, may be considered as on the decline. Nearly the whole of the young people understand and speak English well. And of late years, and in consequence of the new system of farming introduced, converting large tracts of land into one farm, strangers have come amongst us, who do not understand Gaelic, and must therefore bring with them from other parts servants who can understand them.

Some of the tenant farmers and workers who were evicted in the early nineteenth century from Redcastle (and the other local estates) were granted asylum by the Kilcoy estate on the higher ground of the Millbuie [the highest point of the Kilcoy estate reaches about 175 metres]. This ground was allocated proportionately to the various estates and, to this day, some of their names are retained in this part of the Millbuie – for example, Drynie Park and Allangrange Park. Even the Killearnan parish church, as a principal landowner, was allocated a parcel of land. The name of this croft does not seem to have been recorded, but it is referred to as 'a detached part of Killearnan glebe at Drynie Park' in some of the national censuses.

The evictees were taken into the Kilcoy estate on condition that they cleared an acre of land each year so that it could sustain food crops and pasture for animals. It would have been back-breaking work but was funded by a Government Land Improvement Gratuity, which paid £5 for each Scots acre cleared and funded rent-free use of the land during its initial lease (usually nineteen to twenty-one years). Rev. John Kennedy in the New Statistical Account asserts that 'they are accommodated on liberal terms, and where it is expected that they may make for themselves, in a few years, pretty comfortable settlements. Those who first settled on these parts of the Kilcoy property after I became minister of this parish [in 1814] are now able to keep a horse, a cow, with a follower, and a few sheep'. [A 'follower' was a calf, still dependent on its mother.] An article entitled 'A Day in the Black Isle', published in the *Inverness Courier* of 4 June 1874, also describes the wasteland clearances and improvements that were undertaken by farm evictees during this period.

1.9   The Baillies of Tarradale and Redcastle

The Baillie family has a long pedigree that originates from Bailleul in French Flanders.[137] They crossed the English Channel with William the Conqueror in

1066 and, after the Battle of the Standard (where the Scots under David I were defeated by the English at Northallerton in 1139), they became established as landowners when Guy de Balliol was granted the Barony of Buiveld and lands in Northumberland. The family had already extended its land ownership into Scotland when John Balliol was selected by Edward I as King of Scotland in 1292. For example, coincidentally, the de Balliol family is recorded in the twelfth century in ownership of the eponymous Redcastle in Angus.

When John Balliol renounced his allegiance to Edward I in 1296, he was taken prisoner to the Tower of London but was subsequently allowed to return to his family estates in Bailleul in 1299. Meanwhile, Edward I plundered Scotland, reaching Elgin before turning south to Scone where he removed the Stone of Destiny, the traditional coronation stone of the Kings of Scotland. The stone remained in Westminster Abbey until Christmas Day 1950, when it was stolen. It was discovered four months later in Arbroath Abbey and returned to Westminster. On St Andrew's Day (30 November) 1996, it was relocated to Edinburgh Castle where it currently rests.

During the reign of John Balliol, his great-uncle, Sir Alexander de Balliol, became Lord Chamberlain of Scotland. Alexander's son, William, married William Wallace's daughter, and their son, William of Lamington, changed his name to Baillie when Robert the Bruce took the Scottish crown in 1306. William's great-grandson, Sir William Baillie of Lamington, had four sons. The eldest, Alexander, and two of his brothers perpetrated a horrible crime when they castrated their clergyman tutor and, fearing the retribution of the Church, fled from Lamington. Alexander went to Inverness, where he was taken in by his cousin, the Earl of Huntly. They fought victoriously at the Battle of Brechin in 1442, for which Alexander was rewarded with the Barony of Dunain and Dochfour. In 1667, David Baillie (the second son of the 7th Laird of Dunain) married Margaret Fraser (the daughter of the 8th Lord Lovat) and was created the 1st Baron of Dochfour.

David Baillie's great grandson, Col Evan Baillie, succeeded as 4th of Dochfour in 1799. He was MP for Bristol and a merchant. In reality, he was a slave trader who owned 3,000 slaves in the West Indies and amassed a vast fortune, including a handsome compensation payment of £91,632 when his slaves were legally freed in 1834. His brother, James, was also an MP who lived mainly in Grenada and St Kitts. James holds the distinction of having given only one speech in the House of Commons in 1792, during which he opposed the abolition of slavery on the basis that life aboard a slave ship was no worse than life on many other ships, and that a life of slavery in the West Indian plantations was no tougher than that endured by the poor in some parts of London.

Col Evan Baillie (4th of Dochfour) had two sons, Peter (5th of Dochfour) and Hugh, born on 31 May 1777. By the time Hugh purchased Redcastle, he already owned Tarradale as well as a London house, and had become MP for

Rye and Honiton and the Lord-Lieutenant of Ross-shire. [Tarradale had been purchased by Col Evan Baillie of Dochfour from the geologist Roderick Impey Murchison in 1818.] Col Hugh Baillie not only invested heavily in improving the woodland and farmland of the estate, but also renovated and extended the castle. Indeed, according to his factor, Dr John MacKenzie,[138] he expended so extravagantly on his Redcastle and Tarradale estates that he was obliged to borrow money from his brother out of the compensation package that his father, Evan Baillie (4th of Dochfour), had received after the abolition of slavery. John Mackenzie quotes from William Shield's 1883 operetta, *The Poor Soldier*, in describing the Colonel: 'How happy the soldier who lives on his pay; and spends half a crown out of sixpence a day.'

In 1840, Hugh Baillie commissioned the Scottish architect, William Burn, to draw up plans and carry out work on the castle. As rebuilt by Colin Mackenzie (4th of Redcastle) *circa* 1765, it was an L-plan tower house (Figure 5, page 33), with its shorter wing directed approximately to the south and its longer wing to the east. Burn's original plans, which have survived as a series of nine architectural drawings,[139] show that it was intended to make extensive alterations and additions (Figure 11).

Figure 11: A part of William Burn's 1840 architecture drawings of Redcastle, commissioned by Hugh Baillie, owner of Redcastle 1839–66 (© RCAHMS, William Burn Collection)

The alterations included redesigning the cellars, building a new two-storey 'utilitarian' northern wing at the rear of the castle (with an entresol for women servants' apartments), infilling the re-entrant angle with a new stair tower, extending the eastern wing so that it balanced the southern wing, building an arcaded loggia across the southern-facing elevation, enlarging the windows and adding some decorative features (such as door and window pediments). However, not all of these alterations were carried out, nor were they completed as designed. In particular, the eastern wing was not extended, so the castle today still retains its L-plan appearance when viewed from the south. Nevertheless Burn's alterations remodelled Redcastle from an austere L-plan tower into a mansion in the Scots baronial style.

On 9 August 1842, it was reported in *The Times* that Sir Robert Peel, the Prime Minister, was to visit Redcastle during the summer parliamentary recess. However, four days later on 13 August, *The Scotsman*[140] reported that 'it has been rumoured that the Premier is expected in Ross-shire this season on a visit to Colonel Baillie of Redcastle, MP. We understand that the report is entirely without foundation – Sir Robert will be too busy even during the Parliamentary recess to permit his being absent at such a distance [three days' journey] from London'. Despite this report, Hugh Baillie's granddaughter, Philippa Baillie (writing under her married name of Mrs Frank Russell), in her book *Fragments of Auld Lang Syne*[141] claims that Sir Robert Peel had visited Redcastle and had described the view from the castle as 'a magnificent panorama'. Whether the Prime Minister visited Redcastle or not, Hugh Baillie seems to have ensured that the extended castle and the estate grounds were maintained in excellent condition. In an article[142] on the Barony of Redcastle published in 1850, it is surmised that 'there is no estate in the Highlands of equal extent as Redcastle that is so valuable, as, exclusive of the arable land, there are hundreds of acres of thriving wood' and Col Hugh Baillie is described as 'one of our best Highland lairds, never giving occasion to either tenant or cottar to murmur'. *The Times* of 20 December 1842 also reported on the excellent condition of the estate in the following article:

> Some English sportsmen were present at battues [driving of wild game by beaters] held recently at … Redcastle … where pheasants, hares, rabbits, woodcock, blackgame and roe were found in such abundance as to convince them that a thorough knowledge of destroying vermin and rearing game has made many of these preserves to resemble the best English manors.

Although Col Hugh Baillie was responsible for a great many improvements to Redcastle and its gardens and woodlands, he lived there relatively rarely. He died in London on 21 June 1866 at the age of eighty-nine. In his obituary, the

Inverness Advertiser of 29 June recalls that his father, as a young boy, had witnessed the Battle of Culloden from a hill above Dochfour, had made his fortune as a merchant in the West Indies and Bristol, and had represented that city as its MP. Hugh Baillie was married twice, initially in 1796 to Elizabeth Raynett, by whom he had a son and three daughters, and secondly to Mary Smith of Castleton Hall, Lancaster, by whom he had three sons and a daughter. He seems to have been a popular and respected man, of whom the obituary states:

> Few men have passed through a long life more sincerely respected than the deceased. At one time he was prominent in the higher circles of London society, and up to a very advanced age he was assiduous in the discharge of his future as a landed proprietor and Lord Lieutenant of the county in which his fine estate lay.

Redcastle was inherited in 1866 by Hugh's only son by his first marriage, Henry James Baillie, born in March 1804,

Figure 12: Henry Baillie, owner of Redcastle 1866–85
(from Russell, Fragments of Auld Lang Syne*)*

He represented Inverness-shire as MP from 1840 to 1868, and had served as Under-Secretary of State for India. Like his father, he was married twice, firstly (in 1840) to Phillipa Sydney of Strangford, and secondly (in 1857) to Clarissa Rush of Elsenham, Essex. He had four children by his first marriage: two sons, Francis Henry and Hugh Sidney; and two daughters, Philippa Augusta Marie and Elizabeth Ellen. Philippa Baillie's book[143] features several family portraits (Figure 12) and recounts the legend that Redcastle was haunted by a 'green lady' [traditionally a Scottish witch]. However, she admits that she never encountered the lady, despite always sleeping in the 'green lady's room'. She also recalls how her father (and, before him, her grandfather, Col Hugh Baillie) had extensively renovated the castle and had engaged Dr John MacKenzie of Gairloch as factor to oversee the design and construction of its gardens 'on the model of an old French chateau, with terraces and Portugal laurels cut to imitate orange-trees and sugar-loaf yews'. The head gardener was Thomas Fraser, the first of three generations of Fraser to hold that post, and together they planted trees and shrubs, including many exotic varieties, such as figs, peaches, ilex and cork, some of which can still be found today in the now overgrown grounds.

The Right Honorable Henry James Baillie died in Cannes on 16 December 1885. He had been in poor health and had gone to the south of France, where he had hoped the climate would be more beneficial. He was a wealthy man, having inherited the great wealth of his father and grandfather, but was also generous. For example, there is a sasine abridgement[144] of December 1876 which issues a bond for £6,228-6-10d to the Society for the Relief of Indigent Gentlewomen of Scotland. [This organisation still exists to assist 'ladies of Scottish birth or education with professional or business backgrounds who exist on low incomes and have limited savings'.] The purpose of Henry's donation is not recorded, but perhaps he was providing for a relative of his second wife who had fallen on hard times.

Henry Baillie's will, which had been written in June 1885 before he moved to Cannes, details how he wished his considerable wealth to be distributed[145] by his executors: Philippa; Hugh (his half-brother); Sir Charles Grant (his son-in-law); and James Leman (solicitor). As both of his sons and his second wife had died before him, the only family beneficiaries were his two daughters and a granddaughter (Constance, the only child of Francis Henry). The younger daughter, Elizabeth, who had already in 1879 been in receipt of a trust deed, was left the Strangford family portraits; Constance was left £6,000 in trust for her education and a one-third share of an annuity of £16,666; and Philippa, who had no trust fund, received the balance of his cash reserves, plus all the household effects in Redcastle. These included the gold and silver, china, glass, furniture, pictures, books, and garden and farm stock. He also left money to others: £1,000 to his half-brother, Hugh Smith Baillie; £400 to his butler, James Pitt; an additional year's wages to his housekeeper, Mrs Stiles; and an additional year's wages to his head gardener, Thomas Fraser. He had also in 1876 generously pensioned Dr MacKenzie, giving him £85 per year in reward for forty years' service as factor in both Redcastle and Tarradale.[146]

Although his daughters could inherit their father's moveable property, they could not inherit the estate land or the castle itself. In consequence, these were inherited by Henry's cousin (twice removed), Col James Evan Bruce (JEB) Baillie of the Dochfour branch of the family. However, Henry had been astute and had previously ensured that his daughters and his half-brother would be financially secure by assigning them £10,000 each as the executors of his will and issuing bonds of provision, binding on his heirs, of a further £5,000 each. The money was derived from a Special Act of Parliament passed in 1881 and reported in both the *Inverness Courier* (16 August 1881) and *The Times* (30 August 1881).

The article in *The Times* explains that the Redcastle estate was:

> ...placed under strict entail [a deed to secure or alter a specified succession of heirs] in 1865 in favour of Col [Hugh] Baillie in liferent and of his son, the Rt Hon Henry J Baillie, and his heirs male in fee. Failing heirs male, the estate was entailed on Mr Baillie of Dochfour, and after him on the same series of heirs entitled to succeed to the Dochfour estate. By the same predecease of the heirs male of Mr Henry Baillie, it became apparent that the Redcastle estate would devolve upon the Dochfour family to the exclusion of Mr Henry Baillie's family, and that the extensive improvements effected by Col [Hugh] Baillie and his son would be lost to the family unless some remedy were meanwhile provided. For many years prior to the deed of entail, and up to the period of his death, Col [Hugh] Baillie had expended large sums of money and exercised great care in planting and cultivating the timber upon the estates, and Mr Henry Baillie since his succession had followed the same course of management. The property had thus become greatly enhanced in value and had been made peculiarly attractive as a residential property. The timber, on a recent valuation, was found to be of the intrinsic value upwards of £32,000, while the matured and marketable timber was worth upwards of £22,000. The present heir, being entitled to cut down the matured timber, had been advised to reimburse himself for his own and his father's expenditure by selling the same, but being unwilling to affect the peculiar beauty and attractiveness of the estate, he offered to abandon all right to cut down the timber for a sum of £20,000. The next heir seems readily to have closed with this offer and the Act now passed sanctions the agreement, and empowers the present heir to charge by bond as freely as if the property were held in fee simple with the sum of £20,000, and £1,000 as the expenses of the Act, the heir binding himself not to cut timber

during his occupancy, except for estate purposes. Provision is made for the gradual extinction of the debt by means of a sinking fund spread over a period of 25 years, but in the event of the timber being cut sooner, the proceeds are to be applied to an earlier discharge of the burden.

The Special Act of Entail therefore allowed for the enhancement in the value of Redcastle that had arisen from the investment in its woodlands to be put in bond (rather than to be realised by felling, thereby ruining the beauty of the estate). The value of the marketable timber, set at £20,000, was the amount Henry Baillie assigned to his daughters as his executors. Furthermore, the 'intrinsic' value of the woodlands in which he and his father had invested was estimated at £32,000, from which amount his heirs (the Baillies of Dochfour) would provide the bonds of provision.

Henry Baillie's will is of further interest, because attached to it is an inventory of the entire contents of Redcastle taken on 13–14 January 1886 by John Paxton, Valuator, Inverness. Every room is documented, and the value of each article is listed:[147]

- Drawing room, £120-14-6.
- Back drawing room, £44-2/-.
- Dining room, £2-16/-.
- Best bedroom, £22-6-6.
- Extra bedroom, £14-6/-.
- Dressing room 1, £19-9-6.
- Dressing room 2, £1-9-6.
- Mr Baillie's bedroom, £15-4-6.
- Miss Baillie's room, £11-2/-.
- Prince Charlie's bedroom, £18-14-6.
- Lobby, £1-18-6.
- Bedroom, £7-15-6.
- Nursery, £9-12/-.
- Turret bedroom, £2-4/-.
- Men's bedroom, £5-10-6.
- Maid's bedroom 1, £6-4-6.
- Maid's bedroom 2, £7.
- Bath room 8/6d.
- Top lobby, £30-3-6.
- Business room, £25-2/-.

- Housekeeper's room, £5-15-6.
- Lobby, 12/6d.
- School room, £3-19-6.
- Butler's bedroom, £2-18/-.
- Servants' hall, £2-8-6.
- Front hall, £7-5-6.
- Butler's room, £9-19-3.
- Linen napery, £15-16/-.
- Servants' linen, £23-8-6.
- Lobby, 4/6d.
- Valet's room, £5-18-6.
- Front green bedroom, £10-11-3.
- Dressing room, £2-17-6.
- Back green bedroom, £18-?-9
- Stair lobby, £2-15-6.
- Front entrance, £2-8-9.
- Laundry, £3-2-8.
- Laundry maid's room, £1-13/-.
- Kitchen, £10-17-3.
- Housemaid's bedroom 1, £1-16-9.
- Housemaid's bedroom 2, £3-6/-.
- Housemaid's pantry, £4-19-9.
- Gun room, £11-13-6.

The contents of other estate buildings were also included:

- Redcastle Mains, £21-15-6.
- Seafield, £96-19-3.
- Parkton, £115-12/-.
- Stable, £61-10-3.
- Byre, £83-6/-.
- Dairy, £2-2/-.
- Carriage shed and harness room, £130-7-6.
- Garden, £12-6-9.

With the silverware separately valued at £207-12/-, the value of the entire contents was estimated for Probate Duty at £1,271-6-2d. Additionally, there was silverware at Trescott and Co. of London valued at £613.

1.10 The Kessock Ferry

The proprietorship of the Kessock Ferry had belonged to the owner of the Redcastle estate since May 1589, when Sir William Keith of Delny, Earl of Ross, made a charter to Ruairidh Mor (1st of Redcastle) of 'all and whole the lands and village of Easter Kessock with the ferry of Kessock'. However, in a statute of 1661, responsibilities for the regulations and charges applying to any ferry were given to the Justices of the Peace of the shires in which the ferry operated. This meant that there should have been joint responsibility for the Kessock ferry between Ross and Inverness but, as stated in a legal opinion[148] of 1835, 'the Justices of the Peace of Ross-shire seem to have long exercised a jurisdiction over the ferry by fixing the rates of fare and prescribing other rules to be observed in its management'. This is confirmed in a letter from 'A Black Peninsular' to the *Inverness Courier* published on 18 June 1874, which claims that 'for at least a century back, the Ross-shire Justices have claimed and exercised the privilege of regulating the fares and rates exigible on Kessock Ferry'. It further records that the passenger fare during the eighteenth century had been a 'hearth-bannock of oatmeal' but by the beginning of the nineteenth century it had become 1d. It seems, however, that the ferrymen generally ignored the prescribed regulations; for example, in April 1779 a fine for 'non-compliance' (presumably overcharging) had been imposed on Andrew Paterson, the tacksman of the ferry. [Many of the Patersons of North Kessock became ferrymen. There is a myth told by MacLean[149] that one of them married a mermaid. She later escaped back to the sea, but provided her family with plentiful supplies of fish which she left on the shore near their house.]

In April 1788, it was minuted by the Commissioners of Supply[150] that 'having learned that the pier of Kessock was in a state of disrepair, the Clerk of Police was ordained to inspect the same, and, if he found it in the state reported that he should order it to be forthwith repaired'. As the Redcastle estate was in sequestration at that time, no action was taken until the new proprietor, James Grant, was in residence. In April 1793, he submitted a set of proposals to improve the ferry, which he described as 'the direct and shortest communication from the town and county of Inverness to the shire of Ross, its three burghs and Cromarty with all that part of Scotland north of the Frith of Beauly … the great and most frequented thoroughfare between the five more northerly counties and the rest of the Kingdom'. He also described the pier at North Kessock as 'a partial accommodation chiefly for foot passengers … from the beginning inadequate for the purpose of landing or embarking conveniently such horses and carriages as have for the last forty years been more generally used in this township'; and was less than complimentary about Inverness Town Council which had 'hitherto opposed on some pretended obsolete prescriptive right the erection of anything like a pier on their side of the Frith'. His proposals were to construct two new stone piers of sufficient size to accommodate boats from high to low water mark on both sides of the ferry, to supply two boats (one on each side of the ferry), to procure ground on the Inverness side of the ferry, to build ferrymen's houses as close to the piers as possible and to enlarge (into a hotel) the public house close to the Ross-shire shore.

It was estimated that the capital cost of these proposals would be £700 (£400 for the piers, £100 for the ferrymen's houses and £200 for the hotel), which would be paid for through a temporary fare increase of ½d (to 1½d per foot passenger) and a proportionate increase for horses and carriages, to be in force until such time as the capital outlay had been recouped. The proposals were unanimously agreed by the Commissioners of Supply, and in October 1794 James Grant reported that all the improvements had been made and that the new charges were now in operation. Ten years later, in April 1805, the Commissioners appointed a committee to investigate whether James Grant had now recouped his capital. However, they reported back in October 1805 that they were 'dissatisfied with the accounts kept by Mr Grant as being inexplicit' and although being remitted to 'obtain the necessary explanations from Mr Grant', no resolution was reached and the 'temporary' charges remained in force.

The dispute over ferry charges had again been raised in June 1820, when Patrick Grant objected 'that the Justices of the Peace of Ross-shire had not the exclusive jurisdiction of the ferry of Kessock, which was by the statute, shared with them by the Justices of the Peace of Inverness-shire'. The Commissioners of Supply had to agree, and remarked 'that no communication appeared by the records to have been made at any former period with Inverness-shire, on the subject of the regulations of the ferry of Kessock'. This new dispute had arisen because Patrick Grant wanted to raise the fares in order to improve the piers 'for substituting a steam boat for the sailing boats on Kessock ferry'. It seems not to have been resolved because, after the sale of Redcastle estate in 1825, Sir William Fettes also applied to raise the fares and prepare the piers for steam boats. Finally, in October 1825 the new fares (3d per foot passenger) were sanctioned and a steam boat was introduced. However, the steam boat was found to be unreliable and, in April 1830, Sir William Fettes announced his intention to discontinue with it and revert to sailing ships. The foot passenger fare was accordingly reduced to 2d.

A further request by Henry Baillie for a fare increase was presented to the Ross-shire Justices in June 1874. This was met with considerable opposition from both Inverness and Black Isle traders, who argued that the annual rent (£570 in 1874) received by him was more than sufficient to cover any capital expenditure on boats and piers and that the current fare (of 2d per foot passenger) was sufficient for the tenant of the ferry to manage the service and pay his boatmen. A full report was published in the *Inverness Courier* on 2 July 1874. The request was refused.

It was not until 1880 that there was another attempt to use a steam ship at the Kessock ferry. The *Inverness Courier* of 27 May carried an article in which it announced that 'a handsome little steamer, the *Redcastle* ... was being placed on the ferry through the enterprise of the ferry lessee, Mr Hector Stewart'. She was forty-five feet long and fourteen feet broad, with a draught of four and a half feet aft and three feet at the bow. She was expected to average eight miles per hour but 'only time will tell how she may suit the peculiarities of Kessock ferry – the strong tidal currents, the frequently high winds, and the nature of the traffic'. Time *did* tell, because less than a year later the *Inverness Courier* of 3 March 1881 reported that the *Redcastle* had been sold and, on its way to London, had put into Berwick 'with sternpost and rudder carried away, having struck something off the Fern Islands'.

Only in 1906 were steamships finally put into reliable regular service at Kessock. These were the *Nellie* and the *Maud*, which served the route during World War One and until 1921. Although the Redcastle estate sold its rights to the ferry in 1898, the steamers were named after two members of the Baillie of Dochfour family, the owners of Redcastle from 1885.

1.11 The Baillies of Dochfour and Redcastle

James Evan Bruce (JEB) Baillie was the 8th of Dochfour. He was the great-grandson of Col Hugh Baillie's brother, Peter Baillie (5th of Dochfour). Peter had died in 1812 and his eldest son, Evan Baillie (6th of Dochfour), had died in 1883. Evan's eldest son, Evan Peter Montagu Baillie (7th of Dochfour), had also died (in 1874); therefore his son, James Evan Bruce Baillie, fell heir to the Redcastle estate.[151] James' date of birth is not recorded, because he was born in Paris, France. In national census returns (1891 and 1901, when he was resident in Dochfour), his age is given as thirty-two and forty-two, suggesting that he was born in 1859.

Probably because of further mechanisation on the estate farm lands and, therefore, a dwindling population with less need for estate workers' accommodation, Henry Baillie had commenced disposal (by leasehold sale) of some of his estate properties, a practice that seems to have been accelerated by James

Baillie. Quarry House in Quarry of Redcastle was the first to be put up for sale. It was a three-storey house built *circa* 1830. The sasine extract[152] describes the property as '2 roods 14 poles of ground, with Quarry House, etc. thereon, bounded on the south or south-south-east and on the south or south-south-west by the Foreshore of the Beauly Firth'. However, the sasine abridgement[153] records that James Baillie required the consent of James Hogg for the sale because, in June 1862, Col Hugh Baillie had transferred to him the ninety-nine-year tack on both the quarry and the house that had originally been granted in 1837. It was purchased in 1880 by James Nicol and his wife, Lillias, who lived in Milton of Redcastle and had farmed at Blairdhu since 1870.

Throughout the nineteenth century, fishing rights in the Beauly Firth had been the source of several disputes between the local landowners, particularly those of the Redcastle, Tarradale and Lovat estates. For example, in March 1817 Thomas Alexander Fraser of Lovat and other 'curators and proprietors of the fishings in the River Beauly' had successfully petitioned[154] against Patrick Grant of Redcastle 'from using stakenets where the sea ebbs and flows for the purpose of catching salmon'.

In May 1860, the Chairman of the Ross-shire Police Committee[155] received a letter of complaint about the 'interference' of the Chief Constable in a local fishing dispute. It transpires that Duncan Chisholm, who was in charge of Lord Lovat's mussel scalps, had given permission to John Currie and James Riach, two fishermen from Buckie, to take mussels from the Firth and pay Duncan for them on behalf of Lord Lovat. The Chief Constable had personally interfered, because he was of the opinion that Col Hugh Baillie of Redcastle had exclusive rights to the mussel scalps and that he should have received the payment. The minutes of the Committee do not record how the issue was settled, but it seems that Duncan had formerly managed Col Baillie's scalps before changing his allegiance to Lord Lovat. The Chief Constable was disciplined and received a warning about his future conduct. He resigned a year later; apparently he had an alcohol problem.

The castle that Henry Baillie had inherited in 1866 was described in the Valuation Rolls of that period as a 'mansion-house and garden with shootings, woodlands, mussel scalps and fishings'. For the right to harvest the shore of the Beauly Firth, the Redcastle estate paid a feu (of £25) to the Crown. However, the mussel scalps and fishings were sublet to George Colvill of Kessock Cottage, Inverness. The sublet was soon to be discontinued, and thereafter the estate employed managers to look after the scalps and fishings. They were to become the cause of several disputes in the latter years of the nineteenth century. For example, on 4 October 1878 the *Inverness Advertiser* reported that James Baillie was suing James Souter and nine other fishermen from Lossiemouth for taking mussels from the Firth. However, he was unsuccessful, as the fishermen claimed that they had taken the mussels from tidal waters, not from the estuarine intertidal waters over which he held the fishing rights.

James Baillie was more successful when he had to defend his rights from Lord Lovat. On 23 January 1890, the *Scottish Highlander* reported that Lord Lovat was taking legal action against James Baillie and others over two issues, firstly for 'shooting or sweeping salmon nets' in the stretch of the River Beauly opposite Tarradale and, secondly, to have declared illegal the shoreline embankment built at Tarradale by Henry Baillie in 1869, which, Lovat claimed, had altered the flow of the River Beauly, adversely affecting his fishings. James Baillie won on both counts, firstly by proving that he (and his predecessors) had fished that section of the Firth for over twenty years, hence establishing statutory rights in law and, secondly, by proving that the embankment had been built with the consent of Lord Lovat's predecessors and that Henry Baillie had purchased the reclaimed land from the Board of Trade for £388-16-4d. To rub salt in the wounds, James Baillie sold all his fishing rights (excluding those opposite Redcastle estate) to Lord Lovat in April 1900.[156]

James Baillie lived in Dochfour, and shortly after he inherited Redcastle he decided that it was surplus to his requirements. He therefore put the estate (together with the Tarradale and Craigton-Kessock estates) up for sale in 1890. Advertisements placed in the national newspapers described the estates as follows: 'Residential, agricultural and sporting subjects … situated on the Beauly Firth … for sale by private treaty as one subject or in three portions'.

The sales particulars[157] presented the Redcastle estate in glowing terms:

Redcastle is said to be the oldest inhabited mansion in the North of Scotland. It is built in the Scotch Baronial style, and is picturesquely situated on an eminence overlooking the Beauly Firth. It contains three public rooms, library, twelve bedrooms, an ample kitchen, servants' and other accommodation, and is fitted up with every regard to modern requirements, yet without detracting from the charm and dignity of its ancient character. There is no district in the Highlands which possesses a more salubrious climate, and, from its peculiarly sheltered situation and southerly exposure, the winter and spring seasons are unusually mild and agreeable. The grounds surrounding the mansion house are extensive, and contain splendid walnut and other trees of great age. The gardens are large and are in the highest state of cultivation. There are also vineries and peach-houses. The estate extends to about 3,745 acres, whereof 2,115 acres, or thereby, are arable, and the remainder woodlands and pasture. The arable land comprehends twelve farms representing a rental of £2,368.

Despite the sasine extract[158] transferring the ownership of the estate to James Baillie in 1886 describing Redcastle as 'a town near the sea having a commodious port and harbour and a station or pier erected thereat', there is no reference in the sales particulars to either the quarry or the pier. The quarry had closed *circa* 1875, and the pier was therefore more or less redundant.

Figure 13: The vignette of Redcastle from the 1890 sales particulars (reproduced from an original, D303, held by the Highland Council Archive Service)

The document describing the sales particulars is noteworthy for a striking vignette of Redcastle and its gardens drawn by Percival Skelton (Figure 13). It also provides a breakdown of the annual feu and rental income that the Redcastle estate gained in 1889–90 from each of the occupants of its properties. In Milton of Redcastle, Quarry of Redcastle and Chapelton, the twenty-one listed properties collectively raised £59-19-6d, whilst the crofts and glebe at Spital, Garguston, Blairdhu and Milton collectively raised £69-19/-. All tenants are named, although it is not always clear which is the specific house they occupy. The document is also supported with a map of the estate, drawn up in 1889 at a scale of 6 inch:1 mile. Unfortunately, the map is disappointing in showing only the six local farmhouses (Whitewells, Garguston, Blairdhu, Fettes, Parkton and Redcastle Mains), Greenhill House, the Killearnan Public School, the parish church and both the Established and Free Church manses, in addition to Redcastle itself. No houses are shown in either Milton of Redcastle or Quarry of Redcastle and, even stranger, the Free Church at Newton crossroads is absent, despite having been built in 1866.

As it transpired, only the Craigton-Kessock estate was sold. The price of £19,000 was agreed in 1898, although the sasine abridgement of the purchase is dated December 1901. The purchaser was Donald Macdonald, who was a shipbroker and coal merchant at North Kessock. He became Provost of Inverness in 1918, and was knighted in 1922. The sale included the Kessock ferry, thus ending over 300 years of operating rights by the proprietors of Redcastle. No purchaser was found for Redcastle, and therefore the estate remained in the ownership of the Baillie family of Dochfour. It is probable that the marriage on 31 January 1894 of James Baillie to the Hon Nellie Lisa Bass (Figure 14) may have influenced its withdrawal from the market. Born in December 1873 as the only child of Michael Bass, Lord Burton of Rangemore, she seems to have fallen in love with Redcastle – as well as its owner.

Figure 14: (left) Col James Baillie, owner of Redcastle 1885–1931; (right) Nellie Bass, Baroness Burton (reproduced with permission from the collection of the late Frances [Ada] McDonell)

At their lavish wedding in London, there were ten bridesmaids and 700 guests but, according to the *Scottish Highlander* of 1 February 1894, the event was equally celebrated in Inverness and throughout the Baillie estates in Scotland. The merchant traders of Inverness gathered at the Station Hotel where the chairman, wearing a buttonhole of violets (the favourite flower of the bride), presented a toast to the bride and bridegroom which was 'most heartily pledged, and accorded Highland honours'. A telegram was sent to the couple:

'Mr and the Hon Mrs Baillie of Dochfour, Chesterfield House, London. Merchant traders of Inverness assembled at Station Hotel send true Highland greetings and hearty congratulations – Macdonald, Chairman; Keeble, Secretary'. Later that afternoon, a reply was received: 'Many thanks for kind congratulations and greetings from the merchant traders of Inverness, which have given us great pleasure – Nellie and James Baillie'.

On the estates, there were huge bonfires. At Redcastle, the celebratory arrangements were placed in the hands of Robert Trotter, the tenant farmer of Garguston. Four hundred trees were felled and piled seventy feet high on the summit of Gallow Hill. The employees, servants and tenants of the estate mustered at Greenhill House and, headed by a piper, processed with lighted torches to the summit of the hill. The fire was lit, aided by eight barrels of tar and paraffin, by Colin MacDonald of Linnie Wood. [He was the second oldest person on the estate and was standing in for the oldest, his brother Roderick, who was ill.] Before toasting the married couple, Robert Trotter read a letter he had received from James Baillie.

> I have to thank you for your letter of 16 January. I regret to say I shall not be in the North before the wedding. All the presents we have received are to be exhibited in this house [Chesterfield House in Mayfair] on the 29th and 30th January. Do you not think it would be a pity if the present that the Redcastle and Tarradale tenants are so kindly giving to Miss Bass were not exhibited there also? We shall probably be coming to Dochfour about the 3rd week in February. If you would settle a day and let me know a little later on … we would come over to Redcastle and receive the address. Please convey to all those who have so generously joined on this occasion our very warmest thanks for this token of their good wishes.

A firework display and copious amounts of refreshment followed.

This was not the first Baillie marriage at which bonfires were lit on the estate hilltops. Over twenty years earlier, *The Scotsman* of 30 April 1870 recorded the marriage in Inverness of Capt Hugh Baillie (Henry James Baillie's eldest son) and reported that it 'occasioned great rejoicing over the family estate in Ross-shire. On all prominent points flags were displayed, and at night half a dozen huge bonfires blazed from the surrounding hill tops. At the castle, fifty gentlemen sat down to dinner, presided over by Provost McKenzie, Inverness; and the proceedings were afterwards wound up with a ball'. Unfortunately, Capt Hugh did not live to inherit his father's Redcastle estate.

Despite his wife's love of Redcastle, James Baillie's policy of disposing with some of the estate properties continued after his marriage. The most significant sale was that of the freehold of Garguston Farm, which was purchased in June 1899 by its long-term tenant, Robert Trotter. Sasine abridgements of June 1899 also record that the leaseholds of both Fettes and Blairdhu farms were sold to Kenneth MacDonald, who farmed at Redfield (near Tore). Other properties were also sold on a leasehold basis, for example, Quarry Cottage in 1899 and the smithy at Chapelton in 1901.

Surprisingly, and unfortunately, the castle is omitted from the 1901 national census; therefore it is not possible to determine whether any of the Baillie family was in residence, nor to what extent Redcastle was used by them at the turn of the century. In all probability it was a third home, well maintained but irregularly used (the main homes were in London and Dochfour). The estate was a subscribing member of the Ross-shire Squirrel Club, which had been formed to reduce the numbers of red squirrels on the participating estates. Red squirrels had been reintroduced into the Highlands by Lady Lovat in 1844. They had multiplied rapidly, and by the end of the century had become regarded as pests. However, during the period 1903–05, the Redcastle estate could not have been overrun with squirrels, as it recorded only seventy-one killed compared, for example, to Kilcoy estate, which recorded 759 killed during the same three-year period. The Squirrel Club paid 4d per tail.[159]

In the period 1910–15, the Inland Revenue carried out a valuation of every house in the UK, on a parish-by-parish basis. It is sometimes referred to as the 'New Domesday' survey. The boundaries of every property are marked out and numbered on copies of the relevant 1:2,500 (*circa* 25 inch:1 mile) second edition Ordnance Survey maps[160] and the data is fully documented in associated field books.[161] Redcastle is described as a twenty-nine-acre estate with mansion house and garden owned by James Baillie of Dochfour, and is recorded as being in excellent repair and in first class condition, with walls in the old portion seven feet thick. The accommodation is described as follows – but, surprisingly, the basement (which comprised two servant's bedrooms, two cellars, a laundry and the back entrance) is not included:

- Ground floor: entrance hall, bedroom, housekeeper's bedroom, store room, kitchen, scullery, larder, two bedrooms, store, cellar, wine cellar, butler's room, butler's pantry, boot room, servants' hall, two WC.
- First floor: front hall, study and room, smoking room, dining room, drawing room, bathroom and WC, housemaids' pantry, boudoir, bedroom and dressing room, two bedrooms, WC, cupboard.
- Second floor: six bedrooms, two dressing rooms, WC.
- Third floor: five bedrooms.
- Tower: bedroom.

External to the castle were the lodge house (West Lodge), gardener's house, stables, garage, kennels, laundry, potting sheds and glasshouses, but these are not separately described. Some buildings in Redcastle Mains (or Redcastle 'Home Farm', as it is named in the survey) were also considered to be part of the castle. These included a stable (eight stalls), two looseboxes, four groom rooms with hay loft over, a harness room, a garage for six cars, a wash house and ironing room and kennels for six dogs. The woodlands around Redcastle were divided in the survey into three woods. Linnie Wood chiefly contained good thirty-year-old Scots fir, Redcastle Burn Wood was mixed timber and hardwoods, whilst Gallow Hill Wood mainly contained Scots fir, larch, oak and beech.

Whether Redcastle was occupied at any time during World War One does not seem to be recorded, but after the end of the war James Baillie attempted to let Redcastle. An advertisement in *The Scotsman* of 21 February 1923 reads:

> To let with entry at Whitsunday 1923, Redcastle Mansionhouse, Home Farm and Shootings, Ross-shire, one mile from Redcastle Station and 5 miles from Inverness. The mansionhouse contains 5 reception rooms, 21 bed and dressing rooms, and is comfortably furnished. There is a large fruit and vegetable garden. Redcastle Farm extends to 127 acres arable and 700 acres or thereby of pasture. The shootings consist of 1,500 acres arable and woodlands near the house, and the game consists of partridges, woodcock, snipe, wildfowl, hares, roe-deer, etc.

There does not appear to have been any uptake, because later that year HRH Edward, the Prince of Wales, stayed with Col James Baillie and Baroness Burton at Redcastle during his visit to unveil the Seaforth war memorial at Fort George on 22 August.

The preparations were frenetic. In a letter to her husband sent from Dochfour and dated 8 August 1923, the Baroness describes the preparations for the visit.[162]

> The work has been tremendous, but I have all in order, everything was to blazes at Redcastle, even the mowing machine was broken that I diddled by sending over the one from here in the garden float. I think it will look quite nice but I have had to take on two extra men in the garden for a fortnight – it was a hay-field. I have grabbed some things from Dochfour and looked out the best dinner service we never use and so on. He stays two nights. It is for the unveil-ing of the Seaforth Memorial at Fort George. He was asked to stay at Moy but he would not go. He also wants to see the dogs. He wrote himself rather as if he was my long lost brother. The Elgins come just then so that is splendid, and I've got Evan and his Maud and have asked Georgie Chetwode. He wishes no neighbours asked to dine as he is on holiday, and wants to be as peaceful as he can. I have about worked myself to death and shall come South on Saturday to

Curzon Street, arriving on Sunday morning and go to Maud's ma-in-law on Tuesday to Friday and then back North. Coming South will be a rest. I shall be glad to see you. We had an awful storm here yesterday, tropical rain and all the drains blocked at once! Such fun – backyard flooded and so on.

On his departure from Redcastle, the Baroness presented Prince Edward with a pale cream cairn terrier called 'Dochfour Molly'. Framed photographs of Molly (and some of the other cairns belonging to the Baroness) still hang in Greenhill House. The Prince showed Molly at the Caledonian Canine Society's Championship in January 1924, where she won the reserve bitch certificate. He successfully bred cairns from Molly until his succession to the throne as Edward VIII (on 20 January 1936) and his abdication (on 10 December 1936). 'Evan and his Maud' in the Baroness's letter was a reference to her eldest son, George Evan Michael Baillie, and his fiancée, Lady Maud Cavandish. They were married on 15 November 1923, and were presented with a silver tea-kettle as a wedding gift from the tenants and employees of Redcastle. The estate manager, Donald McDonell, presided over the event and said that 'the gift had been subscribed for with a heartiness that reflected the popularity of the young couple in the district'. The presentation was made to Evan, in the absence of Lady Maud, who was not able to be present due to illness, by Rev. Alexander Cameron of the Killearnan United Free Church. Photographs of the event show that around ninety estate employees and guests (Figure 15) were present and the archways at the front door of Redcastle had been specially decorated with laurel by the head gardener, Hugh Fraser.

Figure 15: The 1923 wedding gift presentation from the employees of Redcastle to Evan Baillie and Maud Cavandish (reproduced with permission from the collection of the late Frances [Ada] McDonell)

James Baillie died on 6 May 1931, and Baroness Burton remarried in 1932 to Major William Melles. They lived mainly in Redcastle and, in consequence, the house and the gardens were maintained in superb condition. The castle was also rented out on occasions; for example, the Duchess of Somerset was briefly a tenant in the early 1930s. There are numerous photographs from this period that testify to the condition of the castle and its gardens, including postcards by Urquhart of Dingwall, Mackay of Inverness, Forbes of Muir of Ord (dated 1926) and Tuck and Sons of London dating from *circa* 1930. A copy of the Urquhart postcard is held at RCAHMS and copies of others are known to be in private collections, such as the Brian Maclennan (Munlochy) collection. There is also an album (currently in Greenhill House) that contains superb photographs of the interior of Redcastle from the inter-war years.[163] In December 1936, the Baroness instructed Mackenzie and Moncur Ltd, Heating Engineers, Edinburgh, Glasgow and London, to draw up plans to install central heating. A plan of the proposed installation[164] shows the recommended positions of the radiators superimposed on a plan of the castle, at a scale of 1 inch:10 feet, that details the room layout on each of the five floors (the tower is not included). It is interesting to compare this plan with the schedule of accommodation that was detailed in the field books of the 1911 Inland Revenue valuation survey (page 101):

- Sub-basement: two bedrooms, wine cellar, laundry, cellar (where the boiler was to be installed).
- Basement: main hall, servants' hall, servants' bathroom, three bedrooms, kitchen, scullery, two larders, wine cellar, pantry and lamp room.
- Principal floor: business room, dining room, drawing room, ante room, three bedrooms, two bathrooms.
- Bedroom floor: five bedrooms, dressing room, two WC.
- Attic: five bedrooms.

Some earlier plans drawn up in 1929–30 by J R McKay, Architect, Melville Street, Edinburgh, show designs for new fireplaces in the drawing room and breakfast room – but also, in anticipation of the installation of central heating, proposed alterations to the ground floor required to accommodate an oil store and boiler house.[165] A 250-volt electrical power supply had already been installed into Redcastle using a turbine powered by water piped from the mill dam below Parkton. A turbine, driven by the Redcastle burn, had also been installed *circa* 1925 to provide electricity to the Gardener's Cottage in Milton of Redcastle, and this is thought to have been the first electrically lit house in the area.

During the last week of June 1931, HRH Edward, Prince of Wales, again visited Inverness and Ross-shire, during which time he undertook so many engagements that the *Ross-shire Journal* of 3 July 1931 remarked 'was ever in so short a space so many functions crammed', whilst one Black Isle spectator is said to have likened his schedule to 'a cloud o'stour and a flash o'Mackenzie tartan'. During that week, he resided at Lovat Castle but is known to have made a private visit to Redcastle (where he had stayed in August 1923), probably to convey his condolences on the recent death of Col James Baillie (who died on 6 May 1931) but also because, in common with Baroness Burton, he was particularly fond of cairn terriers. It is recorded that he brought two with him to Inverness. They had probably been bred from 'Dochfour Molly', the cairn terrier that had been presented to him during his visit to Redcastle in 1923.

Each September in the early twentieth century, the gardens at Redcastle (Figure 16) were opened to the public, who were charged 1/- entry fee. The head gardener was Hugh Fraser, who lived in the Gardener's Cottage at Milton of Redcastle and was also the parish registrar. He died in September 1926, and is buried in Killearnan churchyard. His father, Thomas, had helped Col Hugh Baillie and his son, Henry Baillie, to redesign the gardens of Redcastle from 1865 onwards. Hugh was succeeded by his son John, who therefore became the third generation of the Fraser family to hold the position of head gardener at Redcastle. He and his family also lived in the Gardener's Cottage and tended the gardens until 1958. Throughout his tenure, John kept a daily log of the work carried out in the gardens.[166] It comprises a set of three notebooks and offers a remarkable insight into village life in Redcastle during the middle years of the twentieth century, not only as a record of the complexity of managing a large estate garden and the associated daily programme of work, but also for the additional entries about the weather and the various events taking place in the parish.

Figure 16: Redcastle and its gardens circa 1930 (reproduced with permission from the collection of the late Frances [Ada] McDonell)

105

The first entry, recorded only as 'digging', was made on Monday 21 February 1927. Thereafter, the seasonal routine unfolds and is repeated year after year: clipping beech hedges and ivy, box, holly, laurel and yew bushes; carting away clippings; cleaning the greenhouses; riddling earth; tying up and pruning peaches, figs and vines; manuring plots; sowing lettuce, beetroot, parsnips, cauliflowers, carrots, leeks, peas, turnips and cabbages; potting and planting out tomatoes, onions, potatoes, begonias, dahlias, delphiniums, hollyhocks, sunflowers, gladioli, lobelia, antirrhinums and carnations; weeding and Dutch hoeing borders; pruning roses; staking and tending to strawberries, raspberries, gooseberries, redcurrants and blackcurrants; mowing and raking grass; trimming verges; picking and storing apples, pears, plums and cherries; lifting potatoes; brushing, carting and burning leaves; etc.

On 17 December 1954, John records the arrival of a motor plough. From that date onwards, the phrase 'ploughing with motor plough' replaces 'digging' – clearly a welcome purchase. John Fraser seems also to have been the estate beekeeper. He often records sightings of queen bees, when the bees swarmed, when the bees were fed, when honey was extracted and when the hives were cleaned. On 20 August 1949, he records that 368 jars of honey were obtained.

Not surprisingly, John Fraser's log books also provide a commentary on the prevailing weather, especially when it was exceptional. Thus snow, hail and thunderstorms, high winds and particularly wet, cold or hot weather are noted. In the sheltered location of the castle gardens, extremes of temperature could occur – for example, the coldest record seems to have been 4°F (-16°C), which is recorded on two occasions in 1955 (20 January and 26 February), while the hottest record seems to have been 90°F (32°C), which is recorded on 6 July 1932.

Many other events of both local and national importance are noted in the log books. Of local interest are references to days: when John travelled to Inverness, Dochfour, Fortrose, Kingussie, Dingwall or Glasgow; when coal was delivered; when the castle was empty; when the Duchess or her servants arrived; when the garden was opened to the public; when seals were beached (for example, 7 November 1935 and 24 July 1947); when the church sale was held and the amount that was raised (for example, 20 August 1936 – £55, and 22 July 1950 – £165); when foot and mouth disease broke out (26 December 1942); when seagull eggs were collected (for example, 6 May 1950 and 26 April 1952); when John was required for grouse and pheasant beating; and two occasions when the dam below Parkton broke and caused flood damage in the valley of the Redcastle burn (29 September 1945 and 14 August 1957). Also recorded are: the dates of the Dingwall, Munlochy and Muir of Ord shows; the opening of Tore Hall (5 December 1931); and the funerals of many local people including Col James (JEB) Baillie (10 May 1931), Rev. Aeneas

Macdonald (1 December 1932), Rev. James MacDonald (24 December 1946), Miss Augusta Bruce (23 December 1949), Donald Riggs (13 May 1950), Major William Melles (26 February 1953) and Donald McDonell (27 October 1955).

Some of the national events and holidays that are noted include: the Royal Jubilee (3 May 1935); the abdication of King Edward VIII (10 December 1936); the coronation of George VI (12 May 1937); the VE day celebrations (8/9 May 1945); the Victory Day celebration (8 June 1946); and the coronation of Queen Elizabeth II (2 June 1953). Notably, apart from the New Year Holidays on 1 and 2 January, and some occasional fast days, John never seemed to take any annual holiday until after World War Two, when he is recorded as taking one week, usually in October or November. On some occasions, he records going on holiday to Edinburgh or Aberdeen.

Some personal events are also noted. For example, on 22 November 1940 he records that his son, Hugh, was called up. This is the sole instance, other than the victory celebrations, of any event related to World War Two being recorded. The Third Statistical Account of Scotland[167] written by Rev. George Ballingall in September 1954 records that Redcastle 'is unoccupied, but the gardens and policies are kept in good order and are beautiful'. Unfortunately, regular entries to Hugh Fraser's log book end on 20 March 1958, when it is recorded that general garden work was undertaken inside due to 12 degrees of frost (-7°C). Poignantly, the log ends in the week 29 March–5 April 1958, when it is noted that he was flitting to Raddery, near Fortrose. Sadly, from that day onwards the gardens at Redcastle have been left to nature and, fifty years on, their former glory can be experienced only in the many surviving photographs[168] (see, for example, Figure 16, page 105).

Redcastle was requisitioned by the War Office for military purposes in 1939, and Baroness Burton relocated to Greenhill House. Clearly, this was a hasty decision, because it had been offered as an unfurnished let from Whitsunday 1939. The advertisement in *The Scotsman* of 8 April stated that it offered '2 public, 6 bed rooms, bathroom, boxroom, kitchen, &c, garage'. After the war, on the death of her father in 1952, she inherited the Barony of Burton-on-Trent and Rangemore in her own right under a 'special remainder' that came into effect because there were no sons. Greenhill House remained her Highland retreat (although less so after her second husband died in 1953) until she died in May 1962. Tragically, her eldest son by her first marriage, George Evan Michael (GEM) Baillie, 9th of Dochfour and known as Evan, had died of war injuries in 1941. Evan had a distinguished military career, having fought in World War One and been awarded the Military Cross and having risen to the rank of Brigadier in the Royal Artillery. His death meant that Baroness Burton's eldest grandson, Michael Evan Victor (MEV) Baillie, who had been born in 1924, inherited Dochfour as the 10th Baron. Michael was often at

Greenhill after World War Two, and was well known to the local youths, but he seems to have preferred Dochfour. Although it would not have been obvious at the time, this signalled the demise of Redcastle.

There are two paintings of Redcastle in Greenhill House. They are both painted from the direction of the gardens and are therefore views of the front of the house. One is undated, and the artist's signature is just discernable but not legible (Figure 17). It contains a group of three persons in Highland dress in the middle foreground and, from the appearance of the castle, it was painted prior to William Burn's modifications in 1840 (Figure 11, page 86). The other was painted in October 1948 by a Polish ex-prisoner of war, M Azepeckj, but it is not clear how (or why) the painting was commissioned. There is also a tapestry, framed in a fire screen, depicting a similar view of Redcastle. It is not known who embroidered it. Other paintings of the castle are held in private collections.

Figure 17: Painting of Redcastle, artist and date unknown but probably late eighteenth century (© Burton Property Trust)

After World War Two, the castle was briefly rented by Capt Jack MacLeod, the Independent Liberal MP for Ross and Cromarty in 1945–64. His wife gave birth to twins in the castle, and the family were the last people to live there. Until then, Redcastle had claimed the distinction of being the longest continuously inhabited castle in Scotland. It is said that Michael Baillie shortly afterwards had the roof removed for property taxation purposes, but this is not substantiated and it is likely that the real reason was for safety. In consequence, it quickly fell into disrepair during the 1950s through a combination of water ingress and a fire, accidentally caused by local youths. The Valuation Rolls first describe Redcastle mansion house as 'uninhabitable' in 1957. Today, it is an empty shell and its walls are crumbling dangerously (Figure A, page 13, and Figure 18).

Photographs of the castle dating from 1959 onwards are held by the RCAHMS, and record the decline in its condition.[169] Some show the superb stonework in detail, particularly on three of the inscribed dormer pediments. Some remnants of the stonework are still stored at Redcastle Mains. Redcastle is now in the ownership of the Burton Property Trust, who, to date, have been unwilling to consider selling it, since it lies in the middle of the estate. It was placed on the Buildings at Risk Register[170] as a category B risk (critical) in June 1990. A proposal to consider the use of some of the woodlands around the Redcastle burn as a Country Park was included in the (draft) 2005 Ross and Cromarty East Local Structure Plan.[171] The castle was last used in 2006, when a marquee was erected to hold the engagement party of Hamish Michael Baillie, the younger son of Evan Michael Ronald (EMR) Baillie and grandson of the current proprietor of Redcastle, Baron Michael Evan Victor (MEV) Baillie (10th of Dochfour). More recently, a proposal has been made to create a conservation area around the castle that would include many of the buildings that owe their existence to the Redcastle estate.

Figure 18: Aerial view of Redcastle in 2008 (reproduced from an original by permission of Mr Jim Bone)

What will transpire is unknown. Meanwhile, the ancient Redcastle stands in ruins on its twelfth-century foundations, a sad relic of 800 turbulent years, awaiting its future – or final demise.

NOTES

[1] Evidence for a tsunami on the east coast of Scotland is given in Dawson, A G, 'Evidence for a tsunami from a Mesolithic site in Inverness, Scotland', J. Archaeological Sci., 17, 509–12 (1990) and in Perry, D, 'Inverness: an historical and archaeological review', Proc. Soc. Antiq. Scot., 128, 831–57 (1998).

[2] Archaeological studies carried out at Tarradale are described in Jones, G D B, 'Tarradale: Investigation of a Cropmark Site near Muir of Ord, Ross and Cromarty', Manchester Archaeological Bull., 13–19 (1991) and in Gregory, R A and (the late) Jones, G D B, 'Survey and Excavation at Tarradale, Highland', Proc. Soc. Antiq. Scot., 131, 241–266 (2001).

[3] There are several texts on the history of the area that contain information on Redcastle, Killearnan, the Black Isle and Easter Ross. These include: Alston, D, 'Ross and Cromarty, A Historical Guide' (1999); Alston, D, 'My Little Town of Cromarty: the History of a Northern Scottish Town' (2006); Baldwin, J R (ed), 'Firthlands of Ross and Sutherland' (1986); Marshall, E, 'The Black Isle, A Portrait of the Past' (1992); Meldrum, E, 'The Black Isle: Local History and Archaeology Guidebook No. 3' (1984); Robinson, A and Courtney, H, 'Kilcoy Castle – a short history' (2001); Bain, R, 'History of the Ancient Province of Ross' (1899); and Miller, J, 'Inverness' (2004).

[4] Information on all ancient and historical monuments and sites in Scotland is available from the Royal Commission for the Ancient and Historical Monuments of Scotland (RCAHMS) website www.rcahms.gov.uk using the 'Pastmap' and 'Canmore' facilities. The RCAHMS hold numerous photographs of archaeological sites in the Redcastle area, for example, the excavation of Carn Glas (RCAHMS C82896) and the food vessel that was found (RCAHMS RC/1885). Many of the website pages are linked to www.ambaile.org.uk and http://ads.ahds.ac.uk. The Highland Council Archaeology Unit has recently launched a fully searchable 'Historic Environment Record (HER)' at the website http://her.highland.gov.uk. It provides information about historic buildings and sites in the Highlands using an interactive map facility similar to 'Pastmap'.

[5] Excellent descriptions and ground plans of the Neolithic and Bronze Age cairns at Kilcoy are given in Henshall, A S and Ritchie, J N G, 'The Chambered Cairns of the Central Highlands' (2001). Earlier accounts are given in Woodham, A A, 'A Survey of Prehistoric Monuments in the Black Isle', Proc. Soc. Antiq. Scot., 88(7), 65–93 (1954–56).

[6] An early account of the 'artificial islands' in the Beauly Firth is given in Fraser, J, Phil. Trans. Roy. Soc., 21, 230–2 (1699) and a review of subsequent examinations can be found in Blundell, Rev. O, Proc. Soc. Antiq. Scot., 44, 12–33 (1909–10).

[7] The excavation of the Redcastle crannog is detailed in Hale, A, 'Scottish Marine Crannogs', BAR British Series 369 (2004); 'Marine Crannogs: Previous Work and Recent Surveys', Proc. Soc. Antiq. Scot., 130, 537–58 (2000); and in Coastal Archaeology and Erosion III, Focal Study No 17, 'Seeing the Unseen: Locating Marine Crannogs', 155–162 (2003). These articles contain photographs of the excavations and aerial photographs taken in 1966 (RCAHMS B80299/CN/po) and in 1993 by Prof G D B Jones of Manchester University.

110

[8] A brief report of a presentation by Col Angus Fairrie on the Roman Campaign to North Britain in AD 84–85 is given in the *Ross-shire Journal* of 10 November 2006.

[9] Ptolemy's 'Geographica' map of 'Albion Britannica Insula' of AD 150 is reproduced in J G Bartholomew's 'Survey Atlas of Scotland' as Plate 9 of the 'Historical Maps of Scotland' (1912). It can be viewed online at www.nls.uk/maps.

[10] See note 3.

[11] A series of articles and letters concerning the possible Gaelic origin of the term 'Black Isle' was published by Sinclair, Rev. J, *Celtic Monthly*, Vol 6, pages 153, 163, 190 and 210 (1898). The conclusion favoured the probable origin to be 'Allan Duth'.

[12] The original Act of William I (the Lion) that established a castle at Etherdouer is recorded in Barrow, G W S and Scott, W W, 'Regesta Regum Scottorum, Vol 2: The Acts of William I, King of Scots, 1165–1214', pages 11 and 292 (1971). The reference to the Act of 1211 is given on page 454. Another source is Watt, D E R (ed), 'Scotichronicon' Vol 4, pages 337 and 465–7 (1994). This text is a translation of Vol VIII (William I) of Walter Bower's original Latin manuscript written *circa* 1440 and describes Etherdouer as being 'rebuilt' in 1179. A further source which describes Ederdover as being 'strengthened' in 1179 is Anderson, A O, 'Early Sources of Scottish History: AD 500 to 1286', Vol II, pages 301–2 (1990).

[13] An excellent account of 'Mottes in North-East Scotland' is given by Yeoman, P A in Scot. Arch. Rev., 5 (parts 1 and 2), 125–33 (1988). Redcastle (Etherdouer) is described as one of a defensive line of mottes guarding Inverness from attack from the north.

[14] A detailed and well-referenced account of the medieval history of Redcastle is given in 'Origines Parochiales Scotiae: The antiquities ecclesiastical and territorial of the parishes of Scotland', Vol II part II, pages 524–31 and Appendix pages 840–42 (1855). Shorter accounts are given in 'History of Redcastle', Trans. Inverness Sci. Soc. and Field Club, 2, 240–43 (1882) and 'Excursion Round the Black Isle', Trans. Inverness Sci. Soc. and Field Club, 8, 185–6 (1913).

[15] The reference to the original location of Redcastle (Eddydor) being at Chapelton is in MacLean, J, 'Historical and Traditional Sketches of Highland Families and of the Highlands' (1895). The chapter on 'The Mackenzies of Redcastle' is on pages 119–37. (NB This text contains a fanciful account of the life of Kenneth Mackenzie [8th of Redcastle] as well as several other improbable stories, so the validity of its contents may be suspect.)

[16] The reference to the sixteenth-century L-plan tower house of Redcastle incorporating the twelfth-century castle is given in Coventry, M, 'The Castles of Scotland' (2006). Other architectural texts that describe Redcastle include: Gifford, J, 'The Buildings of Scotland; Highlands and Islands' (1992); Tranter, N, 'The Fortified House in Scotland', Vol 5 (1970); and MacGibbon, D and Ross, T, 'The Castellated and Domestic Architecture of Scotland', Vol 3 (1889). The original Redcastle was known as Eddyrdor or Edradour, which translates (according to

www.scottish.parliament.uk/vli/language/gaelic/pdfs/placenames)   as   *Eadar   Dha Dhobhar*, meaning 'between two waters'. See also note 4.

[17] A well-documented account of the establishment of Beauly Priory by the Bisset family of the Aird is provided in Chisholm-Batten, E, 'The Charters of the Priory of Beauly' (1877). Some other texts which describe the origins of the early 'de la Ard' landowners of Redcastle and the clans associated with Ross are: Mackeggie, J A, 'Beauly Priory and its Associations', a series of three articles published in *Celtic Monthly*, Vol 20, pages 191, 204, 222 (1912); Mackenzie, A, 'History of the Chisholms' (1891); Sellar, D, 'Highland Family Origins' in Maclean, L, (ed) 'The Middle Ages in the Highlands', pages 103–116 (1981); and Grant, A, 'The Province of Ross and the Kingdom of Alba' which is Chapter 5 (pages 88–126) of Cowan, E J and McDonald, A, (eds) 'Alba: Celtic Scotland in the Medieval Era' (2000). This latter text is particularly detailed and extensively referenced.

[18] The Beauly Charter of 1278 granting Redcastle (Eddyrdor) to Sir Andrew de Bosho (or Bosco) is No. VII in NLS AdvMS35.2.4. It is also recorded in Chisholm-Batten, E C, 'The Charters of the Priory of Beauly', pages 63–73 (1877).

[19] See note 3.

[20] See note 12.

[21] The Wardlaw manuscript was originally written in 1666 by Rev. James Fraser of Kirkhill (previously known as Wardlaw). A translation was published by the Scottish History Society under the editorship of Mackay, W, 'Chronicles of the Frasers (AD 916–1674): The Wardlaw Manuscript' (1905). The original manuscript was entitled 'Polichronicon seu Politcratica Tempora' and is held at the NLS (MS3658).

[22] Descriptions of the many medieval and post-medieval metal-detector finds from fields around Redcastle are contained in MacLeod, C, 'Unearthing Redcastle's Hidden History' (2007). This text is also available on the website of the Ross and Cromarty Heritage Society at www.rchs.uhi.ac.uk. Several of the finds are described in Weeks, P and MacLeod, C, Discovery Excav. Scot., 3, 71 (2002) and 4, 89 (2003). Many are also recorded in the websites www.rcahms.gov.uk and www.ambaile.org.uk.

[23] The guerrilla campaign conducted in Northern Scotland by Robert the Bruce against Edward II and John Comyn, Earl of Buchan, is described in McNeill, P G B and MacQueen, H L, 'Atlas of Scottish History to 1707' (1996). A fuller account is given in Barnes, P A and Barrow, G W S, 'The movements of Robert the Bruce between September 1307 and May 1308', Scot. Hist. Rev., 49, 46–59 (1970).

[24] The Acts of the Kings of Scotland are collected in Paul, J B, 'The Register of the Great Seal of Scotland' (1882). The first record of 'Eddirdule' (Redcastle) is in Charter 43 (1426) reproduced in Vol 2 (1424–1513), page 8. Other subsequent references to early custodians of Redcastle can be found in: Vol 2, Charters 1470 (1481), 1472 (1481) and 3625 (1511); Vol 3 (1513–46), Charters 411 (1526) and 3117 (1545); Vol 4 (1546–80), Charters 947 (1554) and 1618 (1565). References to the ownership of Redcastle by the Mackenzies commence from: Vol 5 (1580–93), Charters 707 (1584), 1331 (1587) and 1625 (1587); Vol 6 (1593–1608), Charters 861 (1598) and 2177 (1608). The Great Charter of Inverness, which refers to the 'boyes-fair' of St Andrew on 7 July at Redcastle, can be found in Vol 5, Charter 2001 (1591–92). The royal

pardon given to Colin and Ruairidh Mor Mackenzie in October 1586 is recorded in Vol 5 (1580–93), Charter 2362.

[25] 'The Exchequer Rolls of Scotland' published by Burnett, G, (1883) reproduces the Act of Annexation of certain lands, including 'Eddirdule' (Redcastle), to the Crown (1455) in an Appendix to the Preface of Vol 6 (1455–60). Detailed accounts of the rentals paid by each of the farms within Eddirdule are recorded from Vol 8 (1473–78) onwards. The first record under the name of 'Reidcastell' is in Vol 14 (1513–22). The record of Gargastoun and Reidcastell being in 'few-ferme to Rorie Makenze' is in Vol 23 (1595–1600).

[26] See note 13.

[27] See note 25.

[28] See note 24.

[29] The royal charter by Mary, Queen of Scots assigning the Mill of Redcastle and other neighbouring lands to Johanne Stewart on 8 July 1554 is written in Latin and is archived in AUSLA MS3470/15/1/1. Mary's 'Progress through the Northern Highlands' and her visit to Redcastle in the summer of 1564 is documented at www.marie-stuart.co.uk and in McNeill, P G B and MacQueen, H L, 'Atlas of Scottish History to 1707' (1996).

[30] The 'Inventory of the Title Deeds of the Barony of Redcastle' (1790) was commissioned by James Grant. It contains details of the various charters and sasines associated with the Redcastle estate from 1578–1790. Known as the 'Redcastle Writs', the inventory is held at NAS GD23/10/603. The original charter of land by James VI to Sir William Keith of Delny in August 1587 (which included Garguston, Newton of Redcastle, Easter Kessock and the Kessock ferry that were assigned to the Redcastle estate in 1589) is held at NAS GD305/1/29/1.

[31] See note 24.

[32] The trial of Colin Mackenzie of Kintail and his brother Ruairidh Mor (1st of Redcastle) for the capture of the house of the Bishop of Ross in Chanonry (Fortrose) and the apprehension of several of his servants in 1577 is recorded in Masson, D, 'Register of the Privy Council of Scotland (1578–1585)', Vol 3, page 88 (1880).

[33] See note 24.

[34] See note 30.

[35] See note 30.

[36] The 'Acts of the Parliaments of Scotland' is a fully searchable database of the records of the parliaments of Scotland from the first surviving Act of 1235 to the Union of the Parliaments in 1707. It is available at www.rps.ac.uk and contains both the original Latin, French or Scots texts as well as modern translations.

[37] See note 25.

[38] See note 15.

[39] See note 24.

[40] The genealogy of the MacKenzies of Redcastle is described in several texts. Probably the most reliable is Warrand, D, 'Some Mackenzie Pedigrees', 68–79 (1965). Others include: Douglas, Sir R, 'The Baronage of Scotland', 398–400 (1798); MacKenzie, A, 'History of the Clan MacKenzie with Genealogies of the Principal Families', 398–403

(1879) (the 1894 edition of this text was digitised by 'Project Gutenberg' in 2003 and is available online); 'History of the Clan Mackenzie' authored by the editor (Alexander Mackenzie) of 'The Celtic Magazine', a series of twenty-three articles in Vols 3 and 4 (1877 and 1878); and a genealogical chart (sheet no. 7 of the Findon Tables, 1879) entitled 'The Families of Redcastle and Kincraig from Kenneth 'Na Cuirc', 10th Baron of Kintail' (NAS RH16/206). There are also numerous texts that contain some of the genealogy of the Mackenzies of Redcastle. They include: Fraser-MacKintosh, C, 'Antiquarian Notes: a series of papers regarding families and places in the Highlands', second edition (1913) [This text also contains reference to the 'Valuation Roll of the Sheriffdom of Inverness, including Ross' (1644); and a booklet entitled 'The Genealogy of the Mackenzies preceding the year 1661, written in the year 1669 by a Person of Quality', page 16 (1843) (HCRL 929.2). Two websites that contain information on the histories and heritage of the MacKenzies of Redcastle are www.clan-mackenzie.org.uk and http://freepages.genealogy.rootsweb.com. NB Many of the vital dates in the latter do not correspond with those given by other sources.

[41] See notes 14 and 40.

[42] The charters from Oliver Cromwell (Lord Protector) providing authority to Colin Mackenzie (4th of Redcastle) to re-enter Redcastle in 1651 and to recollect rentals in 1656 are archived at BL Add.Mss.61570. They form part of a collection of Mackenzie family charters (1350–1866) relating to possessions in Moray, Inverness and Ross and Cromarty held at BL Add.Mss.39187–39211 and 61231–62170. The 1559–60 charter of the 'Viccars Croft of Killiernan' is located at BL Add.Mss.61568.

[43] See note 36.

[44] See note 36.

[45] See note 22.

[46] See note 30.

[47] Texts in which the arms of the Barony of Redcastle are described include: Pryde, G S, 'The Burghs of Scotland, a critical list', Section 3: Burghs of Barony and Regality, page 76, No. 410 (1965); and Bute, J. (Marquess of), Stevenson, J H and Lonsdale, H W, 'The Arms of the Baronial and Police Burghs of Scotland' (1903). A description can also be found at www.visionofbritain.org.uk and the crest can be viewed at www.heraldic-arts.com.

[48] Listings of members of the Scottish Parliament and of Scottish members of the UK Parliament are given in Young, M D, 'The Parliaments of Scotland' Vol 2, (1993) and Foster, J, 'Members of Parliament, Scotland 1357–1882' (1882).

[49] See note 40.

[50] The document of 'reduction' and transfer of Redcastle estate by Roderick (Ruairi Dearg) Mackenzie to his son, Roderick (Ruairi Mor) and his wife Margaret Calder is held at NAS CS226/6344.

[51] See note 40.

[52] I am indebted to Dr David Alston for information on the slave trade involvement of the Mackenzies of Redcastle. An account of the lives of Kenneth Francis Mackenzie, owner of the Lusignan cotton plantation in Demerara, and his son, Charles Kenneth Mackenzie, is given in http://victorianresearch.org/obscure_contributors.html.

[53] Documents relating to the various legal actions surrounding the disputed sale of land in Easter and Wester Kessock by Roderick (Ruairi Mor) Mackenzie to Col Hugh Fraser are held at NAS CS194/151 (act for the first term, 1747); CS205/36 (act and commission, 1747); GD255/1/12/1 and 2 (instruments of protest, 1729 and 1732); GD255/1/18/2, 3 and 4 (instruments of protest, 1730, 1733 and 1736); GD255/1/18/8 (memorial, 1749); and at BL ESTC T22113 (legal advice, 1731).

[54] The petition drawn up by Roderick (Ruairi Mor) Mackenzie in 1739 against Sir Thomas Calder of Muirtown and Colin and James Graham of Drynie naming several local witnesses is located at NAS CS181/7512.

[55] The bill of account from William MacIntosh of Inverness to Roderick (Ruairi Ban) Mackenzie for Lady Hannah's funeral on 25 April 1755 is held at NAS CS96/1/158.

[56] The extended legal case regarding the non-payment by Roderick (Ruairi Ban) Mackenzie of an account for barley purchased from a ship in Inverness is described in a paper entitled 'Information for William Mackintosh of Balnespick, pursuer; against Roderick Mackenzie of Redcastle and John Dingwall, Writer in Edinburgh' dated 4 March 1761. The original is in the Bodleian Library (Oxford) and a copy is held by the University of Leeds, referenced as BL ESTC T216778.

[57] The Court of Session case involving the heritable bond and trust fund set up by Sir Robert Munro of Fowlis in 1738 is recorded in Home of Kames, H, 'Select Decisions of the Court of Session from 1752 to 1768', second edition (1799). It can also be viewed in 'Eighteenth Century Collections Online' available in NLS.

[58] An account of a visit to Redcastle is described in Craven, Rev. J B (ed), 'Journals of the Episcopal Visitations of the Right Rev. Robert Forbes, 1762 and 1770', page 224 (1886). References to Rev. Hugh Campbell and Rev. John Williamson are on pages 71 and 114.

[59] The background to the complex 1784–91 land disputes between the four Mackenzie-owned estates of Redcastle, Kilcoy, Allangrange and Pitlundie bordering with the Fraser-owned Wester Kessock, Kilmuir and Easter Sligo estates is described in the 'memorial' at BL ESTC T477847 (RB.31.b.284. No.11). A map of the disputed area with the boundaries claimed by each of the estates marked in various colours (but now faded) was drawn up by Hugh Kinnaird in 1783. It is entitled 'Plan of the Controverted Marches betwixt Lady Erskine's Lands of Wester Kessack, Kilmuir and Easter Sligo and the conterminous Properties' and is held at NAS RHP117/3.

[60] The boundary between the Redcastle and Allangrange estates was surveyed in September 1776 by Hugh Kinnaird and is recorded in detail in a document entitled 'Boundarys of muir and hill pasture between the property of Redcastle and Allangrange', held at NAS GD23/9/25. The exact locations of the fifteen march stones along the boundary are described.

[61] The references to Kenneth Mackenzie's 'opprobrious' youth are in Fraser-Mackintosh, C, 'Letters of Two Centuries from 1616 to 1815', page 26 (1890).

[62] A good introductory text on the military records held at TNA is 'An Alphabetical Guide to certain War Office and other Military Records preserved in the Public Record Office' (1963). Kenneth Mackenzie's army career can be followed in the annual 'List of the General and Field-Officers as they rank in the Army; and of the

Officers in the several Regiments of Horse Dragoons and Foot on the British and Irish Establishments' (known as the Army Lists). Sets are held at TNA and, locally, at the Archive of the Regimental Museum of the Highlanders, Fort George. The TNA set is annotated with handwritten updates. Kenneth Mackenzie first appears in the 1768 edition and was not removed until 1799, nine years after his death. His appointments as Ensign (26 August 1767) and Lieutenant (27 February 1771) in the 33rd Regiment of Foot and as Captain (26 October 1775) in the 37th Regiment of Foot are also recorded in the Army Notifications of Commissions at TNA WO25/153 and 144. His appointment as Captain (15 January 1778) in the 78th Regiment of Foot (Seaforths) 'from the Dutch Service' is in TNA WO25/148. These appointments are also noted in the annual Army Lists. The Army Muster Books and Pay Lists log Kenneth's career in the 33rd Regiment of Foot from August 1767 to September 1775 in TNA WO12/4802 and 4803 when he transferred to the 37th Regiment of Foot (TNA WO12/5101).

[63] Kenneth Mackenzie's bill of November 1768 and receipt of October 1769 for expenses incurred in the election of the Marquis of Lothian as a Scottish peer are held at TNA T1/466/217-8.

[64] See note 62.

[65] See note 15.

[66] The best source of primary records of the American War of Independence is 'American Archives' at the fully searchable website http://dig.lib.niu.edu/amarch. The record of Capt McKenzie been paroled on 18 September 1776 from Philadelphia jail on grounds of ill health is in Series 5, Vol 2, page 1360.

[67] Some records, mainly of marriages of Scots Brigade soldiers and baptisms of their children in Holland, are contained in Ferguson, J, 'Papers illustrating the History of the Scots Brigade in the Service of the United Netherlands, 1572–1782', published in three volumes by the Scottish History Society (1896–1901). Vol 2 contains a chapter on 'The Last Days of the Brigade, 1750–82' but does not name Capt Kenneth Mackenzie, who was on attachment from the 37th Foot. Vol 3 is entitled 'The Rotterdam Papers, 1709–82' and contains the reference to 'Capt Mackenzie and his Lady' attending a Communion Service in Nijmegen in August 1777. A copy is held at NLS JRM.505.

[68] A 'Historical Record of the 72nd (originally 78th) Regiment of Highlanders (the Seaforth Highlanders)' has been written by Major I H MacKay-Scobie and is held in the Archives of the Highlanders Museum at Fort George. It consists mainly of extracts from articles originally published in the regimental magazine Cabar Feidh (1922–60). Two earlier histories are MacVeigh, J, 'Historical Records of the 78th Highlanders' (1887) and Davidson, Major H, 'History and Services of the 78th Highlanders' (1901). The 'Revolt of the Wild Macraes' is described in these texts and Lieut Kenneth Mackenzie's role in defending the Tolbooth is described in Grant, J (ed), 'Cassell's Old and New Edinburgh' Vol IV, Chapter 37, pages 307–10 (1880). A brief article on the career of Capt Kenneth Mackenzie in the 78th regiment was published by Lieut-Col Angus Fairrie in the 'Queen's Own Highlander', 22–3 (1980). The 'Return of Arms, Accoutrements and Clothing, etc. received for the Right Honourable Lord Seaforth's Regiment', sent from Elgin on 15 May 1778, is listed in TNA WO17/199.

This file of records also contains the May 1781 monthly staffing return of the 78th Regiment. See also note 62.

[69] Transcripts of the Proceedings of the General Court Martial held in Guernsey in September/October 1779 are held at TNA WO71/90/233–284 and WO71/150/box B.

[70] Witness statements and other court papers pertaining to the divorce of Lieut Kenneth Mackenzie and Jean Thomson are held at NAS CC8/6/38 and the proceedings of the Consistorial Court hearing held on 12–13 September 1780 are at NAS CC8/5/16. A promissory note regarding payments of the divorce settlement is held at NAS CS271/31041.

[71] The letter from Kenneth Mackenzie to Lord Amherst, Commander-in-Chief, requesting an inspection of his Independent Company is held at TNA WO34/172/38. The 'Return of the Age and Size of the Men of Captain Mackenzie's Independent Company inspected by Col Samuel Townsend at Chatham Barracks, 7 February 1781' is held at TNA WO34/172/102–4 and the appointment of Kenneth Mackenzie as Captain of an Independent Company is recorded in the Army Succession Book for 7 February 1781, at TNA WO25/35/246. The staff surgeon's 'Return of Recruits enlisted by Captain Mackenzie for his Independent Company' sent on 16 February 1781 is held at TNA WO34/172/295 and Capt Mackenzie's letter to Lord Amherst confirming the formation of his Company was sent on 16 February 1781 and is held at TNA WO34/172/267.

[72] The letter of 9 February 1781 from Capt Kenneth Mackenzie to Lord Amherst, Commander-in-Chief, recommending Thomas Hawkshaw as his Ensign and enclosing a character reference is held at TNA WO34/172/155 and 158.

[73] See note 62.

[74] See note 68.

[75] The letter of 10 July 1781 from Capt Kenneth Mackenzie to Lord Amherst, Commander-in-Chief, requesting the appointment of Alexander Fraser as his Lieutenant is held at TNA WO34/172/156-7. Lord Amherst's negative reply is annotated to the letter.

[76] Letters of instruction to Capt Kenneth Mackenzie regarding his mission to West Africa are collected in Crooks, J J, 'Records relating to the Gold Coast settlements from 1750 to 1874' (1973), chapters 4 and 5, 47–81. This text also describes the events leading to his arrest for murder.

[77] A day-by-day account of the activities of the *HM Leander* over the period June 1780–April 1784 is given in the Captain's log held at TNA ADM51/527.

[78] Capt Kenneth Mackenzie's affidavit sworn on 13 December 1708 requesting the return of the possessions confiscated at the time of his arrest by Capt Wickey and naming the persons he wishes to be brought back from West Africa to act as witnesses at his trial is held at LMA CLA/047/LJ/13/1784/009.

[79] The action taken in 1784 by Capt Kenneth Mackenzie against Commander John Wickey to recover property confiscated at his arrest in West Africa in 1783 is held at TNA TS11/892/3034. The letters to the Foreign Secretary from Comte de Kageneck, the Belgian ambassador, and Capt Hagueron of the *Compte de Flandres* are held at TNA FO95/8/2/34–37.

[80] See note 62.

[81] The Army Half Pay Ledgers for 1784–88 record Kenneth Mackenzie's salary as ex-Captain of the No. 1 Independent Company (disbanded in 1783) in TNA PMG4/35–41.

[82] George III's request to his Commissioners of Oyer and Terminer to try Capt Kenneth Mackenzie for the murder of Kenith Murray Mackenzie is held at TNA KB8/80, and Capt Kenneth Mackenzie's petition of October 1784 to HM Justices of Oyer and Terminer requesting bail is held at LMA CLA/047/LJ/13/1784/009.

[83] The trial papers of Capt Kenneth MacKenzie are held in TNA TS11/1016 (4213) and TNA PC1/3103. A transcript of the trial can also be viewed at www.oldbaileyonline.org.uk and is also published in two pamphlets available at BL ESTC N10462, T107529 and T213529, and also in digital form in '18th Century Books online' (available at NLS). The pamphlet entitled 'The life and complete trial of Kenith Mackenzie Esq for the wilful murder of Kenith Murray Mackenzie…' (1785) also contains an account of the life of Kenith Murray Mackenzie, alias Jefferson. The various notices of respite are held in [TNA HO13/2].

[84] Articles from *The Times* (1785–1985) can be viewed through the indexed and searchable Times Digital Archive. This is available as a subscription service but is free of charge to registered users of libraries such as the NLS. References to Capt Kenneth Mackenzie in issues of *The Times* published during 1785 are also indexed in the 'Times Index, Jan–Dec 1785'.

[85] The 'Address to the Officers of the British Army' (1785) written by 'An Officer' is held at NLS ABS.2.201.015.

[86] The voyage undertaken by Capt Kenneth Mackenzie and 350 convicted prisoners in 1781–82 is described on page 17 of the 'First Report from the Committee appointed to enquire what Proceedings have been had in the Execution of an Act passed in the 24th Year of the Reign of His present Majesty entitled an Act for the effectual Transportation of Felons and other Offenders, and to authorise the Removal of Prisoners in certain Cases; and for other Purposes', published 9 May 1785. A copy of the report is held at TNA HO42/6/373–83.

[87] See note 84.

[88] The letter sent by Capt Kenneth Mackenzie from Newgate prison on 23 August 1785 to the Right Honourable Lord Sydney, Home Secretary, requesting his release from prison is held at TNA HO42/7/344–6.

[89] Capt Kenneth Mackenzie's royal pardon is held at TNA HO13/3, page 260.

[90] The 'Bucks of the City' portrait of Capt Kenneth Mackenzie and a short biography is published in Paton, H, 'A Series of Original Portraits and Caricature Etchings by the late John Kay', Vol 1, No CXX, 292–7 (1877). The biographical details are not entirely accurate. The caricature was also used by Major I MacKay-Scobie in a spoof 'composite' illustration of Capt Kenneth Mackenzie dressed in the uniform of the 78th (Seaforth) regiment published in *Caber Feidh*, (IV)27, (1928).

[91] The circumstances of the death of Capt Kenneth Mackenzie in a duel in Constantinople were reported in letters to the *Edinburgh Advertiser* on 26 and 30 June 1789. The articles can be viewed at NLS and online at www.ancestry.co.uk.

[92] See note 40.

[93] Acts and Warrants in favour of the various creditors of the Redcastle estate can be found at NAS CS111/258, 305, 339, 391, 393, 396, 404–5, 407, 422, 529, 532, 575, 588 and 637. The Acts and Warrants in favour of Kenneth Mackenzie's divorced wife, Jean Thomson, can be found at NAS CS111/631–3, 635–6 and 638 and the 'Act and Warrant in favour of James Grant of Redcastle for getting up his Bond of Caution (January 1793)' can be found at NAS CS111/258. Further papers relating to William Chalmers, Town Clerk of Dundee, Lieut-Col Colin Mackenzie and other creditors are held in AUSLA MS3175/364.

[94] The inhibition of John Mackenzie (6th of Kincraig) is recorded in the General Register of Inhibitions, Vol 206, pages 858–62 (NAS DI8/206). Adjudications in favour of various creditors of the Redcastle estate are held in the Records of Abbreviates of Adjudications for the years 1788–92 (NAS DI14/122/244, 260 and 382; DI14/123/105, 194 and 202; DI14/124/70; DI14/125/305 and 384; DI14/126/55, 159 and 450). The complexity arising from the different claims of creditors against the Redcastle superiority and the property is explained in the adjudication of Catharine Mackenzie against Ross and Ogilvie and others held on 1 June 1791 in the Court of Session and which can be viewed at 'Eighteenth Century Collections Online' available in NLS.

[95] The action in February 1792 of the creditors of Kenneth Mackenzie against his younger children is recorded in Steuart, W and Craigie, R, 'Decisions of the Court of Session from 1787 to 1792' (1795). It can also be viewed on '18th Century Books online', available at NLS.

[96] The decisions of the House of Lords on the appeal by John Peter du Roveray and the objections of the younger children are held at BL ESTC T214086/7 (L.3.a.1. Vol 23, Nos. 77 and 78). These items also provide useful summaries of the history of the Mackenzie bankruptcy.

[97] See note 94.

[98] The circumstances surrounding the claim of Alexander Mackenzie against his brother, Ruairi Mor, is contained in a paper entitled 'State of the process, poor Alexander Mackenzie, tidewaiter at Strontian; against Roderick Mackenzie of Redcastle, and Alexander Monro, tacksman of Dunvoronie' (1761). The paper is held at BL ESTC T220006, and a digital version can be viewed in '18th Century Books online', available at NLS.

[99] The division (in 1798) amongst the creditors of the sequestered assets of Roderick and Capt Kenneth Mackenzie, elder and younger of Redcastle (both deceased) is fully documented in NAS CS96/4733. There are also numerous legal papers relating to the sequestration of the Redcastle estate and the division of the assets, in particular the Register of Acts and Decreets (NAS CS18/660–1) and the Act approving the Scheme of Division (NAS CS111/532).

[100] See note 94.

[101] There are different explanations of the origin and meaning of the stone carving above the entrance to the Mackenzie vault at Fortrose cathedral. Versions claiming that it represents 'Death holding on to his castle at Redcastle' are given in Turner, L B,

'Fortrose Cathedral', Groam House Leaflet No. 2 (1984) and in www.blackisle.org/historic.

[102] The novel entitled *The Last Mackenzie of Redcastle*, loosely based on the exploits of Capt Kenneth Mackenzie of Redcastle, was written in 1888 by his granddaughter Rosa Mackenzie Kettle. A copy is referenced at NLS but has gone missing.

[103] See note 15.

[104] See notes 62 and 68.

[105] The original 'Statistical Account of Scotland' contained descriptions of every parish in Scotland written mainly by the parish ministers and was published in 1799 by its originator and compiler, Sir John Sinclair MP. Grant, I R and Withrington, D J edited the individual accounts through the 1970s and published them in twenty volumes entitled the 'Old Statistical Account of Scotland (1791–99)'. The 'Parish of Killearnan' was written in 1794 by Rev. David Denoon (II) and is published in Vol 17, Chapter 23. The author's name is incorrectly spelled as Dunoon. The OSA is also available online at www.edina.ac.uk/statacc. A text that provides an excellent summary and review of the contents of the OSA is Steven, M, 'Parish Life in Eighteenth-Century Scotland' (1995).

[106] The description of the living conditions of eighteenth-century Killearnan farmers is contained in Mowat, I R M, 'Easter Ross 1750–1850; The Double Frontier', page 97 (1981). The uses made of Black Isle quarry stone are described on page 64.

[107] The Crown charter of the Barony of Redcastle issued to James Grant on 5 July 1790 is held at NAS GD23/4/212.

[108] The minutes books of the Ross and Cromarty Commissioners of Supply (1765–1926) are held in HCA CRC1/1/1–6. Some committee minutes are also available, for example: the 'County Record of Ross-shire' (1733–1864) (HCA CRC1/2/1–6); the Police Committee (1757–1890) (HCA CRC1/2/9); and the Prison Board (1840–78) (HCA CRC10/4/1–2).

[109] See note 30.

[110] See note 60.

[111] The letters and papers of James Grant of Redcastle to his factor (James Grant of Bught) are held in the 'Bught Papers and Letters, Nos. 285–305' (1793–1807) at NAS GD23/6/300/1–10. The indenture of Donald Mackay as a writer for seven years is held at NAS GD23/4/214. The account for trees supplied by George Brown in 1802 is held at NAS GD23/6/396/1.

[112] The poultry rental assessment paid to James Grant by each farmer on the Redcastle estate in 1790 is contained in NAS GD23/8/7/1. The documents entitled 'List of Rent received at Redcastle, 16/17 March 1803' and 'Rental of the Estate of Redcastle, crop 1804' provide details of rentals paid by the farms and businesses of the Redcastle estate. They are at NAS GD23/8/7/2 and 3.

[113] A copy of the 'Tack betwixt Roderick Mackenzie of Redcastle and Mr David Denoon' (1764) is held at NAS GD23/4/191. It defines the extent of the minister's glebe and details the land taxes payable by him as a heritor of the parish.

[114] Dr William Kennedy's bill for medicines dispensed to James Grant between July 1796 and December 1806 is held at NAS GD23/5/373(1).

[115] The 'Petition of Col Alexander Grant of Lochletter and Col Hugh Grant of Moy regarding the death of James Grant of Redcastle' (1808) is held at NAS GD23/7/36.

[116] The 'Inventory of Title Deeds' (1800) of James Grant and the 'Bond of Provision by James Grant to Maria Jane Grant, Charity Emelia Grant and Sybilla Christina Grant' (1808) are held at NAS GD23/4/231 and 245.

[117] An extensive pedigree chart with short biographies for the Grants of Sheuglie (and Redcastle) is given in Fraser, W, 'The Chiefs of Grant', Vol I Memoirs, 516–7 (1883).

[118] The signed regulations for the tenant farmers of Redcastle estate drawn up by Lieut-Col Alexander Grant are in the collection of 'Bught Papers and Letters, Nos. 476–500' (1811) at NAS GD23/6/482.

[119] The Testament and Bonds of Provision (of 1814) in favour of the children of Col Alexander Grant are at NAS GD23/7/44/1 and 2.

[120] Issues of the *Inverness Courier* (1807–date), *Inverness Journal* (1817–49), *Scottish Highlander* (1855–98), *Ross-shire Journal* (1877–date) and *Inverness Advertiser* (1849–85) are available on microfilm at HCRL. A searchable keyword index to nineteenth century articles is available at www.ambaile.org.uk.

[121] The pencil drawing of Redcastle by Alexander Nasmyth, entitled 'A castle, Inverness-shire', is held in The National Gallery of Scotland under reference D3727/84.

[122] A description, with photographs, of a 'caman' is given in *Celtic Monthly* Vol 5, 64 (1896). The 'camach' between the Chisholms and other natives of Strathglass is described in Hutchinson, R, 'Camanachd! The Story of Shinty', pages 102–3 (1989).

[123] The Grant tartan design, originated by Patrick Grant of Redcastle and registered as WR 1385, can be viewed at www.tartans.scotland.net. The identification number is 430.

[124] Details of the proposal by the trustees of Patrick Grant to issue a bond for £120,000 using the Redcastle estate as security are contained in NAS GD113/5/380/17.

[125] The original of the 'Plan of the Lands of Redcastle' (surveyed by Edward Sang and Sons of Kirkcaldy in 1824 and submitted to Patrick Grant in 1825) is owned privately by Mr Michael Martin of Garguston. A photocopy is deposited at NAS RHP49495. The deposit is also recorded in the National Register of Archives as microfiche No. 2751 (1986) at NLS.

[126] The instrument of sasine transferring ownership of Redcastle from Patrick Grant to Sir William Fettes is held at NAS GD23/4/269. The title deed extract about the holding of St Andrew's Fairs comes from the 'Trust Disposition Settlement and Eight Codicils' by Sir William Fettes (1830) held in Fettes College Archives, Edinburgh.

[127] Records of Sir William Fettes' activities at Redcastle are contained in his private notes and a brief history of his life is described in 'The Fettes College Registers 1870–1953'. Both are held in Fettes College Archives. A brief description of the life of Sir William Fettes is also given in Whitson, T B, 'The Lord Provosts of Edinburgh' (1932).

[128] The 'Reduced Chart of that part of the Eastern Sea or Moray Frith from the East boundary of the Lands of Sir William Fettes, Baronet, to the River Beauly' (1832) is held at NAS RHP117/1.

[129] See notes 30 and 126.

[130] See note 22.

[131] The stories of the Duff brothers fighting at Redcastle market and of the Hossack toast are told in Miller, H, 'Scenes and Legends of the North of Scotland', pages 342 and 481–3 (1881 edition) and pages 326–7 and 459–6 (1994 edition). The reference to Hugh Miller's wife is in Sutherland, E, 'Lydia', page 158 (2003).

[132] The 'New Statistical Account of Scotland' (1834–45) contains descriptions of every parish in Scotland written by the parish ministers. The 'Parish of Killearnan' chapter was written by Rev. John Kennedy (in 1837–38) and is published in Vol 14, pages 63–72. The NSA is also available online at www.edina.ac.uk/statacc.

[133] A description of the geography of Killearnan is given in Lewis, S, 'Topographical Dictionary of Scotland', Vol II, pages 35–6 (1846).

[134] See note 3.

[135] An extensive article on the 'Barony of Redcastle' appeared in the *John o'Groats Journal* on 4 October 1850. It describes the Redcastle estate when owned by Col Hugh Baillie, provides a brief history of the Redcastle quarry, details the conflict between Rev. Donald Fraser and the Killearnan witches in the eighteenth century, and describes the improvements made to Fettes Farm in the early nineteenth century.

[136] The introduction of new farming methods and the consequent depopulation of Redcastle estate is described in Omand, D (ed), 'The Ross and Cromarty Book', page 173 (1984). Ross, D in www.electricscotland.com/webclans describes the decline in the use of Gaelic in the area.

[137] The Baillie lineage is detailed in Burke's 'Landed Gentry of GB, the Kingdom of Scotland', nineteenth edition, Vol I, 38–40 (2001). A short summary of the history of the Baillie family is given in www.dochfour.co.uk/history and short biographies of family members can be viewed at www.thepeerage.com.

[138] Dr John MacKenzie's biography is contained in 'Pigeon Holes of Memory. The Life and Times of Dr John Mackenzie (1803–1886)' edited from his manuscript memoirs by Christina Byam Shaw (1988). Comments related to Col Hugh Baillie of Redcastle are mainly contained in pages 194–200.

[139] The set of nine architectural drawings prepared by William Burn, dated 22 January 1840, are held at RCAHMS RCD28/1–9. Not all the additions and alterations shown on the drawings were carried out.

[140] Articles from issues of *The Scotsman* from 1817 to 1950 can be searched and viewed using the subscription-based digital archive service http://archive.scotsman.com.

[141] Philippa Baillie recounted her experiences of being brought up in Redcastle writing under her married name, Mrs Frank Russell, in the book *Fragments of Auld Lang Syne*, pages 81–85 (1925). The book also contains etchings and early photographs of some of the Baillies of Redcastle.

[142] See note 135.

[143] See note 141.

[144] Summaries of the legal documentation associated with all property transfers in Ross-shire are contained in the series of annual 'Sasine Register Abridgements' (1781–

1970) available in HCA CRC10/5/1–92. Each volume contains a surname and place index.

[145] The will and codicil of the Right Hon Henry James Baillie, written in June 1885, is located at BL IOR: Mss.Eur. E308/62. Attached to the will is an inventory by John Paxton of Inverness of the entire contents of Redcastle in January 1886.

[146] See note 138.

[147] See note 145.

[148] The legal opinion about who should draw up the regulations and fix the charges for the Kessock Ferry was presented to the Ross-shire Commissioners of Supply on 10 October 1835 by E Douglas Sandford of Edinburgh, and is reproduced in the Commissioners' minutes at HCA CRC1/1/3. The opinion contains a useful documentary of the ferry from October 1774 to April 1835.

[149] See note 15.

[150] See note 108.

[151] See note 137.

[152] Extracts from the Register of Sasines are available from the NAS and also digitally at Erskine House, Queen Street, Edinburgh or at www.registers-direct.ros.gov.uk.

[153] See note 144.

[154] The dispute in 1817 between Patrick Grant of Redcastle and Lord Fraser of Lovat over salmon fishing in the Beauly Firth and River is documented at NAS CS271/63509.

[155] See note 108.

[156] See note 144.

[157] The document entitled 'Particulars of the Estate of Redcastle and of the Kessock and Craigton, for Sale, July 1890' is held at HCA D303. This copy contains the vignette of Redcastle by Percival Skelton but the 6 inch:1 mile plans of the estates have been detached. A complete copy is held privately by the heirs of the late Frances (Ada) McDonell of Redcastle and Dochfour.

[158] See note 152.

[159] The Reports of the Ross-shire and Highland Squirrel Clubs (1903–46) can be viewed at www.ambaile.org.uk. For each participating estate they tabulate the subscriptions paid, the numbers of squirrels killed and the bonuses paid. From 1906, Redcastle estate is not reported separately but only as a composite total with Dochfour.

[160] The Inland Revenue Valuation Office (Scotland) survey used Ordnance Survey of Scotland second edition 1:2,500 (circa 25 inch:1 mile) maps (originally surveyed in 1872, revised 1904). The sheets covering properties in Redcastle are available to view at NAS IRS126/440 and 428.

[161] The Inland Revenue Valuation Office (Scotland) survey, Killearnan Field Books are archived at NAS IRS80/66 and 67.

[162] Private scrapbook mainly of newspaper cuttings and other documents belonging to the late Frances (Ada) McDonell of Redcastle and Dochfour. The collection includes a programme of the unveiling of the Killearnan war memorial in 1923, the accounts book of the Killearnan Volunteer Training Corps (1915–17), the gold medal presented to Donald McDonell and several early photographs of Redcastle and the Baillie family.

[163] The postcard showing a photograph of Redcastle *circa* 1930 by Urquhart of Dingwall is held at RCAHMS RC1044PC/B8353. Many other photographs of Redcastle and its gardens are held by various private individuals. There is also an album containing photographs of the interior of Redcastle during the inter-war years in Greenhill House. Photographs showing general views of Redcastle since it has no longer been inhabited are held at RCAHMS, for example: C96936 and SC400809, undated; B96935po and C22224, dated 1959; RC/416–7, dated 1967; A110–2, dated 1984; and B53306–7, dated 1989.

[164] Copies of the 1 inch:10 feet plans of Redcastle showing the 'Proposed Heating Apparatus' drawn up by Mackenzie and Moncur Ltd for Baroness Burton and dated 28 December 1936 are held at AUSLA MS2918 and at RCAHMS RCD28/1–10.

[165] The architectural drawings of new fireplaces and an oil fuel store at Redcastle drawn up by J R McKay of Edinburgh in 1929–30 are held at RCAHMS DPM1920/170/1/1–10.

[166] The set of three log books detailing work carried out in the gardens at Redcastle was compiled daily by John Fraser, head gardener at Redcastle from February 1927 to April 1950. They are part of a collection of items held by Mr Fred Fraser, to whom I am indebted for allowing me access. Also in the collection are the transcript of an article about a whale caught at Redcastle in 1877 which was submitted to the *Inverness Courier* but never published, and John Fraser's National Registration Identity Card, National Insurance Card and World War Two 'Certificate of Residence in a Protected Area'.

[167] The 'Third Statistical Account of Scotland' contains descriptions of every parish in Scotland written mainly by the parish ministers. The project was launched in 1946 as a review of the state of the country after World War Two but the 'Parish of Killearnan' chapter, written in 1954 by Rev. George Ballingall with a postscript written in 1982 by D P Willis, was not published until 1987 under the editorship of Alexander Mather in Vol XIII, pages 26–38. It can be viewed at HCRL. The Third Statistical Account is not available online.

[168] See note 163.

[169] See note 163.

[170] The 'Buildings at Risk Register for Scotland' can be viewed at www.buildingsatrisk.org.uk. The reference for Redcastle is SCT 0920. It contains a useful bibliography to sources of more detailed architectural information.

[171] Redcastle as a potential location for a Country Park was contained in The Highland Council, Ross and Cromarty East draft Local Structure Plan, Vol 1, Chapter 6, paragraph 68 (2005).

Chapter 2

THE CHURCHES

2.1 Early Ecclesiastical Killearnan

There are different accounts of the origin and meaning of 'Killearnan', the name of the parish in which Redcastle is located. It has been suggested that it originates from a Norse prince, named Irenan, who died in a battle nearby and is said to have been buried in Carn Irenan (Figure 1, page 19). [The Redcastle crannog (Figure 2, page 20) has also been cited as his burial place.] Another suggestion is that the church was founded by St Ernan (or Earnan), a nephew of St Columba. According to the *Highland News*[1] of 9 January 1904, St Ernan is the patron saint of Killearnan parish and his anniversary falls on New Year's Day. However, the currently favoured explanation is that the name comes from the Gaelic *Cill-Iurnain* and is probably a reference to a monastic cell that served as St Iurnain's place of worship.[2] Iurnain (who is also known by variants such as Iturnan) was probably a missionary and a disciple of Columba, who is said to have come to the area in AD 640 and *circa* AD 665 'died amongst the Picts'.

It is also worthy of note that the Irish warrior priest St Kessog, who founded a monastery on the island of Inchtavannach in Loch Lomond in AD 510, travelled around Scotland as a Christian missionary several years in advance of Columba, Ernan and Iurnain. It is thought that Kessog may have visited the Black Isle, where he is remembered in the name of North Kessock. Two other seventh- to eighth-century contemporaries of Iurnain who are known to have preached in the Black Isle were the Irish saint Maelrubha – who probably founded churches in Contin and Strathpeffer – and Curadan (also known as Boniface), who is thought to have founded a monastery at Rosemarkie and several churches, including Kilchrist at Tarradale.

Many of the medieval charters referring to the castle at Eddyrdor (or its variant spellings) refer to a St Palmer's chapel, and this is generally accepted as being the earliest site of Christian worship in the area. It may have originated as a Culdee chapel of the early Celtic church [from the Gaelic *ceile De'* meaning 'companion of God']. Culdee monks were Christian missionaries and hermits, and are known to have been well established in Ross-shire during the late Pictish period (the eighth to tenth centuries) before the Celtic church gradually gave way to Catholicism during the eleventh and twelfth centuries.

Unfortunately, there have been no archaeological surveys undertaken to locate the actual site of St Palmer's chapel. It has been suggested that the present Killearnan parish church stands on the site, and *Origines Parochiales Scotiae*[3] suggests that it was about half a mile (one kilometre) to the west of the church. However, it seems more likely that it was located about one kilometre north of Milton of Redcastle and that the hamlet of Chapelton was named after it. It is said to have been dedicated to St Andrew, and it is thought to have been here that the annual St Andrew's fair was originally held on 7 July each year. Nearby there was a well, also dedicated to St Andrew, which was famous for its curative properties. This well can still be seen under the old bridge over the Redcastle burn at Chapelton. There was a drinking ladle attached to the bridge by a chain until the 1960s. The ladle is thought to have been donated to Dingwall Museum, but it seems now to be lost.

The origin of the name of St Palmer is also something of a mystery, as no saint of this name appears to be recorded. 'Palmer' is an old word for a pilgrim, predating the Reformation and possibly originating from the custom of pilgrims praying with their palms together for a safe journey and touching palms with the effigies of saints at roadside chapels. Juliet, in Shakespeare's *Romeo and Juliet*, Act 1 Scene 5, refers to this practice in the lines 'for saints have hands that pilgrims' hands do touch, and palm to palm is holy palmers' kiss'. It is possible that this particular chapel was on the pilgrim route to St Duthac's shrine (at Tain), and it may therefore have become known as St Palmer's chapel.

According to *Fasti Ecclesiae Scoticanae*, the parish was created in 1275 and, like its royal castle, was originally named Etherdouer.[4] However, other records[5] show that in 1235 Pope Gregory IX authorised Robert, Bishop of Ross, to found and endow new canonries in Ross-shire. In a letter of 1238, the same Pope confirmed that one of the churches created by Robert was at 'Edderdover'. Later, in a Papal Bull of 1256, Pope Paul IV confirmed the establishment of 'Edderdor' church within the Archdeaconry of Moray and Ross. Thus the most reliable date for the establishment of the church in the parish now known as Killearnan is 1238, and although Robert can be claimed as its first minister, responsibility for the parish would have been delegated to one of his priests (or rectors). That rector would have been responsible for collecting the teinds [one-tenth of the produce of the parish which everyone was supposed to give to support the church], most of which he would have appropriated for himself and the cathedral, originally at Rosemarkie and later at Fortrose. Ministerial duties in the parish would have been delegated to a local vicar, whose stipend would have been paid from the teinds.

The existence of a 'hospital-house' is recorded in a charter of 1299 granting 'patronage, rents and pertinents of the house along with the barony of Edirdouer' to William, Earl of Ross, by Elizabeth Bysett (one of Sir John Bysett's three daughters, who had inherited Redcastle and its lands in 1259).[6] The hospital was at Spital Shore and is thought to have been a refuge for pilgrims who crossed the Beauly Firth near that point on their way to the chapel marking the birthplace of St Duthac in Tain. St Duthac was born *circa* 1000 and died in Ireland in 1065. His remains were transferred to the original St Duthac's chapel *circa* 1250, thus initiating the pilgrimage route to Tain. James III (1460–88) founded St Duthac's Memorial Collegiate Church in Tain in 1487, and in the reign of James IV (1488–1513) the hospital is known to have been in the hands of the Knights Hospitallers, who were formed in the eleventh century to provide care for Christian pilgrims, initially to the Holy Land. Its location is recorded[7] but no excavations have been carried out. The east wall, which contained a 'very elegant triplet lancet window', was still standing when the site was visited by the Inverness Field Club in 1882.[8] No visible trace remains, and the site is currently marked by a cairn of field clearance stones.

Fasti Ecclesiae Scoticanae provides short biographies of all the Killearnan parish ministers from 1560 onwards,[9] but there is little recorded of the earliest vicars of Eddyrdor. Some appear as witnesses on various medieval charters, for example: William, Vicar of Eddyrdor was a witness to the Beauly Charter of 1278, in which Eddyrdor castle was granted to Andrew de Bosco; and Richard Muirhead was a signatory to the charter of 1487 by which James III founded St Duthac's Memorial Collegiate Church in Tain. Fortunately, the known records relating to the life of every minister of Eddyrdor were thoroughly researched by Rev. Aeneas Macdonald (parish minister, 1890–1932) and compiled into a remarkable manuscript[10] entitled *The Succession of the Beneficed Clergy in the Parish of Killearnan 1226–1906*.

The early ministers at Eddyrdor were Roman Catholic, but during the Reformation of 1560–1690 – led initially by John Knox and later by Andrew Melville – they became increasingly protestant. The first to have converted appears to have been Mungo Monypenny, who was minister in 1543–60 and is described by Rev. Macdonald as 'a self-assertive, pugnacious man and not quite above using his fists when occasion arrived' – an approbation that derived from March 1543, when he had attacked Gavin Dunbar, treasurer of the diocese of Ross, 'laying hands upon him and cruelly wounding him to the effusion of his blood'. It seems also to have been around this time that the parish was renamed. Post-reformation documents generally spell the parish name as 'Kilernane', but many variations are found, such as Kilurnan, Killernan, Kilearnan and Kiliurnan. Two early maps dating from 1727–30 refer to the parish and the kirk as 'Killurning', and during the nineteenth century most records consistently refer to 'Kileaurnan'.

The minister at the time of the initiation of the Reformation in 1560 was Rev. Donald Fraser (I), who is therefore accredited with being the first reformed minister. In 1566, he became Archdeacon of the Diocese of Ross but was murdered in Alford, Aberdeenshire, by his servant (unnamed) whilst returning from Edinburgh in 1572. Ruairidh Mor Mackenzie (1st of Redcastle) seems to have grasped the opportunity to seize his land in Artafallie – an act that was avenged 150 years later by Rev. Fraser's descendants and led to the bankruptcy of the Mackenzies of Redcastle. From 1566, he was succeeded by two ministers of doubtful status, being recorded respectively as 'vicar' and 'reader', so the next reformed minister is generally accepted to have been Rev. Robert Grahame, who was parish minister from 1573 to 1602. However, he had originally been ordained in the Church of Rome and seemed to have only partially embraced protestantism, being described by Rev. Aeneas Macdonald as a 'pluralist of the old type [that is, embracing elements of both the catholic and protestant denominations, and probably also earning income from sources other than the church] … [holding] more offices than he could discharge … [and] doing the minimum of work'. He was the second son of Patrick Grahame and a grandson of the Earl of Montrose; as was normal for second sons of the junior nobility, he became a minister. He had a reputation of not being diligent in his work, but nevertheless became the Archdeacon of Ross and the founder of the Grahame family of Drynie by virtue of a liferent lease of Drynie that he (and his heirs) obtained in 1579, and which was confirmed by James VI in 1585. It is worthy of note that Rev. Macdonald seems to have had little respect for the McLeans, who purchased the Drynie estate in 1874, because he was somewhat disparaging of them in his manuscript, referring to one of them 'as a clodhopper of a self made carter' and another as 'a long-legged creature and a perfect specimen of the genus cad'. It is said that because of these statements his manuscript was never published.

The visible foundations of the present parish church building appear to originate from a medieval (Catholic) church dating from *circa* 1390. However, there is no evidence of a church having been located anywhere else, so it is generally thought that it is built on the site of earlier, probably Pictish, foundations. In the graveyard (Figure 19), whose monumental inscriptions have been recorded by the Highland Family History Society,[11] there is one medieval (fourteenth-century) grave slab on which is sculpted a calvary cross about twenty inches high and twenty-five inches in diameter at the head. A tablet recording the deaths of Collin McKenzie of Muirtoun and Anne Grant, his spouse, has the years of their deaths apparently chiselled out but is thought to be from the late seventeenth century. It is highly likely that other medieval gravestones lie undiscovered under the turf. Other visible gravestones date back to at least the eighteenth century, but their dates are no longer legible.

One such grave records 'John MacKenzie, Minister at Killearnan'. There have been four ministers by the name of John MacKenzie in Killearnan, the most recent of whom was in post during 1700–16, although he seems never to have been ordained or recognised by the Presbytery, presumably because he was episcopalian and had been 'planted' by the heritors. The earliest inscription with a readable date is '1720 Donald McDonald – Janet Campble'.

Figure 19: Killearnan parish church and graveyard, with the old manse in the background

Unusually, the church remains cruciform in design, because successive heritors refused to fund alterations to its 'papist' shape, despite vigorous protestations by several of its ministers, especially Rev. John Kennedy in the early nineteenth century. The bell is said to date from 1676, when it was gifted by Colin Mackenzie, 4th of Redcastle. There have been several partial rebuilds, during which the walls have been raised, the roof slated and a wooden floor inserted about three feet above the original floor (which was earthen until 1838, when it was flagged with stone). The earliest recorded renovation was in the late seventeenth century during the tenure of Robert Williamson, the last episcopalian minister. An internal redesign, including the installation of the present pulpit, was carried out in 1838. During substantial renovations in 1892, there was a search for the 'foundation stone', under which it was said that there was a jar containing historical parchments. No jar was found, but a commemorative flagstone was discovered. It reads:

This stone is here placed in memorie of Mr Robert Williamson, Minister at Killearnan, who departed the ... of ... 16— and his spouse Margaret Burnet where there only sone Mr Alexander is buried the 2nd of Februarie 1678. My body rest in grave as in a cell. My soul is filled with joy no tongue can tell. In that last day united with great glory He sing God's praises aloude for ever more. Repent, believe, lost sons of Adam's race. That Heaven with me may be your dwelling place. Memento mori.

It is thought that several other gravestones lie under the raised floor, including those of some of the early Mackenzies of Redcastle.

Killearnan parish church remains one of the few churches still in use in the Black Isle on its original medieval site. The red sandstone is probably from the adjacent Redcastle quarry. The architecture is mainly Gothic, but the window in the east gable is perpendicular (somewhat unusual in Scotland) and was from the pre-1796 church. There are signs that there was an arched doorway, possibly medieval, in the south wall. Also on the south wall is a plaque but, except for a few words, the Latin text is now unreadable due to weathering of the stone (Figure 20). It is said[12] to commemorate Rev. Robert Williamson (1664–86), but the initials 'A.W.' are clearly readable on the plaque and the only minister with those initials was Alexander de Waghorn during 1381–99. The architrave surrounding the plaque is also lightly carved with the initials 'M.P.', which could signify Mungo Moneypenny (1543–60).

Figure 20: The 'A.W.' plaque of unknown date, mounted on the south wall of Killearnan parish church

Inside the church, there are three brass wall plaques listing all fifty-one ministers of the parish from 1226 to the present. Although the church is relatively austere, there are a few interesting artefacts. One of particular interest is a *circa* one-metre-high stone statuette holding a sword (Figure 21). It is much weathered and was dug up from the graveyard in the early twentieth century. Its origin is unknown, but it is thought to be from the sixteenth or seventeenth century and may have been buried to avoid discovery during or after the Reformation. Outside the church gates, two old stone fonts of unknown age are currently used as flower pots.

Figure 21: The pre-reformation statuette dug up from Killearnan parish church graveyard

The nearby late nineteenth-century manse is now in private ownership and called Killearnan House. Several older manses are known to have been located on the same site, although it does not seem to be recorded when the first was built. In 1587, Robert Grahame[13] was accused at the General Assembly of having 'a Highland kirk that he served not', and responded in his defence that he had 'neither manse nor gleib [glebe]'. This suggests that the first manse was probably built in the early seventeenth century after Ruairidh Mor Mackenzie, 1st of Redcastle, had been granted the charter of 'Redcastle and its lands' by James VI in 1608. There appears to be an earlier record of a glebe when, in 1559–60, a charter of the 'Viccars Croft of Killiernan' was given to Alexander Mackenzie of Killichrist.[14] This may account for there being no glebe attached to Killearnan in 1587.

2.2   The Presbyteries of Dingwall and Chanonry

There is evidence[15] that an episcopal style of hierarchical organisation began to take over from the essentially monastic Celtic church from *circa* AD 850 onwards. By 1100, the Diocese of Ross had been established, with bishops – appointed by the king – being based in the cathedral at Rosemarkie and with boundaries roughly corresponding with those of the Earldom of Ross. Around 1240, Bishop Robert (who had founded the church at Eddyrdor in 1238) moved the cathedral to Fortrose and created a chapter (council) of nine prebends [canons (or rectors) in receipt of a stipend, one of whom represented Eddyrdor]. By the early fifteenth century, the chapter had increased to twenty-one prebends and the cathedral buildings at Fortrose had been substantially extended, with a bell tower, a south aisle and a Lady Chapel created for the spiritual welfare of the Earls of Ross (especially the Countess Euphemia, who died *circa* 1394 and is buried there).

As a consequence of the Treaty of Edinburgh which initiated the Reformation in 1560, the Church of Scotland alternated between being presbyterian and episcopalian in outlook. The matter was not settled until 1688–89, when the National Convention of Estates drew up a new constitution for the Church of Scotland (a process that is generally referred to as the 'Revolution'). This led to the final abolition of bishops in Scotland and to the restoration of the General Assembly, with a substructure of synods, presbyteries and kirk sessions comprised of elders, deacons and the parish minister. The new constitution was ratified by William III in 1690, when he finally proclaimed the Church of Scotland to be Presbyterian, and the Scottish Parliament enacted the abolition of 'prelacy and all superiority of any office in the church of this Kingdom [Scotland] above presbyters'. Despite this, mainly because of the Anglican leanings of many of the heritors, the episcopalian movement was significant in Easter Ross and the Black Isle well into the early eighteenth century (and, to this day, remains active in St John's at Arpafeelie).

The earliest minutes of the church in Ross-shire are contained in the proceedings of the Presbytery of Dingwall, which date back to June 1649 and exist up to October 1687 (with a gap from March 1658 to May 1663). They are in poor condition and difficult to read due to bleeding of the ink into the paper but, fortunately, they were transcribed in 1896 by **Rev. William Mackay**.[16] There is a reference in this transcription to an 'old pbrie [Presbytery] booke being at the beginning thairoff of the daite 12 Novemb 1633 zeires [years] and ending at the daite 18 Octob 1637', but this minutes book has not survived. There were probably earlier minutes books, as an Act of the Scottish Parliament created Presbyteries in 1592 and it is thought that a Ross-shire Presbytery was formed at that time. Few of the minutes from 1649 onwards mention Killearnan, because the parish still retained strong episcopalian leanings and its ministers seem rarely to have attended the Presbytery meetings. Indeed, the first mention – on 19 February 1650 – records that 'the Kirk of Kilernan is diseused with because yr [there] is no minister yr'. The next two entries, both on 18 June 1650, indicate that presbyterian ministers were sometimes sent to Killearnan to preach, the first stating that 'Mr Murdo McKenzie, late minister at Dingwall, satisfied for his malignance ane Lords day in y' [the] Kirk of Killairnain', and the second stating that 'Mr Jon Monro reported yt [that] Rorie McKenzie of Redcastle satisfied for his malignancie in ye Kirk of Killurnain, and yt he receaved him according to ye ordinance of ye Comission of ye grail [General Assembly]'. ('Malignant' was a term used by early Protestants to refer to persons who retained allegiance to Roman Catholicism after the Reformation.)

By 1687, there were insufficient presbyterian ministers to constitute Presbytery meetings, hence there are no minutes. In July 1693, there was an attempt to form a 'Presbytery of Ross and Sutherland', but it was dissolved in November 1701. Recorded minutes[17] recommence in January 1707 in the form of the 'Rolls of the United Presbitry of Chanonry and Dingwall'.

The first occasion on which 'Kilurnan' parish appears is on 1 December 1708, when it is minuted that 'Presbitrie appoints Mr Hugh Campbell [of Kiltearn parish] to supplie at Kilurnan the second Sabbath of this month'. There was a vacancy at Killearnan, and (as in 1650) it was the custom for the Presbytery to send occasional supply preachers. However, visiting presbyterian ministers were not always well received by the congregation of Killearnan so, not surprisingly, Rev. Campbell's preaching did not go down well. According to the Right Rev. Robert Forbes,[18] he was 'rabbled there in time of divine worship' and assailed in the pulpit 'to the endangering of his life'. The incident was brought to the attention of the Presbytery meeting of 2 February 1709, and it was reported that 'they had drawn up a representation of the rabbling at Kilernan and had given the same to the Justices of the Peace'. However, it does not seem that any action was taken, and several other ministers (for example, the reverends John Munro, John McKilligin, Thomas Inglis and Thomas Chisholm) are recorded as undertaking supply at Killearnan. In general, these seem to have been carried out without provoking indiscipline from the congregation, except on one occasion in March 1717, when it was reported that John Munro 'could not find the kirk-officer and was obliged to make use of his own servant to officiat for him and also reported that in time of divine worship he was disturbed by a mixt multitude crying out in a most tumultuous manner'. The Presbytery resolved to write 'to the Laird of Redcastle elder requiring him as principall heritor of the paroch to countenance and assist the minister who is sent to supply the same, conform to his engagement to the Synod of Ross and Sutherland to that effect', but it seems unlikely that any response would have been made by Ruairi Dearg Mackenzie, 5th of Redcastle, whose episcopalian sympathies would have lain with the 'multitude' – indeed, he probably orchestrated the disturbance. The vacancy at Killearnan was of considerable concern to the Presbytery, especially as it appears that an episcopalian, John Mackenzie (IV), was in receipt of a stipend from the heritors and was also in residence in the manse. In May 1709, they recorded 'the desolation of the parish of Kiliurnan for the space of eight or nine years', and expressed the view that the:

> ...right of calling a minister to that parish is now of a long time devolved into the Presbyteries hands and further considering that there is no expectation of a call from that parish to anie minister or probationer of the present establishment, notwithstanding that several of the brethren have dealt with him to that effect and being well informed that a considerable number of the common people there are desirous to have the gospel planted among them notwithstanding of the disaffection of the heritors, therefore agreed to plant the said parish, jure devoluto, by giving a Presbyterial call to Robert Munro, probationer now in their bounds.

Church patronage had been abolished at the 'Revolution' in 1690, but was restored in 1712 with provisos that the Presbyteries had the right either to overrule the presentation of a minister by the patron (or heritors) on behalf of the Crown, or to appoint a minister to a parish, *tanquat jure devoluto*, if no appointment to a vacancy had been made by the heritors or the Crown within six months.

Why Robert Munro was not ultimately appointed does not appear to be recorded, but it is likely that the heritors objected to a presbyterian adherent being planted to oust John Mackenzie (IV). Another factor may have been the split of the Presbytery of Dingwall and Chanonry into its two components in

1714. In consequence, it took many more years before any further attempt was made to fill the vacancy. In March 1715, Rev. Thomas Chisholm was sent to speak to the heritors and discourage them from attempting to plant a minister who would be unacceptable to the Presbytery. He reported back in April 1715, stating that he had conversed with the heritors but had been informed that 'the Patron had the power of calling a minister to their parish and that they [the Presbytery] could not meddle with it'. Four years later, in January 1719, after the 'resident' episcopalian John Mackenzie (IV) had died, the Presbytery took:

> ...to their serious consideration the desolate state of the paroch of Killernan (which is within their bounds) in the want of a gospel minister planted among them and that the right of calling and presenting a minister to the said paroch is by law devolved into the hands of this Presbytery they therefor did after mature deliberation unanimously agree ... and hereby do appoint ... Mr John McArthur their preacher of the gospel to be minister of the said paroch of Killernan.

The heritors attended the February 1719 meeting of the Presbytery so that members could 'converse with the said heritors to signify to them the Presbyteries design of planting Mr John McArthur in the said paroch of Killernan and to ask their concurrence therein'. The heritors' response was 'that they would go in the more readily to the said settlement, that their proposition of the union of the churches was granted. But that since the said proposition did suppose of Killernan to stand and remain as one of the two churches and consequently to be planted they have no objection against that young man'. Killearnan, at last, had a presbyterian parish minister, and at their meeting at Killearnan on 26 March 1719, the Presbytery:

> ...did by prayer and imposition of hands ordain and set apart the said John McArthur to the work of the ministerie and did admit him minister of the said paroch of Killernan whereupon all the brethren present did give to the said John McArthur the right hand of fellowship and the parochiners present did come and take him by the hand in token of their cordial accepting of him to be their minister and then the action was closed by prayer and singing of psalms.

The 'union of the churches' referred to a proposal to merge the parishes of Kilmuir Wester, Suddy and Killearnan, which had first been raised by the heritors in July 1718. It was subsequently approved, but did not take place until 1756.

Immediately following his appointment at Killearnan, Rev. McArthur became engrossed in a succession of incidents and events in the parish. In January 1718, Laughlan Mackenzie and Isobel Fraser were cited to appear before the Inverness kirk session to confess their 'alleged adultery together ... whilst the said woman's husband is yet in life and she hath not sought nor obtained a divorce'. Both confessed their sin, but it emerged in February 1718 that Isobel's father, John Fraser, had been 'harbouring and protecting the said persons who were reputed to live together in adulterie'. Furthermore, he had advised the couple to marry and had been the witness to their marriage in Redcastle on 12 February 1718. The marriage had been conducted by John Williamson, who was an episcopalian preacher in Kilcoy. Twenty months later, in October 1719, the moderator of the Presbytery wrote to the other Presbyteries in the Synod of Ross to request advice on John Williamson's conduct in carrying out the marriage, which was described as 'irregular'. By January 1720, all of the replies had been received and it was 'their unanimous opinion that the said John Williamson should be prosecute for his irregular preaching and particularly for the irregular marrying of Laughlan Mackenzie to Isobel Fraser'. The Presbytery's response was to send a deputation:

...to go this day to Chanory and avail of the Sherriff Deputising in Ross and give in to him a subscribed information by the Moderator and Clerk against John Williamson, Episcopal preacher at Kilcoy, for his irregular marrying Laughlan Mackenzie and Isobel Fraser at Redcastle the 12th day of February 1718 while the said Isobel's husband was still in life and she having obtained no divorce that the said John Williamson be put in the Portuis Roll. [The official list of persons drawn up by a sheriff for indictment before a Circuit Court of Judiciary.]

It was not until November 1726 that the Presbytery minuted that 'John Williamson did not compear before the said Court [at Dingwall] nor any witnesses except one, and that the Sherriff ordered the said John Williamson to be seized and incarcerat till he would answer to the libel against him'. It was also reported to that meeting, in what initially appeared to be unconnected business, that a woman by the name of Anne Fraser, who 'had fled from discipline out of the parish of Killearnan sometime ago' was now in the parish of Kirkhill and was to be cited to compear to the next diet [meeting] of the Presbytery. [Kirk sessions were responsible for the maintenance of civil order, and had powers to rebuke and discipline sinners and wrongdoers. When parishioners would not submit to a discipline (which usually took the form of a public rebuke from the pulpit and possibly a fine), their kirk session could cite them to appear at the Presbytery, which had ultimate powers of excommunication if necessary. The process of summoning a miscreant to appear before a statutory authority – for example, a court, a presbytery or a kirk session – was called a 'compear'.]

Anne consistently failed to compear at subsequent Presbytery meetings but, in April 1727, Rev. John McArthur presented a minute from the kirk session of Kirkhill held on 17 March 1727 at which Anne had made an extraordinary confession. She stated that she had been an unmarried servant in Redcastle and had:

> …brought forth a child in uncleanliness some years ago [in 1722] … [and] being asked who was father to the said child answered it was John Williamson, Episcopal preacher that resides at Kilcowie, and being asked where the said child was begotten answered it was at Redcastle, and being asked how she came so long to conceal the father of the said child, answered that she was obliged to do so and acknowledged it was her sin and prayed the Lord to forgive her, and being asked if she believed that John Williamson would acknowledge his being the father of her child answered she did not know but feared he would not for that she had conversed with him when she found her self with child and that then he told her he could not help it and that he would acknowledge it before God and seek forgiveness of his sin from him but would not confess it before man.

The response of the Presbytery to this revelation was to compear Anne Fraser to their next diet and to request the Killearnan kirk session to compear John Williamson whilst they sought advice from the Synod of Ross. Neither Anne nor John seemed inclined to comply with these or several subsequent compears. In the case of Anne, it was discovered that her continuing non-appearance was because she had moved to Lochcarron in the Presbytery of Gairloch. The minister of Lochcarron parish was Rev. Aeneas Sage, who was requested to take up the issue and, over the next twelve months, issued three public admonitions and three public prayers from his pulpit. Anne still did not compear. The final prayer was made in August 1728, and on 24 September 1728 the Presbytery wrote to the Presbytery of Gairloch, desiring them 'to deal seriously with the said Anne Fraser and her conscience, holding forth the awfulness of the sentence of excommunication and to assure her, if she continues contumacious [wilfully disobedient], that this Presbytery will undoubtedly proceed to pass the said sentence against her'.

Rev. Aeneas Sage was a native of Redcastle, born in March 1694 at Chapelton, where his father was a farmer. He was appointed in 1726 as the first presbyterian minister of Lochcarron and, like John McArthur in Killearnan, came up against initial opposition to presbyterianism from his congregation and heritors (who initially refused to pay his stipend).[19] Sage is also known to have originally supported the Jacobite cause at college in Aberdeen, where he had been 'head of a furious Jacobite mob' during the 1715 uprising (of the

'Old Pretender'), an event for which he had his bursary stopped. In Lochcarron, he became well known for his outspoken and cantankerous behaviour, not only towards his heritors but also to the General Assembly.

A response from Rev. Aeneas Sage was received in April 1729. It stated that Anne 'had again and again confessed to him ingenuously that John Williamson was father to the child brought forth by her and that she professed a willingness to submit to censure in any congregation except Kilearnan where the said guilt was committed'. The Presbytery considered this response and decided to request their clerk to write to Rev. Sage 'that he would endeavour to get the said confession from her judicially and untill essaye be made this way the further consideration of her case is delayed'. In June 1729, Rev. Sage responded that 'Anne Fraser would not make any more judicial confessions in these bounds that are under Mackenzie influence'. Why Anne had declared such animosity to Ruairi Mor Mackenzie (6th of Redcastle) is not clear, but the Presbytery had run out of patience; on 21 October 1729, they elected to:

…proceed to the highest censure against her. At which the Presbytery taking under serious consideration and having reasoned fully thereupon, they did appoint the Rev. George Gordon minister of the gospel at Cromarty [and the Moderator of the Presbytery] to pray for sight and direction in the affair, which being accordingly done, the Presbytery did again resume consideration of the affair whereupon the vote was stated thus: excommunicate the said Anne Fraser or not. Being called to vote, marked it carried unanimously to excommunicate. Wherefor the Presbytery did thereby do, in virtue of that power and authority committed to them by the Lord Jesus Christ the King and head of the Church, excommunicate the said Anne Fraser and deliver her over to Satan for the destruction of the flesh that the spirit may be saved in the day of the Lord. And the Presbytery recommend to the very reverend Presbytery of Gairloch to pronounce the said sentence of excommunication in the parish where the said Anne resides and that they exhort and beseech all the Lord's people to have all due regard to the said sentence and to carry towards her as ane heathal and excommunicate person.

John Williamson received the same ultimate sentence, having refused on several occasions to appear in front of the Killearnan kirk session. The Presbytery sought advice in October 1727 on how to proceed from the Commission of the General Assembly.[20] The letter, signed by the moderator Robert Finlay, describes John Williamson as a:

…profligate wretch … [who conducted] a Schismatical meeting house … [and who] seduces poor ignorant people from attending upon the ordinances of the Gospel, baptises the children of scandalous persons and others who withdraw from their own Ministers up and down thro' the whole country, and has been guilty as an accessory to a great many irregular clandestine marriages to the detriment of several considerable familys there, and been supported and influenced by Donald Mackenzie of Kilcoy in all his extravagant preaches.

It also describes how the Episcopal Church in Scotland had been:

...so touched by a sense of guilt that a considerable time ago he was suspended by the pretended Bishop of Edinburgh upon which he desisted publick preaching for a little time. But he continued to baptise notwithstanding the said suspension ... and we are told that last month he was again suspended by a pretended Bishop called Dunbar but he continues to baptise.

The advice given by the General Assembly does not seem to be recorded, but John Williamson was subsequently given three public admonitions and three public prayers, and in December 1728 he was offered a final opportunity to 'profer submission'. He failed to respond to this offer, and the Presbytery proceeded to excommunicate him at their meeting of 28 January 1729.

The minutes of the proceedings describe how John was now residing in Kishorn (on the Applecross estate of Ruairi Mor Mackenzie's cousin) and how 'all the neighbourhood were, and still are, deeply impressed of his being the father of the said child brought forth by the said Anne Fraser sometime in 1722'. However, it also states that Anne Fraser had originally 'endeavoured to impose on us in this country, alleging that one Donald McKenzie, son to Rorie Mackenzie tenant in Applecross a man not in being (for no such man was ever known there as appears by the frequent testimony and declaration of the minister of the place and Presbytery of the bounds of the diligent search) being influenced so to do by the said Mr Williamson and the gentlemen who support him'. Despite this, the members of the Presbytery were convinced that John Williamson was the father of 'the child in the highlands of Applecross and Lochcarron and thereabouts commonly designed the minister's daughter'. Accordingly, they voted and pronounced John Williamson excommunicated, 'unless the said John Williamson, or some in his name, signify some relevant ground for delaying the same'.

It appears that excommunication did not deter John Williamson (who, presumably, did not recognise the Presbytery), because he was subsequently reported to have moved on from Applecross, this time to Lewis, where in 1738 he was still pursuing his episcopalian beliefs and was 'zealously active in perverting and drawing aside the people from attending the ordinances'. Although his original misdemeanour, in the view of the Church of Scotland, had been to perform an irregular marriage in 1718, eleven years later he suffered excommunication for allegedly fathering Anne Fraser's illegitimate child.

It remains uncertain that John Williamson actually was the father of Anne Fraser's daughter. What seems quite probable is that the real father was Ruairi Mor Mackenzie (6th of Redcastle), and that John Williamson allowed himself to be cited in return for retention as an episcopalian minister on Mackenzie-owned lands. In this respect, Ruairi Mor seemed to have something of a reputation. For example, another servant of Redcastle, Mary Young, was compeared to the Presbytery in April 1727. She confessed that:

> ...by bad advice she gave Duncan McRae for father of her child, yet said that he was never guilty with her, and that Roderick Mackenzie the Laird of Redcastle was the father of her child. She, being asked if her child was baptised, answered that it was baptised in Strathglass by Alexander McRae a popish priest, and that she and the child were brought to Strathglass by Collin McAllaster, taylor and cottar to the said Laird of Redcastle.

Mary was 'earnestly dealt with and rebuked for her atrocious sin in being guilty of adulterie and wronging an innocent man and baptising her child by a popish priest'. Predictably, no action was ever taken against Ruairi Mor.

Another action undertaken by Rev. John McArthur soon after his appointment as Killearnan parish minister was to alert the Presbytery of Chanonry (no longer united with Dingwall) to the state of his manse and to petition them for a visitation. Since the Reformation, by several Acts of Parliament, ministers serving in any parish with the Church of Scotland were 'allowed sufficient manses situated near to their churches not above a thousand pounds nor below five hundred merks Scots money in value', and Presbyteries had the power 'with the advice of two or three honest men of the paroch, to design and appoint competent manses for the minister in every paroch'. According to Rev. McArthur's petition in June 1719, his manse was 'ruinous and not habitable until it be repaired and wants the necessary office-houses'. It appears that Ruairi Dearg Mackenzie (5th of Redcastle) and several other parishioners had destroyed it in protest against the calling of Rev. John McArthur as the parish's first presbyterian minister. However, Ruairi Dearg and seven others[21] were each required to compensate Rev. MacArthur the sum of £10 Scots (or the equivalent in farm produce) 'within 15 days ... under pain of poinding' by the Sheriff Principal of Ross for what he described as a 'riot'.

The Presbytery duly agreed to Rev. McArthur's petition, and issued a:

> ...warrand to advertise and warn the Heritors to be present at the said visitation and also grant warrand to your Officer of Presbyterie in that part [John Glass]

to warn and cite two or three of the most honest and discreet men of the paroch with some honest tradesmen of each necessary craft whom the Presbyerie shall think fit to name to be present at the said visitation that they may concur with and assist the Presbyterie in the foresaid designation in manner prescribed by Law.

Although no heritor attended, the visitation was held on 24 June 1719 in the presence of Roderick Tuach and James Kale (honest and discreet men of the parish), Donald Watson and Alistair Mackenzie (masons), and Alexander and John Clark (wrights). The manse was described as 'fourty foot in length and fifteen foot in breadth ... the side walls to be only two foot in height above the second storey ... the roof and lofting with the partitions and the stair to be altogether ruined ... and that it wanted glass windows'. In the 'office house', the kitchen was found to be 'altogether ruinous', and 'there was no barn, stable nor byre'.

The required repairs included rebuilding of the walls, reflooring of the second floor with a garret above, partitioning to provide two rooms and a cellar on the ground floor and two rooms and a closet on the second floor, building two new stairs and rethatching the roof. As for the 'office house', this was to be 'built single-storey thirty-two foot in length for a kitchen and brew house. That another be built thirty foot in length for a barn and a third to be built twenty-four foot in length for a stable and a byre and that all the said office house to be six foot in height in the side walls and thirteen feet wide, that they have highland couples [twelve-foot rafters] with doors and that they be thatched'. When asked how much the work would cost (under oath), the masons stated that it would be £210 Scots to build the walls and the office house, plus 1,600 loads of stone and mortar at 1d per load (£80 Scots). The wrights stated that their costs would be £389-2/- Scots, with timber and thatch amounting to £113 Scots. The whole scheme was approved, and in their minutes of the visitation the Presbytery recorded that they:

> ...hereby do appoint the Heritors of the said paroch of Killearnan to meet and to stent [proportion] and tax themselves conform to their respective interests ... and to advance and pay in to the said Mr John McArthur minister of the gospel at Killearnan for making the foresaid reparations their respective shayre of the said sum betwixt this and the fifteenth day of August next to come wherein if they faill is hereby recommended to, and the Presbytery humbly entreats, the Right Honourable the Lords of Council and Session to grant letters of horning and other executionals needful they pass hereupon.

What nobody knew at the time was that it would take eighty years to complete the repair work to satisfaction!

Ruairi Dearg Mackenzie and the other heritors had no option but to pay the total repair bill of £792-2/- Scots to renovate the manse. They also agreed to pay Rev. McArthur a stipend of £100 Scots money, £30 for communions, and six chalders, eight bolls and three firlots of victual (half meal and half barley). This can be compared with the stipend of Robert Grahame, which in 1574 was recorded as twelve chalders of victual and £12-13-4d Scots in cash.

In 1730, Rev. John McArthur transferred from Killearnan to the parish of Logie Easter. His replacement was John Robertson, who was previously the minister of Contin parish. The appointment was not without issue, as his Presbytery (Dingwall) objected and his presentation to the parish was declared 'null and void'. However, Ruairi Mor Mackenzie, 6th of Redcastle, supported the nomination and the General Assembly ultimately approved the transfer in July 1731. John Robertson quickly drew attention to the inadequacy of the 'office house' at the manse. Another Presbytery visitation was convened on 6 June 1732, when it was found that the roof of the stable required new couples, cabblers and rails [wooden supports], whilst both the kitchen and the byre would also require roof strengthening and new thatching. The total cost was estimated to be £139-3-4d Scots, and the heritors were again directed to pay the minister under penalty of horning if they failed to do so. However, it seems unlikely that these repairs were carried out, as the issue of the condition of the 'office house' would surface again ten years later.

The alleged practice of witchcraft was still not uncommon in rural Scotland in the early eighteenth century, although the law requiring 'proven' witches to be put to death was repealed in 1735. [The last instance of a witch being burned in Scotland was Janet Horne in 1727 in Dornoch. A commemorative stone in the town is erroneously dated 1722.] There appear to have been only two recorded instances of trials of witches in Killearnan. The first was in 1696–97, when Donald Moir and others were tried 'anent [about] the witches in Kilernan'. No papers seem to have survived, but Donald Moir is known to have been found strangled in prison.[22]

In the second instance, twelve members of an extended family were 'alleged guilty of the diabolical crimes of and charms of witchcraft'. Seven of the accused lived in Killearnan: John Glass of Spital; Barbara Munro (wife of John Glass); Margaret Munro (mother of Barbara); Mary Glass of Newtown; Barbara Rassa and Margaret Munro of Milntown; and Donald M'Kulkie of Drumnamarg. The others were named as Agnes Desk, Agnes Wrath, Christian Gilash, Mary Keill and Erick Shayme. They were tried on 18 July 1699 by Commissioners for the Privy Council, chaired by Robertson of Inshes, but verdicts were not issued until 2 January 1700. John Glass and Mary Keill were released, as nothing could be proven against them, although John Glass was re-arrested and imprisoned in Beauly Priory until he was taken to Edinburgh for a trial on 10 January 1700 – at which he was again found not guilty. Agnes Desk and Margaret Munro made confessions and were 'recommended some arbitrary punishment'. The others were found guilty, but their punishment was remitted to a local committee 'to appoint what they thought proper'. There is no known record of what punishments were imposed, but it is known that Agnes Wrath, Margaret Desk and Margaret Munro (and presumably the others) escaped the death penalty and were imprisoned in Fortrose. The victim of this episode is not detailed in the surviving records, but it is possible that it was Rev. John Mackenzie (III), the parish minister from 1686 until 1700, whose death was alleged to have been caused by witchcraft.[23]

A case of 'charming' involving a woman named Anna Bouie (or Buy) arose in 1732. In 1723, Anna had been remitted by Killearnan kirk session to compear at a Presbytery meeting because she had been declared contumacious in not undertaking a discipline for fornication with Donald McIan in Braes of Garguston. She had failed to attend on three occasions, and had been publicly declared a fugitive from discipline by Rev. John McArthur. It has to be assumed that she had subsequently submitted to public discipline, because in November 1732 she appeared before the Presbytery and was interrogated in connection with a charm she had allegedly used on cattle owned by John McConchy of Kilmuir Wester. When asked if she charmed cattle, she answered that she had some skill in keeping cattle from straying or being stolen, and for that purpose used to repeat some words in Irish [Gaelic] which in English were as follows:

> The blessing which St Comin gave ye cattle which St Patrick left in the field nae thief shall touch them in the fields they shall not be lost in the waters or drown in the seas from rocks and weather and bare footed … they shall ly down in the name of the cross of Earnan and rise in the cross of Christ till they come again in peace.

Anna's reference to the 'Cross of Earnan' appears to be the only reference in the records of Killearnan parish to its patron saint. She seems to have escaped any more serious punishment than a solemn lecture on 'the heinousness of her crime and greatness of her delusion … [and] was exhorted to take the matter to heart, to attend frequently of John Robertson [the new parish minister at Killearnan] twixt and next Presbytery to which she was cited'.

That next citation was in March 1733, when she 'was seriously dealt with' to make a confession that she had also charmed other cattle, but she denied that she ever had. Thereafter she was remitted back to Killearnan kirk session to 'satisfy discipline'.

Amongst the various parishioners whom Rev. John Robertson referred to Presbytery for contumacy in failing to undertake discipline for fornication and adultery were Jean Barber and Hugh McLay. They had confessed to fornication at the Killearnan kirk session, but were referred to the Presbytery in August 1739 because 'this was suspected to be incest in regard it was alleged that she had been guilty formerly with a brother of the said Hugh McLay and that she had proven contumacious to the session whereupon she had been cited to the Presbytery'. However, she failed to compear 'due to being in childbirth of another child brought forth in uncleanliness to John MacKeddy or MacLeod, now in the military'. However, she did compear in April 1740 to be:

> ...seriously dealt with anent [about] these influences of guilt laid to her charge she adhered to her former confession, acknowledged her relapse in fornication and being rebuked for her contumacy was seriously exhorted to repentance and remitted to the session of Killiurnan to undergo discipline. In the meantime Mr Robertson was appointed to inquire into the matter of the incest that was suspected of the said Jean Barber and to report to the Presbytery as soon as possible what light he could find thereon.

Presumably, he found no evidence, because there does not appear to be any further citation in the Presbytery records.

Rev. John Robertson died suddenly on 25 February 1743 and was replaced by Rev. Donald Fraser (II), who had been the parish schoolteacher in 1728–30. Like his two presbyterian predecessors, Donald was quick to quote from Acts of Parliament passed during the reigns of Mary, James VI and Charles II concerning the upkeep of churches and manses, and to call for a Presbytery visitation to the inadequate buildings at Killearnan – both the parish church itself and the manse. The visitation took place on 26 March 1745 and was attended by Rev. Hugh Campbell (the moderator of the Presbytery) and all three heritors (Ruairi Ban Mackenzie, younger of Redcastle, Colin Mackenzie of Kilcoy and George Mackenzie of Allangrange), as well as Rev. John Munro (Presbytery member), Rev. Donald Fraser (II) (parish minister), four masons (Robert Nicolson, James Munro, Alexander Mackenzie and Donald Mackenzie), two wrights (James Russel and William Glass), a glassier (John Littlejohn) and two honest men of the parish (Donald McWilliam-Riach and Rory Mitchel).

The party's inspection of the church, manse and office house 'found that the kirk must be thrown down all save the wester gavel [gable], that it must have an additional breadth of six feet, that the manse and office houses need to be repaired', and the tradesmen and honest men were requested to estimate the costs that would be incurred. They reported that the total cost of rebuilding the church would be £110-16-10d sterling (comprising: £74-6-4d for the masonry; £30-10-6d for the joinery; £4-5-4d for the glazing; and £1-14-8d for thatching, assuming the heritors would supply and transport the heather). It was further reported that the total cost of repairing the manse would be £8-1/- sterling (comprising: £7-4-4d for joinery; 10/- for masonry; and 6/8d for glazing) and that the cost of the office house repairs would be £8 sterling for joinery. The grand total of £126-17-10d was required from the heritors 'in three different proportions at the terms of Lammas 1745, 1746 and 1747', and a committee was formed to 'stent [levy a tax on] the different heritors according to their valuations, an attested list of which was produced as follows: Redcastle's valuation in the parish of Kilearnan is £822-15/- Scots money, Allangrange's valuation is £452-10/- Scots, Kilcoy's valuation is £295 Scots'. It was also decided that the work would be overseen by an 'undertaker', who would receive from the heritors a £10 allowance for 'his trouble and charges in managing the said work'.

The next day (27 March 1745), the Presbytery received two letters. The first, signed by Roderick Mackenzie elder of Redcastle (Ruairi Mor, 6th of Redcastle) and Colin Mackenzie of Kilcoy, named Roderick Mackenzie, younger of Redcastle (Ruairi Ban) as undertaker for the repairs. The second letter, signed by Ruairi Ban, stated that he accepted the appointment and that he would 'finish the said work sufficiently according to the several condescendences given in by the tradesmen before the end of October 1746'. The appointment and timescale were accepted. At a subsequent meeting of the Presbytery held in August 1745, the agreed division of the responsibility for payment was received. The total cost had been amended to £120-16-10d, of which Redcastle would pay £62-16/-, Allangrange would pay £34-0-10d and Kilcoy would pay £24. The undertaker, Ruairi Ban Mackenzie, was appointed to 'collect, ingather and receive the sums of money above written from the above heritors … [and to] employ masons, wrights and glassiers and to provide the materials necessary for the said work, to oversee the same and pay the workmen'. For their part, the heritors were appointed:

> …to make payment of their said proportions to the said Roderick Mackenzie and in case either of delay or of not payment in due time, the Presbytery does humbly intreat the Right Honourable the Lords of Council and Session to interpose their authority and direct their letters of horning and other executorials needful thereto, according to Acts of Parliament thereanent, and thereby oblige the heritors of the said parish to make payment forthwith of the said sums as shall be demanded by the said Roderick Mackenzie.

Eighteen months later, Ruairi Ban appeared at the Presbytery to explain that 'the troubles of the times and the confusion the country was in by the late rebellion was the reason why he had neither collected the money, nor provided any materials'. He also explained that 'the price of several articles particularly timber and glass is considerably raised by certain intervening events since the passing of the decreet [of February 1743]', and requested that 'he may be indemnified as to any extraordinary charges he may be put to in finishing the work'. Accepting this as good reason, the Presbytery agreed to arrange for him to be 'reimbursed in what overplus of charge he shall be put to' and exhorted him 'now that the country was peaceable to proceed without delay'.

It comes as no surprise that nothing happened, and in February 1753 Rev. Donald Fraser (II) informed the Presbytery that his manse and office house at Killearnan remained 'ruinous and insufficient', whereupon the Presbytery again resolved to carry out a visitation to which the heritors were compeared (on 14 March 1753). Unfortunately, it is not possible to determine what happened, because the Presbytery records for March 1753 to September 1762 have not survived. However, it has to be assumed that there was no progress, because the matter of the inadequate manse was again raised in 1765!

2.3 Killearnan Parish Kirk

The minutes of the parish kirk session of Killearnan[24] (or 'Kileaurnan', as it is consistently spelled in the minutes) commence on 2 April 1744. This is because the parish was strongly episcopalian and did not have a constituted eldership until 1744. Rev. Donald Fraser (II) was the minister, but is always referred to as the 'moderator'. His stipend, payable by the parish heritors, is recorded on the first page as 'six chalders and an half, three firlots, a lippy and a half of victual [corn or grain], with one hundred and ninety-five merks of money'. The total monetary value of this stipend was calculated in 1755 to be equivalent to £49-5-10½d (sterling). The members of the kirk session are not listed in the initial minutes, but they are detailed on the first page of the Old Parish Registers,[25] which also commence in April 1744. They included: Roderick Mackenzie (Ruairi Mor, 6th of Redcastle); four tacksmen (Farquhar Murchison of Newtown, Thomas and Kenneth MacLennan of Chapeltown and Alexander MacKenzie of Blairdow); James Calder, a brewer in Miltown; and John Munro, a miller in Redcastle, who was the nominated representative to the Presbytery (where he was known as a 'ruling elder').

Apart from the maintenance of civil order, the kirk session was responsible for the organisation and administration of the parish's affairs, the routine upkeep of the church's property and the welfare of the poor. It was also responsible for the recording of births, marriages and deaths (although many parishes, including Killearnan, did not record deaths). These are commonly referred to as the 'Old Parish Registers'. The first recorded baptism in Killearnan parish was that of Katherine Ross of Kilcoy, which took place on 11 April 1744, a day that was noted to be 'a national fast appointed by publick authority for the Spanish war'. Amongst the notable early records is the baptism on 11 November 1744 of Murdoch Mackenzie, the eldest son and heir of Ruairi Ban Mackenzie, 7th of Redcastle, and his wife Margaret Calder. Unfortunately, Murdoch died in July 1746. Another notable early entry was the baptism on 13 January 1745 of Kenneth and Jannet MacKenzie, the first twins to be recorded. Their father was a servant to Ruairi Mor Mackenzie, 6th of Redcastle.

A feature of the early Killearnan records is that almost all the people mentioned were living in the western part of the parish in the immediate area around Redcastle and the parish church. This may indicate that the eastern parts – around Tore, Drumnamarig, Croftnacreich and Lettoch – were minimally populated at that time (although 100 years later they were heavily crofted and sustained a greater population than Redcastle). The locations commonly recorded up to 1750 include Miltown, Chapeltown, Newtown, Burntown, Blairdow, Gargieston and Corrighrain, as well as many instances of Redcastle and Killearnan. It is not clear whether the terms Redcastle, Killearnan and Miltown were interchangeable and synonymous in referring to the vicinity of Redcastle or whether there was a real distinction. The professions recorded in these early records include miller, shoemaker, gardener, wright [craftsman], excise officer, tacksman, piper (to Redcastle), mason, weaver, surgeon, merchant, smith, tailor, brewer, ground officer, square wright [carpenter], butcher and chapman [pedlar].

Another document that also names some middle eighteenth-century residents and their occupations is a petition to the Court of Session in 1739 by Roderick Mackenzie (Ruairi Mor, 6th of Redcastle). The purpose of the petition is not specified, other than that 'the nature of his submission required proof by witnesses' and that he seeks a warrant for them to appear.[26] Several of the persons named are Ruairi Mor's tenants and servants; for example, Alexander Bizet (tenant), Roderick Borvie (tenant, Blairdow), Hugh McKey (servant), Donald McKey (late servant and gardener) and Donald Fraser (late servant). Others are local businessmen; for example, Alexander Mackenzie (vintner) and Florance (spouse), Colin Finlayson (tailor), David Duncan (dyster [dyer]), Alexander Juner (weaver) and William Glass (wright).

Welfare of the poor became the responsibility of kirk sessions after the Reformation *circa* 1560. It was financed through fines and ceremonial fees, and topped up with voluntary contributions from heritors. Amongst the first recorded names in the Killearnan Roll of the Poor (1744–46) are many residents of Miltown and Chapeltown, including Kenneth Glass, Katherine MacKenzie, Margaret Munro, Katherine Chisholm, Mary Ross, Donald Bayne, Alexander Grey's twins and John Briscanach's orphans. Another was Mary Tuach, who is recorded as 'a blind lass in Newton'. Other place names are rare, suggesting that the poorer inhabitants of the parish lived mainly in Milton and Chapelton.

Prominent in the early records of rebukes issued for various sins, particularly extramarital fornication and adultery, were Margaret MacLennan (who was 'with child' in Chapelton), Margaret Davidson (who was a 'servatrix to Redcastle with child') and Alexander Bain and Isobel Biset (who were married but had 'brought forth a child' only six months into the marriage). Adulterers were particularly severely disciplined. They were required to sit on a 'cutty stool' wearing sackcloth and be publicly rebuked at length by the moderator on three successive sabbaths. Minutes from 1745 show that the kirk session paid 4/4d to fabricate a garment for adulterers from a new sheet of sackcloth, suggesting that its predecessor had been well worn! Miscreants could also be fined by their kirk session (usually up to 8/-), but there is no evidence that fines were imposed in Killearnan.

The Old Parish Registers[27] also recorded illegitimacy in the baptism records. For example, it is noted on 15 December 1744 that a child, Alexander Bayne, was presented for baptism by Thomas Fraser because 'the parents were under scandal for ante-nuptial fornication', and in the baptism record of Mary MacLennan on 17 March 1745 it is stated that she was 'daughter to Kenneth MacLennan, late servant to Redcastle, and to Margaret Davidson, late servatrix there, begot in fornication. Alexander MacLennan weaver in Redcastle, the said Kenneth's uncle, became sponsor for the Christian education of the child'. It is worthy of note that Margaret Davidson had been a servant when she was disciplined for fornication, but was an ex-servant when her child was baptised. Women with young children were not considered employable in the eighteenth century.

Another concern that occupied the kirk session in the mid-eighteenth century was the prevention of 'the profanation of the Lord's day particularly by fishing the yares upon that day'. In 1746, five men from Miltown were 'long and seriously dealt with anent the nature of the Sabbath profanation and having solemnly promised to be guilty of no such practice hereafter, they were rebuked before the Session and dismissed'.

It is sometimes claimed locally that Prince Charles Edward Stuart (the 'Young Pretender') visited Redcastle in 1745. Although it is recorded that he used the Corryairack Pass on his route south to avoid the English garrisons based in Inverness, it is possible that he, or one of his entourage, made a secret recruitment visit to Redcastle. The bedroom provided at Redcastle supposedly had two exits, one of which connected to a staircase which led directly outside, thus providing a rapid means of escape if necessary. Ruairi Mor Mackenzie (6th of Redcastle) was in financial difficulty and may have been thought to be receptive to financial inducement or reward for joining the Jacobite cause. It is said that the visitor was on the point of succeeding when Ruairi's wife, Katherine, 'accidentally' spilled a kettle of boiling water over her husband's foot. This diversion is said to have prevented any change of allegiance, so the Mackenzies of Redcastle remained loyal to the British Crown and supported the Duke of Cumberland at the Battle of Culloden on 16 April 1746 – allegedly at a respectful distance, to allow their loyalty to switch should the Jacobites have been victorious.

In consequence, few people from Redcastle took part in either the uprising or the final battle. However, there were exceptions. For example, twelve men from Redcastle were listed as part of the Earl of Cromartie's forces and one was enlisted with Fraser of Lovat. These men were from Miltoun (three), Chapeltown (two), Spital (two), Newtoun (two), Burntown, Gargastown, Blairdow and West Culmore. The three from Miltoun are described as Finlay and John Glass, brogmakers [shoemakers], and Caluin Stuart, servant to James Calder.[28] Five of these men are known to have been taken prisoner, and eleven of them are also listed in the compilation of 'Persons concerned in the Rebellion'.

Another Redcastle rebel was John Ross, a mason from Chapelton. He was with Lord Cromartie's force of 200 men who had pursued some of the Duke of Sutherland's militia into Caithness. On returning from this fruitless mission, they were ambushed near Dornoch on the day prior to the Battle of Culloden. John was one of the few who were neither killed nor taken prisoner. He is said to have taken refuge in north-west Sutherland, but he appears to have returned to Chapelton some time after Culloden, as he is recorded acting as a witness at a baptism in Killearnan in September 1749. John was the eldest son of Alexander Ross. Alexander had inherited an old silver quaich when the Chief of the Ross clan had died in 1711, impoverished and without children. He had the quaich remade in Inverness in 1720, and it was inherited by the 'rebel' John. To this day, the quaich is said to be passed down through the eldest surviving sons.[29]

Killearnan kirk session was hastily convened on 21 April 1746, five days after the battle. The minutes read:

> The Moderator represented that though there was a prospect now of having the exercise of discipline restored by means of the victory obtained by his Royal Highness the Duke of Cumberland over the Rebel Army at Culloden

Wednesday last, being the 16th current, yet he was sorry that the madness and folly of some of this parish in joining with the Rebels had made them abnoxious, so that when many of the neighbouring parishes do already enjoy peace and tranquility, this is far from being our case. That the reason of his calling a Session this day was that a party of the Earl of Sutherland's men were detached from Beauli, with orders from the Duke of Cumberland, as they say, to take up the persons and effects of the Rebels in this parish, that two or three of them had called at him and said that they were to ... [act against] all except such as had Certificates from their parish minister.

Rev. Donald Fraser (II), the parish minister, had been absent from the parish for six weeks prior to the Battle of Culloden, apparently 'for his own safety'. The kirk session, therefore, had to advise him regarding those who should be given certificates but, unfortunately, no names are recorded in the minutes. Several parishioners were already at the church door, waiting 'certificates of their not being in arms' and complaining that the Sutherland men had already 'served the persons and were pillaging the effects of several innocent people'. With some urgency, the kirk session adjourned their meeting and went to Milton of Redcastle to confront the Earl of Sutherland's men and 'write certificates for those who were not concerned in the rebellion'. There are no further references to Culloden in the parish records and, in consequence of not taking part in the battle, the Redcastle estate was exempted from annexation to the Crown.

Rev. Donald Fraser (II) seems to have given support to the Jacobite cause. After a short period as the schoolmaster at Killearnan, he had taken the position of missionary in Strathglass and subsequently as private tutor to the younger son of Lord Lovat. Both Lovat and Strathglass had joined the Jacobite rebellion and, clearly, this was where Rev. Fraser's allegiance lay. In 1747, he was called as a witness to the trial of Lord Lovat in London. Lovat had written in a statement that he had 'a minister of the gospel, a very honest man, whom they designed to make a witness against me', suggesting that Rev. Fraser (II) had been prepared to 'turn King's evidence'. In the event, he was not called to testify.

The Presbytery also met shortly after the Battle of Culloden and recorded their views of the rebellion, leaving little doubt about their loyalty. Their minutes of 29 April 1746 record that they had been unable to meet since February:

...because of the troubles and confusions occasioned by the unnatural rebellion ... [and] taking to their serious consideration the merciful and reasonable deliverance which God has been graciously pleased to grant this nation by the signal defeat of the rebels at Culloden the sixteenth day of this month by the King's forces commanded by his Royal Highness the Duke of Cumberland, they did resolve to supercede all other business at this dyet and to spend the rest of it in prayer, which was accordingly done.

It is worthy of note that the Presbytery had also recorded on 4 January 1715 their royal allegiance after the claim to the throne made by the 'Old Pretender'. On that occasion, they had proclaimed 20 January 1715 to be:

…kept for a day of solemn thanksgiving for his Majesties safe arrival to the throne of these dominions and thereby disappointing the designs of the Pretender and the united contrariness of his adherents, did appoint that all the ministers of this Presbyterie make timous intimation of the said act and proclamation and observe the said day.

Another 'delation' [accusation] of witchcraft in Killearnan occurred in October 1747, when it was reported to the kirk session that Florence MacKenzie, spouse to Coline MacKenzie of Chapelton, had 'reproached and scaldalised' Isabel MacFarquhar of Burntown for witchcraft. It was claimed that Isabel had 'cut handfuls of the said Coline's standing corn and by that had taken away the substance of a field'. Florence offered to produce witnesses to corroborate her assertion, but they refused to testify. The kirk session therefore requested the moderator to meet with Florence and Isabel and 'accommodate the differences betwixt these women'.

In January 1748, the moderator intimated that he had failed to resolve the matter and that Florence, who now 'in all appearance had not long to live, being brought very low by a consumption', was still determined to continue with her accusation by further asserting that Isabel had 'caused her [Isabel's] servant cut off a sow's head on the threshold of her [Florence's] house which she [Isabel] carried to a field of corn belonging to the said Florence and buried it there and that this was one instance of the diabolical arts she [Isabel] used'. Unable to determine the truth of the matter, the kirk session finally 'did not judge it for edification to proceed against Isabel MacFarquhar as such practices deserve if found proven, but … that she should be seriously exhorted to act more suitably to her Christian character for the future'.

Interestingly, some of the MacFarquhars of Burntown are recorded on two of the oldest gravestones in Killearnan churchyard. One records a John McFarquhar, 'tacksman of Burn Town', who died in March 1730, and his son Colin McFarqr [sic] who died in March 1742. Colin's wife was Mary McKenzie, perhaps suggesting that the accusation of witchcraft in 1747 might have been part of an old family feud between the Mackenzies and MacFarquhars of Burntown and Chapelton.

The kirk session in 1756 became concerned about 'vagrant beggars strolling from place to place'. It was resolved that no poor aid would be dispensed to these strollers, but in order to help out the parish's own beggars they would create a list and issue badges. The badges were to be marked 'Redcastle' or 'Kilcoy', and only those beggars who had been issued with a badge would be entitled to financial assistance from the Poor's Fund in future. None of the badges appear to have survived.

Rev. Donald Fraser (II) was not a popular minister at Killearnan, partly because the majority of the population of Redcastle, led by their heritors, still retained episcopalian beliefs and partly because he had a somewhat shady past – for example, he seems to have left his post at Killearnan School in 1730 in curious circumstances to become a missionary in Strathglass. In 1735, he was appointed as tutor to Lord Lovat's younger son Alexander (nicknamed the 'Brigadier'), and in 1737 he became a probationary minister at Tain, in which post he was proposed as a candidate for the ministry at the parish of Fearn. However, in May 1741 he was 'charged with very serious misdemeanours' by the Presbytery of Tain. The charges were brought by Simon Ross of Aldie and Robert Ross of Achnacloich, both being heritors of the parish of Fearn, who opposed his candidature. The case was heard by a Committee of the Provincial Synod of Ross and is detailed in an extensive set of records and papers[30] of the proceedings held in October 1741. There were three original charges:

(i)   That he used scandalous familiarities in 1734 with Mary Grant, the spouse of Roderick McGilligan of Alness, in particular that he had gone to Mary's house several times when her husband was away and had stayed with her most of the night and was seen lying in bed with her.

(ii) That in like manner, he had frequented the house of Margaret MacLeod, spouse to Robert Robertson, minister at Edderton, when he had been away during May–August 1736.

(iii) That in October–November 1736 he had frequented ale houses, had been in a state of drunkenness on several occasions, had used offensive language and had asserted that witches did not exist.

A large number of witnesses were called, and their evidence is recorded in great detail on 184 pages of extracts from the records of the committee's meetings. The conclusion of the hearing was that Rev. Fraser (II) and Mrs Robertson were guilty of 'scandals of a mutual nature' and this decision was forwarded to the General Assembly, who appointed another committee to consider 'the proof on the lybell [libellous charges] against Rev. Donald Fraser'. This committee not only considered the original three charges but also a further three charges of:

(iv) Laughing in church in April 1736.

(v) Using undue means to get himself to be minister of Fearn.

(vi) Scandalous irregularity in May 1740 of kissing William Ross's daughter and asking if she would 'lie with him'.

Although several of the individual incidents associated with each charge were ruled to have been proven, the committee also concluded many to be not proven because of inconsistencies in the witness statements. Nevertheless, Rev. Donald Fraser (II) was not entered into the leet [shortlist] of candidates for the Fearn ministry. This prompted a series of appeals in which he mainly argued that 'the articles of the lybell were not relevant' to his candidacy. In the event, he was not considered a suitable candidate for Fearn but, curiously, was appointed unopposed to Killearnan two years later in 1743.

It is said that Rev. Fraser (II) was eventually driven from the parish by witchcraft.[31] Two incidents are recounted. In the first, it is said that a woman named Mhairi Alie made a *corp creada* [a bodachan or clay effigy] of him and placed it by a rivulet that ran at the side of the manse. When Rev. Fraser (II) retrieved it, one of its fingers fell off. Not long after, the minister also lost one of his fingers. The second incident is recalled in an article on the Barony of Redcastle written in the *John o'Groats Journal* in 1850.[32] To speed his departure, it is said that a group of witches made a clay effigy of Rev. Fraser (II) and stuck pins in it. One of the witches, who was 'of higher sort' and wore a red cloak, was in the act of placing it in the manse dunghill when she was spotted by Rev. Fraser (II). The effigy was confiscated and Rev. Fraser (II) 'sharply and severely reproved her, at the same time intimating that an exposure of her doings would be made from the pulpit on the Sabbath'. The spell did not kill him but, apparently, it caused him to fall asleep during his own church services. Soon afterwards (in 1757), he was offered the ministry at Ferintosh parish. It is said that he announced from the pulpit that he would not take up the post if one member of the Killearnan congregation asked him to stay. Nobody did.

Rev. David Denoon (I) became the minister of Killearnan parish in 1758, shortly after the three parishes of Killearnan, Suddy and Wester Kilmuir had finally become merged in 1756 into an enlarged Killearnan and a combined Wester Kilmuir and Suddy (which subsequently became retitled as Knockbain). The average Sabbath congregation was only twenty-four, a measure of the still strong opposition to presbyterianism in the parish.[33] The extent of the support for episcopalianism can be gauged, for example, by the actions of the Presbytery in 1751, when they reported Donald McKay, a preacher in Kilcoy, to the Lords of Judiciary in Inverness for 'unwarrantable practices ... in officiating to non-jurors in Arpaphilie ... [by] reading prayers and sermons every Lord's Day to a numerous crowd of people in the parishes of Kilmuir Wester, Killearnan and Suddie'. [The original 'non-jurors' were a group of Anglican clergy who, after the deposition of James II in 1688, refused to take an oath to William and Mary and the subsequent Hanoverian kings. The movement gradually died out, particularly after the death in 1788 of Prince Charles Edward Stuart. Because the Church of Scotland was established in Scots law, they were technically guilty of 'unlawful worship' and were sometimes prosecuted.]

Rev. Denoon's stipend was reassessed in 1764, when it became nine chalders and one boll of bear [barley], three chalders and three bolls of oat meal and £98-9-8d of Scots money. In addition, the Kilmuir Wester glebe was equally divided, its value at that time being seven bolls and three firlots of bear (in comparison, schoolmasters' salaries were set at £100 Scots, although they could earn a further £20 plus perquisites as kirk session clerks). Rev. Denoon (I) was also given a tack[34] for 'the lands of Peckmore … half the oxgate at Killearnan with the kiln … together with houses, biggings, yards, mosses, muirs and part pendicles in Killearnan', but he had to pay rent for these. For example, he paid £12 Scots for the kiln, 18/- Scots for the vicarage and 18/- Scots for his share of the schoolteacher's salary, as well as his poultry rent.

Another case of incest arose in 1761. Elizabeth Sinclair of Chapelton was accused of fornication with her nephew (who is not named). This sin was considered of such seriousness that the Rev. Denoon (I) and the kirk session referred the case to the 'Presbytrey of Chanry' [sic]. However, she had failed to appear, as a result of which she was excommunicated. Five years later, in December 1766, the Presbytery recorded that she had come 'praying to have the sentence taken off and being seriously dealt with and suitably exhorted to a sincere repentance, the Presbytery remitted her to the session of Killearnan to act as they see proper for edification'. She was readmitted to the church in January 1767.

Rev. David Denoon (I) was an earnest and able preacher who gradually converted growing numbers of his parishioners to presbyterianism. In 1766, he petitioned[35] the Royal Bounty Committee of the General Assembly for a catechist. [The Royal Bounty Committee, which oversaw the distribution of royal funds to the Church of Scotland, had been allocated special funds to encourage presbyterianism in the Highlands after Culloden.] The petition states that the parish contained 1,025 'catechisable' persons over the age of seven but 'owing to two nonjurant meeting houses in the parish until the Battle of Culloden, the parish minister would not have forty hearers on Sunday'. Despite the apparent lack of interest in presbyterianism in Killearnan, the rising numbers in Rev. Denoon's congregation caused a problem that grieved the kirk session in 1763. This was the issue of people 'profaning the Lord's Day by much idle talk' whilst strolling about in the churchyard on the sabbath until public worship began. The proposed solution was to employ Donald Munro (who was the church reader) to read scriptures to them, for which he would be paid an additional £8 Scots per year. However, that did not seem to work for long, because in 1771 it was minuted that 'the kirkyard was like a market place every Sabbath until the preaching begins'. The new solution was that worshippers were now required to enter the church as soon as they arrived!

The issue of the manse and the 'office house' was again raised at the Presbytery in October 1765, when Rev. David Denoon (I):

> ...produced a letter addressed to him by Roderick Mackenzie of Redcastle [Ruairi Ban] as the principal heritor of the parish bearing that he agreed to have a manse built directly at Kilearnan on the same plan with that at Knockbain and had reason to think the Tutor of Kilcoy and Factor of Wester Kessock would likeways agree for their respective interests, and as proof of his willingness to forward said manse directly he proposed Lachlan Ross, a square-wright to be Undertaker for it.

The Presbytery were not satisfied and requested that a letter be sent to the other heritors indicating that 'if they refused to join with Redcastle in building a manse at Kilearnan that they will proceed as Law directs'. By April 1766, both of the other heritors had agreed the plan at a total cost of £204-16-2d sterling, and Lachlan Ross vouched that he would have the work completed by Candlemas next (2 February 1767). The work was completed on schedule, but it transpired that no 'office house' had been included, so Rev. Denoon (I) again petitioned the Presbytery in February 1771. He had already agreed with the heritors that the total cost of 'two wings ... contiguous to the manse ... [for a] kitchen and cellar, a byre and a brewhouse' would be £20, if timbers from the old manse were used. The Presbytery approved the proposal and requested the works be completed by 1 June 1772. However, the financial plight of Ruairi Ban Mackenzie was such that it is doubtful that he was able to pay for any works. In consequence, the office house was reported twenty years later as still being 'ruinous'.

The next issue that Rev. David Denoon (I) took to the Presbytery was that of an upgrade to the County 'High Road' between Beauly and North Kessock that had been proposed by the Commissioners of Supply.[36] The proposal from the Commissioners' overseer was to alter the route of the old road, which ran around the edge of the glebe, by cutting 'a straight road twenty-four feet in breadth thro' the glebe of Kileaurnan'. Rev. Denoon had enclosed his glebe with a stone dyke and claimed that the 'encroachment is comprised to injure the minister about four bolls annually besides the expense of his enclosure'. However, the Presbytery's procurator [solicitor] advised him that the overseer would require the agreement of three Justices of the Peace to proceed with such a plan and that, if they were inclined to agree it, they would need to 'set down meiths [boundary markers] for the new in place of the former road and upon oath estimate the damage of the parties prejudiced'. Rev. Denoon was successful; the new road was laid on the route of the old road around the glebe.

An example of 'pauper apprenticeship' is recorded in 1776. Donald Cameron, an under-miller at Redcastle, had died suddenly, leaving four children, two of whom were very young. Rather than support the whole family from the Poor's Fund, the kirk session resolved to 'bind the eldest to a trade and thereby qualify the orphan boy for gaining his bread when he arrives at manhood'. The trade to be taken up is not recorded, but a grant of £2 per annum was agreed as his 'prentice fee'. Although there were exceptions, most pauper apprenticeships in the eighteenth century seem to have been effectively a form of slavery, commonly in the form of an indenture as a servant or a farm labourer. Other entries in the Poor's Roll around that time also show little respect for individuals with physical or learning difficulties. Amongst the recipients named are: 'the orphan'; 'the blind in Miltown'; 'the dumb'; 'the fool in Croftnacreich'; 'Donny the fool'; 'the cripple in Drumnamarg'; and 'the fools above Lettoch'.

From 1755 onwards, the Killearnan kirk session minutes show that the parish's principal heritor, Ruairi Ban Mackenzie (7th of Redcastle) was in financial trouble. In that year, Ruairi Ban borrowed £100 from the parish poor fund, promising that he would pay annual interest for distribution amongst the poor. In 1759, he offered ten bolls of oatmeal in lieu of the interest, and in 1765 he repeated this offer to cover interest payments for 1763–65. He was appointed as Collector of HM Taxes at Inverness harbour in 1768, but this appears to have made little difference to his personal financial position, because in 1770 it is minuted that he was due four years of arrears, and in 1773 his arrears were converted to seventeen bolls, three firlots and one lippy in discharge of all his dues up to 1769. In 1773, it is recorded that Redcastle was 'not in readiness to give meal or money at present', and a further minute of the kirk session refers to Redcastle being in 'factory' in January 1776 and the need to apply to a 'writer [WS] in Dingwall for arrears from 1773'. Ruairi Ban died in 1785, when it was recorded that the Redcastle estate had been sequestrated 'some time ago' and that 'creditors were to produce claims to be ascertained by the Court'. Only in 1796 was the kirk session informed that it was to receive '£150 for Redcastle's dues'.

Despite a shortage of parish funds due to the financial and other problems befalling Ruairi Ban Mackenzie and his son (Kenneth, 8th of Redcastle), in November 1773 it is recorded that 'the Session considering it their duty to adorn the House of the Lord in a decent manner asked the Moderator to contrive the most expedient method for buying two silver communion cups with the balance of the ash trees lately cut in the churchyard'. The ash trees in question had raised £6-6/- from a local carpenter, and at its next meeting the kirk session was informed that Rev. David Denoon (I) had spent £16-10/- on the cups. However, he offered to make up the shortfall by lending the cups to neighbouring parishes at a rate of 2/6d for both! An addendum to the kirk session minutes book[37] covering the period 1744–97 registers these cups along with several other items of communion ware: 'two silver and two pewter communion cups marked Kileaurnan ... two pewter communion ashets [plates] marked as above ... two pewter baptism basins ... two pewter decanters for the balance of wine and three trenchers or plates for the offering marked Killearnan'. The 1773 silver communion cups are still in the possession of the Killearnan parish church, and their uniqueness and value would be raised 200 years later as a cause of some concern in the kirk session minutes of 1969.

A further note written in the back of the 1744–97 kirk session minutes book records:

(i)   The two pewter communion plates (bought in 1774), two pewter communion cups and two pewter decanters for wine.

(ii) The two silver communion cups (recorded as bought in 1784, but actually 1773).

This note also lists:

(iii) Two silver-plated communion cups and one silver plated decanter attached to the West U P Church, Galashiels 1891.

(iv) One pewter communion plate, two pewter communion cups and one pewter decanter attached to the Free Church of Scotland, Banchory Ternan.

The date of 1891 indicates that this note was appended at a much later date, as the minutes book closed in 1797. How the articles listed in (iii) and (iv) came into the possession of Killearnan parish church is not clear.

Rev. David Denoon (I) was also the instigator of the annual communion season in Killearnan. The first reference to a proposed communion is in the kirk session minutes of May 1762, when the Rev. Denoon (I) announced that he 'intended to administer the sacrament of the Lord's Supper in this parish sometime next month if the apparent scarcity of meal would not prevent him'. This was because worshippers who travelled great distances to communions needed food, and it appears that the lack of sufficient supplies in the parish did delay the inaugural communion until 1764. It is not recorded where the initial communions took place, but it seems that the annual communion season in Killearnan became so popular that some time after 1764 Redcastle quarry was brought into use as an amphitheatre. A typical communion season is described by Rev. John Kennedy in his book *The Days of the Fathers in Ross-shire*.[38] The events lasted up to five days through Thursday (fast day), Friday (self-examination day), Saturday (day of preparation), Sabbath (communion day) and Monday (day of thanksgiving). Without specifically mentioning the services at Redcastle, he states that 'on the Sabbath, the day of communion, an immense crowd is gathered before the tent [the temporary pulpit]. As many as 8,000 are there.'

Kirk session minutes of May 1784 also refer to the problem of feeding the large congregations that attended these events and to the Rev. Denoon's somewhat innovative solution to reduce the burden on the parish:

> The Moderator signified to the session that as he annually dispensed the sacra-ment of our Lord's Supper about this time of year, he had fixed upon the eighth day of August for solemnising that holy ordinance in order to co-incide with Inverness, and as the parish is very poor because of the scarcity of meal, he intended to have only the Gaelic language upon that occasion in order to prevent a crowd from thronging the parish.

According to Susan Thomson in her book[39] on Killearnan, up to 10,000 worshippers gathered in or near the Redcastle quarry in 1799, and Margaret Oag states in her book[40] on Killearnan that 2,000 of these took communion. However, there seems little basis for claims of such large attendances. For example, the kirk session minutes of August 1777 state that 817 communion tokens were issued, and those of September 1786 state that there were 720 communicants.

In March 1796, the moderator reported that 'he had employed Collen Young to make a new tent [pulpit] for the quarry where the sacrament is generally dispensed in the Gaelic language, for which in consequence of the advanced price of wood he had paid four pounds sterling'. This 'tent' is also recorded in September 1797, when the kirk session compiled a list of 'articles bought at different times and now belonging to this parish of Kileaurnan for the use of the kirk'. The list includes the following entries: 'six planks or long deals for the quarry'; 'sixteen forms or long seats for kirk and quarry at the communion'; a 'wooden box or tent for the quarry'; a 'communion cloth for the quarry, 50 feet long marked Kileaurnan'; and 'six more planks or thick seats for the quarry'. Whatever were the actual numbers in attendance, the scale of these late eighteenth-century communion events was clearly substantial.

Rev. David Denoon (I) retired in February 1790 when, according to the kirk session minutes, his 'health had broken'. He died soon afterwards in January 1792 and is interred with Mary, his wife, who had died in 1767, in Killearnan churchyard (Figure 22). He was succeeded as moderator by his son, Rev. David Denoon (II), who had been appointed by the Presbytery as assistant and successor to his father in November 1789. Immediately after his father's death (and the purchase of Redcastle by James Grant), Rev. Denoon (II) petitioned the Presbytery, stating that 'true it is, and of verity, that the manse which your petitioner now inhabits requires several repairs to make it tolerably comfortable, and that the office-houses are ruinous, and the church seems also to want repairs'. How often the Presbytery had heard that plea throughout the eighteenth century!

Figure 22: The 1792 grave tablet of Rev. David Denoon (I)

A Presbytery visitation was arranged for 24 April 1792. Present were: James Grant of Redcastle and Charles Mackenzie of Kilcoy, now the sole heritors of the parish since the merger of the parishes; Rev. Roderick Mackenzie, moderator of the Presbytery; Rev. Robert Arthur, Rev. James Smith, Rev. Robert Smith, Rev. Alexander Wood, members of the Presbytery; Rev. David Denoon (II), parish minister; Alexander McGillivray and James Nicol, masons; David Christie and Hector Douglas, wrights. All agreed that the offices at the front of the manse were inadequate; that the manse required extensive renovations; and that the church roof needed to be slated and the churchyard to be enclosed with a stone dyke. Estimates were called for the next meeting on 29 May 1792. These were deemed to amount to £176-19-10d sterling, comprising: £62-18/- for masonry; £94-4-6d for joinery; £17-15-4d for thatching; and two guineas for the Presbytery's costs. The monies were to be paid in two halves, one half by 11 November 1792 and the remaining half when the work was completed. On 26 November 1793, Rev. Denoon (II) 'intimated to the Presbytery that the reparations of his church, manse and offices at Kileaurnan are now completed, but as some demur had been made by the heritors about paying up the sum decreed to the workmen, he requested a visitation of the repairs'.

The second visitation was held on 17 December 1793. Charles Mackenzie of Kilcoy and James Grant, the Redcastle estate factor, were present, as were Alexander McGillivray, mason at Milntown of Redcastle, William Grant, house-wright at Redcastle, and Alexander Davidson, wright at Knockbain, as judges to inspect the work. The wrights reported that 'the repairs of the church are sufficiently executed except a few slates wanting on the back of the roof – as to the repairs of the manse and the offices they declared themselves, in the like manner, perfectly satisfied that every part of the work belonging to their trade has been properly and substantially executed'. The mason reported that:

…the repairs of the church itself are, in his judgement, sufficiently executed, but that the churchyard dyke instead of being pinned with lime as specified in the estimates is only harled on the outside – as to the manse, he reports, that the lime wherewith it has been harled was not sufficiently tempered, which makes several parts of said harling insufficient already, and the whole of it less durable than if the lime had been rightly prepared – as to the new offices, he reports, that the mason work of them is sufficiently done, excepting two scuncheons [door jambs] of the meal cellar door, which have not been built perpendicular, or have already shifted out of plumb – and that the pillar between the doors of the kitchen is in like manner out of plumb; and that the top of the kitchen gable has not been harled in the inside; also that some parts of the harling of the kitchen wall will require to be supplied or made up with additional lime on the outside.

The Presbytery requested that these repairs be undertaken by the end of August 1794 and payment was not to be made until the repairs had been verified by Alexander Munro, factor of Kilcoy, as overseer and judge for the heritors. These repairs were duly completed, so – for the first time since Rev. John McArthur had petitioned eighty years earlier that his manse was 'ruinous and not habitable ... and wants the necessary office-houses' – the Presbytery were satisfied that the church, manse and offices at Killearnan were at last in an acceptable condition. However, their satisfaction would last for only three years!

Unfortunately, the minutes of Killearnan kirk session between 1797 and 1841 have not survived; therefore many of the details of the continuing ministry of Rev. David Denoon (II) and his successors are not recorded. However, the minutes of the Presbytery[41] have survived, so many of the major issues are recorded. The first of these again concerned the fabric of the church. In November 1797, the Presbytery was informed that:

> ...the roof of the church is declared by judicious tradesmen to be insufficient and dangerous, that the whole galleries and seats are ruinous, that the windows and doors are decayed, that there is reason to apprehend that a part of the wall begins to totter – that there are no proper tables or benches for dispensing the sacrament of our Lord's Supper.

Once again, a visitation was convened and an inspection carried out. It was agreed that major renovations were required, including: making watertight the wall angles of the south aisle; enlarging the windows and restoring the stone-work; and repairing the roof valleys between the aisles and the main roof. In the light of the latter, Rev. Denoon (II) also suggested that consideration might be given to pulling down both the south and north aisles and widening the main body of the church. At its next meeting, the Presbytery received a letter from Rev. David Denoon (II), presumably aimed at keeping up the pressure on the heritors, 'indicating the now ruinous state of the parish church of Killearnan makes it quite uncomfortable and dangerous for himself and his flock to convene therein for public worship in wet or stormy weather'. However, at the next meeting on 5 March 1799, Mr James Grant, acting on instructions from the Laird of Redcastle:

> ...objected to any enlargement of the windows ... and insisted that the said church and both its aisles shall be kept up in their present form, repairing and renewing only such parts thereof as the masons and wrights inspectors have declared insufficient: but agreed that a new roof be given to the whole church, as the present roof has already been condemned.

Estimates for the agreed work were sought and presented on 25 March 1799 to be: £46-4/- for masonry; £152-14/- for joinery; and £40 for slating. The meeting also received a communication that 'Mr Grant of Redcastle may possibly on more mature consideration of the business, be induced to prefer the more eligible plan of widening the church and taking away the aisles', but this cannot have been progressed, as the church to this day retains its cruci-form shape. Although it is not recorded, the slating of the church roof was carried out and there is no further mention of Killearnan parish in the Presbytery minutes until 31 March 1807, when it is recorded that Rev. David Denoon (II) had died 'on 30 or 31 December 1806' [actually 31st]. He was only forty-one years old, and is interred in Killearnan churchyard, where his broken memorial stone – with parts of the inscription missing – currently stands in the undergrowth at the side of his father's tablet.

At that same March 1807 meeting, the patroness of Killearnan, Mrs Maria Hay-Mackenzie of Cromarty, nominated Rev. Dr Thomas Ross, late minister of the Scots Church at Rotterdam, for the vacancy. However, at the next meeting in May 1807 it was recorded that there was 'a competition of patrons in the present case as to the right of presenting a minister to the vacant parish of Killearnan; and considering that it is not by law competent for … [the Presbytery] to give judgement with which of the two patrons now exercising it … a final decision by the proper civil court shall take place'. It transpired that the opposing patron was no less than the king, whose nominee was Rev. William Macrae of Barvas (Isle of Lewis). No immediate replacement to the parish ministry would be possible until the dispute was resolved.

The Presbytery tried to make interim appointments to supply the parish with suitable preaching, but found that 'there was a paucity of their numbers who are able to preach in Gaelic … [so could only] supply the parish once in a fortnight … [and] exhort parishioners to attend divine service at any of the three nearest Gaelic parishes most convenient to themselves on the inter-mediate Sabbaths'. There was also the problem of who should preside over the kirk session, and the Presbytery had to make arrangements for Roderick Mackenzie, minister of Knockbain parish, to act in this capacity and also to officiate at baptisms and marriages. In June 1808, two of the elders (John Dingwall and Colin Gilmour) made a representation to the Presbytery:

…that in the present distress of the poor and the small sum collected for their relief for a year past, owing to the infrequent supplies … especially in winter … [it] would be proper for Presbytery … to require payment of two years interest due to the kirk session by Mr Laughlan, land waiter [official who watched over the landing of cargo from boats] of the customs at Inverness, upon his heritable bond of £2,000 sterling being the stock or Poor's Fund of the parish.

Fortunately for the poor of the parish, it is minuted in July 1808 that Mr Laughlan had 'timely paid'.

An example of the problems encountered in supplying preachers arose in May 1808, when it is recorded that the congregation of the parish had 'convened numerously at the church in expectation of divine service being performed by Dr Ross'. However, Rev. Dr Ross did not turn up, and a letter was later received by the moderator of the Presbytery:

> Reverend Sir, In consequence of a letter from Mr Smith of Cromarty mentioning to me, though not officially, that the Presbytery of Chanonry had, at their last meeting of the 3rd inst, appointed me to preach at Killearnan on the 3rd and last Sabbaths of May – I have to request the favour that you will have the goodness to say to the Presbytery of Chanonry that I wish to be relieved from the necessity of preaching in Killearnan until my presentation to that parish shall have been sustained by the Presbytery.

In November 1808, William Young WS, representing Rev. William Macrae, the Crown's presentee to Killearnan, objected to the presentation papers for Rev. Dr Ross on the basis that:

(i)   They were not accompanied by a certificate from his patron with regard to his government qualification.

(ii) That he had signed his letter of acceptance before the date of his government qualification.

(iii) His certification was not signed by a JP or a magistrate.

He also announced that HM Advocate was about to make an appeal to the House of Lords and that any decision would therefore be delayed. In January 1809, it was also noted that Mrs Hay-Mackenzie had entered a 'cross-appeal' to the House of Lords in favour of Rev. Dr Thomas Ross. The heritors of the parish (Lieut-Col Alexander Grant of Redcastle and Charles Mackenzie of Kilcoy) also got involved. In March 1809, they wrote to the Presbytery explaining that:

> …they and their people had been deprived of the benefit of having the ordinances of the gospel regularly dispensed among them … [as only two of the Presbytery preach in the Gaelic] and now as the disputed right of patronage twixt the Crown and the Hon Mrs Mackenzie of Cromarty is appealed to the House of Lords … great reason to apprehend that the parishioners may remain in their present forlorn and melancholy situation for a considerable time unless the reverend Presbytery in their superior wisdom should adopt some method of expediting the settlement of the parish.

They also wished it to be 'made known to Presbytery their wish for the success of the Crown … as they are most anxious to have the Rev. William Macrae, the Royal presentee, for their minister'.

However, the Presbytery wished to remain impartial and responded to the heritors that they would 'transmit their petition to the Lord High Chancellor of Great Britain … urging a decision as early as possible'. The appeals progressed slowly through the House of Lords, and in December 1811 the Presbytery received two letters from the parish (one from Lieut-Col Alexander Grant, the other from three of the elders) requesting permission 'to employ the Rev. Neil Kennedy, late minister of the Gaelic chapel at Aberdeen, assistant for some time to the late worthy minister of Urray, to preach regularly in the parish of Killearnan until some other minister or preacher shall be appointed'. Given that the parish had been 'desolate … [and] five years without', the Presbytery unanimously agreed and offered to pay 'one guinea per week for his trouble'. Six months later, in June 1812, Mrs Hay-Mackenzie temporarily agreed to engage Rev. Neil Kennedy's brother, Rev. John Kennedy, a missionary minister in the North, as locum minister.

In September 1814, Rev. Dr Ross withdrew his nomination and finally, in November 1814, the verdict of the Court of Session in Scotland and the 'Order and Judgement of the House of Lords in the process of His Majesty's Advocate against the Hon Mrs Maria Hay-Mackenzie of Cromarty' was settled in favour of the patron. With her original nominee (Rev. Dr Ross) having recently withdrawn, Mrs Hay-Mackenzie entered a nomination in favour of Rev. John Kennedy. The Presbytery immediately agreed and called 'the heritors, liferenters, wadsetters, elders and heads of families to meet in the church of Killearnan upon Thursday the 17th current [November 1814] when a call to the said Mr John Kennedy to be their minister, is to be presented to them'. The call was sustained and Rev. John Kennedy was formally admitted to the ministry of Killearnan parish on 8 December 1814.

As a result of the eight-year vacancy, a 'very considerable sum of vacant stipend had become due', but it took until July 1816 before an agreement was reached about its distribution: £250 (sterling) to Mrs Denoon, the widow of Rev. David Denoon (II); £150 to Rev. John Kennedy, the locum preacher; £300 to the heritors to endow a catechist; and the balance (less £12-5-5½d for Mrs Hay-Mackenzie's expenses) to the heritors for repairs to the church, graveyard dyke, manse, garden and schoolhouse. However, Patrick Grant of Redcastle and Colin Mackenzie of Kilcoy (the heritors of the parish) and Rev. John Kennedy had to take Mrs Hay-Mackenzie to court on 15 May 1818 to petition for the £300 for the catechist.[42] They were successful and, under penalty of a poinding, she finally discharged her debt on 25 May 1818. [A catechist was a teacher of religion who assisted the minister in preparing people for entry to the church, for example, as communicant members or prior to baptism of their children.]

Rev. John Kennedy proved to be a very popular minister whose preaching was renowned. It is said that some worshippers walked up to eighteen miles to hear him, even though the facilities he could offer were poor because the improvements to the Killearnan church and manse promised in 1816 had not been carried out. In eventual frustration at the heritors' broken promises, Rev. Kennedy approached the Presbytery with a petition for a visitation in December 1830. It explained that he had:

> …wanted comfortable church accommodation for himself and congregation ever since he was inducted into his parish – that he was frequently by the heritors encouraged to believe that they would be made more comfortable, both before the estate of Redcastle was sold, and since the sale of that property took place – that in the first week of November last, the heritors, without your petitioner's knowledge or concurrence, by shutting two of the doors of the church and building a stair inside the southern jamb leading to a decayed gallery, have induced the church more inconvenient and uncomfortable than it was before; so that your petitioner was obliged to preach in the church-yard and continued to do so until the gale of the 20th of last month threw down his tent [wooden pulpit] and rendered it unfit for further use – that since then he preaches in the church to the no little confusion of the solemnity of public worship and the inconveniency of the hearers – that your petitioner beseeches the Presbytery to issue their orders for serving edict for an early visitation of the church and manse accommodation of your petitioner, that both may be inspected by respectable tradesmen, in order to put them in a respectable, sufficient and comfortable state of repair, and also a respectable and legal fence around the burial ground of the parish.

The visitation took place on 29 March 1831 at which John Mackenzie, a banker in Inverness, represented Sir William Fettes of Redcastle and Alexander Sheppard, a solicitor in Inverness, represented Sir Colin Mackenzie of Kilcoy. Also present were Hector Douglas and William Bain (house-carpenters), John Matheson (mason) and John Watson (builder). The verdict of the workmen was that the masonry and roof-slating were 'sufficient', except for some leadwork in the windows. However, there was no agreement with regard to the carpentry, and Donald Mackintosh of Inverness was appointed as an 'umpire'. His verdict was that there was much decay to rafters, joists and flooring due to water ingress, that many of the timbers were undersized and that the seating in the gallery was temporary and inadequate. The Presbytery therefore requested the heritors to submit proposals for the necessary repairs. These were presented and approved in July 1831.

Over six years later, in November 1837, Rev. John Kennedy again petitioned the Presbytery, stating that:

> ...his congregation are entitled to safe and comfortable church accommodation and that the present uncomfortable and dangerous state of the parish church compels him to bring it under the notice of the Presbytery that many of the parishioners of Killearnan have already discontinued their attendance in church on the Sabbath and others are likely to follow their example from the fear of cold and discomfort as well as of accidents that may be apprehended in a building which they consider ruinous.

Once more, a visitation was arranged for 27 March 1838. On this occasion, the Presbytery first heard a petition from John Ross of Coulmore and Robert Trotter of Garguston on behalf of 'upwards of three hundred individuals, heads of families and other parishioners of Killearnan', stating that they had:

> ...for many years laboured under the most serious inconveniencies from the dilapidated and ruinous state of their parish church. That its original construction was such as to render hearing exceedingly difficult in many parts of it and also to cause it to be so very cold as in the winter season seriously to endanger the lives of the aged and infirm. That of late years to these defects in the original building which were probably beyond the power of the Presbytery to remedy, there is now added the uncomfortable feeling that their lives are in actual and imminent danger from the probability that the church may fall upon them, not to mention the lesser annoyance of being subject to be drenched with rain whenever a shower falls during their attendance in church, thus preventing them from paying due attention to the services and rendering them subject to bodily ailments.

They further added that, in their opinion, their church was incapable of being repaired and that, if the Presbytery were acquainted with the real state of matters, they would not withhold 'timely redress of this crying grievance'. The Presbytery's visitation party then requested William Robertson (architect), Donald Mackintosh (house-carpenter) and George Russell (mason and slater) to inspect the church and report 'as to its safety, sufficiency and comfort'. Once again, their report pointed out serious decay due to water ingress to the woodwork of the flooring, the roof rafters and the stairs leading to the balcony. They also criticised the general construction of the church and the layout of the seating, which they described as 'inconvenient and uncomfortable'. The heritors agreed to consider the tradesmen's report and 'state at the next meeting what repairs they are willing to agree to execute'. At that meeting, the heritors produced 'a statement of the repairs which in accordance with the minute of the last meeting they were willing to agree to execute and an estimate of the expense of doing so, which amounted to £20-16/-'. Not surprisingly, the Presbytery's response was that the offer was 'quite inadequate and unsatisfactory'.

One of the factors relating to the internal design and 'comfort' of the church was that it was claimed by some to contain too few seats (pews) for the potential number of worshippers. The Presbytery therefore set up a committee to determine the population of the parish and the seating capacity of the church. The committee reported in June 1838 that 'the population of the parish of Killearnan above twelve years of age, fully certified, from which it appeared that the examinable number of persons in that parish was 1,211'. They also presented a plan of the church, showing the measurements of the pews and the total floor space available. However, there had been a disagreement about 'the number of inches in a legal sitting', so they had not been able to determine the capacity of the church. However, they reported to the next meeting of the Presbytery that the Court of Session had set a custom and practice of eighteen inches sideways and twenty-seven inches from back to front, from which they calculated that there was 'legal accommodation for 580 sitters'. It was also announced that Col Hugh Baillie of Tarradale MP had purchased Redcastle estate and further consideration of the work required at Killearnan church should be delayed until the September meeting, to allow the new laird to be present or represented.

At that meeting, a review of the previous minutes and the tradesmen's report was held and it was found that:

> ...besides the insufficiencies specified in that report there are other serious defects which render the building very inconvenient and unsuitable as a place of worship; more particularly, being old and built in the form of a cross with the pulpit awkwardly placed at one of the internal angles, the house is very unfavourable for hearing. It is very ill lighted even about the pulpit. The ground floor is neither flagged nor floored with wood, is always damp, and in rainy weather is flooded with water, and is even used occasionally as a place of burial.

The heritors were again requested to provide 'plans, specifications and estimates obviating and removing these defects in addition to those noticed in the tradesmen's report'. Mr Hugh Cameron, representing the heritors, stated that the heritors 'were willing sufficiently to repair the church comfortably ... [but] objected to any alteration of the construction or fabric of the building or addition to it going beyond a sufficient repair bone fide of the existing church'. The plans and specifications were presented on 27 November 1838 and detailed the repairs that would be carried out to the masonry, slating, carpentry, glazing, lathing and plastering as well as a proposed remodelling of the interior of the church. All details were approved, the plans were signed and there was agreement to proceed without delay. This time the work was carried out and Killearnan, at last, had a 'sufficient' and 'convenient' church. To this day, the interior design has changed little.

In 1837–38, Rev. John Kennedy wrote the Killearnan chapter of the New (Second) Statistical Account of Scotland,[43] which was not published until 1845, some time after he suddenly died in January 1841 having, according to *The Times*[44] of 19 January 1841, been 'seized with croup in the throat'. In a section of his chapter on the ecclesiastical state of the parish, Rev. Kennedy is highly critical of the 'Popish form' of the church building, the unsatisfactory condition of his 'far from … comfortable or commodious' manse, and of his inadequate stipend which he claims was the 'smallest stipend in the Synod of Ross', having been unchanged since 1756.

A commemorative tablet erected in the church in 1892 records Rev. John Kennedy as 'cherished in highest esteem by the people of the Highlands as a preacher of the cross and a teacher of righteousness'. His gravestone in the churchyard, which is not the original but a replacement erected in 1937, describes him as 'a man of God, sent forth into the vineyard with the fullness of Gospel Blessings, the peculiarly honoured ambassador of Christ, through whom shone forth the excellency of the Power in conversion of many a soul to God'. According to Noble,[45] there were 300 episcopalians in Killearnan in 1803, but by 1841 only a few remained, a statistic that well illustrates John Kennedy's power to convert but hides the reality that episcopalianism in Killearnan and the neighbouring parishes of Urray and Knockbain remained strong. In his visits to the area in 1762 and 1770, Bishop Forbes[46] had respectively confirmed 197 and 250 people at the episcopal chapel of St John's at Arpafeelie (in Knockbain parish), and the Old (First) Statistical Accounts[47] of 1790 states that one-quarter of the population of Killearnan and Urray were episcopalians. The chapel at Arpafeelie (which became the church school) was replaced by a new St John's church in 1812. By the end of the nineteenth century, St John's Episcopal Church in Scotland still had sixty communicant members and the school had a pupil roll of forty-four. The church remains active to this day.[48]

Rev. John Kennedy was succeeded in September 1841 by his son, Rev. Donald Kennedy, who was to become one of the leaders of the Free Church 'Disruption'. This was to have serious implications for the parish church in Redcastle.

2.4 The Free Church Disruption

Since the Reformation in 1560–1690, the presbyteries of the Church of Scotland had, from time to time, been in conflict with heritors over the appointments of parish ministers. The issue was further inflamed in 1712 when a Patronage Act, giving powers of appointment to heritors (or a nominated patron) was passed. According to the General Assembly, this was in direct contradiction to the terms of the 1707 Treaty of Union and for many years it called for repeals of the Act. As in many Northern parishes, this was a particularly divisive issue in Killearnan during the eighteenth century. The strongly held episcopalian beliefs of the Mackenzies of Redcastle, the principal heritors, had often caused appointments to be blocked, with the consequence that there had been several periods of vacancy – for example, in 1700–16 and 1806–14. This opposition to the Presbytery also resulted in the heritors refusing or delaying refurbishments of the church and the manse, with the consequence that they became derelict on several occasions.

Eventually, the issue of patronage or 'intrusion' in the appointment of ministers by heritors or patrons became such a serious schism in the Church of Scotland that 450 ministers, who regarded the practice as state interference in the internal affairs of the church, segregated and formed the Free Church of Scotland in 1843 – an event that became known as the 'Disruption'. In many parts of the country, the split was acrimonious. For example, a letter written by Lord Panmure and published in *The Scotsman*[49] of 19 August 1843 is self-explanatory:

> You foolish men. Return to your good old Kirk, where there is plenty of room, and when more is necessary you will be provided with it. Return to that moderate, useful and harmonious Church, for the establishment of which your forefathers fought and bled. Pay due and proper respect to that Minister placed in the parish by her most gracious Majesty. Let peace, and comfort, and harmony surround your firesides, and you will always find in me (as principal heritor) a friend ready to promote your welfare and happiness.

As patronage had been enshrined in law, in effect, the conflict was between the church and the state (or the 'establishment'). In consequence, the part of the Church of Scotland that adhered to patronage became known as the 'Established' Church of Scotland. Needless to say, the Presbytery of Chanonry was quick to expel those of its members who transferred to the Free Church. This included Rev. Donald Kennedy of Killearnan, who was included in a list of adherents to the deed of cessation issued by the General Assembly of the Established Church. On receiving this list in June 1843, the Presbytery appointed their clerk 'in conformity to the instructions already referred to, to write a letter of citation to him requiring his compearance at the ensuing meeting ... for the purpose of ascertaining whether he had so subscribed and still adhered – the said letter to be with certification'. It is no surprise that Rev. Kennedy neither answered this letter nor attended the ensuing Presbytery meeting on 5 July 1843.

Rev. Sage of Kirkmichael and Rev. Fraser of Cullicudden were also compeared to that meeting and, on their non-appearance, the Presbytery's response was to declare:

> ...in terms of the deliverance of the General Assembly that the said Messrs Kennedy, Sage and Fraser have by their own acts and deed ceased to be ministers of the Church of Scotland as by law established ... that their respective churches have become vacant ... that they are disqualified for receiving any spiritual care in this church. Their names were accordingly ordered to be struck off the roll and the Clerk was instructed to intimate the vacancy of these churches to the respective Patrons, namely John Hay-Mackenzie, Esq of Cromarty, the Patron of Killearnan.

Mr James Gibson, the Clerk to the Presbytery, was then appointed to preach at Killearnan on the next sabbath and to declare from the pulpit that the church and parish were vacant. In contrast to most other parishes, the Free Church in Killearnan was formed with the support of its heritors, particularly Col Hugh Baillie of Redcastle, who leased land for a church, a manse and a school. In the Annals of the Free Church of Scotland,[50] it is recorded that 'Donald Kennedy, Minister of Killearnan and nearly all his people came out in 1843. A large double-roofed church was forthwith erected' and, according to Barron,[51] the offer of land by Col Baillie to one of the 'non-intrusion churches' was 'almost a solitary instance among the extensive proprietors in the North'. One of the plots of land was at Newton crossroads, where initially a 'tent' (in effect, a large shed) and then the 'double-roofed' church were erected as places of worship (Figure 23).

The *Inverness Courier*[52] of 12 October 1848 carried an advertisement seeking estimates for 'slating, mason, carpenter, plaster and lead works' (presumably for the 'double-roofed' church, although this is not stated) and indicated that a plan and specifications could be viewed at A and W Reid, Architects, 45 High Street, Inverness.

Figure 23: Sketch of the 'double-roofed' Free Church at Newton crossroads, erected in 1848 (The National Archives of Scotland, CH3/1200/11/5)

At the creation of the Free Church of Killearnan, the roll of communicants totalled 145, compared to only five who remained with the Established Church of Scotland in Killearnan. To entitle them to attend a communion service, Free Church communicants were issued with communion tokens which had to be surrendered at the church door. These, of course, had to be distinguishable from those of the Established church. A sketch of an 1844 token[53] shows that the Free Church in Killearnan initially put 'Redcastle' on their tokens rather than 'Killearnan'.

Somewhat surprisingly, the Free Church Deacons' Court held its early meetings in the Redcastle Inn. In 1845, it considered 'the necessity for taking steps for the securing of a site for a manse and a school'. On 15 May 1846, an advertisement was placed in the *Inverness Journal*[54] requesting estimates for the 'mason, carpenter, slater, plaster and plumber works of a Free Church manse to be erected at Redcastle'. The site was actually at Linnie Wood, about a kilometre east of the Newton crossroads where the 'double-roofed' church was sited. A minor dispute over glebe land at the manse would emerge in 1883.

Several residents of Redcastle feature in the early records of the Killearnan Free Church.[55] For example, Lewis MacKenzie (a tailor) was appointed by the Deacons' Court as 'Collector' for the District of Quarry. He died in 1860 and his gravestone in Killearnan parish church graveyard records his long-standing eldership of the Free Church. At its first meeting, the Free Church Parochial

Board registered a Roll of Paupers. Three widows in Quarry of Redcastle are named (Janet Thomson, Sarah MacKay and Mary McRae).

The Free Church session minutes of 1846 record the 'compearing' of Catherine Logan of Quarry of Redcastle. Catherine confessed to the session that 'she brought forth a male child in uncleanliness' and declared that a William MacKenzie from Ballivaird was the father. The session rebuked Catherine and resolved to call on the Inspector of the Poor to secure aliment for the child. The case was to re-emerge in 1849–50. [Kirk sessions of all denominations were always keen to establish the paternity of an illegitimate child, because a deserted mother and child were a major burden on the poor funds. If fathers could be identified, they could be fined and made to agree to maintenance payments. In England, such agreements were called 'bastardy bonds'.]

The customs of 'target shooting' and 'raffling' during the winter months concerned the Free Church. In 1847, the session alleged that these activities were accompanied by 'much profanity and sin', and the moderator was requested to warn the young of the congregation from the pulpit. This is probably an early reference to the use of Redcastle pier as a shooting range and as a place for the youth of the area to wager on their proficiency with a rifle. The pier would later be used as a 'Volunteers' Rifle Range', with a marker's butt and a target located at the far (southern) end.

Three years later, the continuing case of Catherine Logan and her son, fathered by William MacKenzie, is fully documented in the session minutes of 1849. It offers a detailed insight into the processes that parents had to endure to get illegitimate children (or children born from 'ante-nuptial fornication') baptised. William attended a session meeting in October 1849 and confessed that he was the father of Catherine's child, and 'being solemnly rebuked and having expressed his desire to be cleared of the scandal of his sin' was required to meet with each of the elders at their respective dwellings and then appear before the next session meeting. Catherine was also summoned to that meeting and an elder (James Urquhart) was appointed 'to converse with her with a view, if found qualified, to receive a discipline'.

William and Catherine again attended the session in November 1849, at which they were instructed 'to appear before the congregation on the following Sabbath to be publicly admonished'. The moderator was authorised 'to free them on the third Sabbath from the scandal of their sin'. Thereafter, William had 'to wait on the Moderator about the baptism of his child' and, if permitted by the moderator, he and Catherine would be further summoned to appear at the session meeting of January 1850 'that their child may be baptised'. At that meeting, they 'were absolved from the scandal of their sin' and the child was baptised. Throughout the various minutes stretching from 1846 to 1850 the name of the child is never recorded, nor is it noted whether William and Catherine had married. In fact, they had married and the child was named John. They are recorded in the 1851 census living in Quarry of Redcastle with another two-month-old baby, named after her mother, but known as 'Katie'.

The story has a bittersweet ending. Katie died in September 1853, aged two, but her mother, Catherine Logan, lived to reach the age of seventy-seven. Both are recorded on a tombstone erected by John in the Killearnan parish church graveyard. There are later additions to the inscription, but William MacKenzie, John and Katie's father and Catherine's husband, is notably absent.

Another example of a resident of Redcastle being recorded in the Free Church records is afforded by the case of Mary MacDonald. She is not recorded in the 1841 census, but was resident in 1847 when the Parochial Board reduced her allowance to 1/6d per week because she was receiving rent from a tenant (named as 'Alexander Loban's son'). In 1849, Mary applied for an increased allowance, but she was refused on the grounds that the Board:

> ...considered her present allowance of 1/6d per week quite adequate if she remained in the parish to which she is chargeable, having in it a free house and garden part of which she let to tenants and received the rent from same. That having left of her own accord the parish to which she is chargeable without just cause and gone to Inverness where she may pay dear for her lodgings and may make her allowance very inadequate. But then the Board don't consider themselves ... [obliged] to meet the views of paupers who leave their own parishes without cause and who may go to Inverness, Glasgow or Edinburgh where they may occupy houses rented at from £10 to £20 per annum.

It seems that even in the nineteenth century city living was expensive.

It is surprising that the minutes of neither the Free Church session nor the Deacons' Court record the building of their new church at Newton crossroads that replaced the double-roofed corrugated iron church (Figure 23, page 171). It was commenced in 1864 and completed in 1866 at a cost of £1,000. It was designed (seating around 800 people) by Mr Rhind of Inverness and built by Messrs Urquhart and Maclennan. The stone may have come from Redcastle quarry, but is more probably from either Tarradale or Kilcoy quarry. The *Inverness Advertiser*[56] of 16 February 1866 records the opening services, which were conducted by Rev. Donald Kennedy in Gaelic at 11 a.m. and English at 1 p.m. The building is described as:

> ...imposing and most pleasing in appearance ... the door handsomely finished off and there is over it a large and exceedingly handsome gothic window with rich traceries ... the principal ornament is a circular window over the pulpit at

the farther end with glass stained after a beautiful pattern … it has, although small, a very fine effect … the pulpit is of the platform construction considerably elevated, and enclosed on both sides … the vestry, a snug erection in harmony, outside and inside with the rest of the building … it is proposed to provide immediately a good bell.

Both services attracted 'audiences quite filling the building and including members of almost all families in the parish, of both denominations', and the collection at the door raised £84-7-6d.

Rev. Donald Kennedy, the minister who had taken most of his congregation from the Killearnan parish church to the Free Church during the disruption of 1843, died from a heart attack in May 1871 at the age of fifty-eight. A plaque mounted on the wall of the Free Church at Newton crossroads (now Tore Art Gallery) commemorates his ministry (Figure 24). It reads:

Ordained minister of Port Glasgow in 1838, succeeded his venerable father the Rev. John Kennedy whose name will ever be fragrant in the church as minister of the parish of Killearnan in 1841. During the thirty years of his ministry was a faithful preacher, a diligent pastor, a wise counseller, a warm and true friend to all his people. His death they mourn.

The Deacons' Court of the Free Church[57] received a letter in 1883 from John MacLennan, styled as the under-factor at Redcastle estate, stating that the piece of ground adjoining the (closed in 1873) school at Quarry of Redcastle was being used as a garden by 'former teachers'. Henry Baillie, the owner of Redcastle estate, wished it to be known that the feu did not include this piece of ground and demanded that the Deacons' Court 'give up possession immediately', making this 'an indispensable condition to his entertaining any offers in connection with glebe lands'. The glebe lands in question were at Linnie, adjoining the site of the Free Church manse, and the former teachers were, presumably, the MacIntoshs who had retired in 1876.

The Deacons' Court requested their moderator, now Rev. Neil Gillies, to consult with the 'Custodian of Title Deeds'. At the next meeting, he quoted from the lease, dated 5 February 1864:

All and whole that part of ground containing [0.72 acres] or thereby upon part of which is built a School in connection with the Free Church, bounded as follows: On the north and east by the lands of Milton Inn Farm presently occupied by Alexander Campbell, on the west by Redcastle quarry and on the south by a road leading from said quarry to the Milton of Redcastle.

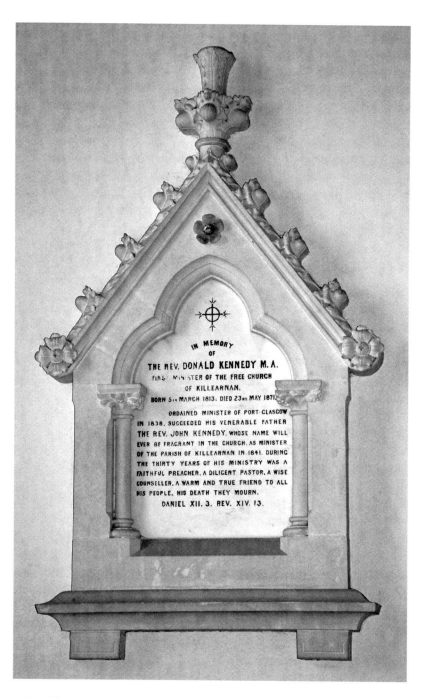

IN MEMORY
OF
THE REV. DONALD KENNEDY M.A.
FIRST MINISTER OF THE FREE CHURCH
OF KILLEARNAN,
BORN 5th MARCH 1813; DIED 23rd MAY 1871.

ORDAINED MINISTER OF PORT-GLASGOW
IN 1838, SUCCEEDED HIS VENERABLE FATHER
THE REV. JOHN KENNEDY, WHOSE NAME WILL
EVER BE FRAGRANT IN THE CHURCH, AS MINISTER
OF THE PARISH OF KILLEARNAN IN 1841, DURING
THE THIRTY YEARS OF HIS MINISTRY WAS A
FAITHFUL PREACHER, A DILIGENT PASTOR, A WISE
COUNSELLER, A WARM AND TRUE FRIEND TO ALL
HIS PEOPLE, HIS DEATH THEY MOURN.
DANIEL XII. 3. REV. XIV. 13.

Figure 24: The commemorative tablet to Rev. Donald Kennedy, Free Church minister of Killearnan 1843–71, in the ex-Killearnan Free Church of Scotland (now Tore Art Gallery)

175

Henry Baillie clearly had no case, and the new glebe land was duly presented to the Killearnan Free Church.

It is not clear why Henry Baillie had raised the issue. Perhaps he was not such a strong supporter of the Free Church as his father, Col Hugh Baillie. Similarly, it is also not clear why the Free Church Deacons' Court was determined to retain a piece of ground that they no longer required since their school at Quarry of Redcastle had closed in 1873, ten years earlier. The ground in question, immediately to the south-east of the quarry, was the site of the original L-shaped building that was the residence and garden of the quarry 'overseer' during the construction of the Caledonian Canal. Perhaps the Free Church had sublet it to the MacIntoshs or perhaps Henry Baillie wanted the ground for sheep, cattle or crops.

2.5 The Established Church of Scotland in Killearnan

After the Disruption of 1843 and the creation of the Free Church of Scotland, the Established Church of Scotland in Killearnan struggled to survive. Indeed, it probably would not have done so but for its statutory role – for example, in maintaining the parish school and appointing the parish registrar. At the last meeting of the kirk session before the disruption (held on 26 December 1842), it is recorded that Kenneth MacKenzie of Milton of Redcastle, John Dingwall of Prescaltin and Robert Trotter of Garguston had stood for election as elders.[58] They had all received considerably fewer votes than the three candidates from the eastern part of the parish, so were not elected. However, the result was meaningless because the Killearnan parish church subsequently lost all but five of its communicant members at the Disruption.

The next meeting of the parish kirk session was not held until 10 April 1845, over three years later. This was because of problems in replacing Rev. Donald Kennedy, who had transferred to the Free Church. In November 1843, the post was offered to Rev. Alexander McIntosh, but there were objections raised by several parishioners, and the General Assembly of the Church of Scotland ordered the Presbytery of Chanonry to recommence the appointment process, whereupon Rev. McIntosh resigned in July 1844. He was replaced in December 1844 by Rev. John Macrae. The kirk session meeting in April 1845 was his first meeting and there were only two items of business, the first being to appoint John Corner of Kilcoy as church officer, and the second being to write to the previous session clerk and parish school-master, Kenneth MacKenzie, to demand the return of 'the records, books, papers and documents pertaining to the Church Session'. However, Kenneth MacKenzie refused to return the documents until he had been paid his outstanding salary arrears. It appears that this was never done and, unfortunately, the books have not survived.

There were further problems retaining a minister. Rev. Macrae resigned in September 1847 when he transferred to Stornoway. He was replaced by Rev. Patrick Campbell, who had previously been in British Guiana. He was unmarried and died of a brain disease at the age of forty-five in January 1860. Surprisingly, there is no mention of his sudden death in the kirk session minutes, although there is a wall plaque in his memory in the parish church. It describes him as 'an Israelite indeed, in whom was no guile'. One might surmise whether he was the subject of the well known pipe tune 'Campbell's Farewell to Redcastle'. Some sources suggest that the Campbell referred to in the title may have been Capt Robert Campbell of Glen Lyon, who led troops in the massacre of Glencoe in 1692. However, his connection with Redcastle is not obvious. Also, the composer of the tune is not known but it has been attributed to a Colin Mackenzie and seems to have been first published in 1875.[59] It is also possible that neither Campbell nor Redcastle pertain to Killearnan. They could, for example, refer to the Redcastle near Tain which was demolished in 1870.

Patrick Campbell was succeeded by Rev. William MacKay in May 1860. Throughout his thirty-year tenure (to 1890), his kirk session comprised only three members, these being himself, Donald McLeod Esq and the parish schoolteacher, (Rev.) Hugh Skinner, who was also the session clerk. They had so little business to transact that they met in the manse only once per year. After July 1879, these annual meetings were held under the aegis of the Presbytery, generally at Chanonry (Fortrose). The attendees were commonly only the moderator and two 'assessors', who were usually the ministers of Fortrose and Rosemarkie churches. However, despite the minimal membership, the Established Church of Scotland in Killearnan continued to provide church services and run the parish school. According to Fullarton's *Imperial Gazetteer*[60] of 1868, the parish church was 'of large capacity but very uncomfortable', whilst the Free Church had 'a very large attendance and its receipts in 1865 amounted to £153-13/-'. In contrast, Rev. William MacKay of the parish church reported to his kirk session that their total income for 1868 had been £3-3-9d, of which the ordinary collection receipts had been only £1-16-9d.

Throughout the remainder of the nineteenth century, a constant population decline in Redcastle had an adverse effect on both churches. For example, the Roll of Communicants[61] for the July 1883 communion in the Killearnan parish church contains only five names, which included Rev. William MacKay and Robert Young, a Presbytery assessor from Fortrose. Although numerically much larger, the Communicants Roll of the Killearnan Free Church also showed decline, reaching a nineteenth-century low of forty-one in 1890–91.[62]

Like the Free Church, the Established Church of Scotland would not baptise illegitimate children until the parents (and particularly the mother) had repented. However, the Established Church no longer submitted its miscreants to the discipline of public rebukes over three successive sabbaths. One of the few residents of Redcastle who was an adherent of the Established Church, Elspet (or Elizabeth) MacKenzie, is recorded in 1868 as having borne an illegitimate child. She was compeared to the kirk session:

> …having been guilty of the sin of fornication, and said Elspet MacKenzie having expressed her deep sorrow for the sin of which she had been guilty, and her resolution that henceforth thro' divine grace she will walk in newness of life and endeavour to adorn the doctrine of God her Saviour. The Moderator, after a serious rebuke and solemn admonition, did in the name of the session absolve her from the scandal of her sin and restored her to the privileges of the Church. The Moderator then baptised her child in the presence of the session.

As in the compearing of Catherine Logan by the Free Church in 1846–50, there is no mention of the name (or sex) of the child or of Elspet MacKenzie's marital status. However, the 1871 census records her as living unmarried in Quarry of Redcastle with her elderly parents and a four-year-old daughter, Jessie MacKinnon. What the census also reveals is that she had a ten-year-old daughter, Mary MacGlashan. Jessie had been Elspet's second illegitimate daughter.

Another family living in Quarry of Redcastle consisted of three generations, all named Isabella Gray. The seventy-year-old grandmother was the widow of Alexander Gray, an agricultural labourer. Their marriage is recorded in the Killearnan Old Parish Registers[63] for November 1839. They lived at Redcastle Mains but appear to have moved to Quarry of Redcastle by 1871. Their (unmarried) daughter was also an agricultural worker who had two children, a daughter Isabella, aged seven, and a son, Alexander Robinson. She was 'craving baptism for her illegitimate child' and was compeared in 1881 to the Killearnan kirk session, where she confessed that 'she had given birth to a male child on the 21st February 1876, and that James Robertson [named as Robinson in the 1881 census], a farmer residing in Quarryfield, Avoch, was the father'. The moderator was authorised to deliver 'a solemn rebuke and admonition', and on receiving 'her expression of her penitence and her resolution by divine grace to walk henceforth in newness of life, to absolve her from the scandal of her sin, and to baptise the child'. The date of Alexander's baptism is not recorded, but in 1884 Isabella gave birth to another illegitimate child, Helen. Her resolution 'to walk henceforth in newness of life' made in 1881 had lasted all of three years! The small gravestone of the grandmother, Isabella Gray, is in Killearnan parish church graveyard. It is undated but of interest for its spelling of 'Quary'.

Rev. MacKay died in April 1890 and is buried in Killearnan churchyard. He was succeeded as moderator by Rev. Aeneas Macdonald, elected by the congregation as patronage had been abolished in 1874. For reasons that are not entirely clear, it was decided at that time to raise the walls of the church by four feet (and the level of the floor), attach a new roof and build a new manse. Plans were drawn up in April 1891 by the Inverness architects Ross and MacBeth,[64] for which their quotation was £1,050-7/-. However, this turned out to be remarkably inaccurate, the finished cost being £1,409-19-9d, of which the alterations to the parish church were £658-9-9d. The parish heritors financed the work by borrowing £2,200 from the North British and Mercantile Bank at four per cent over ten years. Despite the cost overrun, there were issues with the quality of the work in the manse, with shrinking plasterwork, ill-fitting skirting boards, an uneven kitchen floor, and an ineffective boiler being major problems. In the 'offices' [the building now known as Finlaggan], there was no hay loft or poultry house, and the byre required partitions. However, by far the most problematic issue was the water supply, and the various attempts to resolve it would become an ongoing saga over the next sixty years.

Two residents of Milton of Redcastle provide an illuminating insight into the problems of the welfare of older people who were unable to earn a living and required financial support from the poor funds administered by the Parochial Board.[65] In 1891, Susan Hogg was awarded 1/- per week. In 1898, this was increased to 2/- per week and supplemented by a 15/- clothing grant. She seems to have developed mental health problems and increasingly received her allowance in kind – for example, a cartload of firewood and 6d cash in 1900. By 1901, Widow MacLean was being paid 1/- per week to attend her, and in 1904 it was decided to commit her to an asylum or otherwise to find 'suitable arrangements for her safety'. It is recorded that her son, who was a salmon fisherman, took her to live with him in Nairn, where she died in 1905. Another Milton of Redcastle resident, Mary Ross, was single and unable to work at the age of sixty in 1896. She, too, received a small cash allowance and help in kind (boots, shoes, blanket, coal and flannel) during the period 1899–1908. She was also allowed an attendant (Mrs Bisset) during an illness in 1907 and a nurse from 1915 until 1916, when she died.

An alternative to receiving financial support in cash or kind from the Parochial Board was the poorhouse. Killearnan was one of seven parishes that contributed funding to the Black Isle Combination Poorhouse in Fortrose.[66] It had been built in 1859 to comply with the Scottish Poor Law Act of 1845 but, in reality, was never more than half full. There were two reasons for this.

Firstly, unemployed paupers on the Black Isle were rare due to the excellent soil and thriving agricultural economy. Secondly, the rural communities of the Black Isle were traditionally self-supporting and looked after those who were genuinely too ill or frail to earn a living.

Life was strictly regulated in the poorhouses. Inmates wore a uniform, had weekly baths and regular haircuts, and there was a prescribed daily routine that required them to work according to their capabilities. Diet was also prescribed and mainly consisted of broth, meal and bread with a small amount of boiled meat. Although some of the paupers of Killearnan were offered relocation to the poorhouse, this seems to have been quite rare and was generally rejected in favour of local help. Hugh MacLeod, an ex-quarrier from Quarry of Redcastle who had become paralysed and unable to work, is one example of a person who was offered a place in 1874, but he preferred to remain at home, living on 2/6d per week until he died in 1888. Indeed, in the forty years from 1861 to 1901, only four inmates of the Black Isle Combination Poorhouse are recorded as coming from Killearnan. They were: Janet Paterson, a seventy-four-year-old farmer's widow; Alexander Fraser, a seventy-two-year-old ex-quarryman, Dardinna Bain, a forty-nine-year-old pauper; and Jessie-Ann Stewart, the three-year-old illegitimate child of Ann Stewart, born in June 1867 and the only child born in the parish known to have been abandoned to the poorhouse. None of these came from Redcastle.

2.6   The United Free Church of Killearnan

The United Free Church of Scotland was created in 1900 when most of the Free Church of Scotland merged with the United Presbyterian Church. At that time, the Free Church minister in Killearnan was Rev. Neil Gillies, who had been appointed in 1872 after the death of Rev. Donald Kennedy. Rev. Gillies transferred to the United Free Church, but only a minority of his congregation joined him. The first meeting of the Killearnan United Free Church Deacons' Court was on 3 October 1900, and the first record of a meeting of the kirk session[67] is dated 17 December 1900, although there are references to earlier meetings of which no minutes have survived. Hugh Fraser, the head gardener at Redcastle, was one of the 'ruling elders' present at the first kirk session meeting, at which only forty-two members were entered on the communicant roll.

In July 1902, Rev. Gillies announced that due to failing health he wished the kirk session to commence the process of appointing his successor. He was provided with a pension of £60 from the sustentation fund, in addition to what his 'time of service' entitled him to receive from the Aged and Infirm Ministers' Fund. Rev. James MacLeod of Knockbain acted as an interim moderator until Rev. Charles Matheson was appointed in February 1904. However, he resigned four years later and Rev. Kenneth Cameron stood in during the interim. Rev. Alexander Cameron was appointed in July 1909 and remained moderator until June 1933.[68]

The congregation of the United Free Church initially worshipped in the Free Church at Newton crossroads. However, when the House of Lords ruled in 1904 that all former Free Church of Scotland buildings should remain in their ownership, it was handed back. Thereafter, the United Free Church hired the Killearnan public school, but in January 1908 the kirk session was informed that the trustees of the Kilcoy estate 'had granted a site for the new church near Redcastle railway bridge at the rate of £4 per annum'. Furthermore, a letter had been received from the Special Building Committee 'promising a grant for an iron church to accommodate 182 persons'. It is not recorded in the kirk session minutes when the new church opened, but the *Inverness Courier* of 5 June 1908 recorded that it was opened on the previous day by Rev. Dr Macgregor of St Andrew's Church in Edinburgh. The church is described as being a corrugated iron structure erected by Messrs Spiers of Edinburgh and 'quite handsome in appearance, and the internal arrangements are as comfortable as possible' (Figure 25). The Deacons' Court minutes of January 1909 refer to a special collection at the opening of the new church which had raised £10-13-5d. The building was extended in 1922, but this also is not recorded in the session minutes.

Figure 25: The former United Free Church, subsequently Church of Scotland, at Redcastle Station (reproduced from an original by permission of Dr Kenneth Mackay)

Soon after Rev. Alexander Cameron was appointed, Donald MacDonald of Fettes Farm on 20 October 1910 signed a feu charter[69] for a lease of ground at Redcastle Station for the building of a United Free Church manse. It was completed in 1911, and is now named Newlyn House.

Whilst the Deacons' Court concerned itself solely with financial matters, the United Free Church session seemed to meet for only two purposes. The first of these was to set the dates of communion services and maintain the communicant roll. The roll of members previous to 1910 has not survived and that for 1910–11 is incomplete; however, from 1911–12 onwards the names of the communicant members are individually listed. They generally totalled between thirty-five and forty-five, and normally included about sixteen residents of Redcastle – for example, Donald and Annie MacDonald of Redcastle Mains, Hugh Fraser of Redcastle Gardens, Mrs Lily Jack of Quarry of Redcastle, Mrs Spence of Garguston, and Williamina McIntosh, George and Lizzie Forbes and Mrs MacLean of Milton of Redcastle.

The second purpose for meetings of the kirk session was to undertake an annual review of the 'State of Religion and Morals' within the parish. In 1902, their review recorded that 'there is a gratifying disposition on the part of some of the younger members to engage in Christian work and to manifest greater interest in the services of the Sanctuary ... the moral tone is good, generally speaking ... [however] the young men labouring at the larger farms are difficult to reach and influence for good owing especially to frequent changes'. In 1908, the review was reassuring in stating that 'the moral tone of the people is on the whole a high one. Drunkenness is apparently on the decrease and indeed the habits of the people are commendably temperate'. The session of the United Free Church in Killearnan may have been viewing the parish through rose-tinted spectacles, but it does seem to be true that the moral state of the parish was (and always had been) high.

The United Free Church of Scotland disbanded when the Church of Scotland (Property and Endowments) Act of 1925 allowed for its union with the Established Church of Scotland, and transferred all responsibility for their combined ecclesiastical properties to the new unified Church of Scotland. In Killearnan, the merger did not occur until June 1933, when Rev. Alexander Cameron resigned 'in the interest of the Union of the congregation with that of the congregation of Killearnan, under the name of Killearnan congregation'. At the union, the United Free Church in Killearnan had an 'electoral roll' of thirty-six members and ninety-six adherents, a much greater number than had been in the Established Church of Scotland.

2.7 Water, Water, Everywhere, but not at the Manse

When the renovated manse of the Established Church of Scotland in Killearnan was completed in 1892, the water supply was collected from a shallow drain (sometimes called a well) in the field above the manse and piped to an underground tank set in the manse lawn. From there, it was hand-pumped to a tank above the kitchen. Neither the Presbytery nor Rev. Aeneas Macdonald was satisfied with this supply, which was often of poor quality and tended to dry up during the summer. For example, a report from the Presbytery in December 1893 noted that 'the water supply to the manse is insufficient, failing as it did for two months this year, and will be unsatisfactory until brought in by gravitation'. This solicited an immediate response from the heritors:[70]

> With regard to the water supply we respectfully submit to the Presbytery that the normal supply from the existing well and force pump cannot be fairly judged by the past year, which was one of exceptional dryness. No doubt a supply by gravitation would be more satisfactory, if that were possible, but this question was fully considered by the Heritors while the manse was under repair and they came to the conclusion that the most reliable means of supplying the manse was by a force pump as at present.

This seemed to settle the issue, with the exception of a repair to the pump in January 1905 for which the heritors paid £9-5-6d to R Black and Sons, Plumbers, Inverness. However, the saga of the water supply would re-emerge with a vengeance in 1920.

It is not apparent whether the water supply to the manse was a matter of contention between Rev. Aeneas Macdonald and the Killearnan heritors in the period up to 1920. This is because there are no heritors' minutes for the period between 1912 and 1920. However, it has to be concluded that by the end of World War One the issue had been raised. Included in a long list of repairs required at the manse submitted by Rev. Macdonald to the heritors in April 1920 was also a demand for 'a house for his man ... [and] a desire to get a supply of water by gravitation that might be got from ¾ mile distant from the manse'. In reply, the heritors restated that 'as the question of the water supply was already considered before the pump was put in [in 1892], not to re-open the question'. Furthermore, they did not admit any liability for a 'man's house'. This did not satisfy Rev. Macdonald, but he appeared to offer a compromise when he stated that 'if the heritors ... carried out the repairs to the manse ... consideration of the water supply could be left off for a future occasion. The alternative is the calling in of the Presbytery and insisting on a water supply by gravitation as well as a man's house'. This only fuelled the heritors' resolve to affirm again that they were neither liable for a gravitation water supply nor for a man's house.

Figure 26: Rev. Aeneas Macdonald, minister of Killearnan 1890–1932 (circa 1920)
(reproduced from an original by permission of Alan Macdonald)

However, Rev. Macdonald (Figure 26) was a man of determination. He had already approached the Presbytery (a simple task, as he was now its moderator) to commission from George Gordon and Co., Queensgate, Inverness, an 'Engineer's Report on the Water Supply to Killearnan Manse'. This report is transcribed into the heritors' minutes:

> In accordance with the instructions of the Presbytery of Chanonry conveyed in your letter to us of 26 August 1920, we made a careful inspection of the existing water supply system at the manse of Killearnan and of possible sources for an improved supply and now beg to report.
>
> The present supply is derived from a shallow drain in the arable field situated immediately to the north of the manse. From a small open collecting well at the edge of the field the water is conveyed in a ¾ inch lead pipe to an under-

ground cistern placed in the lawn about 15 yards from the house and thence the water is raised by a pump placed in the scullery to a service cistern in the roof of the kitchen wing. As mentioned above, the source of the present supply is a shallow field drain collecting surface water which will no doubt be subject from time to time to manurial pollution from fertilisers used in the soil and from cattle grazing in the field. We are of the opinion that this is not a suitable source for a domestic water supply.

For an improved water supply we have examined numerous suggested sources within a radius of a mile or two from the manse. The sources with elevation sufficient to take a supply to the manse by gravitation were found to be deficient generally in the matter of volume during the dry months of the year. The best available source which we have been able to discover within a moderate distance of the manse is a spring which issues from the face of the rock in the bottom of the old quarry some 400 lineal yards east of the manse.

The present yield of this spring is at the rate of 5,400 gallons a day whilst the maximum supply required at the manse would probably not exceed 600 gallons a day.

The works required to introduce a new supply to the manse from this source, as indicated generally on the enclosed plan, would include a small gathering well at the eye of the spring, a windmill pump with the necessary piping to raise the water to a concrete cistern of about 3,000 gallons capacity, placed in the corner of the field on the north side of the road at an elevation sufficient to allow the water to gravitate from there to the manse.

We estimate the cost of these works at £350.

The heritors' response was brief and predictable:

As regards the water supply, the Clerk pointed out to the Heritors that the matter came up before the Presbytery in December 1893 and that, in a reply made by the Heritors to the Rev. Macdonald dated 11 January 1894, it was pointed out that the water supply for Killearnan Manse was from a well and not surface water as stated in Messrs Geo. Gordon and Co's report.

However, they did decide to contact Mr Knowles, Water Manager and Sanitary Inspector for the Burgh of Inverness, to ascertain if 'in his opinion, any improvements should be carried out on the supply so that no complaint could be made against it'.

On 11 February 1921, the Presbytery took the issue of the water supply and the man's house to the Sheriff Court in Dingwall. Rev. Macdonald's hand-written notes prepared in response to the 'Statement of Facts for Appellants' still survive.[71] The first notes refer to the original (February 1891) report from Ross and MacBeth, the architects chosen to undertake the works, which states 'that a reservoir be formed on the glebe where a good supply can be had at a height sufficient to supply the ground floor of the manse and offices by gravitation'. However, the tank had been placed under the manse lawn and no water had ever been brought into the manse other than by pumping. The next note refers to the architects' report of March 1894, in which it had been stated that 'the water supply is sufficient except in time of drought and that the only means of continuing the water supply was by increasing the storage capacity'. This had been done but, according to Rev. Macdonald, the enlarged tank 'was getting choked with gravel every other year and one year the lawn was so flooded as to make access to the manse difficult'. A further note refers to a heritors' meeting of April 1905, at which it was claimed that Rev. Macdonald was now 'thoroughly satisfied with the work done and hoped it would not be necessary further for 30 years'. His response was categorical: 'I deny having ever uttered these words'!

Rev. Macdonald also refers in his notes to the house for the minister's man. He suggests that it could have been built on a plot of land which he claimed had belonged to the glebe, 'in which belief I was confirmed by several old residenters then living'. There is also a note referring to an 'affidavit by an old residenter', which claimed that the house adjoining the churchyard was formerly the house of the minister's man. This presumably refers to the house known at the time as Manse Cottage (or sometimes Manse Park), located between the churchyard and the edge of the quarry. There do not seem to be any records of it being a house for a minister's man, although its name does suggest that it may have served this purpose. Also, the parish did employ a catechist at various times; for example, from 1766 when Rev. David Denoon (I) successfully petitioned the Royal Bounty Committee,[72] and from 1816 when the heritors were allocated £300 to endow such a post for Rev. John Kennedy.[73]

The decision of the Sheriff Court was that the minister was not entitled to a man's house, but it did decide to refer the matter of the water supply to 'a man of skill'. It was agreed that such a man was Mr Mackenzie, the sanitary inspector for Dingwall, but it appears that Mr Charles Manners, a civil engineer in Inverness, actually provided the report. On 8 April 1921, the sheriff reconvened the court hearing and found for the Presbytery on the matter of the water supply, but reaffirmed against them on the matter of the man's house. The heritors were therefore required to install a water supply that would provide a reliable supply of water to the manse, and in September 1921 secured Mr Munro, an architect and surveyor in Inverness, to report on how this could be achieved.

Rev. Macdonald had consistently argued that the best source would be the spring in the quarry face about 400 yards east of the manse (marked as a 'well' on the 1:2,500 [*circa* 25 inch:1 mile] second series Ordnance Survey map of 1907) that was used for drinking water by the residents of Quarry of Redcastle. From there, he proposed that the spring water could either be pumped to a tank in the field where it could supply the manse by gravity or directly to the cistern under the manse lawn. However, in January 1922, Mr Munro reported to the heritors that he considered that the best and cheapest way would be to supply the water from the quarry by means of a ram. Astonishingly, the heritors deferred the decision whilst they commissioned Col Rose of Kilravock to examine the ground around Blairdhu Farm to determine whether the water could be supplied from there. At that same January 1922 meeting, the heritors also received two letters. The first was from Messrs Baillie and Gifford, Solicitors, acting on behalf of Col James Baillie of Redcastle (and Dochfour), requesting an annual payment of £10 should the water supply be taken from his quarry. The other was from Rev. Macdonald, requesting payment of the expenses incurred by him during the Sheriff Court case. The heritors denied any liability other than for the report produced for the Presbytery by Messrs George Gordon and Co.

Mr Munro, the architect and surveyor, reported to the heritors in February 1922 that he had obtained two estimates for the ram scheme: £356-8/- from Mackenzie and Son of Dingwall; and £370 from Mr Urquhart of Beauly. The heritors were also informed that Col Rose of Kilravock had not been able to undertake the examination at Blairdhu but had suggested the use of a 'practical diviner', and that a firm in Bath were highly recommended and would charge twenty-one guineas if they were already in Scotland or £30 for a special visit. As it turned out, both Col Rose and a local diviner visited Blairdhu and confirmed the availability of water there. However, there was also a requirement to put a water supply into the Killearnan school, so the heritors decided to confer with Dr Philip, Director of Education for Ross-shire, to ascertain if a common source of water sufficient for both the manse and the school could be found.

On 11 April 1922, a professional water diviner, Mr Mullins from Kent, visited Blairdhu (at the cost of £21). His report found 'there are no means of obtaining a water supply for the manse by gravitation, the whole of the water available (at Blairdhu) being at a much lower level than the roof of the house'. To thoroughly confuse the issue, he also suggested that (at a cost of only £80) a 1,000-gallons-per-day supply could be tapped by excavating an eighteen-foot-deep well at the site of the existing source in the field above the manse! Excavations were immediately carried out by Mr Urquhart of Beauly, and the heritors reported to the Sheriff Court on 12 May 1922 that they 'now propose to make a well as advised by Mr Mullins and thus give a plentiful supply of water to the manse'. However, the sheriff's verdict – based on the report from Mr Manners that he had commissioned in August 1921 – was that:

...the existing water supply to the manse of Killearnan was defective both in respect that it is subject to manurial pollution and that it cannot be depended upon as an adequate supply ... [this being] sufficiently condemnatory of the existing water supply to the manse and offices both as to adequacy and wholesomeness to justify my ordering a fresh supply to be installed ... [however, I am not entitled] to prescribe to the heritors any particular source of supply though doubtless they will be wise to take the minister with them in this matter, having regard to the future.

Rev. Macdonald had been victorious, so the heritors reverted to their ram scheme. However, the purity of the quarry water had first to be analysed and this was undertaken by S Hendry Esq., Pharmacist, Bridge Street, Inverness, who reported:

This sample has a very slightly opalescent appearance and gave a slight deposit of organic matter of an innocuous character on standing 48 hours. The sample showed a normal degree of acidity and was found to be quite free from poisonous metals, nitrites and phosphates. The proportions of both free and albuminoid ammonia are well within the limits usually prescribed for a good potable water. The organic content of the water, as indicated by the amount of oxygen absorbed in 4 hours, was low. Judging from the quality of the sample this water is of excellent quality and is well suited for domestic use.

However, the ram scheme was in trouble at the Sheriff Court, as it required manual labour to work the ram. On 20 October 1922, the sheriff-substitute found:

...in law that such labour in pumping is not obligatory on the defender [Rev. Macdonald] and that he is entitled to obtain from the pursuers [the heritors] an adequate supply of good water delivered to the upper stories of the manse ... without and independent of such labour on his part or that of his household. Therefore ordains and discerns the pursuers to install ... an adequate supply of good water, capable of continuously rising whether by gravitation or mechanical contrivance ... and to complete such installation within a period of six weeks.

Rev. Macdonald may again have been victorious, but he did not leave the court totally unblemished when the sheriff-substitute remarked that 'though the defender has doubts as to the sufficiency of the supply [from the quarry] I fear he is inclined to asperse, in the figurative sense, any offer made by such hands as the pursuers'. With the manual ram scheme now discredited, another method of pumping the water out of the quarry had to be found. A petrol engine was initially suggested, but it was refused by Rev. Macdonald. The heritors therefore petitioned the sheriff-substitute. He visited the site, and on 24 November 1922 found for the heritors, on the condition that they guaranteed 'an ample and sufficient supply of lubricating oil and petrol ... free of charge ... and to keep said engine in good running order and in good repair'. However, Rev. Macdonald and the Presbytery were not happy and in February 1923 they requested the heritors to abandon the petrol engine in favour of a windmill. This 'entailed an entire alteration in the plans', but Mr Newlands, the engineer-in-chief of the Highland railway, offered to draw up a new plan 'showing the exact location required for the windmill and the disposition and necessary length of piping'.

Procurement of a windmill proceeded immediately. One at the Nigg depot of the Board of Agriculture was inspected, but its purchase was considered 'too speculative'. Estimates were obtained for the cost of the mill and its erection, the tank and pump, foundations and plumber works. The lowest estimate for supply and erection of the mill was from Mr Mullins of Kent and for the plumbing was from R Mackenzie and Sons, the total amounting to £141-3-4d.

Surprisingly, the building of the windmill and the completion of the new water supply to the manse is not recorded in the Killearnan heritors' minutes. However, a Deed of Servitude in favour of the Church of Scotland General Trustees dated 21 May 1928 is recorded. It refers to the windmill, the storage tank and the pipes; therefore it can be assumed that it was in operation by then. Unfortunately, Rev. Aeneas Macdonald lived to enjoy the fruits of his efforts for only a short time, as he died in November 1932. A commemorative plaque in the church describes him as 'a faithful pastor, a sound and instructive preacher, a wise counsellor and a loyal friend'. The bible that he had used at the communion table remains in the church. It was rebound and fully restored by his grandson in 1984.

The windmill was located in the field above the manse, but it was fated not to stand there for long. In November 1936, it was described by the kirk session to be in a 'precarious condition' when repairs to the wheel cost £17-10/- and an overhaul of the pump cost £6-7-6d. Unfortunately, the expense of those repairs proved fruitless, because the windmill was destroyed a month later in a gale on 15 December 1936. The kirk session decided that it would be inadvisable to repair 'the total wreckage of the wheel of the windmill' and that a gravity supply should be found. As a temporary solution, the hand pump in the manse was brought back into service and a man was employed for two hours per week (at a rate of 1/3d per hour) to pump water into the tank. The remains of the windmill remained in the field above the manse throughout World War Two and were finally removed in 1944.

In June 1937, a formal application was made by the kirk session to the County Council 'to participate in the water scheme for the school' and, in the meantime, a request was made to Redcastle estate for permission to use the reservoir that supplied Fettes Farm. Both applications failed, at least in the first instance. In January 1938, the Director of Education wrote to the kirk session indicating that he had now initiated an investigation into a water supply to the school, but nothing happened, so the hand pump continued to be used.

After Rev. Aeneas Macdonald's death in 1932, Rev. Julius McCallum had been appointed as the parish minister. However, he resigned and entered the ministry of the Episcopal Church in Scotland in November 1939, and a new minister, Rev. George Ballingall, was ordained and inducted in April 1940. It took Rev. Ballingall only three years to intimate to the kirk session that he had been in consultation with a local plumber about 'the unsatisfactory state of the water supply to the manse'. The response provided a solution that had not previously been considered: 'If a ram were installed on the burn passing through the grounds of the manse, water could be raised to a sufficient height to enter the tank in the manse.' The cost was estimated at £30 and, although it is not recorded, this solution was put in place.

The issue of the connection of the manse to the proposed schemes to bring water to Garguston and Blairdhu farms and the Killearnan school was again raised with the kirk session almost ten years later in March 1949. At the same meeting, the moderator also submitted estimates for 'wiring the manse and supplying other fittings in connection with the installation of electric light, the cost being £129-12-6d and an estimate for supplying and fixing an electric pump for raising water from the underground tank in the manse grounds to the tank in the attic'. True to form, the kirk session agreed to the electric light but not to the electric pump. The response from Rev. Ballingall was to contact another plumber and request him to 'inspect the ram and the pipe leading from the ram … and advise on the matter'!

In 1951, a piped water supply was installed in the school, so once again, in January 1952, the kirk session agreed 'to ask the Proprietor of Redcastle estate for permission to lay a pipe from near Killearnan school, so that a gravitation water supply may be laid on to the manse and the glebe steading'. No reply is recorded in the kirk session minutes, but in October 1954 they recorded their 'grateful thanks to Mr John Fraser for so kindly keeping the ram which supplies water to the manse in working order'. Then finally, on 1 April 1955, the kirk session agreed 'to install an electric water pump in the manse, to lay copper pipe from the tank in the manse grounds and make the necessary connection'. Rev. Ballingall must have been tempted to treat this as an April Fool, but in September 1955 he reported that 'the electric water pump which had been installed in the manse on June 10th was giving satisfaction'.

It had taken over sixty years to provide a satisfactory water supply to the manse. It seems ironic that mains water was installed four years later!

2.8   Killearnan Parish Church

In Killearnan, the Established Church of Scotland and the United Free Church merged in June 1933. The session minutes of the parish church record that 'it is hereby declared by authority of the Presbytery of Chanonry and Dingwall at its meeting on 2 May 1933 that a Union of the congregations of Killearnan and Redcastle has been agreed upon, to take place from today the 11th June under the name of Killearnan Congregation'. Rev. Brechin and Rev. Craig were initially appointed as joint interim moderators, but in September 1933 Rev. John Reid from East Wymss was offered the unified post. However, he declined the appointment when the Presbytery refused to accept conditions that he had tried to impose, and Rev. Julius McCallum was duly appointed in December 1933. The joint communion roll in January 1934 was just fifty-five, of which thirty-five had come from the United Free Church.

Rev. Julius McCallum chose to live in the Established Church of Scotland manse at Redcastle rather than in the United Free Church manse at Redcastle Station. In March 1934, the latter was rented by Rev. George Burnett, who had retired from Cromarty. He was at constant loggerheads with the kirk session over responsibility for the erection and repair of fencing that he demanded to protect his garden from hens belonging to his neighbour at Rosebank Cottage. Agreement was finally reached in June 1937. The kirk session wanted to dispose of that manse, but could not agree with the Presbytery the distribution of the rental income or any proceeds that would entail from its sale. However, in October 1940 both the parties finally agreed that the manse should be sold. An advertisement in *The Scotsman* of 28 December 1940 describes it as 'standing in its own grounds; 2 public rooms, 4 bedrooms, kitchen, pantry, scullery, coalhouse, bathroom (hot and cold); outhouses; good water supply; railway station, shop, post office, telephone close at hand; assessed rent £24; feu duty £2-1/-. Immediate entry. Apply Rev. George Ballingall, Manse, Killearnan'. In June 1941, it was purchased by Angus Urquhart, a veterinary surgeon, for the sum of £882. The kirk session's share of the capital would eventually be used to fund Killearnan manse renovations in 1956.

Many other issues attracted the attention of the Killearnan kirk session, not least the difficulties of ejecting 'tinkers in the glebe' and of finding choir members (disbanded in 1961) and organists. (It didn't help the recruitment of organists that one resigned in 1972 after 'her capabilities had been called into question' by the moderator.) However, the principal recurring problem was the condition of the manse at Killearnan. Apart from the long-running issue of the water supply, renovations were regularly requested by successive moderators, some of whom seemed almost unreasonably demanding in their desire for domestic comfort. Major structural renovations commenced in 1950, and heating and cooking systems were modernised after the electric supply was upgraded in 1955. Requests for refurbishments continued unabated and it was becoming obvious that, with diminishing funds, a point in time would be reached when building a new manse would be financially more sensible than continuously expending on the old manse. This was first raised in December 1966, when Wylie Martin of Garguston Farm, who had become an elder in 1965, suggested that 'the Thomson family would be re-housed sometime in future and he believed that the ground on which their house stood belonged to Lord Burton and we should ask him to reserve this ground for us in case we would want to build a new manse on it'. (The Thomson family lived in Manse Cottage [or Manse Park], the house that Rev. Macdonald had suggested in 1921 could be made available for his minister's man.)

Heating and lighting in the churches also became a recurring problem. It was recorded in the 1911 Inland Revenue survey field book[74] that the parish church contained a heating chamber, which presumably was coal-fired. It is also recorded in the kirk session minutes that paraffin 'Tilley' lamps were used for lighting prior to the 1950s. Electric lighting was connected in 1958, but the installation of electric (or oil) heating was considered too expensive (£270) and a Calor Gas system was purchased at a cost of £122. This was used until electric heating was finally installed in 1969, although the Calor Gas radiators were retained as backup.

The insurance of the church's property had exercised the kirk session from time to time, but in May 1969 the moderator intimated that he had taken the two communion cups to a silversmith in Inverness, 'only to discover their uniqueness and value', estimated at £1,000 for the pair. They were the cups dated 1784, made by 'T.B.' (either Thomas Baillie or Thomas Borthwick) and inscribed: 'This communion cup was bought for the Parish of Kileaurnan, Ann Dom 1784, by Rev. Mr David Denoon being Minister'. Actually, they had been purchased in 1773 and presumably had been engraved in 1784. At a later date, they had been recorded in the 1744–97 kirk session minutes book[75] together with the other communion ware (the estimated value of which in 1969 was £1,356). Included in the other communion ware were two silver-plated cups inscribed 'West UP Church 1891 Galashiels'. They were valued at £45, and it was decided to offer them to any new congregation in need of communion vessels.

Although the United Free Church had provided the majority of the communicant members of the merged churches in Killearnan, the attendances at services in its 'iron church' (Figure 25, page 181) at Redcastle Station were problematically low. The issue of its eventual closure was initially raised in

November 1942 when it was decided to discontinue communion services there. Another lengthy saga was about to begin. This one would take fifty years!

Rev. Ballingall was requested by the kirk session in July 1954 to announce from the pulpit that 'unless there was an improvement in the Sabbath attendances, it would be necessary to close the Redcastle [Station] church for regular Sabbath services'. To ease the problem of travel across the parish, a bus was laid on (for which a grant of £11 per year was provided by the Presbytery). This seems to have provided a workable solution, at least temporarily. A new moderator, Rev. Richard Bolster, was appointed in October 1956 and he seems to have attracted sufficient attendances at both churches by bussing the congregation to services at 11.30 a.m. at the Killearnan parish church and at 6.30 p.m. at Redcastle [Station] church. However, the issue re-emerged again in December 1966 when the kirk session decided to 'seek guidance of the Presbytery in regard to closing Redcastle [Station] church' and, as an experiment, transfer all services to the parish church at Killearnan. The bus continued to be provided to transport members of the congregation.

This seems to have been successful, because on 5 March 1967 the kirk session minuted that it had 'decided by a majority vote to close Redcastle [Station] church'. However, a congregational meeting held on 8 March 1967 appears to have rejected the proposal for closure, because at the ensuing kirk session meeting it was recorded that in the light of 'an unsatisfactory discussion', legal opinion had been sought and had advised that 'ours was an old form of union, therefore the matter could be decided by session alone'. Furthermore, the kirk session was of the opinion that it had always been expected that 'in our union the church at Redcastle [Station] was eventually to be run down and closed'. Letters explaining the situation and balloting all communicant members were sent out, and on 31 May 1967 the kirk session recorded thirty-three votes in favour, five not in favour and one abstention. Accordingly, it was formally minuted that:

> The kirk session unanimously agreed to uphold their decisions of 5 and 23 March 1967 respectively to close Redcastle [Station] church ... in view of the satisfactory attendances during the experimental period ... resolved to ask Presbytery for permission to close Redcastle [Station] church in terms of the basis of union.

If only it had been that simple! In June 1967, Rev. Bolster informed the kirk session that:

Presbytery had put back the application of the Killearnan session for the closure of Redcastle [Station] church as the session meeting of 31 May was not valid as the General Assembly was still sitting and we had a Commissioner attending. We were instructed to call another meeting and re-open Redcastle [Station] church until such time as our appeal was heard.

Then, on 14 November 1967, it is recorded that 'Presbytery after hearing the facts as they were at this present time decided this [Redcastle Station] church remain open'. This caused a considerable financial problem, because the heating system and the paintwork required attention. Wylie Martin was particularly opposed to the expense of installing radiant heaters and time switches at a cost of £166-14-6d in 1969. Only in June 1971 did the Presbytery announce that, in the light of a policy emanating from Edinburgh to reduce the number of church buildings, they 'would be looking at this building in the next three years with a view to closure'. It was to take a lot longer than three years!

2.9   Mergers and Closures

In 1904, the Free Church of Killearnan had regained the use of its imposing church at Newton crossroads (Figure 27) from the United Free Church, but it took until 1919 to find a permanent minister. In the interim, the manse at Linnie was offered for short-term let. The advertisement carried by *The Scotsman* on 25 March 1908 described it as:

> …overlooking the Beauly Firth, delightful situation; 3 large public rooms, 6 bedrooms, good servants' accommodation, bathroom (h & c water): comfortably furnished; pony and double dogcart, boat; wild duck shooting; southern exposure; near station (Redcastle, H.R.) and telegraph office: Aug., Sept., and Oct., or earlier or later if desired; desirous of letting; would consider mod. offer.

Whether any offers were received is not recorded.

The new Free Church minister, appointed in 1919, was Rev. James MacDonald, known locally as 'wee MacDonald' (Rev. Aeneas Macdonald of the parish church, being much taller, was 'big Macdonald'). He died in December 1946 and, as numbers of members were declining, the congregation became linked with Fortrose in 1947. Rev. Robert Murray was appointed to the combined churches in 1950, and he was followed by Rev. Hugh MacKay in 1964 and Rev. Hector Cameron in 1982. Throughout the 1950–70 period, the Free Church had suffered the same problems as the parish church in generating sufficient funds to install heating and lighting and to properly maintain the fabric of the church building and the aging manse at Linnie. However, Rev. Cameron successfully increased membership, and when he retired in 1989 it was decided to unlink the two churches. Rev. Grant Bell was ordained to Killearnan in 1991. He was provided with a new manse in Tore, and the original Free Church manse in Linnie was sold for private ownership. However, the church was again linked in 2000, this time with Maryburgh, whose minister, Rev. Douglas MacKeddie, was destined to be the last minister to preach in the Free Church at Killearnan. The final service was held on 25 January 2004, and this fine building – in which the majority of the residents of Killearnan parish had worshipped from 1866 onwards – has now been converted into Tore Art Gallery.[76]

Figure 27: The ex-Killearnan Free Church of Scotland, now Tore Art Gallery (2008)

Despite the Presbytery's promise in June 1971 to consider the future of the ex-United Free Church at Redcastle [Station], there was little evidence of any progress until June 1974 when there was a discussion at the kirk session[77] of 'Redcastle church's future'. No further reference is recorded until March 1977, when the escalating costs of building repairs and refurbishments gave rise to consideration of the necessity of maintaining a large manse and two churches. In February 1978, a Presbytery property inspection was carried out.

The report reveals the state of the parish church's properties at that time. The exterior of the church at Killearnan is described as satisfactory and the interior was enhanced by a fine wooden roof. However, there were bare bulbs for lighting, open-backed pews, Calor Gas radiators that acted as a standby to the electrical heating, and no water supplies or toilets. The manse was satisfactory, but the east guttering and windows required repair and several rooms were unused, whilst the 'manse steading' was recorded for possible sale to a local buyer. The Redcastle [Station] church (Figure 25, page 181) was built of corrugated iron and used mainly for evening services. There was interior condensation arising from the wall-mounted radiators and no water supply or toilet. Controversially, it was also stated that its 'continuing use should come under discussion', a statement that in the Rev. Bolster's opinion was not within the visitation party's remit. However, it did spur the kirk session to give more consideration to the future of the building, and in April 1979 it was decided to approach the Presbytery for its conversion to a church hall.

The kirk session had previously attempted to obtain a church hall by leasing the Killearnan Primary School building after it closed in 1970. However, they had been forced to retract when a congregational meeting did not approve the proposal. On this occasion they were successful. In October 1979, they received permission from the Presbytery 'to remove the pews from Redcastle church and put chairs in their place, and to use the wood from the pews to make a stage; all this subject to written permission from the Superior'. By this time, the Superior had become the Eagle Star Insurance Company, who had purchased Kilcoy estate in 1975. They raised no objections to the proposal, and the conversion of Redcastle [Station] church into a hall/church was completed in early 1980.

At the same time as the future of the Redcastle [Station] church was under protracted consideration, the conversion of the 'manse steading' into a dwelling house also became a live issue. It appears to have been first raised in March 1977, but Rev. Bolster was not in favour of there being a dwelling house so close to the manse. Only after the Presbytery property inspection of February 1978 was it decided to seek planning permission, and this was granted by the Highland Regional Council in October 1978, subject to access improvements. Briefly, there was a proposal to convert it into the church hall but this proved too expensive at £7,000–£8,000, and in June 1979 it was decided that it should be sold. Private offers were immediately received, but it was advertised and in June 1980 it was announced that the highest offer had come from the grandson of Rev. Aeneas Macdonald, the parish minister in 1890–1932.

Further problems at the Redcastle [Station] hall/church soon emerged. The toilets and washing facilities were inadequate and, even worse, severe dry rot was found at the base of the main wooden pillar. The cost of repairs was estimated in August 1981 to be £10,000 plus VAT, an expense that the Presbytery was unwilling to fund until a proper condition survey had been carried out. In the meantime, the kirk session held a congregational meeting in November 1981, at which financial contributions and voluntary help from willing tradesmen were requested. This idea received little support, which was probably fortunate, because in October 1982 it was reported that the foundations were 'spewing outwards with disintegration in parts' and that 'the building in its present state is not safe for a large gathering of people'. This prompted the kirk session to announce that 'no more money was to be spent on Redcastle church other than roof leaks'.

Surprisingly, despite its serious condition, the hall/church remained in use for several more years. It was not until 1984 that the question of the Redcastle [Station] hall/church re-emerged. It had been decided that the old manse would be sold after the retirement of Rev. Bolster in April 1984, and that a new manse would be built at a cost not exceeding the sale price of the old manse. The old manse was sold in 1985 and is now named Killearnan House. At the same time, it was proposed that Redcastle [Station] hall/church be closed in May 1985, but this motion was defeated by a counter-motion proposing that it remain in use for services until one month before the new minister took up post. Rev. Susan Brown was appointed in June 1985 and, in consequence, the closure of the hall/church was set for 18 August 1985. The *Ross-shire Journal*[78] of 30 August reported that a congregation of forty had attended, several of whom 'had been present when the building was first opened for worship in 1900'. This was a slight exaggeration; the merger that created the United Free Church had taken place in 1900 but the Redcastle [Station] 'iron church' building had actually opened in 1909.

It was also announced in June 1985 that the hall/church had been sold to John Jack for £6,150. However, this was by no means the end of the saga. In December 1986, the kirk session was informed that the completion of the sale was 'still unclear', and in September 1987 they demanded to see a 'precise minute'. However, in May 1990 there was 'still no progress on the sale', and in November 1990 they were informed that 'Redcastle hall/church was not yet sold'. In frustration, the kirk session sacked Mr MacLeod, their solicitor, and placed the matter in the hands of the Church of Scotland solicitor in Edinburgh. There is no further mention of the Redcastle [Station] hall/church in the kirk session minutes, so it has to be assumed that the sale was finally completed shortly afterwards. It had taken almost fifty years! A private house is currently under construction on the site.

Several other issues required the attention of the parish kirk session during the late twentieth century. One was the value of the communion cups and plates, which was again raised in February 1980. In 1969, the silver cups had been valued at £1,000 for the pair, but by June 1980 their insurance value had risen to £7,000. It appears that prior to 1980 they had been kept in the manse, but after revaluation it was decided to keep them in the bank vault at Muir of Ord, where they remain today. The other communion ware was revalued at £1,555, but in November 1994 four of the five pewter vessels that had been on 'extended loan' since 1906 from Banchory-Ternan parish were returned. One pewter plate could not be found.

Another issue was the problem of a very old gravestone which lay flat on the pathway leading to the entrance of the church. It was called the 'old mortality' stone and many of the congregation did not like to walk over it. The kirk session decided in September 1983 to have it removed, and it is now located on the south wall of the church. The session clerk at that time was Wylie Martin of Garguston Farm, who had become treasurer in 1970–76 and session clerk in 1976. He was presented with a Good News Bible at his retirement in November 1983, although he remained an elder until 1995 and is recorded as a member of the kirk session until November 1998. He and his wife gifted the plaques that carry the names of all the ministers of the church from 1226 onwards. They are mounted in the south transcept of the church.

By 1977, the numbers of communicant members had declined to forty, of whom five had not attended for two years and nine lived outside the parish. The effect on finances was becoming critical, and the Presbytery Conference of 1977 produced several suggestions for raising interest in the work of the church. They included: more regular visits by elders; more involvement of the young; variations in the style of the services (they were the same as 100 years previously); a Women's Guild sub-committee to organise more events; quarterly meetings of the session; the congregation to relate their giving to their earnings; a target board for fund-raising; visiting choirs and soloists; a warmer welcome to visitors; and 20p per week more contribution from each member (it was pointed out that a packet of cigarettes cost 50p, a gallon of petrol was 80p, and three stamps were 21p).

This seems to have had some effect, as in 1983 the communicant roll of the parish church was recorded as seventy-one. Nevertheless, the question of the future of the church became an issue at the retirement of Rev. Bolster in April 1984. A joint meeting of the Killearnan and Knockbain kirk sessions was held on 21 November 1984, at which a vote was held on the options of 'deferred linkage' or 'deferred union' between equal partners. The vote was eleven to two in favour of 'deferred linkage', and it was agreed that Killearnan parish would proceed to make a 'terminable appointment' of a new minister. Rev. Susan Brown was ordained in September 1985, although she had to wait until April 1986 before her new manse, a bungalow built just to the west of the old manse, was ready for occupation. She was the first female minister of the parish. (Her husband, Derek, was also a minister and held appointments as chaplain at Raigmore Hospital and at the Highland Hospice in Inverness.). One of Susan's first tasks was to ensure that a new hall was built to replace the Redcastle [Station] hall/church, even if the actual sale of the latter had not been finally concluded. A site for the new hall was finally agreed five years later in May 1991, and the estimate of £58,719 received from W Munro was accepted in November 1992. The service of dedication of the new hall was held on 13 June 1993.

Throughout the 1980s and early 1990s, interest in the activities of the church was resurgent, and by December 1994 there were 145 communicant members and 162 adherents on the roll. The year of 1995 was chosen for a celebration of 700 years of worship at the Killearnan parish church (although the significance of the date is not entirely clear). Various fund-raising events were held and the highlight was a visit of the moderator of the General Assembly, the Right Rev. James Harkness, who officiated at the service of dedication on 2 July 1995. A history of the parish church[79] was also published in 1995. 'Killearnan 700' was reported in October 1996 to have raised £2,250, which was used for several projects – for example, a new large print Bible and a lectern. A plaque on the base of the lectern records that it was dedicated by Rev. Susan Brown on 30 June 1996 (Figure 28).

With the fortunes of the church at their highest for more than a century, on 13 October 1997 the kirk session 'was shocked by the news' that Rev. Susan Brown had been selected as sole nominee for the vacant position at Dornoch Cathedral. It is recorded in the session minutes that 'nobody wanted her to leave, but assured her of their support in doing what she felt to be right'. Susan was inducted at Dornoch on 13 February 1998. At her final Killearnan kirk session meeting, it fell to the long-serving Wylie Martin to thank her:

> ...for twelve years' wonderful work and achievement in the parish. Strengthened by her faith she had been able to inspire people and to motivate them to do more than they thought they were capable of. Many had received tremendous comfort from Susan during illness or bereavement. She had been a friend to us all. Credit for the dramatic increase in the size of the congregation goes to her. Susan and her family will be in the thoughts and prayers of the session and congregation as they start their new life in Dornoch.

On the departure of Susan Brown, Rev. Charles MacKinnon of Urray and Kilchrist agreed to act as interim moderator whilst permission was sought to appoint a successor. This was not forthcoming, because the position of moderator at Knockbain had also fallen vacant and Rev. Dan Carmichael of Ferintosh had been appointed as their interim moderator. With both parishes vacant, the two kirk sessions met on several occasions during early 1999 to consider an 'Act of Linking' and agree a 'Basis of Linking', one clause of which was that a new manse would be made available in North Kessock, a location equidistant between the two parish churches (at Redcastle and Munlochy). As a consequence, the new manse that had been built for Susan Brown in 1986 was sold and is now named Killearnan Brae.

Figure 28: The interior of Killearnan parish church (2008)

On 12 April 1999, Killearnan and Knockbain parish churches were formally linked under the title 'Killearnan linked with Knockbain'. Rev. Dan Carmichael was appointed as interim moderator whilst the search for a new minister was carried out. In October 1999, Rev. Iain Ramsden was named as the sole nominee and he was ordained on 3 December 1999. He remains minister to the linked parishes to this day.

NOTES

[1] See Chapter 1, note 120.
[2] The authoritative text on Gaelic-origin place names is Watson, W J, 'Place-names of Ross and Cromarty' (reprinted 1996). The names of places within Killearnan parish are interpreted on pages 142–6. See also note 4.
[3] See Chapter 1, note 14.
[4] *Fasti Ecclesiae Scoticanae* gives short biographies of all the post-reformation ministers of Killearnan in: Vol 7, 10–14 (1928); Vol 8, 656 (1950); Vol 9, 662 (1961); Vol 10, 379

(1981); and Vol 11, 360 (2000). Another useful text is Noble, Rev. J, 'Religious Life in Ross', Chapter 22, 260–70 (1909). This latter text also contains an interesting chapter on the early Columban, Celtic and Roman churches in the Highlands. A chapter on Killearnan parish church can be found in Longmore, L, 'Land of Churches', 83–8 (2000), and there is also a short account of the history of Killearnan parish church in www.mackenziefamilytree.com/scotland.

[5] See Chapter 1, note 17.

[6] See note 5.

[7] See Chapter 1, note 4.

[8] The visit of Inverness Field Club to the 'hospital' of the Knights Templars in Spital (and also to the 'Temple' near Croftcrunie and Carn Irenan) is recorded in 'Hut Circles in the Black Isle – Castle of Kilcoy', Trans. Inverness Sci. Soc. and Field Club, 2, 236–8 (1882).

[9] See note 4.

[10] Biographies of the ministers of Killearnan parish church are recorded in Macdonald, Rev. A, 'The Succession of the Beneficed Clergy in the Parish of Killearnan from 1226 to 1890' (NAS CH2/918/5). This remarkable handwritten documentary account forms the basis of Thomson, S, 'Killearnan' (1995), a short book on the history of Killearnan parish church published in commemoration of the 'Killearnan 700' celebrations.

[11] The gravestone inscriptions in the Killearnan parish churchyard have been recorded by the Highland Family History Society in 'Monumental Inscriptions, Killearnan Churchyard' (1995) available at HCRL 929.5. The medieval grave slab is described in W Rae Macdonald, 'The Heraldry in some old churchyards between Tain and Inverness', Proc. Soc. Antiq. Scot., 26, 699–700 (1902).

[12] See note 10.

[13] See note 10.

[14] See Chapter 1, note 42.

[15] See Chapter 1, note 3.

[16] The three volumes of handwritten minutes of the Presbytery of Dingwall (June 1649–October 1687) have been digitised and are available at NAS CH2/92/1–3. The records for March 1658 to May 1663 appear to have been lost. Transcriptions of the surviving minutes are available in Mackay, W, 'Records of the Presbyteries of Inverness and Dingwall (1643–88)' (1896). This text also contains an excellent summary of the work of the two Presbyteries during this period. Records of the Presbytery of Ross and Sutherland (in existence during 1693–1701) do not appear to have survived, although there are a few references in General Assembly papers of the period.

[17] The eleven volumes of handwritten minutes of the Presbytery of Chanonry (January 1707–December 1929) have been digitised and are available at NAS CH2/66/1–11. The records for February 1753 to September 1762 appear to have been lost.

[18] See Chapter 1, note 58.

[19] The life of Rev. Aeneas Sage is recounted in 'Memorabilia Domestica or Parish Life in the North of Scotland', Chapters 1 and 2 (1889) (originally edited by his grandson, Donald Sage, in 1840). It can be accessed at http://uk.geocities.com/memorabilia_domestica. Some

facets of his life are also described in Stiubhart, D U, 'The Colonsay Catechist – James Moore, Catechist at Colonsay 1728–36'.

[20] The letter dated 3 October 1727 from the moderator of the Presbytery of Chanonry to the General Assembly is held in a file of papers relating to the Synod of Ross in NAS CH1/2/55, pages 373–4. The extensive collection of papers and letters referring to the charges laid against Rev. Donald Fraser in 1740–1 are held in NAS CH1/2/79, pages 1–189. The petition sent by Rev. David Denoon (I) to the General Assembly Royal Bounty Committee in 1766 is held at NAS CH1/2/107.

[21] The decree against Roderick (Ruairi Dearg) Mackenzie and others for the 'riot' in which the Killearnan parish manse was damaged is contained in the Church of Scotland General Assembly Papers, Main Series (1720) at NAS CH1/2/43/416.

[22] A database of the trials of Scottish witches has been prepared by 'The Survey of Scottish Witchcraft 1563–1736', which can be searched at www.shc.ed.ac.uk/research/witches. Details of the trials of Killearnan witches can also be found in Black, G, 'A Calendar of Cases of Witchcraft in Scotland 1510–1727' (1938) and in Chambers, R, 'Domestic Annals of Scotland', Vol 3, 216–7 (1861).

[23] See note 10.

[24] The minutes and other records of the Kirk Session of Killearnan Parish Church (1744–97) are available in digital format at NAS CH2/918/1–5. Data on the emoluments of earlier ministers is given in 'The Book of the Assignations of Ministers' and Readers' Stipends' (1574).

[25] Births, baptisms and marriages recorded in the Killearnan 'Old Parish Registers' (1744–1854) have been transferred to microfilm and are available to view in HCRL. They have also been digitally scanned and can be accessed online through the subscription service at www.scotlandspeople.gov.uk.

[26] See Chapter 1, note 54.

[27] See note 25.

[28] Names of Redcastle residents who participated in the Jacobite Rebellion of 1745–46 are listed in Livingstone, A, Aikman, C W H and Hart, B S, 'No Quarter Given: The Muster Roll of Prince Charles Edward Stuart's Army 1745–46', 78–87 and 116 (1984). See also 'A list of persons concerned in the Rebellion – transmitted to the Commissioners of Excise by the several Supervisors in Scotland in obedience to a General Letter of 7 May 1746', 80–1 and 332–3, Edinburgh University Press (1890). Owners and tenants of the estates that fought at Culloden are listed in the collection of 'Statistics of Annexed Estates' (1755–56) at NAS 428.01 and 'Reports of Annexed Estates' at NAS 428.000. Redcastle was not annexed.

[29] The story of John Ross and the silver quaich is told by Douglas Ross in www.electricscotland.com/webclans/ntor/ross.

[30] See note 20.

[31] See note 10.

[32] See Chapter 1, note 135.

[33] See note 10.

[34] See Chapter 1, note 113.

[35] See note 20.

[36] See Chapter 1, note 108.

[37] See note 24.

[38] A description of a typical five-day communion season held during the late eighteenth century in Ross-shire is given in Kennedy, Rev. J, 'The Days of the Fathers in Ross-shire', second edition, 116–8 (1895).

[39] See note 10.

[40] An account of the history of the Killearnan area is given in Oag, M, 'Killearnan: The Story of the Parish' (1966). This booklet was originally produced as an entry in a WRI competition on local history and was subsequently published in 1997 by her daughter, Janet Skrodzka.

[41] See note 17.

[42] The notice of discharge for the funding of a catechist at Killearnan to the Honourable Mrs Maria Hay Mackenzie by Patrick Grant, Colin Mackenzie and Rev. John Kennedy is held at NAS GD305/1/134/2.

[43] See Chapter 1, note 132.

[44] See Chapter 1, note 84.

[45] See note 4.

[46] See Chapter 1, note 58.

[47] See Chapter 1, note 108.

[48] A brief history of St John's Episcopalian Church in Scotland at Arpafeelie is given in Page, C B, 'The Episcopal Church in Ross-shire' (1996).

[49] See Chapter 1, note 140.

[50] The creation of Killearnan Free Church is recorded in Ewing, W, 'Annals of the Free Church of Scotland, 1843–1900', Vol II, LXIII Presbytery of Chanonry, page 213 (1914).

[51] An index of articles published in the *Inverness Courier* during the early nineteenth century is given in Barron, J, 'The Northern Highlands in the 19th Century' (1907). Vol I covers the years 1800–24, Vol II (1825–41) and Vol III (1842–56).

[52] See Chapter 1, note 120.

[53] The 1844 communion token is described in Kerr, R and Lockie, J R, 'Communion Tokens of the Free Church of Scotland', Proc. Soc. Antiq. Scot., III, 26–80 (1944–5).

[54] See Chapter 1, note 120.

[55] The minutes books of the Free Church of Killearnan Kirk Session (1843–1900), Deacons' Court (1844–1900) and Parochial Board (1845–1910) are archived at the Library of the Free Church of Scotland, The Mound, Edinburgh.

[56] See Chapter 1, note 120.

[57] See note 55.

[58] The Killearnan Parish Church kirk session minutes book for 1797–1841 has not survived. Minutes for 1842–1979 are available as digital images at NAS CH2/918/7–9.

[59] The origin of the well-known pipe tune 'Campbell's Farewell to Redcastle' is not known, although it is attributed to a Colin Mackenzie and according to www.nigelgatherer.com appears to have first been published in Ross, W, 'Pipe Music' (1875).

[60] Data for Killearnan parish is contained in the Fullarton and Co., 'Imperial Gazetteer of Scotland or Dictionary of Scottish Topography', (ed) Wilson, Rev. J M, Vol II (1868).

[61] The Killearnan Parish Church Roll of Communicants (1866–92) is available digitally at NAS CH2/918/4.

[62] See note 55.

[63] See note 25.

[64] The architectural drawings by Ross and MacBeth of Inverness related to the raising of the roof and floor level in Killearnan parish church in 1891 are held at RCAHMS RCD/34/1.

[65] The Poor's Fund Accounts (1815–42) for Killearnan Parish Church have been scanned as digital images and can be viewed at NAS CH2/918/2.

[66] A brief history of the Black Isle Combination Poorhouse in Fortrose (also known as Ness House) is recorded at http://users.ox.ac.uk/workhouse/BlackIsle.

[67] The minutes books of the Kirk Session and Deacons' Court of the United Free Church of Killearnan (1900–1933) are archived at NAS CH3/880/1–3.

[68] The ministers of the United Free Church at Killearnan are listed in Lamb, J A, 'The Fasti of the United Free Church of Scotland 1900–1929', page 478 (1956).

[69] See Chapter 1, note 144.

[70] The minutes book of the Heritors of Killearnan parish for the years 1891–1928 is available at NAS HR667/1.

[71] Rev. Aeneas Macdonald's undated, handwritten notes about the water supply to Killearnan manse are entitled 'Answers by the Minister of Killearnan to the Statement of Facts for Appellants I.C. The Heritors of Killearnan vs the Presbytery of Chanonry'. They can be accessed as digital images at NAS CH2/918/10.

[72] See note 20.

[73] See note 42.

[74] See Chapter 1, note 161.

[75] See note 24.

[76] A brief history of the Killearnan Free Church of Scotland at Newton (Fettes Crossroads) can be found on the Tore Art Gallery website: www.tore-art-gallery.co.uk/history.

[77] The minutes books of Killearnan Parish Kirk Session for 1972–79, 1979–90 and 1990–99 are respectively located at NAS CH2/918/8, 11 and 12. The 1972–79 book is manuscript and has been digitally scanned, but the two later books, which are typed, were lodged with NAS in 2007 and are currently available only as the original typescript versions.

[78] See Chapter 1, note 120.

[79] See note 10.

Chapter 3

THE SCHOOLS

3.1   Killearnan Parish School

Early education in northern Scotland was provided only to sons and close relatives of the landowners, clan chiefs and other wealthy gentlemen. Many were sent to study overseas (particularly France), but grammar schools existed in the principal burghs such as Inverness and Fortrose. An Act of 1494 required the sons of barons and other landholders to enter these schools at the age of eight and to remain until they were fluent in Latin and 'competentlie founded'. In addition to the grammar schools, the Priory at Beauly was famed as a monastic school. For example, Lord Lovat's four sons are recorded in 1507 as having been 'well educated at Beauly Priory', which at that time was the only such school in the north. Bishop Robert Reid, the most distinguished of the Priors of Beauly (1530–58), improved the school into 'a lamp of learning in the north', and is credited with the creation of 'ane college of cunning and wise men' that was endowed by James V and became the forerunner of the Court of Session, of which Bishop Reid became Lord President.[1]

Initial agitation to introduce parish-based education into Scotland was undertaken by John Knox at the commencement of the Reformation in 1560, when he argued in the 'Book of Discipline' that church and state reformation leading to a 'godly commonwealth' had to be supported by a national scheme of education. However, it was not until 1616 that the Privy Council for Scotland issued an Act for the creation of schools in every parish, so that 'all his Majesty's subjects, especially the youth, be exercised and trained up in civilitie, godliness, knowledge and learning'. However, this Act also required English to be the language taught in the schools and 'the Irish language, which is one of the chief and principall causes of the continuance of barbaritie and incivilitie among the inhabitants of the Isles and Heylandis, may be abolishit and removit'. Since Irish (in the form of Gaelic) was the language of the Highlands, the 1616 Act was largely ignored, as was an Act of 1633 in which the Scottish Parliament made owners of land (the parish heritors) responsible for the financial support of parish schools. However, in 1646 a further Act placed oversight for the creation of a school in each parish on the presbyteries – and although this should have been the springboard for the development of parochial education in the Highlands, initial progress was very slow due to the reluctance of the heritors to provide the necessary finance. The earliest record of parochial schools in Ross-shire seems to be in the minutes of the Presbytery of Dingwall,[2] which refer to schools in the parishes of Dingwall and Kilmorack in 1650.

In 1704, the General Assembly of the Church of Scotland created the Society in Scotland for Propagating Christian Knowledge (SSPCK) to create schools in which English reading, writing and Christian doctrine could be taught, especially in areas where the heritors were reluctant to co-operate fully in providing educational opportunity for the children of all parishioners. The first SSPCK schools opened in 1710, and these were augmented in 1738 by the creation of 'Female Schools of Industry', in which spinning, sewing and knitting were taught.[3]

The first record of the endowment of such schools within the Presbytery of Chanonry[4] was in July 1711, when the Secretary of the SSPCK wrote:

> ...signifying that the Societie are resolved with all diligence to sett about the erecting of as manie schools as the interest of their present stock will be able to maintain as also desiring advice from the Presbitrie as to the most proper places for these schools within their bounds, and to send a list of as many young men as the Presbitrie can find qualified for teaching of the said schools.

In their response, the Presbytery indicated that the parishes in most need were Kilmorack, Gairloch and Kintail.

A further letter was received from the SSPCK in August 1716. It requested:

> ...a distinct account of the number of free schools that will be needful to be erected within the bounds of this Presbyterie and what will be the most proper places as to their situation and contiguitie to other places, the multitude of inhabitants and distance of the places from the legal schools and which of the said places are most infested with papists, what is the length and breadth of the parishes within which it is proposed the said schools should be settled and if any of the said parishes do want legal schools to send ane account of the reason of said want.

The reference to 'legal schools' was to the 'parish schools' that the heritors of each parish were legally required to provide under the 1633 Act.

The response of the Presbytery was to prepare a 'Schools Plann', an extract of which is reproduced in the Presbytery's minutes of 29 April 1718. The plan states that there should be a 'legal' school close by the parish church in every parish, and that the SSPCK should provide additional schools at specified locations in each of the parishes of: Kilmorack and Kiltarlity; Kintail; Lochalsh;

Lochcarron; Gairloch; Lochbroom; Contin; Loggie Wester, Urray and Gilchrist; Kiltearn and Dingwall; Alness and part of Rosskeen; Kilmuir Easter, Loggie Easter and part of Rosskeen; Kincardine and part of Croick; Tain, Fearn and Tarbat; Kirkmichael, Cullicuddin and part of Urquhart; Croick and part of Kincardine; Lairg, North Assynt; Dornoch, part of Rogart and part of Golspie; Clyne, part of Rogart and part of Golspie; and Kildonan.

Significantly, there was no proposal in the Presbytery's 'School Plann' for a school in Killearnan parish, presumably because there was no minister in the parish at that time. However, Rev. John MacArthur, the first presbyterian minister of Killearnan, who had been appointed in 1719, raised the issue at three Presbytery meetings, finally persuading them to visit the parish in October 1721. At the visitation, the younger Roderick Mackenzie of Redcastle (Ruairi Mor Mackenzie) was 'interrogate if he would concurr with the Presbitery in settling a fund for a legal school in the parish of Killiurnan, answered that if the rest of the heritors would concurr he was content'. However, Donald Mackenzie of Kilcoy 'answered that he was but one of the smallest heritors in the said parish therefor was not clear to go on in an affair in which he was altogether unacquainted until he first consulted with Allangrange and Redcastle elder [Ruairi Dearg Mackenzie], therefor declined to concurr at this time'. Rev. McArthur was to discover that getting the 'concurrence' of his heritors was going to be a four-year-long battle.

Having failed to get the matter settled at the visitation, the Presbytery resolved at its next meeting 'to apply to the Honourable Commissioners of Supply[5] of the Shire, that in pursuance of the Laws and Acts of Parliament they may modify and discern a competent legal sallary for mantainance of a schoolmaster for teaching of the youth in the said parish'. However, the response from the Commissioners of Supply was that they could not meet to consider the matter 'sooner than May next'! In reality, the heritors probably never considered the matter, and two years later, in January 1724, the Presbytery decided 'that there is no probabilitie of any success in carrying on the affair befor the Commissioners of Supply' and resolved to pursue the matter through Mr Nicol Spence, Agent for the Church, 'that he carry on the affair befor the Lords of the Session'. In September 1724, it was reported to the Presbytery that 'Mr Nicol Spence had some time agone sent north a summonds with directions to summond the heritors of Killearnan before the Lords on the said affair, and that he advised to give the said gentlemen once more opportunity to meet and agree the said affair at home.'

A meeting between Rev. McArthur and the heritors was arranged for 11 October 1724, but none of the heritors turned up. However, later that month they intimated that they were now 'inclined to agree the affair at home', whereupon a further meeting was arranged for 7 December 1724. On

29 December 1724, Rev. McArthur reported to the Presbytery that the meeting had been held and an agreement had been reached:

> ...that a school be settled in this parish for teaching the youth to read and write and instruct them in the principles of religion, did agree that the parish should give one hundred merks yearly for that end to be payed by the heritors according to their valuations ... viz by Roderick Mackenzie of Redcastle £34-19-4d Scots ... by Donald Mackenzie of Kilcoy £12-10-6d ... by Mr Simon Mackenzie of Allangrange £19-3-4d ... to be payed yearly at the term of Martinmass ... commencing 1725 ... and the heritors are to have relief of the one half thereof from their tenants respective according to the rents they pay anent this sallary is over and above the dues of precentor [lead singer] and session clerk and quarter payments for each schollar which is agreed shall be as follows: for each baptism three shillings (3/-) Scots; for each schollar learning English or Latin 12/-; for writing, arithmetic and mathematick 18/-. And it is agreed that a schoolhouse and a chamber for a schoolmaster to be built at Blardow as the most convenient place for the whole parish. And the heritors do hereby lay on the sum of two merks and a half upon each hundred pound of valuation for the furnishing timber, nails, locks, and paying tradesmen for building the said schoolhouse and chamber and ordain the tenants to give the needful carriages and service for building the said houses proportionally.

The Killearnan parish school had therefore been endowed, and in October 1725 Rev. John McArthur informed the Presbytery that Mr John McLennan had been:

> ...called to be schoolmaster at Kilurnan and had accepted the said call and had come to wait of the Presbytery to have their approbation. The said Mr John McLennan being called and examined was found qualified for the said office and the Presbytery appointed him to read the confession of faith in order to be in readiness to subscribe the same when the Presbytery should think fit to call him.

John McLennan remained as the Killearnan parish schoolteacher only until June 1727. The heritors had the power to call a new teacher within twelve months, but had failed to do so; therefore it fell to the Presbytery to find a replacement. Rev. McArthur reported that:

> ...he had found a young man, Mr Donald Fraser, now serving the doctor in the grammar school of Inverness who was of good report as to his capacity for teaching and of good affection to our constitution in Church and craved that the Presbytery would take tryal of the said Donald Fraser and, as they have cause, proceed to call him to be schoolmaster in the said parish.

The Presbytery gave consideration to Rev. McArthur's nomination, and:

> ...having taken tryal of the said Mr Fraser's knowledge in the Latin and of his other qualifications necessary for teaching a school, did find him sufficiently qualified and well affected to his Majesty King George and for the principles of our church. And laying to heart the great consequence of the education of youth in human litrature and in the knowledge of the principles of the Christian reformed religion and further considering the many good laws appointing a school in every parish and the many pressing recommendations of superior judicatorys to this purpose, did and hereby do call and invite the said Mr Donald Fraser to be schoolmaster in the said parish of Killearnan and appoint a call in due form to be drawn out to him to commence from the term of Martinmass ensuing. And having enquired of the said Mr Donald Fraser if he had read the confession of faith and if he was ready to sign the same confession of his faith he answered that he was educated in the principles of the Church of Scotland and hoped to live and dy in that faith, that he had read the confession of faith and observed nothing in it that could hinder him from signing it as the confession of his faith, only that he craved some little time to consider it more.

Having been granted more time to consider his faith, Donald Fraser duly signed the confession and was appointed as Killearnan schoolteacher on 10 November 1728. He remained only until 1730, and seems to have left under a cloud. Donald Mackenzie of Kilcoy allegedly refused to pay his share of salary and appears to have arranged for him to be 'set upon by a multitude of women convened and employed by Kilcoy and his ladie ... [and] cruelly beat and bruised to the effusion of his blood'. It also is not clear who replaced him as parish schoolmaster. (Donald Fraser was subsequently appointed as Killearnan parish minister in 1743.)

The first record of the parish school in the Killearnan kirk session minutes[6] is not found until July 1749, when John McCall from Penninghame in Galloway was appointed by the heritors at a salary of 100 merks. John McCall did not stay long; he demitted office in May 1753, because he was leaving the country. The real reason emerged in January 1754, when Mary Matheson gave birth to an illegitimate child. She had been John McCall's housekeeper and confessed to having 'administered' to him when he had returned home drunk one evening the previous spring. Mary suffered the usual rebukes from the pulpit on three successive sabbaths, but John McCall could never be found and was declared a fugitive. John MacFarquhar, a student of philosophy, was appointed as his successor in July 1753. He remained until 1759, when William Fraser, another student of philosophy, filled the post temporarily until George Leslie was appointed in 1760.

An early reference to the parish school at Killearnan is found in an entry in the Kilcoy Estate Papers[7] dated 2 March 1786. It records the receipt of £10-15-10¼d by Farquhar Noble of Newton of Redcastle:

>...for a new schoolhouse at Redcastle ... being in full Kilcoy's proportion of £39 sterling being the full amount of making said schoolhouse and repairing the kirk at Killearnan ... attested by Mr Denoon, Minister, and the said sum of Kilcoy's proportion is discharged by me, Undertaker Farquhar Noble.

Surprisingly, there is no record of the building of a new school or of repairs to the church in the kirk session minutes around 1785–86.

Another reference to the parish school is found in the 1794 Old (First) Statistical Account,[8] which states that:

>...the very inadequate salary payable to the parochial schoolmaster is much against the parish, it is only £8-6-8d [sterling]. The office of schoolmaster has been vacant since Martinmas, because no qualified person can be got to accept of it. What a pity is it that the pecuniary reward of a description of men, among the most useful in society, should exceed only, in a mere trifle, the wages of a common hireling.

There is no record in the kirk session minutes of when the vacant post was filled, but George MacCulloch is recorded[9] as the schoolteacher in 1798, although he had been replaced by Donald Leitch by 1802.

The salary paid to the Killearnan schoolmaster was, in reality, higher than that received by many schoolmasters, because the 1649 Act (confirmed in 1696) had fixed parish schoolmasters' salaries at 100–200 merks [100 merks was equivalent to £66-13-4d Scots or £5-11-1⅓d sterling]. Most schoolmasters also took on the role of church precentor and session clerk, for which their salary was augmented by £20 Scots (£1-13-4d sterling). Additionally, they could raise income through the fees paid for registering marriages and births. Pupils also paid fees for each subject they studied at school. Reading and catechism [religious studies] were the subjects that all pupils studied and these were provided free. However, other individual subjects required fees to be paid, usually quarterly in advance. Depending on the expertise of the schoolmaster, fees in the late eighteenth century were typically 1/6d to 3/- for writing, 2/- to 4/- for arithmetic and 2/- to 5/- for Latin, geometry or bookkeeping. Poor families could apply to their kirk session for payment of their children's fees.

Parochial schools were subject to an annual visitation by their presbytery, but the visits seem to have been irregular and superficial, so in practice schools were supervised by the moderator and the elders of the parish kirk. However, in February 1802 the Presbytery of Chanonry conducted an enquiry into its schools and requested a report on each. The Killearnan report stated:

> The parochial school is at Redcastle. The present incumbent is Mr Donald Leitch, regularly called by the heritors and admitted by the Presbytery; has qualified to Government; and subscribed the formula this day coram [in the presence of a quorum]. Teaches English, Latin, writing, arithmetic and book-keeping; holds his school daily; subsists himself by the parochial salary, school fees, and perquisites of session clerkship. Acts under the direction of the Minister and Presbytery; has at present about 80 scholars attending his school.

Donald Leitch was a divinity student, and in 1811 the Presbytery regarded him as 'a youth of good abilities and promise' and he was entered into probationary trials for the ministry. He became licensed as a preacher in 1813.

A Presbytery inspection of Killearnan parish school was undertaken in April 1830 by Rev. John Kennedy (moderator of Killearnan), Rev. R MacKenzie (moderator of Kilmuir Wester) and Rev. R More (Balmaduthy House) accompanied by Colin MacKay of Kilcoy, Thomas MacKenzie of Ord, Capt MacLean of Coulmore and 'several other respectable parishioners'. By this time, the teacher was Hugh MacKay, who was 'certificated and qualified to Government' and had been appointed in June 1828. The *Inverness Journal*[10] of 16 April 1830 reported that during the inspection:

> ...very satisfactory proofs were exhibited of the truly excellent manner in which the seminary is conducted. The number of scholars present amounted to 91, and their neat and tidy appearance presented a scene peculiarly pleasing, while their progress in the different branches of education taught at the school called forth the unqualified approbation of the visitors, and reflected the greatest credit on the ability and efficiency of Mr [Hugh] Mackay the teacher. The Greek and Latin scholars distinguished themselves particularly, and altogether the examination went off with a degree of éclat highly gratifying to those present.

The account of the inspection concludes with a statement that the heritors had lately erected a 'handsome and commodious new school-house at Killearnan'. This was a two-storey building, the ground floor of which was the school and the upper floor of which was the teacher's accommodation. When compulsory education was introduced in 1873 and a new school was built on an adjacent site, both floors of this house were used to accommodate teachers. The house still stands, although it is currently empty.

Hugh MacKay was also a divinity student, who became licensed as a preacher in 1834 and remained as parish schoolteacher until he obtained a parish ministry in March 1837. Kenneth MacKenzie was appointed as his replacement. At the 1843 Disruption, Kenneth transferred to the Free Church and, therefore, had to be replaced as parish schoolmaster. An advertisement was placed in the *Inverness Journal* on 11 April 1845. It stated that 'those concerned with the election are exceedingly anxious to choose the most qualified person they can find … to teach, on the most approved system, all the branches of education taught in the parish schools of Scotland'. Rev. Hugh Skinner was the successful candidate. This was not unusual. In the Highlands, many young qualified ministers took schoolmaster appointments in the hope of progressing to a parish church or missionary post. Those who were not successful became known as 'stickit' ministers. Rev. Skinner's salary at his appointment does not seem to be recorded, but in 1861, when there were around thirty pupils in attendance, it was set by the kirk session at £35 (although Fullarton's *Imperial Gazetteer*[11] of 1868 records that it was £27-11-5½d). Rev. Skinner would remain in post until compulsory education was introduced in 1873 as a consequence of the Education (Scotland) Act of 1872.

3.2 The Schools of the Society in Scotland for Propagating Christian Knowledge

Although an additional school in Killearnan was not included in the Presbytery's original 'Schools Plann' of 1718, many years later the SSPCK financed two schools in Killearnan. One was at Croftnacreich, near Lettoch in the east of Killearnan parish, and the other was a Female School of Industry at Milton of Redcastle. The dates of their founding are not exactly known, but the Presbytery minutes first refer to a 'charity school' at Killearnan (Croft-nacreich) on 26 February 1771, when Rev. Robert Munro was appointed to visit it. He reported in May 1771 that he 'was satisfied … [and] the clerk was appointed to certify the same'. A satisfactory annual report meant that the clerk could sign the teacher's certificate, which would allow the teacher to claim his pay. The first SSPCK teacher in Killearnan was William Fraser, and a Presbytery record of December 1772 indicates that he was to be 'continued at Killearnan with £7 salary'. However, by April 1775 William Fraser had resigned and the SSPCK wrote to the Presbytery offering '£10 to a proper person to be appointed in Killearnan parish in place of William Fraser who is to give up that charge'.

The first record of an SSPCK school to appear in the Killearnan kirk session minutes[12] is in May 1775, in which it is reported that the moderator had applied to the 'Society in Edinburgh to appoint a charity school in the parish'. This was a request to appoint John Noble as William Fraser's replacement. In April 1777, the Presbytery carried out a full inspection of the school and reported that 'having finished the examination they approve of the teacher's method and the scholars' proficiency and appoint the clerk to certify his diligence and fidelity'.

The minutes of the SSPCK state that the school at Croftnacreich had an enrolment of thirty-five boys and five girls[13] in 1780. The school is also recorded in the Old (First) Statistical Account[14] of 1794. By *circa* 1795, the 'society teacher' at Croftnacreich had become John Corbet. He lived on the premises (which he occupied rent-free) but he had to thatch the roof and enclose the garden at his own expense. In the Presbytery's inquiry into its schools in February 1802, the report stated:

> John Corbet, Society's schoolmaster at Croftnacreich in the parish of Killearnan has qualified to Government and subscribed the formula. Teaches English and Gaelic languages, writing, arithmetic, and the catechisms of the Church. Holds his school daily and likewise on the Sabbath. Is supported by the salary allowed him by the Hon Society in Scotland for Propagating Christian Knowledge and by the fees of those of his scholars whose parents can afford to pay a moderate fee for instructing their children. Acts under the Hon Society's direction and that of the parish minister and has at present about 40 scholars regularly attending his school.

A report of an inspection carried out by Patrick Butter in 1824 stated that 'there are no other schools in the parish except the parish school which is not so numerously attended as this'. At that time, there were sixty children (mostly boys) in attendance in summer, and eighty in winter. Some children from Redcastle may have attended this school, especially during the early nineteenth century when the Redcastle quarry was employing up to seventy people, although it is more likely that they attended the parish school. School hours were 7.00–9.00 a.m., 10.00 a.m.–2.00 p.m. and 3.00–6.00 p.m. in summer and 10.00 a.m.–3.00 p.m. in winter. Summer holidays were generally four weeks, and other holidays were taken only at times when the pupils were required for farm work – for example, at harvest time and on market days when animals had to be tended. John Corbet is recorded as a head of family in full communion with the Killearnan parish church in 1834. As there was no evening Sabbath school at the time, he tried to set up Sabbath bible reading evenings. However, he could not attract participants, which prompted Patrick Butter to comment, 'I am afraid there is little of the spirit of religion in this place.'

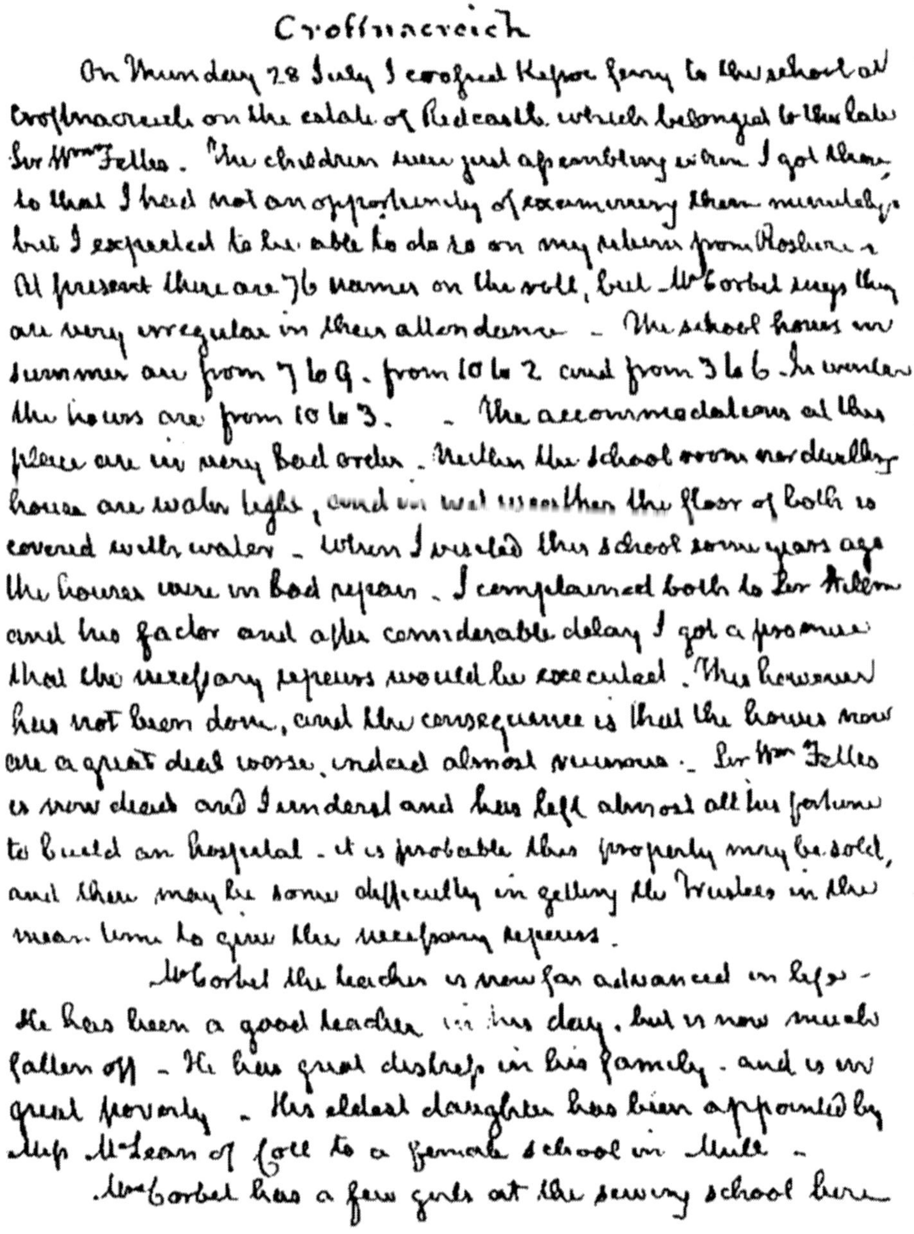

Croftnacreich

On Thursday 28 July I crossed Kepoe ferry to the school at Croftnacreich on the estate of Redcastle which belonged to the late Sir Wm Felles. The children were just assembling when I got there, so that I had not an opportunity of examining them minutely, but I expected to be able to do so on my return from Roshven. At present there are 76 names on the roll, but Mr Corbet says they are very irregular in their attendance. The school hours in summer are from 7 to 9, from 10 to 2 and from 3 to 6. In winter the hours are from 10 to 3. The accommodations at this place are in very bad order. Neither the school room nor dwelling house are water tight, and in wet weather the floor of both is covered with water. When I visited this school some years ago the houses were in bad repair. I complained both to Sir William and his factor and after considerable delay I got a promise that the necessary repairs would be executed. This however has not been done, and the consequence is that the houses now are a great deal worse, indeed almost ruinous. Sir Wm Felles is now dead and I understand has left almost all his fortune to build an hospital. It is probable this property may be sold, and there may be some difficulty in getting the Trustees in the mean time to give the necessary repairs.

Mr Corbet the teacher is now far advanced in life. He has been a good teacher in his day, but is now much fallen off. He has great distress in his family, and is in great poverty. His eldest daughter has been appointed by Miss McLean of Coll to a female school in Mull.

Mrs Corbet has a few girls at the sewing school here

Figure 29: Patrick Butter's 1836 inspection report of the SSPCK school at Croftnacreich (The National Archives of Scotland, GD95/14/29)

A further inspection of the SSPCK school at Croftnacreich was carried out by Patrick Butter in 1836, when there were seventy-six children on the roll (Figure 29). The premises had obviously deteriorated since the 1824 inspection, as it was reported that 'neither the school room nor the dwelling house are water tight, and in wet weather the floor of both is covered with water'. It is further recorded that 'Mr Corbet the teacher is now far advanced in life. He has been a good teacher in his day, but is now much fallen off. He has great distress in his family and is in great poverty.' Although an Act of 1803 had raised schoolteachers' salaries to between 300 and 400 merks, SSPCK teachers received fewer fees from pupils and, unlike their colleagues in the parochial schools, generally were not able to raise additional income as the kirk precentor or session clerk. Hence accounts of their poverty throughout the Highlands were common, especially at times when food was scarce and prices were high. After John Corbet retired, the SSPCK school in Croftnacreich continued to operate with Murdoch MacKenzie as its teacher. SSPCK schools closed when compulsory state schooling was introduced in 1873.

SSPCK schools initially excluded the teaching of Gaelic, believing that the key to educating children in the Highlands was to encourage use of the increasingly available texts printed in English. However, a survey on 'The Moral Statistics of the Highlands and Islands of Scotland' compiled in 1824 by the Inverness Society for the Education of the Poor in the Highlands showed that a high proportion of Gaelic speakers were unable to read.[15] This prompted the SSPCK to introduce the Gaelic bible (translation of which had commenced in 1769 and was completed in 1802) into their schools.

Patrick Butter's report also states that there were 'a few girls at the sewing school'. This was a reference to the Female School of Industry in Milton of Redcastle, which is first recorded in the Presbytery minutes in March 1810 when two members were requested to 'examine the school at Croftnacreich in the parish of Killearnan and the sewing school also there, taught by John Corbet and by Mrs Corbet, his wife'. There are disappointingly few written references to this school, but Mrs Corbet seems to have been the first teacher. Other teachers are occasionally recorded in the early national censuses – for example, Helen Robertson is recorded in 1851 as a 'sewing school mistress'. The 1:2,500 (circa 25 inch:1 mile) First Series Ordnance Survey map of 1872 is the only map that locates the situation of the SSPCK female school at Milton of Redcastle. It was a single-storey thatched building at the western end of the village, between the two rows of houses, and had a teacher's house attached. The school, which had an average attendance of thirty, was supported by school fees, government grant and by the SSPCK, and was 'solely for the teaching of sewing and the rudiments of English, grammar, arithmetic, reading and writing to girls and young children'. Rev. John Kennedy refers to the female school in his Killearnan chapter of the Second Statistical Account of Scotland,[16] in which he states that the schoolmistress in 1837–38 received a salary of £5 Sterling (compared to nearly £30 for the parochial schoolteacher and £15 for the SSPCK schoolteacher). Nowadays, there are no visible remains of the building.

All three schools (the parochial school close to the parish church, the SSPCK female school at Milton of Redcastle and the SSPCK school at Croftnacreich) were located in the south of the parish. This prompted fifty inhabitants of Tore to sign a petition[17] requesting the establishment of a school in the north-east of the parish at Tore. It 'humbly begs that you [Sir Colin Mackenzie of Kilcoy, Baronet] be pleased to furnish us with the necessary accommodation ... venturing to suggest as a suitable place the kitchen of Tore House with the closet adjoining ... being at present unoccupied'.

The rationale offered in support of the request was that, owing to distance, about 100 children were precluded from education. It also stated that the inhabitants of Tore were supporting a teacher at their own expense but had no premises of sufficient size and were unable to raise a schoolhouse. Unfortunately, the petition is undated but it would have been between 1836 (when Colin Mackenzie was created a baronet) and 1845 (when he died). It is remarkable that such an 'unofficial' school existed at that time (such schools are often referred to as 'adventure' schools), but the parents' plea seems to have failed and the inhabitants of Tore had to wait until 1879 before Tore Public School was established.

3.3   The Free Church of Scotland and its Redcastle School

When the Free Church of Scotland was formed at the Disruption of 1843, many of those who transferred no longer wished their children to attend the parish or the SSPCK schools. Thus the Deacons' Court had to give early consideration to the 'propriety of erecting a school house in the west end of the parish as their teacher, Mr MacKenzie, was ejected from the parochial school'. The opportunity arose in 1845 when 'the Moderator intimated his having secured £100 from the Education Committee and had been offered an excellent site for said building from Col Hugh Baillie in Redcastle'. Progress was rapid, as at the June 1846 meeting of the Deacons' Court it was reported that a contract had already been issued to Duncan MacLennan, a house-carpenter from Kilcoy, to build the school. The site was at the east end of Quarry of Redcastle. The value of the contract is not recorded, but it was a single-storey building with a slated roof, and had accommodation for fifty scholars. The date when it opened is not recorded, but a minute of the Free Church session[18] shows that a meeting was held in the school in July 1846.

Special Sabbath collections had been made from 1844 for the 'education scheme', and a schoolmaster's sustentation fund (which contained £13-5-4d in 1846) was set up by the Deacons' Court. The first teacher was Kenneth MacKenzie, who had been ejected as the parochial schoolteacher for going over to the Free Church.

The school was inspected by a committee of the Free Church Presbytery in March 1850, and a quotation from their report was published in the *Inverness Advertiser* of 19 March. It reads:

> The facility and readiness with which the children answered the questions posed, not only by the teacher, but by others in reading, grammar, etmology, geography, history, Latin and Greek, arithmetic, practical mathematics, trigonometry and bible history combined with sacred geography, evidently showed that every thing like superficiality was avoided and that the thinking powers of the children were frequently called forth ... The examination was concluded by distributing prizes to the children, and congratulating the teacher, Mr MacKenzie, on the very efficient manner in which he taught the children.

Kenneth MacKenzie must have retired shortly after being praised in the inspection of 1850, because in 1852 the Deacons' Court recorded that its treasurer, Alexander MacKenzie, had resigned from that office since he had been unanimously elected as 'congregational teacher'. (The teacher was paid from the sustentation fund administered by the treasurer of the Deacons' Court, hence he could not occupy both posts.) However, the tenure of Alexander MacKenzie was short-lived, because in 1854 he resigned as congregational teacher 'on account of continued indisposition'. The school then entered a period in which its teachers lasted only two years: John McRae from Kirkcaldy (1854–56); Robert Stewart from Kelso (1856–58); Alexander MacDougall from Glasgow (1858–60); and in 1860 John Robson from Edinburgh. These successive appointments from the south of Scotland seem strange, as Rev. John Kennedy states in the New (Second) Statistical Account that Gaelic was still the predominant language of the parish at that time. Further appointments are not detailed, but Andrew MacDougall and William Fraser are recorded in the 1860s, and Donald MacIntosh had become the teacher by 1869 and was still in post when compulsory education was introduced in 1873.

3.4   Killearnan Public School

The 1872 Education (Scotland) Act made attendance at school compulsory (though with provisions for 'half-time' work) for all five- to thirteen-year-olds, and provided for local public schools to be created under the general authority of a new Scotch Education Department (based in London, but assisted by a Board of Education in Edinburgh) and day-to-day oversight by School Boards. At Killearnan, the site of the parochial school was selected for the new public school, and in July 1872 the Killearnan Free Church Deacons' Court received a letter from the Commission of Assembly appointed to advise in connection with the 'Transfer of Schools'. It directed that 'as the Congregational School [at Quarry of Redcastle] is not to be taken over as a permanent school for the district, the Deacons' Court should give use of it to the [Killearnan] School Board until a permanent school is provided or for a term of years upon such conditions as may be agreed upon'. There do not appear to be any records that indicate whether the Free Church school in Quarry of Redcastle (or the SSPCK female school in Milton of Redcastle) remained temporarily in use, but it is recorded that the parish church was brought into use to cope with the numbers of children. (The Annals of the Free Church[19] state that their school at Quarry of Redcastle was later used for 'district services'.)

Unfortunately, neither the original Killearnan Public School Board minutes nor the early school attendance registers can be traced. However, the school log book has survived.[20] Its first entry was made in December 1875, when the headmaster was Donald McIntosh, who was assisted by his wife, Isabella, and two pupil teachers, James Macrae and John Tuach. Donald and Isabella had been the teachers in the Free Church school at Quarry of Redcastle and the SSPCK female school in Milton of Redcastle. The parochial school head teacher (and parish registrar) prior to 1873 had been Rev. Hugh Skinner, a clergyman who had taken up school teaching. By the time compulsory education was introduced, Rev. Hugh Skinner was seventy years old and did not transfer to the new public school. He retired to Avoch and died in June 1880.

The first entry in the school log book in 1875 states that 'the small accommodation and bad ventilation interfere very much with the progress of the school'. Another entry in August 1876 states that 'the present place of teaching is very unsuitable, the air being close and unhealthy and consequently materially hinders the progress of the school'. It is not clear whether these comments refer to the schools at Milton of Redcastle and Quarry of Redcastle or only to the previous parochial school, but clearly there was need for new premises. In an inspection of the school carried out in July 1876 by the local His Majesty's Inspector, Mr J Macleod, it is recorded that there were seventy-two boys and fifty-six girls enrolled.

In 1875, Henry James Baillie, the proprietor of Redcastle, granted a feu charter[21] in favour of the Killearnan School Board. This provided land for the building of a new public school and also 'a playground for the scholars, and for a residence for the teacher or teachers in the said school and for no other purposes whatever'. A requirement placed on the School Board was 'to enclose the piece of ground hereby disponed with stone and lime walls of a height not less than four feet six inches, nor exceeding eight feet'. For the use of this land, the School Board (whose chairman was Robert Trotter, the tenant of Garguston Farm) was charged a feu duty of £5-10/- per year, this amount to double every nineteen years. The plan attached to the charter shows the layout of the buildings. The old parochial school was to be converted into a house for the headmaster and a new school was to be built closer to the road, where it still is today. As Redcastle quarry had been worked out by 1875, the new building was constructed with stone from Tarradale quarry (which was also owned by Henry James Baillie). The sasine abridgement[22] is dated 24 May 1876. Also in that month, an entry in the school log book states that 'the new buildings have been begun', and in July 1876 another entry comments: 'Having to teach in the parish church, the want of a suitable apparatus hinders the work.'

A new headmaster, James Davidson (and his wife Eliza), took up post on 1 December 1876. They had responded to an advertisement published in *The Scotsman*[23] on 11 October 1876, which stated:

Teacher (certificated male) wanted by the School Board of Killearnan, Redcastle, Ross-Shire, for the public school, to enter on his duties immediately. Salary £100 and one-fourth of Government Grant, which realised for the last two years upward of £100, with free house and garden. Also female teacher (certificated) wanted for same school. A preference given to teacher's wife or sister. Applications, with testimonials, to be lodged with James McK. Alison, Treasurer to the School Board, on or before 1st November proximo.

It is likely that the new school opened at that time. Although a new building with accommodation for 180 pupils, it was apparently supplied with the furniture from the previous school buildings, because in 1877 Mr Davidson recorded that 'writing classes have not improved, owing to the bad desks'.

Shortly after his appointment, James Davidson's boat was involved in an incident involving a whale that had become stranded in Redcastle Bay in July 1877. Donald Robertson, the village blacksmith, and Hugh Fraser, the estate head gardener, (with the assistance of James Kennedy, a quarrier) had launched the boat and had rowed out sufficiently close to the whale to shoot it. Being members of the 'Volunteers', they were successful and the whale was pulled to the pier, where it was measured to be fifty feet in length. Within days, the carcass of the whale was towed out to sea and taken to Birmingham, where it was drawn through the city streets and put on display on 26 July 1877 in the Hamstead Hall Park, where an admission charge of 6d was levied. An account of the incident is given by Margaret Oag[24] and it is said that an account was submitted to the *Inverness Courier*, but the article seems never to have been published. Copies of the original transcript of the account, headlined 'Exciting Chase and Capture of a Large Whale by Rifle Volunteers in Scotland' are still in private collections.[25] It also seems that the event was not recorded at the time in the local Birmingham papers, but it did become the subject of correspondence in the *Birmingham Weekly Post* over fifty years later.[26] A query about the exhibit, published on 13 February 1932, received three responses from readers who recalled the event. These were published on 20 February, 12 March and 30 July 1932. It appears that the whale, which was advertised as the largest ever caught, was originally displayed in a marquee but, because of the smell, was transported by twenty-eight horses and eight carts to a field near Curzon Street Station. It seems to have remained there until *circa* 1880, when it was taken, as a skeleton, to Curzon Street Hall and again put on display.

Instances of whales entering the Beauly Firth were not uncommon in the latter part of the nineteenth century. For example, there was a very similar incident reported in the *Scottish Highlander* of 6 September 1888, in which a fifty-foot whale 'which got into shallow water near Kessock Ferry was … harpooned by the men employed there, and towed ashore with the advancing tide'. Another article about a whale at Kessock Ferry, published in the *Inverness Advertiser* of 14 December 1880, reported that 'a large whale has been the dread of the fishermen for the last month in Inverness Firth. On Sunday last the monster made its way into the narrows, passed through the ferry, and was all day yesterday seen ranging between the mouth of the canal and Bunchrew. The fish is of a very large size and is still making its way inward'. Whether it reached Redcastle does not seem to be reported.

The new Killearnan Public School was subjected to a 'public inspection' on 23 August 1878. The inspectors were recorded in the *Inverness Advertiser* of 27 August to be: Rev. Neil Gillies, the Free Church moderator and a member of the School Board; Mrs Gillies; Rev. William MacKay, the Established Church moderator; Miss Baillie and Mrs Baillie from the castle; Mr Gillanders, a teacher from Denny; Miss Rose of Rochester; Miss Elder, Miss Bisset and Mr Cameron of Redcastle. Their report was very complimentary, stating:

The appearance made by the school as a whole showed the instruction given by Mr and Mrs Davidson and their assistants to be useful, thorough and well directed, while some of the pupils gave evidence of unusual intelligence. The examination in Scriptural knowledge showed the pupils to have a very intelligent acquaintance with the portion of scripture on which they were questioned, while the standard of efficiency attained in the English and commercial branches does much credit to the energy and ability of the teachers. The specimens of needle work exhibited elicited the praise of the examiners, not only on account of the workmanship but also because the work of this department is such as will demand most attention from the pupils in after life.

It is remarkable that schooling in the 1870s not only prepared pupils for life after school, but also the 'after life'!

On behalf of the Scotch Education Department, the 'Endowed Institutions Commission' (which had been set up to account for the monies voted by Parliament for compulsory education) in February 1879 requested data on the number of pupils and their examination performance from every school in Scotland. Despite the praise given in the public inspection of 1878, the data for Killearnan Public School presented on behalf of the Killearnan, Urray and Muir of Ord School Management Committee by James Davidson, told another story.[27] There were only thirty-eight pupils (sixteen boys, twenty-two girls) in attendance, and the only subjects being taught were: English language and literature (sixteen boys, fourteen girls); mathematics (three boys); Latin (three boys); physical geography (four boys, nine girls); and domestic economy (eighteen girls). Of the thirty-eight pupils, ten (seven boys, three girls) had been entered into the public examinations in English and only seven had passed (six boys, one girl). Furthermore, of the three stages of the examinations, nine pupils had been entered for Stage 1 and only one had entered (and passed) Stage 2. There had been no entries for Stage 3.

Truancy at the new public school was a problem in the early years. This was, in part, due to absences of pupils who were required for seasonal farm work (for example, potato planting and harvesting) but may also have been due to a reluctance of Free Church adherents to send their children to a school that was initially convened in the old parochial school (and the parish church) before moving to its new building, located on the site of the previous parochial school. Illness also caused pupil absence, not always self-referred. The new headmaster, James Davidson, recorded in the school log book in 1879 that, due to a fever in 'Donald MacKenzie's house', he had refused to take in his children. Donald lived in Quarry of Redcastle with his wife, Ann, and three children, Johanna, Kenneth and John. Ann and Johanna were destined to live in the hamlet for some time, and John was to become a policeman and the first private purchaser of the house now known as Quarry Cottage.

Whatever the reasons for the many absences, in 1878 the Ross-shire Commissioners of Supply noted the problem and suggested that a solution might be to authorise local Justices of the Peace to deal personally with defaulting parents rather than use the courts, which in many remote areas were practically inaccessible. However, this advice was ignored and in 1880 the school log book records that 'the compulsory clause has always been a dead letter in this parish'. The average attendance in 1881 is recorded as fifty-eight pupils,[28] only about one-half of the combined total of 110 recorded by the three separate schools in 1872 and of the 128 enrolled pupils recorded in the HMI inspection of 1876.[29] A 'Compulsory Officer' was appointed to tackle the problem in 1882 but this seems to have made little difference, since in 1885 it is recorded that ten or twelve children had been reported to the compulsory officer, and the annual HMI report states that 'the irregular attendance at this school is very disheartening to a teacher, and has a most injurious effect upon the instruction'.

Not only was irregular attendance a problem, but it was compounded by large fluctuations in the numbers of pupils living in the area. When compulsory education commenced in 1873, there appear to have been over 120 enrolled pupils, and the new school building is said to have been designed for up to 180. In 1877, new attendance registers were introduced and 140 names were entered. However, by 1879 there were only eighty-three on the roll, and in 1881 this had further reduced to sixty-four. In 1883 (when the school leaving age was raised to fourteen), the compulsory officer estimated that there were only fifty-four children of school age in the district and commented that 'the population of the district had very much decreased'. One reason for the decrease was the movement away of people due to diminishing numbers of jobs on the farms, but the main reason for the apparent extraordinary decline in the school population at Redcastle is that Tore Public School[30] at the eastern end of the parish opened in 1879 and parents had a choice of which school their children should attend. Although distance would have been the major factor, the poor academic reputation of the school at Redcastle no doubt caused some parents to switch to the new school. However, the decline was soon reversed, because by 1896 there were eighty-eight on the school roll and in 1904 it had risen to 102.

The variable school pupil population also had an effect on the numbers of teachers that could be employed. The funding of the school was dependent on enrolments and registered attendances, as well as 'quality factors' assessed in the annual HMI inspection. This created staff turnover, particularly of the assistant and pupil teachers. For example, in 1879 John Tuach was discharged and a 'monitor' was appointed to replace James Macrae, because declining pupil numbers had deemed it unnecessary to have two pupil teachers. (Later that year, John Tuach was appointed as the first headteacher of Tore Public School.) In 1883, there was a complete turnover of the staff, with William Johnston being appointed as headmaster, his sister Catherine as sewing teacher and Agnes Edward as monitor. These three were replaced in 1889 by William

MacIntosh, Lily Bisset (soon replaced by Jeanie Cruickshank) and James Laing (soon replaced by Mary Edward). As the school pupil population grew around the turn of the century, they were augmented by Isabella Graham as 'Certificated Assistant Teacher' in 1904.

The annual HMI inspection was an important occasion. For example, in 1880 the inspection was carried out by HMI William Jolly, who reported that 'the grant [of £64-14-6d] is only recommended in the circumstances that great improvement will be required'. In 1885, the HMI report states that 'the instruction is in a condition far from satisfactory', and in 1889 it is reported that 'the condition of the school is quite unsatisfactory as regards both instruction and discipline'. On that occasion, the HMI 'ordered a deduction of one-tenth to be made from the grant on account of faults in instruction'. This resulted in the school grant being reduced to £25-4-6d and prompted the swift departure of William Johnston and his staff and the appointment of William MacIntosh as headmaster. The effect was dramatic. By 1896, the HMI report states that 'tone and discipline are faultless ... the general condition [of the junior department] entitles it to the highest grant for excellence ... the upper standards make a distinctly good appearance ... the results in specific subjects are most creditable ... singing and sewing are excellent'.

The school HMI did not inspect Religious Instruction, which was the responsibility of the church ministers. They generally provided glowing reports, that of 1898 being typical: 'By appointment of the School Board, Messrs Gillies and Macdonald examined the school this day in scripture knowledge and the Shorter Catechism and they wish to record their entire satisfaction with the answers returned to the various questions put from the portions of scripture examined on the Shorter Catechism.'

School holidays and occasional closures were determined locally in the nineteenth century, and in Killearnan this meant that the needs of the church and the farms predominated. The school therefore closed for one or two weeks during the biannual communion seasons (February and July) and during planting (April) and harvest (September/October). The school also closed for Christmas and New Year, but these were celebrated on 5 and 12 January, which were referred to as Old Christmas Day and Old New Year's Day. [This arose from the change in 1752 from the Julian to the Gregorian calendar when eleven days were 'lost' by declaring that 2 September would be followed by 14 September – see page 73.] Other shorter holidays were given for various local events, for example: the monthly Muir of Ord market, at which pupils were required to tend livestock; the annual harvest thanksgiving service held on the last Thursday of November; the annual 'soiree' of the Sabbath school; local elections, for which the school was used as a polling station; and the annual tea party given by Miss Baillie at the castle.

Closures could also be imposed by the Medical Officer of Health when outbreaks of childhood diseases occurred. Measles seems to have been the most prevalent, the school being closed from 3 March to 3 April in 1882 and from 26 December 1890 to 19 January 1891 during epidemics. From time to time, low attendance was recorded as being due to chicken pox, scarlet fever, whooping cough and mumps; and occasionally these diseases also closed the school. For example, between 14 November 1905 and 15 January 1906 it was closed because mumps, measles and scarlet fever were prevalent, and on 29 January 1915 Dr Bruce, the Medical Officer of Health, ordered the school to close for scarlet fever. The school was thoroughly cleaned, washed and disinfected, but did not reopen until 22 March 1915, when only fifty per cent of the pupils returned.

From 1890, the school came under the jurisdiction of the Ross and Cromarty County Council, but unfortunately no minutes of the Killearnan School Board have survived. However, the Education Authority minutes[31] date from 1919, when individual school boards were replaced by school management committees that embraced the schools in several parishes. The two Killearnan schools (at Tore and Redcastle) were initially covered by the Knockbain, Killearnan and Urquhart School Management Committee (in 1922, Knockbain transferred to the Avoch Committee). None of the minutes seem to have survived, but the School Management Committee reported to the County Education Authority, whose minutes, from time to time, recorded issues of the day concerning Killearnan Public School.

The first specific mention of Killearnan School is in July 1920, when Annie MacKay was awarded a bursary to attend Inverness Royal Academy. The amount is not recorded, but in the period 1921–29 there were a further nine pupils who received bursaries (to attend Dingwall Academy) of amounts ranging from £7 to £15 per year. Of these, four were children of Alexander Holm, the Redcastle Station master. Davina Holm was a particularly able linguist. In 1934, she won the Dingwall Academy medal for English, Latin and French.

The Ross and Cromarty Education Authority's Staffing Sub-Committee was responsible for the appointment of the teaching and ancillary staff in all of its schools. It undertook a review of all non-teaching staff in December 1920 and recorded their names and functions against each school. Killearnan school, whose roll was sixty pupils, had three such staff: Donald Forbes, the compulsory officer whose salary was £12; Mrs Robertson of Milton of Redcastle, the cleaner who was paid £12 per year; and William Chisholm (of Quarry Cottage) who was paid £7-10/- as the 'office cleaner' (the 'offices' were the toilets). In November 1921, regulations for cleaning schools and offices were issued. They included the requirement to sweep all floors daily, scrub all classrooms monthly, disinfect all walls yearly, empty all office pails daily, clean out all office pits biannually, and limewash all offices yearly.

From time to time, events at the school were recorded in the local newspapers. For example, the *Highland News* of 3 January 1914 reported on the school treat:

> Last week Mrs Robertson, Redcastle, entertained the children attending Killearnan Public School to a Christmas treat. A sumptuous tea was first supplied to the children, after which a display of cinema films was shown on a large screen by Messrs Hercher, Beauly. The *Delhi Durbar*, *King's Coronation* and *Panama Canal Operations* films specially acquired for the occasion from Mr Arnott, Inverness, were a real treat in themselves. Before parting each of the little ones was supplied with a bag of fruit, along with a suitable toy. On the call of Mr Mackintosh a most hearty vote of thanks was accorded to Mrs Robertson for her greatness.

It is not clear who Mrs Robertson was (possibly the wife of Donald Robertson, the village blacksmith, or the wife of the county's chief HMI), but this may have been the first occasion on which motion pictures were shown at Redcastle.

The head teacher, William MacIntosh, and the infant teacher, Isa Graham, were both long-serving (Isa is the teacher in Figure 30). William had been appointed in 1889, and had been responsible for a remarkable turnaround in the reputation of the school and for great improvements in the quality of the education provided, as recorded in successive annual HMI reports. Isa had been appointed in 1904 and also received high praise from HMI. Their signatures are recorded on a commemorative album presented in 1905 to John Robertson, HM Chief Inspector of Schools, on the occasion of his twenty-fifth anniversary of service. Together, William and Isa had also raised the school pupil numbers (although they were destined to suffer from demographic decline after *circa* 1910), and assistant teachers or monitors had been appointed at various times to assist them. These included Maggie Ellis (1905), Annie MacGillivray (1908), Miss Macphail (1909), Margaret MacLennan (1909), M Rose (1911), M Duncan (1913), Miss MacGregor (1920), Robina Cooper (1926) and Margaret Nicholson (1927). Miss Nicholson broke her leg in a motorcycle accident in 1928 and her duties were temporarily undertaken by Sarah Macrae.

William MacIntosh retired in August 1929 after giving forty years of service. His final entry in the school log book is brief and noteworthy for its pathos: 'My age limit expires today; therefore I retire.' On 3 September 1929, his successor wrote: 'I, John Graham, take up duty in this school today as

Headmaster.' On 3 July 1934, he recorded: 'Miss Graham, Infant Mistress, finished after giving 30 years of devoted and loyal service to the school.' William MacIntosh died in August 1936 and, as a mark of the respect in which he was held, the commencement of the 1936–37 school year was postponed in his honour.

Figure 30: Killearnan (Redcastle) Public School pupils and teacher, Isa Graham, in 1930 (reproduced with permission from the collection of the late Frances [Ada] McDonell)

Throughout the years between World War One and World War Two, the school continued to be regularly inspected by HMI, the churches and even the North of Scotland Agricultural College. From 1920, the agricultural college had annually inspected the school garden and had always given it a good report (not unexpected in an agricultural community). For example, in October 1929 they reported that the garden 'is very neatly kept, and the instruction both in practical and theoretical is carried out in a very efficient manner'.

The reports from the inspections of religious instruction were also highly congratulatory. The report for 1929–30 is an example:

We, the undersigned, examined this school today in religious knowledge. The subjects of examination were for the senior division – Samuel, Saul, Jonathan,

David, Absalom and Solomon, with the Shorter Catechism and Psalms for repetition. For the junior division the book of Genesis with Shorter Catechism and Psalms for repetition. We have much pleasure in reporting our entire satisfaction with the appearance made by the whole school. Its reputation is fully maintained and is evidence of the thoroughness with which religious instruction is given. The pupils answered accurately and intelligently the questions put to them.

The inspectors were Rev. Alexander Cameron of the United Free Church and Rev. Aeneas Macdonald of the Established Church of Scotland.

John Graham was a strict disciplinarian, and the outcomes of HMI inspections during his regime were invariably positive and satisfactory, although continuous improvement was always encouraged. For example, in March 1922 the HMI report contains the following paragraphs:

In the lower room the instruction continues to be attended with highly satisfactory results. In this room, however, there are 43 children at five different stages and, in addition, the teacher has charge of needlework and cookery. This constitutes an obvious and undesirable strain, for which some relief should be sought. A more equitable distribution of the numbers in charge of the respective teachers should be effected and arrangements might with advantage be made for the institution of a shortened school day for the infant scholars;

Many of the children in the school are backward for their years. The school population it is true, is drawn to a large extent from an agricultural community, and the personnel of a considerable proportion of the school roll changes annually [in 1922, it was fifty-seven]. It is thus difficult to achieve a completely satisfactory relationship between age and attainment, but it is hoped that a special and sustained effort will be made to reduce as far as possible the disparity that exists at present between chronological age and advancement.

It seems that a degree of success was achieved with this problem, because in 1931 the HMI report records that 'all three teachers are to be commended for the zeal and success with which they have taught their respective sections of the school in spite of the difficulty caused by the migratory character of a considerable portion of the population of the district'.

Just as the difficulty of providing a satisfactory water supply to the parish church manse was a prolonged issue for the kirk session and the heritors during the early years of the century, the lack of any water supply to the school was concerning HMI and the School Management Committee. In June 1924, the Committee had raised the matter with the Education Authority, but it had been 'deferred in the meantime'. It was again raised in January 1926 with a suggestion to approach Donald MacDonald of Fettes Farm for a water supply.

It was agreed 'to keep this in view when considering the replacements and repairs for next year'. Needless to say, it wasn't! However, four years later, in March 1930, the Education Authority agreed to approach Donald MacDonald and, furthermore, approved an estimate of £450 for 'heating classrooms, general repairs, new cooking range for schoolhouse, painting and distempering, new cloakroom, improving lighting and renewing flooring', all to be carried out in the summer of 1930. Needless to say, they weren't!

The Education Authority (together with the Parish Council) was wound up under another local government reform in 1930 and was replaced by the Ross and Cromarty County Council Education Committee. The delay to the Killearnan school repairs was raised in January 1931 and was reported to be 'in the hands of the Works Sub-Committee of the County Council'. Two months later, the Education Committee's estimates for 1931–32 included several items of Killearnan school repairs: 'shifting classroom, improving lighting and lining ceiling (£648); new cloakrooms (£189); heating (£111); 7 chemical toilets (£15)'. Furthermore, there was a note explaining to the Committee that 'the structural formation of this school was bad and seriously affected the light in certain of the classrooms and the improvement of the school was urgently required'. On this occasion, the repairs were carried out.

It is noted in the 1931 HMI report that 'the Education Authority will at an early date take steps both to improve the sanitation and to make the teaching conditions satisfactory for all the classes of the school'. The renovations were carried out during the summer holidays of 1931, and the pupils' holiday was extended for a week whilst they were completed. The school log book for 1 September 1931 records that the:

> …school reopened today – 68 present. During the holidays the school buildings have undergone vast alterations and improvements and the teaching conditions, as a result, will be decidedly more satisfactory. A fact worthy to be recorded is that the Architect, Mr Matheson, who has been in charge of the work, is a former pupil of this school. Mr Matheson is the capable architect employed by the County Council.

Mr Matheson had also been highly regarded by the Education Authority. At their final meeting on 29 April 1930, they had recorded that 'he has rendered noble service … the smallest details are always carefully considered … under his guidance great improvements have been carried out … the new school at Ullapool shall always be an evidence of his architectural skill'.

The Killearnan school HMI report for 1932 remarked that 'the installation of new chemical closets is also noted with satisfaction', but a further comment added that 'the question of a proper water supply for the school and schoolhouse remains a problem which should not be neglected'. Similar comments would continue to be made in successive years by HMI[32] – for example, in 1939 the report states 'the lack of a water supply still exists and calls for attention'. However, it was almost ten years later, in 1941, before the school water supply was again brought to the notice of the Education Committee, and twenty years before any action would be taken.

By 1935, pupil numbers had declined to around thirty-five and the number of teachers had reduced to two, these being John Graham, the head teacher, and Catherine MacKay, the infant mistress. Mary Cameron took over as infant teacher in January 1941. Throughout the pre-war period, good HMI reports continued to be received, typical comments being 'admirably taught ... very good quality ... conscientious and competent teaching'. An interesting comment, which is contained in the report on religious instruction of July 1936, was that 'Gaelic speaking is rarely found in this parish and there is no instruction given in consequence.' Forty years previously, almost every person in Redcastle had been dual Gaelic- and English-speaking.

The saga of the water supply was rekindled in April 1941, when the County Council Education Committee decided not to include the water scheme in their annual estimates, but commented that 'negotiations with the estate should be put in hand'. However, there was no quick outcome. It took until August 1944 for the school log book to record that the Sanitary Inspector (Mr Stewart) and the Medical Officer of Health (Dr Lumsden) had taken away 'a sample of water from a well used by the scholars'. The well in question was the 'Grey Well' (Figure 31) located at the side of the road from Milton of Redcastle to Killearnan parish church, marked (but not named) on both the First and Second series Ordnance Survey maps.

The result of the analysis is recorded in the log book:

The sample was clear and gave no deposit on standing. The proportions of both free and albuminoid ammonia were exceedingly low and well within the limits usually prescribed. The water was slightly alkaline in reaction (pH 8.2) and was free from poisonous metals, nitrites and phosphates. This water is of excellent quality, but possesses a temporary hardness of 16.5 degrees. It would appear, therefore, that it would be quite safe to allow the children to drink this water without it being boiled, but they should continue to use their individual cups.

Needless to say, no progress was made and it would be 1949 before the issue was raised again. Meanwhile, staff changes were taking place. Mrs Grant replaced Mary Cameron in January 1945, and in November of that year Malcolm MacLeod was appointed as an interim head teacher to cover for John Graham, who had been on periodic sick leave since 1943. In February 1946,

Malcolm MacLeod was confirmed as acting head teacher, but John Graham was soon recovered and remained in post until he retired in April 1952 after twenty-two years of service. It is remarkable that there had been only four previous head teachers since the school had opened eighty years previously: Donald MacIntosh (1873–76); James Davidson (1876–83); William Johnson (1883–89) and William MacIntosh (1889–1929).

Figure 31: The 'Grey Well' at Milton of Redcastle

VE Day was observed as a two-day school holiday on 8–9 May 1945, and the school log book records that, to celebrate Victory Day on 8 June 1946, 'a sports day was held in the grounds of Redcastle by kind permission of Baroness Burton' (a similar event had been held in August 1919 to celebrate victory in World War One). The school log book was discontinued from 1 April 1949. By that time, despite the raising of the school leaving age to fifteen in 1945, the school roll had decreased to twenty-two – but the saga of the water supply still had some years to run.

In February 1949 (presumably as a result of the negotiations commenced in 1941), the Education Committee was requested by the county clerk to approve the 'allocation of costs of the proposed water scheme for Killearnan school and the adjoining farms concerned'. Approval was obtained (at a cost of £414), but it transpired that the Department of Agriculture had decreed that the reservoir at Fettes Farm (from which the water supply was to be drawn) was too small and had to be enlarged. This raised the cost to £423 and, in March 1950, when two other participants in the 'joint scheme' withdrew, the Education Committee's proportion of the cost rose to £562. Then, in May 1950, the Education Committee was informed that a regional water scheme would probably be in operation in five to seven years' time. This prompted the Committee to offer to pay a fixed rate per 1,000 gallons to the sponsors of the joint scheme rather than contribute to the capital cost. In December 1951, this was agreed at a rate of 2/- per 1,000 gallons (plus the cost of the branch pipe to the school). So, in early 1952, a drinking water tap was finally installed in the playground. It had taken twenty-eight years!

In May 1951, the Education Committee was approached by Michael Baillie, who had succeeded as proprietor of Redcastle after his father's death in 1941, requesting that the Hydro-Electric Board be pressed into erecting a trans-former in the vicinity of the school so that electricity could be supplied to the school and the adjacent estate properties. This must have been successful, because the school's HMI report for 1954 comments that 'attainment was generally satisfactory ... the premises were greatly improved ... water and electricity supplies had been brought in ... but there were no meals'. School inspectors are never satisfied!

Killearnan Primary School closed in 1970, only three years short of its centenary. The pupil roll had declined to twenty-seven by 1954, and in 1964 the Ross and Cromarty Education Committee transferred the top classes to Tarradale Junior Secondary School in Muir of Ord and reduced Killearnan School to single-teacher status. Mary MacLeod, the head teacher who had taken over from John Graham in 1952, resigned at that time, having been appointed an assistant teacher of modern languages at Dingwall Academy. The new head was Mrs Ann MacKenzie, who had transferred from Lochussie School, which was closing. However, with the pupil roll continuing to decline, the Director of Education met with the parents on 27 October 1969 and permission to close Killearnan School was obtained from the Scottish Education Department on 26 December 1969. The pupils were originally designated for transfer to Tore School, but at the request of the parents it was agreed to transfer them to Tarradale. Mrs MacKenzie transferred to Conon School. She had been only the seventh head teacher in the ninety-seven-year history of the Killearnan School.

The kirk session of the parish church offered to take the lease of the school building as a church hall, but had to retract when a congregational meeting did not approve. In June 1970, the County Commissioner of the Northern Counties Girl Guides Association requested a lease to use the building as a training centre during Easter and summer vacations and at weekends. This was approved, and they still maintain the lease today. The adjoining schoolteacher's house was occupied until 1998, but it now lies vacant (Figure 32).

Figure 32: Killearnan (Redcastle) school and schoolhouse (2008)

NOTES

[1] An account of early education in the Highlands, with particular emphasis on Inverness, Black Isle and Easter Ross, is given in two articles by Mackay, W, in 'The Celtic Magazine', Vol 13, pages 360 and 402 (1887).

[2] See Chapter 2, note 16.

[3] Historical records of the SSPCK are held in the NAS series GD95. The 'Register of Schools maintained by the Society in Scotland for Propagating Christian Knowledge' (1710–61) can be viewed on microfilm at NAS GD95/9/1. Notes of inspections of the SSPCK school at Croftnacreich carried out by Patrick Butter can be viewed in 'Journal of a visit to the Schools of the SSPCK' (1824) at NAS GD95/9/3 and in 'Notes of a visit to SSPCK Schools in Inverness and Ross-shire' (1836) at NAS GD95/14/29.

[4] See Chapter 2, note 17.

[5] See Chapter 1, note 108.

[6] See Chapter 2, note 24.

[7] The extract relating to the refurbishment of Killearnan parish school, dated 2 March 1786, is contained in the Kilcoy Estate Papers held at AUSLA MS3470/15/1/61.

[8] See Chapter 1, note 105.

[9] See Chapter 1, note 112.

[10] See Chapter 1, note 120.

[11] See Chapter 2, note 60.

[12] See Chapter 2, note 24.

[13] See note 3.

[14] See Chapter 1, note 105.

[15] 'Moral Statistics of the Highlands and Islands of Scotland' (1826) is held in HCRL 312.094117. Data for Killearnan parish is tabulated on pages 61 and 68. This document was compiled by the Inverness Society for the Education of the Poor in the Highlands. It is prefixed by a report on 'The Past and Present State of Education in the Districts' which provides a history of church education from 1616. An article on the collection of data for the report was published in *The Scotsman* on 17 November 1824.

[16] See Chapter 1, note 132.

[17] The petition from Kilcoy tenants at Tore requesting the establishment of a school in the kitchen of Tore Castle is contained in the Kilcoy Estate Papers held at AUSLA MS3470/15/1/101.

[18] See Chapter 2, note 55.

[19] See Chapter 2, note 50.

[20] The handwritten Killearnan Public School Log Book was completed weekly by the school's head teacher. It covers the period from December 1875 to March 1949 and is held at HCA R27/5/3/21(a).

[21] The Feu Charter issued by Henry James Baillie to the School Board of Killearnan under the Education (Scotland) Act 1872 is available at HCA R27/57(f). A plan of the original school buildings is attached to it.

[22] See Chapter 1, note 144.

[23] See Chapter 1, note 140.

[24] See Chapter 2, note 40.

[25] See Chapter 1, notes 162 and 166.

[26] Articles on the exhibition of the 'Redcastle whale', published in 1932 in the Birmingham Weekly Post, were kindly researched by *Birmingham City Council*, Department of Archives and Heritage Services.

[27] The return made to the 'Endowed Institutions Commission' by James Davidson, headteacher of Killearnan Public School, in March 1879 is held at NAS ED2/9/55. It shows thirty-eight scholars in attendance during the year ending 31 December 1878, and summarises their entries and performances in national stage examinations.

[28] The reference to pupil attendance at the Killearnan Public School is given in Groome, F H (ed), 'Ordnance Gazetteer of Scotland, a Survey of Scottish Topography' Vol IV (1885). Redcastle is briefly described in Vol VI.

[29] See note 20.

[30] An excellent detailed account of the history of Tore School is given in Bain, S, 'Growing for the Future: The Story of Tore School' (2005).

[31] The minutes books of the Ross and Cromarty Education Authority (1919–30) and the Ross and Cromarty Education Committee (1930–72) are held at HCA CRC5/1/1–4 and HCA CRC3/2/1–18.

[32] School inspectors' reports for Killearnan Primary School (1935–55) can be viewed at NAS ED18/2522.

Chapter 4

THE QUARRY

4.1   Inverness Harbour and Other Early Records

Little is known of the early history of the quarry at Redcastle. An article published in the *John o'Groats Journal*[1] claims that the quarry was in existence 'as early as the beginning of the 12th century … for building purposes, as the stone of the Priory of Beauly, Cathedral of Chanonry [in Fortrose] and Monastery of Inverness is said to have been furnished here'. It is marked on Avery's 'Plan of the Murray Firth' of 1725–30, and the Ordnance Survey name book[2] for the first edition (1873) 1:2,500 (*circa* 25 inch:1 mile) map states that a pier at Redcastle 'is supposed to have been partially constructed by Oliver Cromwell and used for shipping stone from quarries in the vicinity'. The stone was probably shipped mainly to Inverness, where it is said that Cromwell's Fort (or Citadel, known locally as 'The Sconce') was built with Redcastle stone in 1653–58. Stone from Beauly priory and Fortrose cathedral, both of which were demolished for the purpose, was also used. This stone may also have originated from Redcastle quarry.

The earliest documentary reference to Redcastle quarry seems to be in the Treasurer's accounts and journal of the Ale Duty Act[3] of 1719. At that time, Inverness Town Council was in considerable debt and needed to raise funds for public works. The Act gave appointed trustees of the Council the right to charge 'a duty of two pennies Scots or one sixth part of a penny Sterling … on each pint of ale or beer that shall be brewed or sold within said Town of Inverness … for 19 years from and after 1 June 1719 … for paying the debts of the said Town and for building a church and making a harbour there'. By 1724, much of the town's debts had been repaid from the proceeds of the duty and work on the new harbour was commenced. It is not specified why the trustees decided to use Redcastle quarry stone for the harbour walls, but in May 1724 the Treasurer's journal records that they purchased from William Calder:

> …a lease which he had of Reid Castle's quarrie and upon the said Calder's decease they found it convenient to take a new lease from Reid Castle himself for the yearly payment of £1-3-4d. The trustees also continued the quarriers

who were employed therein for some time so that the expense of the quarrie with the tack duty to 10 May 1726 is £20-12-11½d.

However, there appears to have been a dispute over payment of the lease. It is recorded in the Treasurer's journal that 'they [the trustees] have been alarmed with a law suit at Reid Castle's instance', and an entry in the Treasurer's accounts, dated 15 August 1727, authorised a transfer (ordered by Baillie John Steuart) of six guineas to their agents to 'support the tack of the quarrie of Redcastle and suspend the horning raised by Redcastle'. This payment seems to have resolved the issue, but not before Alexander and George Stronach, Masons, had been contracted in May 1726 to 'work in the quarrie and deliver at the shore of Reid Castle as many hewn stones as they judged should be wanted at the rate of 3 pence [3d] for the cubical foot'.

Transporting the stone from Redcastle to Inverness was also a problem. According to the trustees, it was 'impossible without providing a proper method of carriage', so they resolved 'to order the build of a lighter [a large barge] which might transport the stone in a safer and cheaper way than was practicable by the common boats of the County'. The lighter was completed by July 1725, and was 'of 35 tons burden at the expense of £207-6-7½d'. However the lighter 'made less progress in carrying the stones from Reid Castle because the shore there was so flat that the vessel could not come near enough to take in her loading except at Spring tides'. It was therefore agreed to 'have a float made by which the lighter could be loaded at any tide for which they were to pay £42'. So that the float could be loaded at the shore, it was also necessary to have a small pier built at Redcastle. It cost £13-8-6d, comprising £4-14-6d for digging the foundations (189 man days at 6d per day) and £8-14/- for building the walls (using 696 cubic yards of stone at 3d per cubic yard).

With the problem of transporting the stone from Redcastle quarry to Inverness solved, the Stronachs commenced the shipping of a large amount of stone to the new harbour. By February 1731, they wanted their account settled, but it appears that the exact amount of stone that they had delivered had not been calculated. Therefore the trustees:

> ...judging it incumbent to account with Alex & Geo Stronach for the stones furnished for the new harbour of every kind and for materials and work done in the quarrie of Redcastle, and having ordered the master of mathematick to sum up and find the cubical contents of the squared stones, and also having sent (with the proper men) the said teacher of mathematick to the quarrie of Red-castle ... the cashier ... found the following credit due to them.

The Treasurer's account book shows a total of £416-15/- due, comprising £380-19-8d for 566 squared stones (29,077 cubic feet at 3d) at the new harbour; £28-6-1d for 1,205 cubic yards at 5d or 6d at Redcastle pier; £7-9-3d for 396 stones (528 cubic feet) at both Redcastle pier and at the new harbour, and requiring squaring at 2d or 3d per stone.

A further payment of £106-0-10d was made to Alex and Geo Stronach in June 1732 for the supply of 1,566 large stones and for the squaring of 775 stones (4,703 cubic feet) from Redcastle. Then, in August 1732, they were paid a balance of £165-2-9d to compensate for 'having made terms which they were not able to fulfill without apparent loss'. This appears to be the last payment made by the trustees for stone supplied by Alex and Geo Stronach, although the tack of £1-3-4d per year for the Redcastle quarry continued to be paid until May 1743. The Treasurer's journal does not indicate when the new harbour was completed, but it refers to the petition to Parliament in July 1738 to renew the Ale Duty Act for a further twenty-five years, one of the purposes being stated as the 'perfecting of the new harbour'. The accounts were closed in November 1763 and show that the total cost of furnishing the stone for the new harbour at Inverness had been £3,194-12-8d.

In 1760, Pococke wrote that 'near Beaulieu Lough [Beauly Firth] I saw free-stone, and some of it mixed with pebbles' which, in an editorial note, is ascribed either to Tarradale or Redcastle quarry.[4] [The term 'free-stone' refers to a fine-grained, even-textured stone that can be cut in any direction without shattering or splintering.] This suggests that Redcastle quarry stone was still being transported for use in Inverness building projects well after the completion of the new harbour.

The first entries in the Killearnan parish church records that infer the existence of the quarry at Redcastle are in the Old Parish Registers[5] of 1746, which name John Ross as a 'mason in Chapelton'. The first record of a mason in Redcastle is in 1756, when Donald Fraser was a witness to the baptism of Charlotte Young, the daughter of one of the castle gardeners. The next entry does not appear until 1784 but, thereafter, records of christenings that state the profession of the father as a mason become much more common. The reason was probably because James Grant, who purchased Redcastle in 1790, undertook substantial repairs to the castle, undoubtedly using stone from Redcastle quarry. Several names of stonemasons appear with regularity, suggesting that they had settled in the area, in particular John Stewart in Shore of Gargustown and John Ross and Alexander MacGillivray in Milntown (or Miltown) of Redcastle.

The Old (First) Statistical Account[6] of 1791–99 refers to the local quarrying of building stone in describing 'a remarkably thick stratum of reddish free-stone, which extends almost due north to the Frith of Dingwall. It is easily hewn and, when properly selected, very eligible for buildings of any description' but, perhaps somewhat surprisingly, it makes no specific mention of the Redcastle quarry, which would have been the only significant industry at the time (other than agriculture) and must have been a major source of local employment. However, the quality of Redcastle stone is noted by Hugh Miller in his book *The Old Red Sandstone*,[7] in which he states that it 'forms, though coarse, an excellent building-stone, which in some of the ruins of the district, presents the marks of the tool as sharply indented as when under the hands of the workman'.

Redcastle quarry is first recorded in the Killearnan parish kirk session minutes[8] of March 1796, when the moderator reported that he had ordered 'a new tent [pulpit] for the quarry'. This referred to the practice in some Highland parishes of holding annual 'communion season' services that attracted large numbers of people (see Chapter 2, pages 157–159). In Killearnan, these were initiated in 1764 and were held in the Redcastle quarry, presumably because it was already sufficiently large to act as an amphitheatre.

4.2   The Caledonian Canal

One of the most significant events to shape the recent history of Redcastle was undoubtedly the decision to construct the Caledonian Canal. Schemes to build a canal to link Inverness to Fort William had been previously proposed – in particular, one published in a pamphlet[9] of 1772 and described by its editor as 'pregnant with national benefit'. It was finally authorised by Parliament in an Act of 1803 and, in that year, Thomas Telford was appointed as Principal Engineer, at a daily rate of three guineas (£3-3/-) plus travelling expenses. William Jessop was subsequently appointed as Consulting Engineer for the project, and Matthew Davidson and John Telford (no relation) were appointed as Resident Engineers.

The First Report of the Canal Commissioners[10] was presented to Parliament in 1804. It records that 'a free-stone quarry has been opened on the north shore of Loch Beauly near to Red-Castle, from which stone may be carried by water for the works at Clachnaharry, and for the locks to be erected near Muirtown'. Appended to this report is a map delineating the intended route of the canal, on which Redcastle quarry is marked. This map was surveyed in 1803 by John Howell, but was based on Roy's 1750 Military Survey of Scotland, which Thomas Telford had been given special dispensation to access in the King's Library.

It is not clear why Telford decided to use Redcastle quarry. Its location close to the shore and the consequent ease of transportation would have been a factor, just as it had been seventy-five years earlier when Inverness Town

Council had built their new harbour using Redcastle stone. As a youth, Telford had worked as a stonemason, so the quality of Redcastle stone may have been known to him. There is also some evidence that, prior to the passing of the 1803 Canal Act, the availability of local stone for such a project had been investigated. In a letter dated 15 August 1821, the famous civil engineer John Rennie[11] refers to a visit he made to Redcastle quarry 'nearly thirty years since' and advises the Commissioners of the Navy that Redcastle is:

> ...situated on the Beauly Firth where the water is deep and the access easy. The quarry lyes near to the shore and is therefore convenient for shipping.

He further describes the stone as being easily:

> ...raised in blocks of any size ... of a reddish colour ... [with] all the appearance of a durable stone ... [and] fit to be inserted in the specifications where such stone is named.

The purpose of Rennie's visit to Redcastle is not recorded, but he was twice commissioned by the British Fishery Society, in 1792 and 1793, to travel to northern Scotland to investigate possible locations for harbours at Wick and Portmahomack. He would have needed to investigate the availability and price of suitable stone for this work.

It is also possible that Charles Grant, a Director of the East India Co. who had become the MP for Inverness-shire in 1802 and was one of the Canal Commissioners, had a hand in the decision to use Redcastle stone for the Caledonian Canal. James Grant of Shewglie, who had purchased Redcastle estate from the MacKenzies in 1790, was Charles' (third) cousin. James was a linguist and diplomat who had also worked in India and would probably have known Charles well.

In the Commissioners' Second Report (1805), Telford writes:

> No less than two thousand tons [of stone] now lie ready for conveyance to Clachnaharry from the free-stone quarry at Redcastle; where a mound of earth from high-water-mark terminated by a stone pier, has been made, together with all necessary accommodations for lodging the workmen, and preserving the waggons and tools. From the Redcastle quarry, free-stone will be conveyed by water carriage to the Clachnaharry basin, from which it is distant less than six miles.

He further states that 'the iron rail-way from the Redcastle free-stone quarry to the pier extends three hundred and sixty yards'. The map which is attached to the report is the earliest map to show the Redcastle pier (Figure 33). The map hugely exaggerates its length – apparently extending almost a kilometre into the Beauly Firth! [Although it is not recorded, the Telford pier was probably an extension of the pier originally built by the Inverness Town Council trustees in 1725.]

Figure 33: Redcastle pier (2008)

Details of the 'necessary accommodations' built for the workers at Redcastle quarry are not provided, other than that the houses were 'timber-framed'. However, in an Appendix to the Second Report, Telford reports that thirty-six workers were employed at the quarry at the end of 1804, these being thirty masons and quarrymen and six labourers, all of whom were employed 'by measure' [paid according to the amount of stone they produced]. By mid-1805, these numbers had reached a high of seventy in total, represented by thirty-three masons and quarrymen, two blacksmiths, twenty-eight labourers (by measure) and seven sailors.

The sailors were required to transport the stone from the Redcastle pier to Clachnaharry. They used two stone-sloops, one of which was called *Caledonia* and could carry fifty tons. They had been built by Samuel Deadman and John Nichol in Inverness at a capital cost of £1,088. Meldrum[12] refers to a pier in Clachnaharry that was built in 1803 to unload the stone ferried from Redcastle quarry. The first batches were used to construct houses in Inverness for the various contractors, some of which still stand in Telford Street.[13] The price that Telford paid for the cut stone from Redcastle quarry is recorded as 1/7d per cubic foot, somewhat more than the maximum of 6d per cubic foot paid for 'squared stones' by the Inverness Town Council in 1725–35. It was 'excellent free-stone, rather hard to work, but very good for the intended purposes, which are quoins for the locks and copings for the locks and bridges'.

The Third Report of the Canal Commissioners (1806) reveals that:

> The quarry at Redcastle continues to produce plenty of free-stone of excellent quality, though with some occasional interruption from the flatness of the shore, and the small rise of the tide, which delays and sometimes prevents the loaded stone-vessels from sailing. This difficulty is intended to be remedied either by extending the pier further into Loch-Beauly, or by cutting to the side of it a deeper channel from the tide-way.

Then, in the Fourth Report (1807), it is stated that:

> The quarry at Redcastle continues to produce good free-stone in undiminished quantity, but the flatness of the shore has rendered the supply rather uncertain, as the stone-vessels were frequently obliged to wait for spring-tides. A remedy for this inconvenience was at first attempted by making a channel from the side of the pier to the tide-way; but experience having proved that it was difficult and expensive to keep this channel clear of mud, Mr Jessop and Mr Telford, in October last, directed the pier to be lengthened, and it has accordingly been extended two hundred yards. This additional part is formed of timber, which may hereafter be removed and applied to other purposes, when the rubbish from the quarry shall have been brought down and deposited in sufficient quantity to form a less expensive road for the stone wagons.

The delays were obviously serious, as the numbers employed at Redcastle quarry at the end of 1806 had dropped. However, by the time the extension to the pier was complete in mid-1807, numbers employed had again increased – a typical monthly total being around forty, comprising one overseer, twelve masons and quarrymen, seven carpenters, one blacksmith, ten labourers (by measure), two labourers (by day) and seven sailors.

The extension to Redcastle pier seemed to progress without a hitch. In the 5th Report (1808), Telford writes:

> The quarry at Redcastle has been uncovered to a considerable extent, and the rubbish obtained in this operation having been conveyed down by means of the wooden causeway, mentioned in our last report, has served for the formation of a bank and of a road upon it for the stone-waggons, extending from high-water-mark into the sea, almost three hundred yards; and a double object has thus been obtained, the stone being more conveniently quarried, and also sent to Clachnaharry more regularly on board the stone sloops, without waiting, as

heretofore, for the opportunity of spring tides. The timber which formed the temporary causeway has been returned into store at Clachnaharry.

In the Sixth Report (1809), the cost of building Redcastle pier is stated as £1,095, including about £500 for 'carpenters work and other labour'.

It is at this time that the first record of the hamlet of 'Quarry of Redcastle' appears in the records of the Killearnan parish church. On 29 May 1808, it is recorded in the Old Parish Registers[14] that 'Mr Robert Arthur [the minister of Resolis parish, the post at Killearnan being vacant at that time] baptised Fanny, daughter to John Forsyth, mason at the Quarry of Redcastle and his spouse Christina Forbes in the presence of Angus Urquhart of Milntown and Robert Forsyth brother to the parent of the child born 23 May.' John Forsyth would presumably have been one of the masons attracted to the area by the work available in producing the stone for the Caledonian Canal, and may have lived in the original on-site accommodation provided by Thomas Telford. (Interestingly, Fanny Forsyth also seems to hold the distinction of being the first person in the Killearnan marriage records with an address recorded as 'Quarry of Redcastle'. Her marriage to Donald Leitch, a square-wright [furniture maker], is recorded in the Old Parish Registers for March 1828.)

A further problem for Thomas Telford was arising at Redcastle. James Grant died in October 1808 and was succeeded by his cousin Lieut-Col Alexander Grant. It transpired that James had permitted Telford use of the quarry without confirming the rent. In 1807, James had 'expressed a desire to have the rent determined, and a settlement made for the time since getting of the stone commenced', and it had been mutually agreed that George Brown of Elgin would make the valuation. In 1809, Telford wrote to Alexander Grant requesting his acceptance of Brown's valuation,[15] but it is noted in the Sixth Report (1809) that 'owing to the severe indisposition of Mr George Brown' no progress had been made.

In the Seventh Report (1810), Telford writes:

The quarry rent at Redcastle, which we have so long attempted to settle without success, is at length come into dispute with the heir of the late Mr [James] Grant of Redcastle; for the present we shall forbear from stating the demand which has been made on that account; it will be sufficient to say, that on our part we have offered him a liberal rent, or if it is more acceptable to the proprietor, we are willing to pay him in the same manner and at the same rate as we pay for permission to quarry free-stone at Cumbraes in the Firth of Clyde.

Then, in the Eighth Report (1811), it is noted that Lieut-Col Alexander Grant of Redcastle 'has thought proper to reject our offers of payment for the use of his quarry and has taken the decision into the Court of Session, where it remains for decision'.

A fatal accident occurred at the quarry in November 1809. It is not mentioned in the Canal Commissioners' Reports but is headlined as a 'Melancholy Accident' in the *Inverness Journal*[16] of 17 November 1809. In the description, it is stated that 'as several quarrymen were at work, the ground above gave way, and one of them was unfortunately smothered to death before relief could be afforded. Two others, we are sorry to say, have been very much hurt'. Surprisingly, the names of the deceased and injured persons are not given.

Subsequent reports of the Canal Commissioners show that stone from Redcastle quarry was used throughout the period 1812–22. On average, this necessitated a quarry workforce of around twenty-five to thirty, made up of an overseer, up to twelve quarriers and masons, a blacksmith and up to sixteen labourers (by measure). However, the workforce increased at times when stone was required for special purposes. For example, in 1812 it is stated that 'the regulation lock by which the canal will be connected with the varying height of water at Loch Ness … will be faced with free-stone from Redcastle quarry in like manner as the other six locks already built at this end of the canal'. This raised the quarry workforce to forty-four in 1813, and it is reported in 1815 'that the quarry at Redcastle is still in use for furnishing the hollow quoins for the half-cylinders in which the posts of the lock gates will be made to turn'. Redcastle stone was also used 'for constructing the culvert along the western side of the Clachnaharry lock and basin'.

In 1818, the Fifteenth Report states that 'the quarry at Redcastle has been worked from March to July last in order to procure stones for the hollow quoins, square quoins, segment stones and pavement for the lower recesses of the lower lock at Fort Augustus' (Figure 34). Extra stone continued to be taken in 1820, when 'at Redcastle quarry … free-stone has been procured in large quantities for the inverts of the Fort Augustus locks'. This raised the quarry workforce to fifty-four in 1820. Finally, in 1822, Redcastle stone was used for 'the hollow quoins, square quoins, and some other principal stones for the regulating lock at Aberchalder'. This could not have been a large amount of stone, as the workforce at the quarry had by then dropped to a fairly stable fifteen, comprising six quarriers and masons and nine labourers.

From 1818, the north-eastern section of the canal was opened during the summer months, and Redcastle quarry stone was transported through Loch Ness to Fort Augustus and Aberchalder using a stone-sloop and barge that had been repaired, at a cost of £272, in 1811. However, these vessels had been built of 'country timber' and by 1815 they had to be scrapped and replaced with an oak sloop (also called *Caledonia*), which had been built in England and had been used to convey stone from the Cumbrae quarry to build the locks at Corpach in the south-western section of the canal.

Figure 34: Redcastle quarry stone lining the Caledonian Canal locks at Fort Augustus

The question of the rent for the use of Redcastle quarry was finally settled in 1818. The Fifteenth Report of the Commissioners states that 'the legal proceedings and subsequent arbitration which hitherto have prevented us from arriving at a settlement of the sum due by us to Mr Grant of Redcastle, for use of his quarry at that place, have at length been brought to termination, and we are not aware of any obstacle which prevents immediate payment of the amount'. The accounts for 1819 show a payment of £3,000 to Patrick Grant, the eldest son and heir of Lieut-Col Alexander Grant, who had died in 1816.

The sum of £3,000 was an interim payment based on an arbitration[17] by Sheriff Tytler in May 1818. He had based this assessment on the amount of stone taken from the quarry during 1805–16:

- 3d per cubic foot for 'principal cut Ashlar' (94,830 ft^3).
- 2d per cubic foot for 'inferior cut stone' (96,909 ft^3).
- 1d per cubic foot for 'rubble Ashlar' (154,467 ft^3).
- 4d per cubic yard for 'common rubble' (7,043 yd^3).
- ½d per cubic yard for 'mould stones' (12,671 yd^3).

Exclusive of interest, the total amount due by the Commissioners was calculated to be £2,925-13/-, which had risen to £3,215-11-11½ by Christmas 1818.

The arbitration also laid down the terms by which the Commissioners were to leave the quarry when it was no longer required. These included requirements: to pay for any cut, but unused, stone; carry out the removal of all railways, machinery and rubble; and agree with the proprietor of Redcastle (and the Sheriff-Depute of Ross-shire) whether buildings would be taken down or purchased by Redcastle.

The Caledonian Canal was ceremonially opened in 1822 with a two-day 'sail-through' by local dignitaries and landowners, accompanied, according to a surprisingly short report given in the *Inverness Courier* of 24 October 1822, 'amidst the loud and enthusiastic cheerings of a great concourse of people, and the firing of cannon'. At Drumnadrochit, the voyagers 'were joined by Mr [Patrick] Grant of Redcastle', and on reaching Fort William 'a plentiful supply of whisky … did not in the least dampen the ardour'. Thereafter, some stone from Redcastle quarry was used for repairing the locks and basin at Muirton, but the last entry in the Canal Commissioners' Reports of any payment to Patrick Grant for quarried stone was for £10 in 1825.

4.3   Redcastle Quarry Plan (1815)

Apart from the maps that were appended to some of the Caledonian Canal Commissioners' reports, Telford commissioned a map of the Beauly and Moray Firths to show sea access to the canal.[18] This map, dated 1820, also marks the 'Free-stone Quarry at Redcastle', and clearly shows one building close to the quarry and two rows of houses at Milton of Redcastle. This suggests that by 1820 the estate village of Milton of Redcastle had been established at its present-day location, but that the row of houses constituting the hamlet of Quarry of Redcastle had not yet been built.

Another map is of particular interest. It is a remarkably detailed 40 foot:1 inch plan[19] of Redcastle quarry, drawn up on 4 October 1815 in anticipation of the quarry operations being offered for let. It shows two cranes located at the ends of two spurs of the railway that ran out along the pier. Also clearly marked are four buildings. The largest is an L-shaped building with a 'small garden' at the eastern end of the quarry. It consists of two parts, one described as a 'blacksmith's shop' and the other as 'lodgings for overseer and workmen'. Another smaller building at the western end is described as a 'dwelling house for workmen'. Also shown are two 'mason's sheds', one close to the railway, the other towards the north-west in a part of the quarry described as 'Sale Quarry'. Presumably these four buildings were the 'necessary accommodations for lodging the workmen, and preserving the waggons and tools' that had been built by Thomas Telford *circa* 1803 to lodge the quarry workers during the construction of the Caledonian Canal, and hence would have housed the first inhabitants of the embryonic hamlet of Quarry of Redcastle.

A drawing of a vertical section of the quarry face shows that there were three layers of rock. The top layer was *circa* four metres deep and comprised 'hard mountain clay mixed with stones'; the middle layer was *circa* four and a half metres deep and was described as 'useless rock'; and the bottom layer was *circa* five metres deep and contained the 'rock quarried for the canal'. The height of the quarry face in 1815 was therefore only *circa* thirteen and a half metres high, about two-thirds of its present height. The bottom of the quarry was about two metres below high water mark. Presumably, the Redcastle pier (Figure 33, page 239) was constructed from the 'useless rock' of the second layer.

A further feature of the 1815 quarry plan is of interest. At a point opposite where Quarry Cottage is now located, there is marked an 'irregular mound of quarry rubbish as a loading place for Sale Quarry'. This suggests that this may have been the location of the pier supposedly used (or built) by invading Cromwellian forces during their successful attack on Redcastle during 1649. It also suggests that 'Sale Quarry' was the original quarry which would have provided the stone for the construction of the new Inverness harbour in 1725–35. The pier built to transport this stone to Inverness by sea seems likely to have been a little to the east of the 'irregular mound', and was extended by Thomas Telford during his eastward expansion of the quarry to extract stone for the Caledonian Canal.

4.4   Quarry Stone for Sale

By the time of the death of Alexander Grant in 1816, the bulk of the stone necessary for the construction of the Caledonian Canal had been removed from Redcastle quarry, and Patrick Grant decided to let it, rather than continue to work it as an estate business. An advertisement headed, 'To Let, for such a number of years as may be agreed upon, the Free-stone Quarry at Redcastle' was placed in the *Inverness Journal* on 22 November 1816. It continued:

> It is unnecessary to say more of the superior nature of this stone, than that it has been chosen for constructing the mason work of the locks of the Caledonian Canal; and the Contractors of several Public Works in London have been corresponding with a view to obtain supplies from this quarry. Apply to the Proprietor at Redcastle or John Edwards, solicitor, Inverness.

Whether there was a successful applicant is not known, but further advertisements for contractors were again placed in April 1824 and in June 1826. The latter advertisement for the sale of building stone from the quarry stated the seller as Patrick Grant, the proprietor. A later sasine abridgement[20] of 1862 – in which Col Hugh Baillie gave James Hogg a tack of 'an area of ground with dwelling house thereon in Milntown Quarry' for ninety-nine years from 1837 – suggests that no lessee of the quarry was found until 1837, when the Redcastle estate was put up for sale after the death of Sir William Fettes. Failure to find a contractor to operate the quarry did not prevent the continued quarrying and selling of stone, as evidenced by two documents.

The first refers to an incident in March 1824, when five men were drowned after leaving Redcastle with stone from the quarry. The *Inverness Journal* of 26 March 1824 headlined its report 'Melancholy Occurrence' and described how the boat, ferrying stone for a house being built by Hugh Fraser, a blacksmith in Clachnaharry, was overloaded and 'became swamped on her return from the quarry and sunk at a distance of about 300 yards from the Redcastle pier'. A man and a boy in another boat nearby had tried to rescue the men but had been unable to get to them. The blacksmith was found clinging to his sail but did not recover, and the bodies of the others were found as the tide receded. The five men left four widows, fourteen children and several elderly dependents.

This seems not to have been the only occasion when a boat laden with quarry stone became stranded in the Beauly Firth. In his account of his visit in 1908 to Carn Dubh in the centre of the Firth, Rev. Blundell[21] ascribes the existence of angular stones on the cairn (easily distinguishable from the round stones of which the cairn is built) to boats carrying quarry stones having gone aground and discharging some of their cargo in order to get afloat again.

The second document describing a private sale of Redcastle quarry stone is a letter sent in 1826 by Donald Fraser, a boatman from Redcastle, to his brother, Peter, in Inverness.[22] Donald was getting married and was building a house in Redcastle. He had already paid for 'forty trees for deals [flooring and roof timbers]', and wrote an impassioned plea to borrow money 'to pay to the masons next week'. He adds: 'I don't know what I will doo [sic] about scleats [slates] for the house if I would have money to by [sic] them I would put them on but we have no money as you no [sic] brother but mind that yourself be west at Mertinmas'. It is not recorded whether Peter was forthcoming with the money, but the letter is illuminating in showing that a boatman in the early nineteenth century could write understandable (if quaintly spelled) English, and was financially capable (with help) of building a stone and slated house. The Killearnan Old Parish Registers contain a record of a marriage of Donald Fraser of Spital Shore to Margaret Cameron of Kilmorack on 25 January 1828. However, they do not seem to be recorded in Killearnan in any national census, so it is not possible to determine where the house was located or whether it was ever completed.

Another map that shows the extent of the quarry in the years after the construction of the Caledonian Canal is the Redcastle estate map[23] (Figure 8, page 75) drawn up by Patrick Grant's trustees in 1825. It shows that although Thomas Telford had extracted a great deal of stone for the canal, the face of the quarry had not yet reached the road between Milton of Redcastle and Killearnan parish church (where it is today), so a strip of the glebe belonging to Killearnan manse remained between the quarry face and the road. The plan also shows only two buildings in the area known as 'Quarry of Redcastle'. One is the L-shaped 'blacksmith's shop and lodgings for overseer and workmen' near the eastern edge of the quarry; the other is at the location of the house now known as Pier Cottage. It seems probable, therefore, that this was the original house in Quarry of Redcastle, pre-dating Quarry Cottage and Quarry House.

The Killearnan chapter of the New (Second) Statistical Account of Scotland[24] was written by Rev. John Kennedy in 1837–38. It plagiarises from the Old (First) Statistical Account[25] in making reference to the 'reddish free-stone (old red sandstone) easily dressed, and when well selected, very eligible for buildings of any description', but continues with the statement:

> A quarry of this free-stone has been worked for hundreds of years. Inverness has been supplied from it; the locks of the Caledonian Canal were built with stones taken from it. Other smaller quarries have been opened up, of late years, in several districts of the parish, of the same colour and quality, for the purpose of building farm-houses, farm-squares, etc.

Mowat[26] also reports that in the mid-nineteenth century 'there was a fairly steady demand for stone for building and dyking. In addition, quarries in Avoch, Cromarty and Killearnan supplied materials for major projects, eg Fort George and the Caledonian Canal, and on a more long-term basis, provided Inverness with most of its building material'. This is reflected in the 1841 census, which records seven quarriers living in Quarry of Redcastle, all living in the same house, suggesting that this house was a hostel for quarry workers. What is not clear is whether this house was the house now known as Pier Cottage, or the L-shaped house that had been built to accommodate the quarry workers during the construction of the Caledonian Canal in 1803–22. The latter is shown on all three early nineteenth-century maps of the area,[27] and part of it was originally the residence of the 'quarry overseer'. It is a commonly held belief that the house now known as Quarry House was the quarry manager's house. However, if Quarry House was built for that purpose, it was a temporary measure because by 1841 it was occupied by an assortment of sixteen people, including a tailor and his wife, an agricultural worker and his family, five carpenters and various elderly widows.

Almost from the day of its completion in 1822, the banks and walls of the Caledonian Canal suffered damage due to flooding after heavy rain and collapses due to defective workmanship, especially at the western end, where the quality of the stonework had proven to be less than satisfactory. In his book on the history of the canal, Cameron[28] quotes George May, the canal engineer, who had been requested in 1837 to submit a report on the problems to the Canal Commissioners. Mr May was less than complimentary in his report when he stated:

> Had this great work been completed in the manner [originally] proposed, or had the execution of its details at all corresponded to the magnitude and excellence of its design, it would undoubtedly have formed one of the noblest monuments on record of national skill, enterprise and magnificence … the masonry of the whole structure, judged with reference to the purposes for which it is intended, I cannot characterise by any other term than that of execrable; a worse piece of masonry than the Banavie and Corpach locks exhibit is not to be found in connection with any public work in the kingdom.

The Canal Commissioners were initially undecided whether to make the necessary repairs (the estimated cost of which was £144,000) or abandon the whole project (the economic benefits of which had always been considered doubtful). A decision to reconstruct was finally reached in 1843 and the canal was closed for three years before it reopened, without ceremony, on 1 May 1847. The stone for a great deal of the renovation work came from Redcastle quarry. Cameron states that the whole section of the canal from Banavie to Gairlochy was refaced, and 'more spectacular was the rebuilding of the aqueducts … and the construction of the new lock at Gairlochy, where Redcastle free-stone was used, as in Telford's locks from Clachnaharry to Fort Augustus'. Also, the canal was widened above Fort Augustus, where the locks 'had to be stripped down and rebuilt with Redcastle or Tarradale stone' (Figure 34, page 243).

The quantity of stone that was removed from Redcastle quarry for this work is documented in the surviving *Ashlar Book*[29] for 1844. This remarkable book documents the dimensions of every stone that was loaded on to ships at Redcastle pier, as well as the number of stones loaded, the date of shipment and the name of the ship. Sometimes, the destination of the ship and the name of its captain are also recorded. In the course of the year, over 2,500 stones, each of approximately 10 ft^3 (that is, of approximate dimensions 3 ft x 2 ft x 1.5 ft) were loaded in batches of thirty to sixty. The various ships (with their captains, where recorded) included: *The Alfred*; *The Swan* (Captain Lusk); *The John of Paisley*; *The Isabella* (Captain Crawford); *The*

Diana (Captain Gordon); *The Inverness* (Captain Tait); *The Jean Arrat* (Captain MacDonald); *The Jenny Yates*; *The Ann Liza*; *The Industry*; *The Jannet* (Captain McGregor); *The Elizabeth*; and *The Lewes*. The recorded destinations show that the stones were dispatched for the western end of the canal at Fort Augustus, Aberchaldler, Gairlochy and the Sea Lock (at Banavie). Occasionally, it is noted that the ships also carried other materials, for example, timber, rubble and flagstones.

As a consequence of the volume of stone taken from the quarry during this period, the quarry face was cut back to the road that links Milton of Redcastle to Killearnan parish church, thus removing the strip of the manse glebe that is shown on Patrick Grant's 1825 estate map[30] (Figure 8, page 75). In effect, this also heralded the end of centuries of quarrying at Redcastle, as little stone seems to have been extracted after this time (Figure 35).

Figure 35: Redcastle quarry (2008)

The Valuation Rolls[31] for 1855–59 do not list Redcastle quarry. However, it is included in the 1860–61 Roll, its value being recorded as £50 and its 'occupier' being John Hendrie (presumably the manager employed by James Hogg, who held the lease). By that time, activity in Redcastle quarry was declining, although it was still productive and seven quarriers are recorded in the 1861 census residing in Quarry of Redcastle. Presumably, some of these were working at other quarries, particularly Tarradale. Donald MacDonald, who lived at Whitewells Farm near

Tarradale, is recorded in the 1861 census as a quarrier employing eighty men and two boys. This number of quarry workers reflects the number who were employed at Redcastle quarry at the height of its production during the building of the Caledonian Canal, and suggests that, as Redcastle quarry was becoming worked out, Tarradale quarry was being opened up to provide stone for the continuing repairs to the canal and other local building projects.

A freak fatal accident occurred in Redcastle quarry in 1862. According to the *Inverness Advertiser* of 29 July, 'it appears that when raising some stones, the jib of the cran fell, striking John Dingwall on the head and back, from which he received such injuries that he expired'. John Dingwall was only twenty years old. He is recorded in the 1861 census as a quarry labourer living with his parents in Prescaultin, the cottage beside Blairdhu farmhouse.

In 1865, the quarry is recorded in the Valuation Rolls as 'vacant', and it seems not to have produced stone (at least in commercial quantities) ever since. Although there seems to be no formal record of the event, closure appears to have occurred in 1874, as the Valuation Rolls for 1875–76 and the ensuing years describe it as 'unworked'. The first edition 1:2,500 (*circa* 25 inch:1 mile) Ordnance Survey map, surveyed in 1872, shows trees in Redcastle quarry, suggesting that it had not been worked for some years prior.

4.5   The Third Statistical Account of Scotland

The Third Statistical Account of Scotland[32] was launched in 1946 by some of the Scottish universities, and was subsequently published under the aegis of the Scottish Council for Community and Voluntary Organisations. The Ross and Cromarty volume was seriously delayed through lack of chapters from some of the parishes, but interest was revived in 1982. Where they existed, original descriptions were retained and enhanced by addition of brief postscripts prior to publication. The Killearnan chapter had been originally written by Rev. George Ballingall in September 1954, and the postscript was added by D P Willis in 1982 before publication in 1987. It refers to the Redcastle quarry and its pier as follows:

Near the Beauly Firth and about 150 yards east of the Parish Church is the Quarry of Redcastle which ceased operations over 80 years ago. This produced a fine red sandstone which was formerly much used in building, the ramparts of Fort George and the locks of the Caledonian Canal being two examples. From a stone pier about 500 yards long, which had a narrow gauge railway, the stone was loaded on to ships. The pier is now broken in places. About 50 years ago it was customary for volunteers to hold a shooting competition at the pier on New Year's Day. In pre-Disruption days great assemblies were wont to gather in Redcastle quarry for communion. Rev. John Kennedy of Dingwall stated that at one gathering ten thousand were present.

*Figure 36: Aerial view of Quarry of Redcastle (*circa *1995) with Redcastle quarry behind (reproduced from an original by permission of Philip Hodges)*

The size of the communion audience is not substantiated by any factual evidence (Chapter 2, page 157) and the reference to Fort George, although a commonly held belief, is at best confused.

What seems more likely is that some Redcastle quarry stone was used by Cromwell's forces in the construction of the Citadel in Inverness after they had recaptured the town in 1649. They seem to have used (or possibly they built) a landing site near the quarry whilst sacking Redcastle in 1649, and would therefore have been aware of the excellent quality of its stone. The Citadel was destroyed in 1662 after the restoration of the monarchy. The clocktower which now stands near Inverness harbour (and was, at one time, also a windmill) is mainly a modern reconstruction, but its lower courses are thought to be from the original Citadel and therefore are probably built of Redcastle stone. Clearly, stone would have been recycled for other building works within the town, including repairs to Inverness Castle, which had also suffered damage during the various sieges in the 1640s. Inverness Castle was renamed Fort George in 1727 in honour of George I, but it was destroyed (possibly accidentally) by the Jacobites in 1746 just before the Battle of

Culloden.[33] The 'new' Fort George at Ardersier was built by George II in 1748–69 as an impregnable barracks for government troops stationed there to quell any future Jacobite rebellion.

Most of the stone used in the construction of the new Fort George was shipped from the Bennetsfield quarry at Munlochy, but it is likely that some other Black Isle quarries also provided small amounts. The building used 27,480 cubic feet of free-stone, purchased at 1/3d per cubic foot. This can be compared with 1/7d per cubic foot paid by Thomas Telford in building the Caledonian Canal fifty years later. It is said that the ruins of the old Inverness Castle were used as a 'quarry' for many buildings in Inverness before 1836, when the new Inverness Castle (actually law courts) was built using Tarradale stone. The designer was William Burn, who was also responsible for architectural work at Redcastle during the 1840s (Figure 11, page 86). Thus, there is probably some truth in the assertion that Redcastle quarry stone was used to build Inverness Castle and Fort George – but not the castle and fort that we see today!

There is a further interesting reference in the Third Statistical Account to Redcastle pier in relation to the food that was eaten by the people of the parish at the turn of the century. Rev. Ballingall states that 'the place herring took in the diet of the people was indicated by the number of crofters' carts brought to the pier at Redcastle quarry when the word went round that the fishing boats were in the Firth and would be landing fish'. What he did not relate was that the residents of Redcastle were still catching flounders in 'private' fish yairs in the 1950s!

Today, trees conceal the extent of the quarry, which – together with the remains of the pier – must rank as one of the largest industrial heritage sites in the Highlands. Unfortunately, some domestic refuse has been dumped into the quarry from the road above, including the shells of a Morris Minor and a Hillman Minx. The latter is alleged to have belonged to a Redcastle local.

NOTES

[1] See Chapter 1, note 135.

[2] Explanations of the origins and meanings of names used on the first series 1:2,500 (*circa* 25 inch:1 mile) Ordnance Survey maps (sheets 88, 89, 99 and 100) are given in the 'Ordnance Survey Original Object Name Book, Parish of Killearnan' (1873) available at HCA CRC4/2/1–87. The explanations are based on information supplied by educated local people such as the school teacher, minister and parish registrar.

[3] The Treasurer's accounts and journal of the income and expenditure associated with the various public works undertaken in Inverness by the Trustees of the Ale Duty Act (1719) are held at HCA IB2/2/1–2.

[4] The export by sea of Redcastle (or Tarradale) quarry stone is described in Kemp, D W (ed), 'Tours in Scotland by Richard Pococke, Bishop of Meath', Letter XXI (1760) in Pub. Scot. Hist. Soc., Vol I, page 110 (1887).

[5] See Chapter 2, note 25.

[6] See Chapter 1, note 105.

[7] The reference to the excellence of the building stone from Redcastle quarry is from Miller, H, 'The Old Red Sandstone', page 204 (1877 edition).

[8] See Chapter 2, note 24.

[9] The article proposing a canal between Inverness and Fort William was published in 'The British Magazine and General Review', January 1772. The writer is identified only as 'P'.

[10] Detailed accounts of the construction of the Caledonian Canal are to be found in the annual 'Reports of the Caledonian Canal Commissioners' at NAS BR/CCL/1/3–4. Many have maps annexed, for example, the 'Plan of the Friths of Beauly and Inverness' commissioned by Messrs Telford and Downie (1820).

[11] Some papers of John Rennie (snr) are lodged in the Library of the Institution of Civil Engineers; others are held at NLS. The letter of 15 August 1821 to the Navy Commissioners and referring to Redcastle quarry stone is ICE REN/RB/12/182. I am indebted to Peter Cross-Rudkin for information on the purpose of Rennie's visit to Redcastle in 1792–93.

[12] A reference to the unloading of stone from Redcastle quarry at Clachnaharry pier in 1803 is described in Meldrum, E, 'Inverness: Local History and Archaeology Guidebook No. 4', page 50 (1982).

[13] The building of houses in Telford Street, Inverness using Redcastle quarry stone is given in 'The Hub of the Highlands; The Book of Inverness and District', Inverness Field Club Centenary Volume, page 181 (1875–1975).

[14] See Chapter 2, note 25.

[15] The letter sent in 1809 from Thomas Telford to James Grant regarding the rent of Redcastle quarry is available at NAS GD23/6/424.

[16] See Chapter 1, note 120.

[17] The terms of the arbitration on the rent due to Patrick Grant for the use of the Redcastle quarry during construction of the Caledonian Canal are contained in a series of letters from the Clerk of the Canal Commissioners to Patrick Grant's agent. They are held in the Parliamentary Archives in the papers of the Scottish Commissions for Bridges and Highways: SC/1/5/603; SC/1/6/754, 763, 765, 782, 787 and 796; and SC/1/7/809. There is a searchable catalogue at www.portcullis.parliament.uk.

[18] See note 10.

[19] The hand-drawn 40 foot:1 inch map of Redcastle quarry, dated 4 October 1815 and entitled 'Plan and Sections of Redcastle Quarry', is held at HCA D/172/361.

[20] See Chapter 1, note 144.

[21] See Chapter 1, note 6.

[22] A transcript of the letter, dated 5 November 1826, to Peter Fraser from his brother Donald Fraser, a boatman in Redcastle, was provided to the author in a private communication from Dr Jenny Fyfe of Fortrose.

[23] See Chapter 1, note 125.

[24] See Chapter 1, note 132.

[25] See Chapter 1, note 105.

[26] See Chapter 1, note 106.

[27] See note 18, and Chapter 1, notes 125 and 128.

[28] An account of the use of Redcastle quarry stone for repairs to the Caledonian Canal during 1843–47 is given in Cameron, A D, 'The Caledonian Canal', Chapter 11, pages 107–116 (1983).

[29] The Redcastle quarry Ashlar Book (1844), which lists the quantities of stone taken from the quarry and shipped to the Caledonian Canal reconstruction sites, is held at NAS SC25/71/1.

[30] See Chapter 1, note 125.

[31] The original Valuation Rolls for Ross and Cromarty (1855–67) are available in manuscript format at NAS VR115/2. From 1868 onwards, the Valuation Rolls for Ross and Cromarty were printed annually and are available at HCA CR4/2. Valuation Rolls for domestic properties were discontinued after 1989 as a consequence of the introduction of the Community Charge (poll tax) in 1990. [See also Chapter 1, note 40 – 'Valuation Roll of the Sheriffdom of Inverness, including Ross' (1644).]

[32] See Chapter 1, note 167.

[33] The histories of Inverness Castle and Fort George are documented in many sources. Two useful websites containing brief accounts are www.historic-scotland.gov.uk and http://en.wikipedia.org. The estimate drawn up by William Skinner (Director of HM Engineers) in 1752 for the building of Fort George is held at TNA PC1/4518.

Chapter 5

CIVIL ADMINISTRATION

5.1 Early Taxation

In medieval Scotland, all land belonged to the King. Nobles and other land-owners who were granted occupation of castles were required to pay taxes to the King's agents. The earliest record of the land tax due from an occupant of Redcastle is from 1278, when Andro de Bosco was required to pay two merks per annum to the monks of Beauly Priory.[1] In 1455, when Redcastle became a royal property annexed to the Crown, the rental income from the castle and its land payable to James II was recorded in the Exchequer Rolls of Scotland.[2] Initially, this was set at £26-13-4d Scots per year, of which Gillespie of the Isles, the brother of the Earl of Moray, was entitled to retain one half (£13-6-8d Scots) as his fee for acting as its keeper. The Exchequer Rolls also provide accounts of the whole rental income from Eddirdule and the Ardmeanach. For example, from 1473 to 1478 the total amount paid to Arthur Forbes, the king's receiver, was £832-19-6d Scots (less £264-13/- expenses) which included Hiltoun (£30), Gargustoun (£30), Newtoune (£53½) and Culcowy (£39).

By 1523, the Redcastle rental income payable to James V by the Earl of Moray had risen to £30 Scots, and when Ruairidh Mor Mackenzie (1st of Redcastle) was granted Redcastle in the late sixteenth century, the estate was 'set in feu-ferme' for £100 Scots per year. By the late sixteenth century, the Earl of Ross had become responsible to the monarch for the collection of land tax in the Ardmeanach. A surviving charter of *circa* 1591, described by Bain,[3] lists details of rents due from estates in Easter Ross. It is entitled 'Rental of the hail Fermes [farms], Maills [crofts] and Kanes [portions of produce payable as rent] within the Earldom of Ross and Lordship of Armeanach, assignit to the Queen's Matie in compensation'. The Queen in question was Anne of Denmark, who married James VI in November 1590. In recognition of her role as 'the kingis darest bedfellowis', she was given the revenues of the Earldom of Ross, payable in both cash and kind. The list includes: Gargasoun (Garguston) – £10-5/- Scots, eight bolls and two firlots of beir, one sheep, one cow and eight poultry; Newton – £18 Scots, two chalders and two bolls of beir and meal, two cows, two sheep and one poultry; Hilltown – £9-13-7d Scots, one chalder and one boll of beir, one cow, one sheep and eight poultry; and

Milne of Redcastle – £1-6-8d Scots, two chalders and two bolls of beir, two cows and two sheep. It is also noteworthy that the rental of the Kessock Ferry, the rights of which had been given to Ruairidh Mor Mackenzie (1st of Redcastle) in 1589, was £8-4/- Scots.

The earliest record[4] of the 'Valuation Roll of the Sheriffdom of Inverness, including Ross' dates from 1644 and lists Redcastle estate, owned by Rorie MacKenzie (3rd of Redcastle), as having a rental income of £714-13-4d Scots and a 'valued rent' assessment of £193-6-8d. Rental receipts were higher than the assessed valuations, because landowners were permitted to offset repairs and other permitted expenses against the assessment of their valued rent. When the Redcastle estate was erected to a barony in 1680, the amounts payable were set out in a complex *reddendo* attached to the writ.[5] [A *reddendo* is a legal clause in which the services or payments to be given to a superior are specified.] It details the yearly rentals, bondages [payments in lieu of services] and grassums [rent renewal fees] payable to the Crown in respect of each part of the Barony, which comprised eleven parts:

- Town and lands of Newtown of Redcastle.
- Alehouse of Newtown of Redcastle.
- Smiddy Croft of Newtown of Redcastle.
- Milns of Redcastle.
- Lands of Hilltown of Redcastle.
- Town and lands of Gargistown.
- Town and lands of Easter Kessack.
- Frith and ferry of Kessack.
- Fishings at the Stell of Kessack.
- Alehouse of Kessack; lands of Ardafallie.

The total rental was broken down into three components. Firstly, 'all other duties, grassums and services in use to be paid for the said lands, alehouses, milns, tofts, crofts, ferry, fishings, and others specified in old rentals'. Secondly, additional rentals pertaining to each part of the Barony, which amounted to: £61-17/- Scots; two chalders, twenty-six bolls and two firlots of victual; ten sheep; four goats; four dozen poultry; and eighty loads of 'fewel' [presumably wood]. Thirdly, some miscellaneous payments, such as £4-6-8d Scots of 'old rental', plus an augmentation of £1-6-8d Scots yearly for the Barony of Delny (part of which was amalgamated into Redcastle) and £117 Scots to be paid in the first year of every new heir to the Barony.

Other taxes were introduced from time to time. For example, to raise money to fund arrears in army pay and to refund money that had been advanced to the Crown by the Shires and Burghs, the Scottish Parliament in 1690 levied a one-off tax of fourteen shillings Scots on every hearth in the country. The only exemptions were paupers (who were unlikely to have a hearth anyway) and hospitals. Collectors were appointed to make up lists of hearths in their area, the Earl of Cromartie being responsible in Ross-shire. A 'hearth' was defined as a stone-lined fireplace used for cooking or heating, the smoke from which was extracted through a chimney. This, therefore, excluded most of the rural population, who at the time lived in houses with turf walls and heather-thatched roofs, through which the smoke of their peat fires permeated.

The Treasury had great difficulty in collecting the hearth tax, and it was reported in an audit carried out in 1701 that no hearth book had been submitted for Ross-shire. However, a separate list for 'Cilernan' parish had been submitted around 1692, together with some lists relating to other parishes in Easter Ross.[6] It is written in Old Scots and shows that the tax was payable on only fifty-nine hearths, of which sixteen were on the 'Cilcowi' [Kilcoy] estate and forty-three on the 'Reedcastle' estate. The castles themselves accounted for eight and nine hearths respectively, the two owners not being named but entered as 'Himself'. No other entry on the list exceeds two hearths and most are for one hearth. Most of the hamlets had a few hearthed houses, for example: Newtown is listed with five hearths; Blairdow, Hiltown, Garguston and Spital with three each; Chapeltown and Burntown with two each; and Corgrain with one. Strangely, Miltown (of Redcastle) is not listed, suggesting that it may not have existed as a distinct hamlet of that name in the seventeenth century. Many of the names of individuals are not discernable in the hearth tax document for Killearnan, but some of the surnames include Glass, MacAndrew, MacLennan, Gollan, McRae and Noble. These entries represent some of the earliest records of ordinary parishioners, albeit those with sufficient wealth to afford a house with a hearth, and many of their surnames still remain common in the parish.

A poll tax was also imposed in 1694, 1695 and 1698 to pay off debts and arrears of pay of the armed forces. The rate was graduated from 6/- upwards according to rank and wealth. Only the poor and children under sixteen years old were exempt, but unfortunately no records from Ross-shire have survived.

5.2 Commissioners of Supply

The roots of modern local government lie with the administrative bodies known as the 'Commissioners of Supply'. Originally set up in 1667 to collect land tax (known as 'cess'), the Commissioners were mainly landowners (of estates valued at more than £100 Scots), but also included senior judiciary (Justices of the Peace and Sheriffs).[7] They were responsible to Parliament for the administration of their counties and remained in existence until 1930, although their main responsibilities were taken over in 1890 by the County Councils set up under the Local Government (Scotland) Act of 1889. In addition to the collection of local land tax, they were required to maintain roads, raise militia and police, and generally implement systems for the enforcement of laws within their county of jurisdiction. Land tax rolls were compiled in order to establish who owned each property and what it was worth in terms of annual rent. Assessment of the owner's tax liability was then calculated based on the rental valuation, known as 'valued rent'.

A remarkable document detailing the rental income (in both victual and money) from the constituent farms of the Redcastle estate for the 1710 crop year has survived.[8] Furthermore, it not only names the farms but also the farmers and other rent payers in the parishes of Killearnan and Kilmuir. The total rent income amounted to £338-1-10d Scots and 523 bolls of victual, of which £294-11-6d Scots and 436 bolls of victual were derived from seven geographic areas within Killearnan parish. They were: Spittle, Garguston and Braes of Garguston – £50-10/- and 103 bolls; Killernan – £15-10/- and thirty-two bolls; Blairdow – £4 and twenty-four bolls; Milntoune and Prescaltoune – £12-4-8d and 149 bolls; Chapletoun – £8 and thirty-seven bolls; Burntown – £19-6/- and twenty-one bolls; Newtoune – £38-6-8d and seventy bolls. Other rent (in money only) amounting to £35-14-2d was raised from the Croft of Muren, Milntoune mailers, Parktoune, Hiltoun and Corrigrain mailers. Finally, the tolls of 'St Andrew's mercat' and 'St Mathias' mercat' were £93-6-8d and £16-13-4d respectively. [This seems to be the only record of the fair held annually on 24 February being named after St Mathias (or Matthias). He was one of the original disciples of Jesus, and replaced Judas Iscariot as one of the twelve apostles after the Resurrection. His feast day is 24 February, although in 1969 the Roman Catholic church changed it to 14 May.]

It is remarkable that almost one-third of Redcastle estate's income from Killearnan parish came from the tolls charged at the annual St Andrew's Fair on 7 July. It was a substantial event that attracted large numbers of people from the Black Isle, from at least the fourteenth century well into the mid-nineteenth century, after which the Muir of Ord market seems to have overtaken it.

The surviving minutes of the Commissioners of Supply for the County of Ross and Cromarty[9] commence in 1765, although the 'County Record of Ross-shire' dates from 1733. Ruairi Mor Mackenzie (6th of Redcastle) is listed as an attendee at the meeting held on 9 October 1733, when the 'Baron Roll' was drawn up for the purpose of assessing that year's land taxation.

After Ruairi Mor died in 1751, his heir, Ruairi Ban (7th of Redcastle) was required to establish his right of Barony by producing the sasine that legally transferred the estate to him. He did this on 10 October 1753, when the estate's rental income was recorded as £1,490-15/- and the assessed valued rent 'payable in publick burdens' was £822 per annum. This assessment was not altered until 1826, when Sir William Fettes was the owner. At that time, the Commissioners carried out a revaluation and Redcastle estate was re-assessed at a valued rent of £1,133-2-11d. Thirty years later, in 1855, its valued rent had more than doubled to £2,650 per annum, presumably because of the large-scale improvements carried out by Col Hugh Baillie that had raised estate rental income to £3,215 by 1868. By 1895, rental income had increased to £4,666.

The Mackenzies of Redcastle were not noted for their regular attendance or for any significant involvement in the proceedings of the Commissioners of Supply during the eighteenth century. The only exception was Ruairi Ban (7th of Redcastle) who briefly became 'Preses' [Chairman] in April 1769. Each year the Commissioners had to agree the level of their assessment and elect their 'Collector'. For example, in 1765 the assessment was set at £1-18-6d Scots out of each £100 Scots of valued rent for each of eight months, to be paid twice yearly. The collector (who was Kenneth MacKenzie of Kilcoy in 1765) was responsible for agreeing the valuation of each estate and ensuring that each heritor paid the amounts due.

Much of the work of the Commissioners was devoted to the annual assessments and accounts, whilst other matters were put in the hands of their various committees. However, from time to time, important issues of the day were raised. For example, in 1778 an Act was laid before the Commissioners to enable easier recruiting of 'land forces and marines' for the colonial and European wars. They appointed three constables to enlist the 'able bodied, idle and disorderly'. The constables were given powers to bring 'non-enlisters' in front of Justices of the Peace, and bounties were offered for voluntary enlistment into the navy (three guineas for seamen and six guineas for officers). This was followed up in 1779 when a 'Memorialist' plan was devised to raise ten companies of Volunteers (totalling 600 men) from Ross and Cromarty.

A button made of gilt copper alloy and engraved 'Ross Local Militia' set around a royal crown with '1st' underneath was recently discovered by metal detection in the field opposite Chapelton.[10] This field and a neighbouring field near the school, are thought to be the fields where military practice took place, as they also contain large numbers of musket balls and shot. To date, the 1st Ross Militia button is a unique find.

Even in the eighteenth century, the Commissioners of Supply, as a body spending public money, were acutely aware of the potentially contentious matter of their expenses. In 1793, the amount of their tavern bill (which was usually about £30 per meeting) became an issue and it was decided to control future expenditure. Amongst the measures introduced was a limit on dinner entertainment of 2/6d per head (3/6d at Michaelmas), and the requirement that the tavern keeper would produce his bill at a time not exceeding three hours after the Commissioners sat down to dinner. Thereafter, drinks would be chargeable to individuals!

As well as local land tax, many other taxes were levied on houseowners and landowners in Scotland from the middle of the eighteenth century.[11] With one exception, these taxes applied only to those who occupied larger houses with at least seven windows and a rental value of over £5. This meant that in Killearnan only the proprietors of Redcastle and Kilcoy and the parish minister were qualified for assessment. The main tax was the window tax, which was imposed from 1747 to 1798 and was supplemented by a commutation [substitute] tax from 1784 onwards. This latter tax substituted the repealed tea tax. In 1748, Ruairi Mor Mackenzie was levied £1-7/- for fifty-four windows in Redcastle, but by 1749 he paid only £1-1-6d, having managed to reduce the number of windows in Redcastle to forty-three. Like his Mackenzie predecessors, James Grant of Redcastle was subjected to window and commutation tax and, just as his predecessors had done, he also managed to reduce the amount payable by reducing the number of taxable windows in Redcastle. He was assessed under the window tax for £9-1-2d and under the commutation tax for a further £3-11-7d – for thirty windows!

Throughout the later eighteenth century, the government introduced a series of additional taxes to raise money to pay for an increasingly large army and navy. They included inhabited house tax (1778–98), male servants tax (1777–98), female servants tax (1785–92), carriage tax (1785–98) and horse tax (1785–98). To pay for the Napoleonic wars with France, these were further extended in the late 1890s to include farm horse tax (1797–98) and dog tax (1797–98).

The cumulative amounts that were payable were surprisingly large. For example, in 1797–98 James Grant was assessed as follows: £3-7/- for inhabited house tax; £2-0-6d for male servants tax (three servants named as John Graham, a butler, James Boyd, a footman, and Hector MacIntosh, a coachman); £9-12/- for carriage tax (one private carriage with four wheels); £2-14-3d for horse tax (five horses); 13/6d for saddle horse tax (three horses) and £1-0-0 for dog tax (four dogs). He did not seem to employ female servants, so was free of female servants tax. [Only those servants who were personal attendants seemed to be taxable, thus general house servants were not assessed. Of the local proprietors, only Kenneth Murchison of Tarradale was liable for female servants tax. He had a personal chambermaid and a cook, for whom he was taxed 5/- each in 1792]. There was also shop tax (1785–89), cart tax (1785–98), clock and watch tax (1797–98) and aid and contribution tax (1797–98), but the records of these taxes for Ross-shire parishes have not survived.

For taxation purposes, the parish manse and the glebe were regarded as the property of the minister (the Presbytery of Chanonry unsuccessfully tried to get manses exempted from window tax). Until 1766, Rev. Denoon (I) was assessed for seven windows in his manse, but he became exempt in 1767–68 when a note in the assessment book records that the manse had been 'pulled down'. In fact, the manse was being renovated, and Rev. Denoon (I) recommended taxation payments in 1770. The renovated manse also had seven windows and his assessment was 8/8d. Other taxes also had to be paid. For example, in 1797, Rev. Denoon (II) paid a grand total of £2-5-5d for inhabited house tax, horse tax (three horses) and dog tax (two dogs, assessed at 3/- each). However, he was not assessable against other taxes such as carriage tax and male and female servants tax, so it can be inferred that he neither owned carriages nor employed personal servants.

Horse tax was exceptional in being imposed on all horse owners, irrespective of their land ownership status. In Redcastle, there were five other taxable owners (Alexander Paterson, Angus Urquhart, Finlay Noble, Donald MacFarquhar and Colin MacFarquhar), whilst in Burntown there were two (Alexander McKay and William Tulloch). These seven men paid a total of £8-16-9d for nineteen horses liable for duty. They possessed a further thirteen horses, for which no duty was payable – presumably because they were not yet broken in for riding or farm work. (Finlay Noble is recorded on a gravestone in Killearnan churchyard as 'farmer, Newton of Redcastle who died 22nd July 1822 aged 70 yrs'.) The last year in which window tax was charged was 1798. Income tax was introduced to replace the complexity of the previous taxation regime in 1799. It was initially imposed on all incomes over £60 that arose from property rental or the carrying out of a profession or trade. Unfortunately, the early records for Ross-shire were lost in a fire.

5.3 Roads and Bridges

In the seventeenth and eighteenth centuries, the Commissioners of Supply[12] were also responsible for the building and upkeep of district roads, and some of their early minutes refer to the need for better roads and the building of bridges to facilitate travel. For example, in April 1788 the Commissioners received the report of an inspection of the Ross-shire roads, in which it was stated that it was necessary to erect nineteen new bridges, two of these being in Redcastle. The first was:

...on the burn of Burntown of Redcastle at the village of that name which crosses the roads from Redcastle and Beauly to Fortrose, Cromarty and Inverbreaky [Invergordon]. A number of burials pass this way towards the kirk yard of Killearnan, and it is always impassable during speats [spates]. The Rev. David Denoon has lately created a timber bridge here for foot passengers at the expense of the kirk session.

The second was 'at Miltown of Redcastle on the road leading from Beauly to the ferry of Kessock by the shore of Redcastle where the water is always impassable in time of floods'.

To pay for the district roads, the Commissioners of Supply had created a 'statute labour' system which allowed heritors to provide manpower rather than cash. Statute labour could be commuted to 2/6d per day by farmers, some tradesmen, merchants and millers, but otherwise every tenant of an estate could be made available for an agreed number of days, in effect as conscripted labour. For example, in April 1791 James Grant petitioned the Commissioners for the whole of the statute labour of Killearnan to be employed 'on certain publick roads passing through his estate at Redcastle'. He was refused on the basis that the current priorities were the 'great post roads and ferries', but the Commissioners would 'very readily listen to any future application'.

After the Battle of Culloden in 1746, the government created a network of military roads in the Highlands. However, few were ever used for their original purpose and many were abandoned as having little civil use. By the beginning of the nineteenth century, it became evident that a more extended public transport network was required if the economy of the Highlands was to be stimulated and raised to the level of other parts of the country. Therefore, in 1803 Parliament agreed to provide one half of the funding of new roads, the Highland proprietors (in effect, the Commissioners of Supply) being required to contribute the remainder.

To plan and oversee the work, the Commission for Highland Roads and Bridges[13] was created, and Thomas Telford was appointed as Consultant Engineer (in addition to his appointment as Principal Engineer to the Caledonian Canal). This prompted a major phase of road building in which 930 miles of 'parliamentary' roads and 1,117 bridges were built in the Highlands in less than twenty years at a total cost of £540,000, of which £201,799 was contributed by the Commissioners of Supply. In 1814, 255 miles of post-Culloden military roads were also transferred to the Commission.

Telford's initial survey, presented to the Commissioners for Highland Roads and Bridges for their First Report of 1803, did not envisage any parliamentary roads on the Black Isle. However, there were two later developments that had some impact on the Killearnan area. By 1807, it was decided that the parliamentary road west from Inverness (which was originally planned to use Strath Glass and Glen Affric on its route to Loch Shiel) should use a more northerly route through Glen Orrin and Achnasheen to Loch Carron. This required new toll bridges to replace the ferries at Beauly and Scuddel (Conon). The bridge over the Conon was completed in 1811, but it took until 1814 to complete the Lovat Bridge at Beauly. Then, in 1814, it was decided to construct a 'Black Isle parliamentary road' linking the new Conon Bridge with the ferry at Chanonry Point (Fortrose). There would also be two tolled branch spurs to the Kessock ferry, one from the Tore Inn and the other from Munlochy. These were completed in 1817.

Many of the (biennial) reports of the Commissioners for Highland Roads and Bridges are illustrated with maps highlighting proposed routes, sites of bridges and progress with construction. These maps are based on 'The Map of Scotland', published by Aaron Arrowsmith in 1807. Like Telford, who was given authority in 1803 to consult the Roy's (1750) *Military Survey of Scotland*, Arrowsmith was given access for his work on his map. He wrote a 'Memoir relative to the Construction of the Map of Scotland', which is published as an appendix to the Third Report of the Commissioners. It provides a detailed historical review of the early mapping of Scotland.

The best eighteenth-century road map of the area is that of Taylor and Skinner,[14] produced in 1775 (Figure 37). Other maps that are sufficiently detailed to show the area's roads include those of Ainslie and Foden, and Walpoole. The Commissioners' maps also show selected roads that give a picture of the transport links that existed in the later eighteenth century prior to the creation of the Commission. For example, on the Commissioners' 1805 map there are two roads shown in the Killearnan area, one from Beauly to Dingwall via Scuddel Ferry and one from Scuddel Ferry cross-country to Kessock Ferry. However, the route from Fortrose to Beauly that features on Taylor and Skinner's road map of 1775 is not shown. On the Commissioners' 1809 map, the Beauly to Dingwall road is shown but there is no direct road from Scuddel Ferry to Kessock Ferry. Instead, there is a coast road from Kessock Ferry, which joins an inland road from Fortrose near Redcastle and continues to a point midway along the Beauly to Dingwall road (about the location of Muir of Ord). This more or less corresponds to the present-day configuration of roads (but without the A9). However, on the Commissioners' 1821 map, the road from Fortrose to Redcastle is absent and is replaced by the new Black Isle parliamentary road from the Conon Bridge to Fortrose, as well as the branch from Tore to Kessock Ferry. John Thomson's map of 'Ross and Cromarty Shires' (surveyed in 1820, but not published in his 'Atlas of Scotland' until 1832) adds to the confusion by showing all the old and new roads, including the Black Isle parliamentary road.[15]

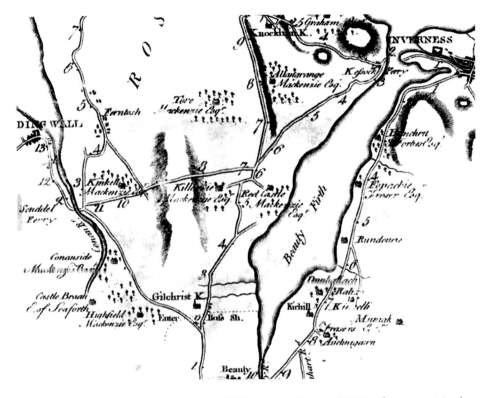

Figure 37: A portion of the Taylor and Skinner road map of 1775 (from an original, D87, held by the Highland Council Archive Service)

The picture is complex but seems to indicate that the coast road from Kessock Ferry to Redcastle was built (or upgraded) in about 1807, and that the old road from Fortrose to Redcastle (which took a route through Allangrange, Arpafeelie, Parkton and Chapelton) was no longer required after the new Black Isle parliamentary road was opened in 1817. Commissioners' minutes stating that 'the portion of road to the east of the bridge at Chapelton till the junction with the old road from Dingwall to Kessock has become unnecessary for the accommodation of the public' are recorded in 1829.

The Commissioners' responsibilities for building new roads ceased in 1821, but they remained responsible for repairs until 1863. Their reports through 1821–63 provide interesting insights. For example, in 1836 they noted that milestones had been erected along the principal roads. The report states that these were provided from Tarradale quarry at a cost of £4-4-6d, but it seems highly probable that this is an error, as the *Inverness Journal*[16] of 3 July 1835 had carried an advertisement for contractors to furnish 80–100 milestones for Ross-shire roads using Redcastle quarry stone. Six of these milestones still stand, the most prominent of which stands on the verge of the B9161 road near Knockbain House, one mile west of Munlochy village (Figure 38).

Figure 38: The Redcastle quarry milestone near Knockbain House

The Twenty-ninth Commissioners' Report in 1843 was optimistic in stating that the surfaces of the roads in the County of Ross were 'generally in very perfect order'. They lived to regret that statement, because extreme winter weather from 1846 to 1849 caused such havoc that it took until 1853 to repair all the damage to the roads and bridges. It is recorded that in 1848 the River Conon rose eleven feet above its ordinary flood level, loosening the rock on which one of the piers of the Conon Bridge was founded. (The same floods washed away the stone bridge over the River Ness in Inverness. It was replaced by a metal bridge.)

The Commutation Road Act of 1807 made each county responsible for collecting the heritors' matching funds for the costs of parliamentary roads and the provision of district roads. This was to be raised by means of a local tax system based on a levy of the heritors' rental income, or the equivalent in labour. In the County of Ross, the Black Isle was District 7. Surprisingly, it is named 'Redcastle District' on the handwritten 'Sederunt Books' [records of meetings], all of which have survived.[17] The first meeting of the trustees of District 7 was convened at the schoolhouse in Redcastle on 1 May 1807. The rental assessment was 'fixed on each heritor at 1/- per day for each of six days of statute labour'. Women living by themselves whose annual rent was less than £5 were exempted from the assessment. In practice, this meant that James Grant of Redcastle was assessed at £58-19-6d, of which, in 1807, he paid £49-12-6d after permitted exemptions and other deductions.

Much of the work of the trustees was associated with the parliamentary roads; thus Redcastle is rarely mentioned in the District 7 minutes. However, a minor dispute arose in 1812, when Lieut-Col Alexander Grant informed the trustees that he had repaired, at his own cost, the road from Kessock Ferry to Redcastle as far as the new road from Scuddel Ferry to Beauly to make it passable by the mail coach from Inverness to Tain. He had applied to the General Meeting of the County for recompense but it had not accepted liability, and had requested District 7 to reimburse his £50 costs. However, District 7 did not have sufficient funds and made a pledge to pay from their next year's assessment. As it turned out, the pledge was not honoured, because District 7 also deemed that it had not been responsible for that road in 1812, although they did adopt it in 1814!

Relationships between the Grants of Redcastle and District 7 clearly soured from that point. In June 1817, there were minutes to the effect that the Clerk to the trustees was to inform Mr (Patrick) Grant or his factor, Mr John Edwards, 'that the circular part of the road below the garden of Redcastle has gone into great disrepair, which road the late James Grant was to keep always in repair as he was allowed to go beyond the Old Road with the garden wall and that Redcastle will cause the said piece of road to be put into immediate repair'. Whether the repairs were completed is not recorded, but from that point the annual rental assessments of Redcastle went into arrears. It was only in 1824, after John Edwards had 'insisted on the payment of £50', that the account from 1812 was finally paid.

This was not the end of the disputes. In 1826, the trustees minuted that they would not sustain an account for 'stones furnished from the Redcastle quarry for drains on the Kessock road', because they considered the benefit 'to the proprietor of Redcastle so great that he may afford these few stones gratis'. Needless to say, Patrick Grant's arrears remained unpaid and, perhaps because of general problems with arrears in many of the heritors' assessment payments, the trustees fell into debt. In 1828, they levied the heritors with 'six pence in the pound Scots' for making and maintaining the roads, and 'eight pence in the pound Scots' towards liquidation of their debts. Finally, in 1834, after Sir William Fettes had purchased Redcastle, it was agreed that the outstanding amounts due from the Grants (for which Sir William Fettes denied all responsibility) should be written off in the accounts.

In 1836, Hugh Baillie of Tarradale complained about the state of the district road between Redcastle and Tarradale, and of the dangerous condition of the bridge in Milton of Redcastle, which had no parapet. It was reported to the next meeting that he and John MacKenzie (representing Redcastle) had agreed a price of £30 with a contractor (Peter MacKenzie) 'for replacing the arches, building parapets and gravelling the two bridges at the village of Redcastle' and for 'the portion of the aforementioned road passing through the estate of Redcastle'.

Ross-shire was obviously not the only county which was experiencing rebellious heritors. In February 1842, the heritors in Inverness accused the Commission of exorbitant expense of repairs, exclusion of competition for repair contracts and excessive cost of management and inspection. A committee was appointed to investigate. Their report of 2 November 1842 concluded with the following paragraph:

> The committee having given their best attention to all the evidence produced before them, and having spared no pains to arrive at the truth, are of the opinion, that the parliamentary and military roads, under the charge of the Honourable Board of Commissioners, are maintained in a very perfect state of repair, and at less cost than any other roads of a similar description. This they conceive to be the best proof that could be obtained of the very high approach to perfection attained in the system of management.

There's no praise like self-praise!

In 1843, it was reported to the trustees of District 7 that there was a danger to travellers on the district road to the west of the glebe at Redcastle. The clerk was instructed to obtain estimates for either a stone parapet or a bank of earth. The latter was chosen at a contract price of 1/3d per yard for 120 yards. The earthen bank is still in place today, although there is also a fence. In 1844, Kenneth Grigor held the contract for repairing the Killearnan parish roads. It was valued at £57 per year, but he complained about 'the heavy cartage of wood and stones on the estate of Redcastle' and intimated that, in consequence, he could not profitably take the contract for less than £80 per year. He was offered £70 in 1847, but in 1852 the contract was issued to Roderick MacKenzie and William McRae for £33 per year! In 1858, it was given to Kenneth Cameron for £40 per year, with an 'allowance for extra metal' of up to £12. James McKenzie Alison, the factor for Redcastle, represented Col Hugh Baillie at the trustees' meetings and was a regular complainant about the state of the roads around Redcastle, especially the shore road from Kessock Ferry and the road from Milton of Redcastle to Tarradale. Responsibility for the upkeep of district roads passed to the Ross and Cromarty County Council, and the last meeting of the trustees of District 7 took place on 22 December 1866.

5.4   Corn Laws and Potato Famine

An issue that generated some concern amongst the Redcastle farmers in 1843 was the emergence of the Anti-Corn-Law League. The League were 'free traders' who had formed in 1838 to lobby for the repeal of the 1815 Corn Laws, which had been enacted after the end of the Napoleonic wars to restrict the import of agricultural produce into Britain. The Commissioners of Supply[18] in Ross-shire called a meeting on 20 February 1844 to consider 'how the mischievous agitation of certain persons calling themselves the Anti-Corn-Law League may best be met and due protection for British industry secured'. It was agreed that a further meeting should be held and that invitations should be issued to the tenant farmers of the area. Snow caused an adjournment of that meeting, but it was eventually convened on 14 March 1844. The attendance list included Robert Trotter of Garguston (who was a JP), Angus Urquhart of Milton of Redcastle, Davidson MacKenzie of Blairdhu and William Dick of Parkton. The meeting resolved that 'the Anti-Corn-Law league, in endeavoring to deprive the British farmer of moderate protection for home grown corn, is highly dangerous in principle and mischievous in effect' and that the Commissioners should exert themselves 'in counteracting the insidious schemes of the League'. Despite this opposition, the Corn Laws were repealed by Sir Robert Peel's Tory government in 1846.

The agricultural improvements described in the New (Second) Statistical Account[19] were achieved at no little cost to the local cottars and crofters, who were deprived of good land and had to depend increasingly on potatoes as the only crop that would grow sufficiently well on poorer soil to provide enough food for their families. As a consequence of years of monoculture, crops became susceptible to disease and in 1846 potatoes in the Highlands became blighted by fungus. The Commissioners of Supply in Ross-shire (whose chairman at the time was Col Hugh Baillie of Redcastle, an MP and Lord

Lieutenant of the County), minuted that there was 'little fear of famine in this County provided the labouring classes determine immediately to exert themselves to overt it'. However, when it was discovered that half of the potato crop was blighted, they resolved to make 'every exertion to procure employment by every individual', to impose the 'strictest family economy' and to encourage proprietors to 'adopt measures to secure to the people a sufficient supply of food at current market prices'.

The Times[20] of 29 September 1846 carried an article on the effect of the blight, in which it is stated that 'on the estate of Redcastle forty farms were examined and two plants were raised from each showing: sound potatoes 240, diseased 178, or nearly ½ of the whole now unfit for human food. On this estate the crop seemed generally about ⅔ grown'. It also quoted Rev. John Kennedy as saying 'about one-half [of the crop] was diseased and there was a great deficiency in the size of the potatoes'. It is surprising that there is no record in the minutes of either the Established or the Free Church to indicate whether the population of Redcastle was severely affected or not.

The winter of 1846–47 was particularly cold and snowy. Malnutrition and financial hardship brought about by the potato famine caused riots in Cromarty and Invergordon, which had to be quelled by troops. In some cases, these were exacerbated by landowners who were still exporting grain despite the plight of their tenants. In an attempt to ease the unrest and provide some famine relief, the Commissioners of Supply resolved to guarantee bank loans of £4,000 in Dingwall and £2,000 in Tain to purchase food. This was not a unanimous decision, some Commissioners believing that it was the responsibility of individual landowners to provide food for their tenants. Perversely, it was only because of the repeal of the Corn Laws (which the Commissioners had opposed in 1843) that cheap Indian grain could be purchased to provide food!

5.5 Valuation Rolls

As a consequence of the Lands Valuation (Scotland) Act of 1854, Valuation Rolls[21] covering all properties were produced by county and burgh assessors' offices annually from 1855–56 onwards. Until 1868, the Rolls for the Ross and Cromarty parishes were produced only in manuscript, but the information they record is identical to those of later years, which were printed. The information contained in the Rolls includes an identification number and description for each property, its proprietor, tenant and occupier, its value (or yearly rental) and the duration of the lease. Unfortunately, the identification numbers are not consistent from year to year, and bear no relation to those used in the national decennial censuses. There is also a tendency to group commercial properties separately from domestic properties; for example, in the 1855–56 Rolls for Ross-shire, the shops and workshops of Milton of Redcastle are numbers 33–40, whereas the houses are 202–217. Furthermore, the descriptions can be vague; for example, in 1855–56 all the houses of Milton of Redcastle are described as 'House and Garden, Milton'. Hence it is not always possible for a property to be uniquely identified.

Throughout the Redcastle estate, in 1855–56, all the farms, crofts (at Spital and Garguston Shores) and business properties (such as the mill, smiddy and inn at Milton of Redcastle), as well as all of the houses on the Redcastle estate, were in the proprietorship of the owner of Redcastle, Col Hugh Baillie. However, most of the business properties were leased out, and it is notable that many of the residential properties in Milton of Redcastle were in 'private' (leasehold) ownership. This is the first evidence of private ownership of residential property in the area and, although the leaseholds were short (nineteen years was normal), this reflects the higher status of the residents of Milton of Redcastle, who, being in better-paid trades and professions, could afford to take leaseholds. Many were occupied by their owners (for example, William Hogg, Margaret MacLennan and Lewis MacKenzie), who also sublet rooms to tenants. Others were owned by people who did not live in the village (for example, Mrs MacKenzie of Avoch, Robert MacFarquhar of Culbokie and Widow Ross of Inverness). Two houses that were not yet in private ownership (around 1860) were rented by the Free Church for its teachers, Andrew MacDougall and William Fraser.

Rental values of the farms and businesses are of some interest. The annual rental value of the Redcastle estate in 1868 was £3,251-5/- (compared to £1,490-15/- in 1750). The individual farms all had nineteen-year leases: Garguston (Robert Trotter) being valued at £461-6/- per year; Blairdhu (James Nicol) at £70; Fettes (George Baillie) at £656; Parkton (William Dick) at £150; and the Redcastle Inn and its farm at £150. Redcastle itself was valued only at £100, whilst the Home Farm (Redcastle Mains) was valued at £134 and the Gallowhill woodlands at £100. By 1875, the annual rental value of the Redcastle estate had risen to £3,746-12/-, mainly because of the increased rental from Andrew Granger, who paid £875 for his lease of Fettes Farm. There had also been a redistribution of value at Redcastle (£80), Home Farm (£200) and the woodlands (£70). Despite being recorded in the 1851 census, the first record of Greenhill House in the Valuation Rolls is in 1873, when the estate factor, James McKenzie Alison, paid only £20 in rent.

5.6   Black Isle District Committee

Until 1889, local government was primarily in the hands of the landowners of the major estates who, with the judiciary, formed the Commissioners of

Supply. The Local Government (Scotland) Act of 1889 allowed for nominees and representatives to participate in decisions about local infrastructure and services at county, district and parish level. For the people of Redcastle, this meant that they could seek election to serve on the Ross and Cromarty County Council, the Black Isle District Committee and the Killearnan Parish Council. Initially, the members serving on these bodies were the same people as had previously comprised the Commissioners of Supply and the kirk sessions, but as property ownership became more widespread in the late nineteenth and early twentieth centuries, a wider range of representation emerged.

The Ross-shire County Council and the Black Isle District Committee records are complete from 1890. There were also various local boards that were responsible either to the County Council or to various national boards. In the context of Redcastle, the Killearnan School Board was of particular importance but there were also boards for roads, police and prisons. Unfortunately, the Killearnan School Board minutes book for 1873–1919 has not survived, but the Ross-shire Education Committee and Education Authority records are available from 1919.

The Black Isle District Committee[22] was primarily concerned with roads and public health in the parishes of Cromarty, Rosemarkie, Resolis, Avoch, Knockbain and Killearnan. The members initially nominated by Killearnan Parish Council were Duncan Cameron of Fettes Farm and Robert Trotter of Garguston Farm (who was also the Chairman of the Killearnan School Board and the nominated County Councillor). For roads, the Committee was responsible to the Ross and Cromarty County Council Road Board.[23] There were four roads around Redcastle which fell under their jurisdiction, described in 1890 as:

- Tarradale Road (1 mile, 1,523 yards) – from the parish boundary near the Ark [the workers' bothy at Whitehills Farm] via Killearnan parish church to Milton of Redcastle.

- Shore Road (4 miles, 1,060 yards) – from Milton of Redcastle to the parish boundary at Lettoch.

- Garguston Road (3 miles) – from Tore Inn to the ploughmens' houses at Garguston.

- Kilcoy Road (2 miles) – from Milton of Redcastle through Newton to the Dingwall road junction below Muillans Wood.

Notably, the minor road from above Redcastle quarry to Blairdhu and the service road to Quarry of Redcastle were not included. Presumably they were only foot or cart tracks in 1890.

Amongst the many problems with the district roads was the section of the Tarradale Road between Milton of Redcastle and Killearnan parish church. In

April 1892, the clerk of the District Committee was instructed 'to communicate with the factor on Redcastle estate pointing out the dangerous state of certain parts of the public road at Redcastle quarry … where the dykes have fallen down and requesting him to have the same duly repaired'. It is reported in July 1892 that the repairs had been carried out, but the dangerous condition of the road would arise again in 1908.

Although many of the roads on the Black Isle had been furnished in the early years of the nineteenth century with milestones made of stone taken from Redcastle and Tarradale quarries (Figure 38, page 265), the road from Kessock Ferry to Redcastle was depleted. This was rectified in 1892 by the purchase of six 'pillars with metal plate, similar to those used by the railway'. They cost 7/6d each, and their positions are marked on the 1907 second edition 1:2,500 (circa 25 inch:1 mile) and 1:10,000 (circa 6 inch:1 mile) Ordnance Survey maps. There was one opposite the shop close to the post box in Milton of Redcastle, another close to the east entrance to Redcastle near Corgrain Point, and two others near Garguston cottages. They were still in place in 1950, but none have survived to this day.

The most problematic issue that the Black Isle Committee had to deal with in the early twentieth century was damage caused by the haulage of wood through Redcastle. In January 1901, there were twelve-inch-deep tracks in the shore road from Redcastle to Kessock, and the repair required large stones to be top-smashed and steamrolled. Then, in October 1901, it was reported that 'damage arising from the excessive weight and by the extraordinary traffic conducted by Mr John MacDonald, Wood Merchant, Inverness on the highway from Milton bridge to Lettoch farm during the years 1900–01 was £251-7-2d'. It was agreed to bill him for that amount and sue if payment was not made. It appears that it was paid, although damage continued to be made over the succeeding years. For example, in March 1904 the County Road Board noted 'great damage which was constantly done to roads through traction engines carrying wood and other material over them immediately after frost', and in April 1907 the Black Isle Committee reported that the shore road was 'very rough and much in need of repair', but that the repairs would be left 'until after the harvest so that better labour may be available'.

The problem of damage to Highland roads caused by increasing motor traffic and the consequent cost of repairs, reached such proportions that the Road Boards of all the Highland counties called a conference in Inverness in January 1908, when it was decided to take a deputation to the Secretary for Scotland in Edinburgh. This seems to have had little immediate effect, as further damage continued to be regularly reported. In 1914, the district road surveyor (who was issued with a motorcycle) stated in his annual survey that 'the district roads and bridges were maintained in good condition and in a satisfactory state except portions of the shore road from Kessock to Redcastle'. In 1922, it was resolved to spend £300 repairing the shore road and to reclaim that amount from John MacDonald. Furthermore, they closed the road to his wood haulage traffic until he settled the bill and agreed to pay for any further damage incurred in the future. Then, in August 1923, an application was made to the Minister for Transport for an order prohibiting 'locomotives, heavy motor cars and vehicles with more than 14 seats' from using this road during winter months. It is not recorded whether the application was successful.

The problem of the safety of the road above the Redcastle quarry re-emerged in April 1908, when the district surveyor reported that 'the retaining wall supporting the road at Killearnan Old Quarry is in tumble-down condition and the road liable to slip away. This must be attended to at once as the road is not safe for heavy traffic'. The repair was noted to have been completed in October 1910.

As road traffic increased in the early years of the century, the Motor Car Act of 1903 required the registration of cars and the licensing of drivers by County Councils. Unfortunately, the early records for Ross and Cromarty have not survived. The Act also required 'dangerous corners, cross-roads and precipitous places' to be signposted. There was much discussion on whether the warning signs should be in 'symbols' or in 'lettering'. Standard symbols were eventually adopted. The list of dangerous places drawn up by the District Committee included: the Milton bridge at Redcastle; the Newton crossroads at the Killearnan Free Church; the road to the west of Killearnan parish church (where a protective bank of earth had been placed in 1843); and the road to Blairdhu Farm from the top of the Redcastle quarry. Although it is not recorded, presumably the first road signs to be erected in Redcastle were at these locations. It is also not recorded when the track from Redcastle quarry to Blairdhu was upgraded for vehicular traffic, but a 'danger' sign was erected outside the Killearnan Public School in 1913, and in 1927 this road was reported by the Killearnan Parish Council[24] to be in a 'bad state for the children attending the school to travel on'. It was repaired with gravel from a pit at Blairdhu.

The Black Isle District Committee's responsibility for public health matters included hospitals, slaughterhouses, sanitary inspections, drainage and water supplies. One of the early issues raised by Robert Trotter in August 1890 was that of the 'total want of water in Drynie Park, the inhabitants of which are under the necessity of carting all they require from a distance'. This same issue had been raised in 1883 by Finlay MacKay, a Drynie Park crofter who had given evidence to the Napier Commission Inquiry.[25] This Commission was set up to inquire into the condition of the crofters and cottars in the Highlands and Islands as a consequence of the clearances of estate lands that had been taking place since the mid-1800s, mainly due to the enlargement and more efficient husbandry of the farms.

Two local crofters gave evidence to the Commission in Dingwall in October 1883. Kenneth Davidson (from Knockbain parish) stated that crofters had regularly cleared new ground, only to find that their rentals had been increased. Furthermore, there had been forty-four crofters on the estate (Kilcoy) in 1850, but there were now only nineteen due to clearances for farm enlargement. Finlay MacKay, who is recorded as a thirty-year-old living at Drynie Park Cottages in the 1881 census, stated that Drynie Park had first been colonised in 1834 due to clearances in Strathconon, that the crofters had rebuilt their own cottages without compensation from the proprietors and that water had to be carried for a mile as their only well dried up in summer.

Landowners were also required to submit information to the Napier Commission.[26] In 1883, Redcastle estate certified that (since 1840) it had neither taken pasture from any crofter nor had transferred or evicted any crofters or cottars. It also reported that its gross rent receipts were £6456, comprising: £4573 from the large farms (26 tenancies covering 2892 acres); £615 from the crofts (84 tenancies, 446 acres); 30 from fishings (2 tenancies); and £1238 from houses (53 tenancies). [For the purposes of the Landlord Returns, a 'crofter' was defined as a person holding agricultural/pastoral land at an annual rent less than £30, and a 'cottar' was an occupant of a house, holding no land privileges, at a rent less than £2.]

As a consequence of the Napier Inquiry, the Crofters' Holdings (Scotland) Act was passed in 1886. This act gave crofters security of tenure and compensation for improvements should they give up their tenancy. It also allowed them to hand on their crofts to their family, and provided for the setting up of a new Crofters Commission to fix fair rents and administer the Act generally. A sitting of the Crofters Commission held in Dingwall is reported in *The Scotsman*[27] of 23 February 1888, when twenty-two applications to fix fair rents were submitted from crofters in the Redcastle District (mainly on the Drynie estate). They had initially been given twenty-one-year leases, for which they were charged 1/3d per acre per year for the first seven years, 2/6d per acre per year for the next seven years, and 7/6d per acre thereafter. They had then been given nineteen-year leases at 10/- per acre per year. This had been raised to 15/- in 1875, but was reduced again to 10/- in 1883 after appeals by the crofters.

The area Medical Officers of Health and the District Sanitary Inspectors provided annual reports and highlighted specific issues as they arose. References to Redcastle are a rarity but, for example, in July 1912 the sanitary inspector reported on houses that were 'unfit for human habitation'. They included the house of Angus Campbell, a labourer living in Chapelton, which was described as 'injurious to health owing to dampness caused by defective roofing'. Similarly, in October 1921 he reported that the house of James Mackintosh at Garguston Shore was 'not in a reasonable sanitary and habitable condition', and that if it was not repaired he would apply to the sheriff for a closure order. It must have been repaired, as the house is still in occupation today!

Standards of housing were clearly of concern to the Committee in the 1920s. Their minutes highlight a report on 'Housing Conditions in the Black Isle' that had been produced by the Scottish Board of Health in April 1928. The minutes suggest that individual houses had been identified in the report and a special meeting of the Committee was convened to discuss it. Unfortunately, the subsequent minutes only record that the special meeting was held and no copy of the report seems to have survived.

The Killearnan Public School log book[28] records numerous occasions when attendance at school was disrupted or the school was closed by Medical Officers of Health due to outbreaks of contagious diseases in the late nineteenth and early twentieth century. Such individual cases were not generally reported to the Black Isle District Committee, but they did express general concern over tuberculosis (in 1904) and venereal disease (in 1917), and an outbreak of smallpox was noted in the Black Isle Combination Poorhouse in September 1920. Surprisingly, the Committee made no reference to the influenza pandemic that hit the UK in 1918.

The Black Isle District Committee was given responsibility for housing and town planning in 1912, but no issues were recorded until 1917 when consideration was given to the 'provision of houses for the working classes after the war'. The only resulting action seems to have involved a few 'army huts', one of which was converted into temporary housing for a road surface-man at Newton crossroads. Another matter that came within the remit of the Black Isle District Committee was the retail price of coal. In September 1917, after much deliberation, it was resolved that best household coal would be £1-12-6d per ton if purchased by the cartload, or £1-16-6d per ton if purchased in hundredweight (cwt) bags. Single cwt bags would be 1/11d (equivalent to £1-18-4d per ton).

In 1920, the decision to install a telephone system in the Black Isle was taken, but it was not until 1924 that the first telephones in the Redcastle area were installed. These were at Garguston Farm and Fettes Farm, where Ralph MacWilliam and Donald MacDonald shared a line with the number Muir of Ord 10. It was not until 1925 that there was an application to erect 'telegraphic lines' into Redcastle. There is an entry in the February 1926 telephone directory[29] under the name of J E B Baillie, showing that the telephone number of the castle was Muir of Ord 14. The northern part of the parish was connected to the Killearnan switchboard – for example, Capt Burton-Mackenzie at Kilcoy Castle had been issued in 1925 with the number Killearnan 2.

By 1925, the planning function was gaining in importance, as private individuals who had purchased houses and land sought subsidies to improve or build. Ralph MacWilliam of Garguston (who, like his predecessor Robert Trotter, was a county councillor) was the first person in Killearnan (in 1925) to request permission to erect an overhead electric cable between his house and his steading (where there would have been a generator). There was already a turbine, driven by the Redcastle burn, which provided electricity to the Gardener's Cottage in Milton of Redcastle, and this is thought to have been the first electrically lit house in the area. A 250-volt electricity supply was originally installed in Redcastle using a turbine powered by water piped from the mill dam below Parkton. From time to time, the turbine had to be stripped down and cleared of eels which had entered through the feed pipe. The remains of the turbine house are still visible at the side of the Redcastle burn in the undergrowth between the West Lodge and the castle (Figure 39). Redcastle Mains was also installed with a water-driven turbine around this time. Instead of a spring-loaded safety valve, this turbine was fitted with a surge pipe, which is still standing just to the north of the Redcastle Mains farm buildings, close to the estate road leading to Greenhill and Chapelton.

By 1928, planning approvals were being regularly sought for properties in the Redcastle area. For example, Ralph MacWilliam sought planning approval to reconstruct two ploughman's cottages at Garguston (for which he was given a subsidy of £495), and William MacAndrew applied for approval to reconstruct the eastern part of Pier Cottage at Quarry of Redcastle (for which he received a subsidy of £96). In October 1929, Catherine Noble of Manse Park (or Manse Cottage) applied for a loan to build a new house. Three of Catherine's sons had been killed in World War One, and she suffered further loss when she was widowed in February 1927. Whether her application was successful is not recorded, as the Black Isle District Committee was wound up in April 1930. However, the first record of a house by the name of Manse Park in the Valuation Rolls[30] occurs in 1936, suggesting that permission was granted. The house now occupying the site of Manse Park is named Woodlands.

Figure 39: The derelict turbine house with Redcastle in the background (2004)

5.7   Killearnan Parish Council

The Local Government (Scotland) Act of 1889 also created the Killearnan Parish Council. Unfortunately, the original minutes book has been lost, but the later book from 1910 has survived.[31] The Parish Council took over responsibility for maintaining the poor roll from the previous Parochial Board, set rates for the welfare of the poor and the upkeep of the school, and generally became involved with any matters of parochial or community interest, although it had limited powers to act, fund or enforce. In 1910, the school rate was set at 11d and the poor rate at 1/11d per £1 of assessable rent on land and heritages. There were three classes of poor: 'ordinary resident' poor; 'fatuous' (idiotic or mentally ill) poor; and 'suspense' (temporary) poor.

Responsibility for the kirkyard transferred to the Parish Council in April 1899, but the Killearnan kirk session had to repair the walls beforehand, at a cost of £15. Management and maintenance of the burial ground was something of a problem for the Council. In April 1913, 'it was unanimously agreed that in future the sexton [the caretaker and grave-digger] will require to be present at the erection of every tombstone which may be put into the church yard, and the parties erecting such tombstone must show the sexton their permission to do so from the Parish Council'.

In December 1915, the sexton (who was James Mackintosh, the crofter at Garguston Shore) seems to have upset some of the Parish Council members, and the clerk wrote to him stating that 'in future he is to place all bones which he may dig out when opening a grave into a small bag and bury the bag and bones in the earth'. It seems that whilst attending funerals some members of the Council had considered it 'very disagreeable to see the manner in which these dug out bones were dealt with'. James Mackintosh was also regularly in trouble with the Parish Council about the condition of the graveyard, and in April 1922 he was informed that he had one month 'wherein to conform with the Council's rules failing which it would be necessary to engage a new man'. The problem was resolved by a formal agreement to cut the grass at least three times per year and to apply weedkiller to the paths, then cover them with gravel from the shore at Coulmore.

The Parish Council also had responsibility for appointing the parish registrar. When Hugh Fraser retired in September 1919, there were four applicants for the vacancy: Donald Robertson, the blacksmith in Milton of Redcastle; Alexander Jack and William Chisholm of Quarry of Redcastle; and John Fraser of Chapelton. Donald Robertson was appointed at a salary of £9 per annum (raised to £11 in July 1921).

The residents of Quarry of Redcastle collectively approached the Parish Council in April 1930 with regard to the state of the road in front of their properties. However, the outcome was not what they desired. The Council was about to be dissolved, and the response was 'no action is now possible by the present Council'. The final meeting of the Killearnan Parish Council was held on 12 May 1930. The main item of business was to congratulate the Chairman, Rev. Aeneas Macdonald, who was about to graduate as a Doctor of Divinity at Glasgow University. Only two years later, in November 1932, Rev. Macdonald died. His gravestone in Killearnan churchyard describes him as 'faithful pastor, learned instructor and wise counsellor, clan historian and celtic scholar, joint author of the Clan Donald, joint editor of the Macdonald Collection of Gaelic Poetry and Poems of Alexander MacDonald'.

5.8 Avoch District Council

The Black Isle District Committee and the Killearnan Parish Council were wound up under the Local Government (Scotland) Act of 1929, and replaced with District Councils in April 1930. Killearnan fell into the ambit of the Avoch District Council, several of whose minutes books have survived.[32] The duties of the District Councils (sometimes called the 'pre-1975' Districts) were partly statutory and partly delegated. The principal statutory duty was the maintenance of minor ('unclassified' or 'parish') roads and, in Ross and Cromarty, the duties delegated by the County Council included water, sewage and drainage, housing allocations, welfare of the poor (to 1948), churchyards and war memorials.

The only two unclassified roads in Redcastle were the road between Blairdhu and the top of the Redcastle quarry, giving access to Killearnan Public School, and the service road from Milton of Redcastle to Quarry of Redcastle. Although the Blairdhu road was improved in October 1935, these were not generally in good condition during 1930–50, and the Avoch District Council consistently recorded their lack of funds to repair and resurface them – for example, in June 1938 (when the Ministry of Transport provided money only for Class II roads), and in January 1939, when they were described as 'in almost impassable condition' and 'seriously hindering the development of the farming industry'. After World War Two, in December 1946, another petition was raised by the residents of Quarry of Redcastle, and this one was successful. However, the service road to Quarry of Redcastle again required attention in 1963, and Kings and Co. Ltd were appointed to undertake repairs costing £406, of which 'Lord Burton and Miss C E Buchanan [of Quarry House] each paid £100 as their contribution towards the cost'. In 1946, the District Council estimated the cost of repair of the Blairdhu road at about £100, and the clerk was requested to 'apply to Redcastle estate per Mr D C McDonnell, Redcastle Mains, for a contribution in view of the fact that the road mainly serves that estate'. This assertion seems not wholly justifiable, as it was the road to the school, but nevertheless a contribution of £50 was forthcoming. This road was taken over by Ross and Cromarty County Highways in 1948, but it was not until 1985 that the Quarry of Redcastle access road was adopted.

As in the years previous to 1930 when the 'General Register of the Poor' was maintained by the Parochial Board,[33] few residents of Redcastle applied for poor relief under any of the various categories for which assistance could be obtained: ordinary poor; able-bodied poor; other area poor; lunatic poor; casual and suspense poor; indoor poor (Ness House in Fortrose); and blind and sick poor (domiciliary assistance). Throughout the 1930s, only three persons from Milton of Redcastle are recorded as receiving assistance: one had two dependent children and received 15/- per week; another was elderly and received 10/- per week; and the third was a young orphan who received 10/- per week. One resident of Quarry of Redcastle was given £1-10/- per week of 'transitional assistance' in 1932–33. Two persons are recorded as lunatic poor: one boarded at Chapelton and received 20/- per week (and later resided at Quarry of Redcastle, before being transferred to Inverness District Asylum in 1943); the other boarded at Greenhill House and received 10/- per week. By 1945, there were no Redcastle residents on the poor roll, and responsibility for poor relief was transferred to the National Assistance Board in July 1948.

A petition from the retail traders in Killearnan was received by the Avoch District Council in December 1934, 'objecting to the system of supplying the poor with clothing and boots, etc., whereby the custom goes outwith the parish and pointing out as ratepayers they are entitled to get a share of the business'. The response was not encouraging:

> The Public Assistance Committee point out that the County must be treated as a whole and that the County Council must, in the interest of ratepayers, make the best terms possible for supplies and that cannot be done unless the goods are supplied in bulk for fairly large areas … [but there was] nothing to hinder petitioners in making an offer for any of the goods required.

The graveyard at Killearnan parish church was a regular item on the District Council's agenda. It was first raised in December 1932, when it was noted that 'additional burying ground will be necessary in Killearnan parish'. In 1935, William MacIntosh (the ex-school headteacher and bone-setter who lived in Rivulet Cottage, and had become a County Councillor in 1932 and Chairman of the District Council in 1935) reported that 'the Baroness Burton of Dochfour is at present doing repairs to the family burying ground of the Baillies of Redcastle in Killearnan churchyard, which the Council approve of'. The Baillie family burial plot in Killearnan graveyard is located in the eastern extension, next to the (inaccessible) Mackenzie of Kilcoy mausoleum. The only recorded Baillie grave in the plot is that of Col Hugh Baillie's wife, Selina, who died in November 1871. There is also an undated gravestone of an Angus Cameron.

However, the state of some other graves was not worthy of the Council's approval – for example, that of Rev. John Kennedy, which needed 'to be put into a proper state of repair', but which could not be repaired until a large tree growing beside it was cut down. The generally poor condition of the graveyard at that time was due to the ill health of James Mackintosh, the sexton. He died in November 1937 and was succeeded by his son, Hugh. In March 1939, the District Council received a letter from a Mr MacKay about 'the deplorable state of the churchyard'. He was assured that the grass was cut three times per year and that the walls would be repaired in the near future.

The question of additional burying ground became more acute in December 1945, when it was reported to the District Council that 'the present burial ground at Killearnan is congested and there is no ground available for new lairs'. It was agreed that tests be carried out either at adjoining ground or elsewhere, and in January 1946 it was reported that 'in view of similar difficulty occurring in Knockbain parish, a site convenient to both parishes be selected instead of having separate burial grounds in each'. This preferred solution was adopted, and by December 1946 the site of the new burial ground had been tested and selected. Rules and regulations for the 'Knockbain and Killearnan Burial Ground' were drawn up in March 1947 – for example: a lair would cost two guineas (£2-2/-); a burial would be 10/- (5/- for children under sixteen); no grave would be dug deeper than six feet; no coffin would be nearer the surface than three feet; and there were to be no rails, walls, fences or chains around graves. The new joint graveyard, which is located on the minor road about one mile south of Tore, was opened for use in April 1949. Thereafter, the Killearnan parish churchyard at Redcastle was restricted to the widows, widowers and unmarried children of persons already interred there.

The District Council also had responsibility for appointing district registrars. Donald Robertson, the Killearnan registrar who had been appointed in 1919, resigned 'owing to age and failing eyesight' in September 1941 (he later became blind). The Council recommended that his daughter take over, as she had acted as assistant registrar to her father. She resigned in May 1945, at which point Eliza Fraser, who lived in Quarry Cottage and was the wife of William Fraser, the head gamekeeper at Redcastle estate, was appointed.

The Avoch District Council also took over responsibility for housing in 1930. One of the earliest applications that it handled, under the Housing (Rural Workers) Act of 1926, was one from Baroness Burton in August 1932 for reconstruction of the Gardener's Cottage at Milton of Redcastle. Her application was recommended but was subsequently refused by the Public Health Committee, for reasons that are not recorded. Charles MacGregor of Chapelton applied in October 1934 for a subsidy to renovate one of the cottages there (and seems to have been successful), but no other applications from Redcastle are recorded in the entire period to 1975.

William Wylie Martin of Garguston Farm was elected to the Avoch District Council in May 1949. Like his predecessors at Garguston, Robert Trotter and

Robert MacWilliam, he was an energetic councillor who represented Killearnan actively. He concerned himself with many local issues, including the proposal to erect a telephone kiosk at Milton of Redcastle in 1949 (he also wanted one at Garguston in 1953, but the GPO turned this down). He was particularly active in transport matters. For example, he was instrumental in the restoration of the road sign at Killearnan school, the realignment of the sharp bends on the A832 at Newton and Garguston to improve visibility, the creation of picnic areas along the Redcastle–Kessock shore road, and the preservation of what was described as the 'old well of interest' [the Grey Well (Figure 31, page 230)] during improvements to the road between Milton of Redcastle and Killearnan parish church.

However, his primary transport concern involved the decrease and the ultimate withdrawal of bus services in the parish. At a special meeting held in Killearnan Primary School on 29 May 1972, he strongly argued that Killearnan parish was hardest hit as a consequence of Highland Omnibuses' proposals to reduce bus services in the Black Isle, citing the difficulties for Redcastle pupils of getting to school in Muir of Ord and other residents of travelling to the doctor, post office and bank. Revised proposals in January 1973 reinstated a bus service to Redcastle, and passing places were constructed on the Milton of Redcastle–Chapelton–Newton road to help the buses to keep to schedule. However, in December 1974 the Muir of Ord–Tore bus service that passed through the village was finally withdrawn due to lack of customers. A post bus service was proposed by Wylie Martin, but this does not appear to have been instated.

The Avoch District Council held its last meeting on 6 May 1975, when yet another local government reform was implemented. Ross and Cromarty County Council, together with its District Councils, was abolished and merged with the other highland counties (Caithness, Sutherland and Inverness) to create the Highland Regional Council.

5.9   Development and Enterprise Boards

The Highlands and Islands Development Board (HIDB) was created in 1965 to establish new businesses, maintain traditional industries and attract inward investment into the area. In 1967, the HIDB appointed a group under the chairmanship of Jack Holmes to study the capacity of the inner Moray Firth area to increase its population, and prepare a plan for urban land use and an infrastructure arising from the building of the aluminium smelter at Invergordon.

In its report,[34] the Holmes Group proposed a 'Tore Option' of new industrial and general residential built-up areas at Munlochy and Redcastle. A subsequent agricultural study for the HIDB reported that a new fast road from

Inverness to Invergordon, passing through Redcastle (and on through Muir of Ord and Dingwall) would open up the possibility of the 'Tore Option' (Figure 40). However, it concluded that 'this was the least likely route to be adopted as its siting led to an expensive crossing of the Kessock narrows with little advantage gained by putting the road along the north shore of the Beauly Firth'. Fortunately, the preferred option was to build the new road by means of a Kessock Bridge, Tore and a Cromarty Firth causeway, as this disturbed less farm land and avoided the creation of traffic bottle necks in Muir of Ord, Conon Bridge and Dingwall. This shorter route was ultimately adopted, so Redcastle was spared the A9!

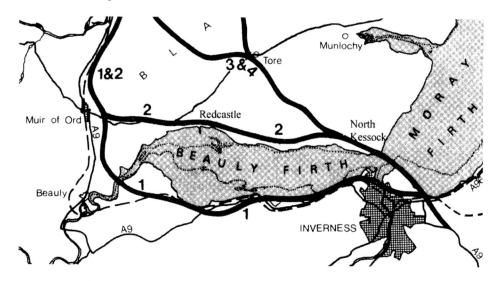

Figure 40: A portion of a map from the Holmes report (1968), showing the option of routing the A9 through Redcastle

The HIDB was dissolved in 1992, when its functions were taken over by Highlands and Islands Enterprise (HIE) and its network of Local Enterprise Companies (LECs). The Killearnan/Redcastle area was served by Ross and Cromarty Enterprise (RACE) until 2006, when – in recognition of the effect of the Kessock Bridge and the integration of the economy of the inner Moray Firth – eastern Ross-shire was merged with other areas to form a new area known as 'HIE Inverness and East Highland', extending over Inverness, Tain, Dingwall, Nairn and Aviemore.[35]

5.10 Killearnan Community Council

In the local government restructure of 1975, the county of Ross and Cromarty was subsumed into the Highland Regional Council and reduced to the status of a 'post-1975 District'. This reorganisation also effectively abolished the old parishes as administrative areas, although the name of Killearnan still survives in the title of the local Community Council.[36] Further local government reform was carried out in 1990, when regional councils were abolished and the Highland Council[37] was formed. At this reorganisation, the status of Ross and Cromarty was further reduced to that of an 'area'. Despite these changes, many local people still include 'Ross-shire' in their postal addresses. At the same date, County and Burgh Assessors were abolished and were replaced by Regional Assessors. This heralded a change in the format of the Valuation Rolls,[38] which were no longer based on parishes but on the new local government districts and electoral wards. Valuation Rolls for domestic properties were no longer produced after the community charge (or poll tax, as it was known) was introduced in 1990, and replaced domestic rates as the basis of local taxation. Poll tax was replaced by council tax in 1994.

The inaugural meeting of Killearnan Community Council took place on 18 October 1977, when Wylie Martin of Garguston was elected as its chairman. The first important business was to comment on the Highland Regional Council's Structure and Local Plans, about which the Community Council commented that 'there should be no great change to the present character of the area, that growth should be allowed for job opportunities for the indigenous population at approximately 20% of the population over 4 years and that housing should be private and not local authority'. Essentially the same response was made four years later in March 1982, but with the addition of a request to ease the difficulty of crossing the A9 at Tore, and for consideration to be given to the creation of parking and picnic areas on the North Kessock to Redcastle shore road, due to its scenic interest for tourists.

The majority of the matters debated at the early Community Council meetings concerned road safety, street lighting and access issues at Tore. However, one issue of direct concern to residents of Redcastle was raised in September 1983, when it was reported that a householder (unnamed) at Quarry of Redcastle had placed obstructions on the path that formed the right of way between Quarry of Redcastle and Killearnan church. The Community Council recorded that 'this path has been used by the public over a long period, at least over the past 80 years', but requested the chairman (now James Hillan) and the secretary (Col Duncan MacDonald) to investigate and report back. They took advice from the Scottish Rights of Way Society and the Ordnance Survey, and informed the next meeting that 'this is a right of way and that several members of the public have been using it'. Although it is not recorded, presumably the obstruction was removed.

Unfortunately, no minutes of Killearnan Community Council meetings from November 1985 to April 1999 seem to have survived. Donald MacKay had become Chairman, but he resigned in May 1999, at which time the creation of the Millennium garden at Tore was almost the only issue under consideration at the irregular and ill-attended meetings. By May 2000, the Council was in crisis and its continuation was in jeopardy. However, on 1 June 2000, an open meeting attended by fourteen people was convened, at which it was unanimously decided to call for nominations and, if necessary, hold a ballot to reconstitute the Council. On 2 November 2000, a new Council, comprising a full complement of seven members, held its first meeting and elected John MacIntosh of Garguston Shore as Chairman. The Community Council has grown in stature since that date. Since April 2003, it has issued a newsletter, which is circulated to every household in the area, and it is now both active and influential in local issues.

Of those issues, several have particularly affected residents of Redcastle. In October 2002, the Council expressed concern at the slow introduction of broadband and prompted the early upgrade of the Muir of Ord telephone exchange that opened up fast access to the internet in 2003. The Council also recorded a notable success in ensuring the retention of the Redcastle telephone kiosk. In August 2004, notices were issued by BT Payphones that the telephone boxes at Milton of Redcastle and Fettes (Newton) crossroads were to be removed. Letters of objection were sent to BT, and the Highland Council was requested to place a preservation order on the Redcastle box. These generated an immediate response from BT in October 2004, that there would be no removal before consultation with residents; with the outcome in March 2005, that the kiosks at both Redcastle and Fettes would be retained. However, the issue of their closure was again raised in 2008, when the Highland Council was requested by BT Payphones to consult on the future of 194 payphones across the Highlands that were deemed to be loss-making. One of these was the Redcastle telephone, from which only fifty-nine calls had been made in the previous year. The *Inverness Courier*[39] featured the Redcastle telephone kiosk in an article published on 13 May 2008.

However, the Community Council's outstanding success was in relation to the water supply in the Redcastle area. In June 2003, nine residents of Redcastle attended the Council meeting and complained of the poor quality of the water supply. At the next meeting in August 2003, a representative of Scottish Water gave an update on proposed water main upgrades and stated that the renewal of the Kilcoy distribution zone (which includes Redcastle) 'was high on the list of priorities', and that 'work would be completed within the next two years'. Two residents of Redcastle protested that this timescale was not acceptable, as 'Redcastle residents should not be expected to continue suffering the frequent bursts [twelve had already been reported in 2003] and subsequent contamination of their water supply. They were paying rates for a very substandard product.' The point had been well made, and in January 2004 Scottish Water informed the Community Council that it 'had accepted the seriousness of the poor water supply to Redcastle and that work on the upgrade had already begun'. By the summer of 2004, the mains water distribution system had been renewed throughout the Redcastle area. In little more than one year, the water supply to every house in Redcastle had been upgraded – a remarkable result in the light of the twenty-eight years it had taken to provide a water tap in the playground of Killearnan school, and the sixty years it had taken to provide a satisfactory water supply to the Killearnan manse!

Environmental issues come high on the Community Council's agenda. A coastal assessment survey of the Inner Moray Firth was carried out for Historic Scotland in 1998 by the Centre for Field Archaeology.[40] It noted that at Redcastle 'the coastal edge is narrow', but that, owing to its sheltered position, 'the condition of the low shore is stable and accreting' and that 'it is the vegetation that is rendering stability in what is considered to be a fairly low wave energy environment'. It also records that the Redcastle pier (Figure 33, page 239) is classified by RCAHMS both as a 'military installation' and as a 'built heritage' site of archaeological interest, but 'remains in a poor state of repair'. Unfortunately, it is exposed to environmental damage, with discarded cans, bottles and assorted flotsam from the Beauly Firth being constantly washed up on it.

None of the houses in the hamlet of Quarry of Redcastle (Figure 36, page 251) are listed by Historic Scotland. On the other hand, the remains of the mill at Milton of Redcastle, together with Redcastle itself, the Lodge House, the stable square and the oval steading at Redcastle Mains, Greenhill House, the parish church and the graveyard (including the walls and gates) are all listed, mainly as category B [buildings of regional importance or major examples of some particular period, style or building type]. Also listed are the bridge over the Redcastle burn at Chapelton (which incorporates St Andrew's well), the Redcastle crannog (Figure 2, page 20) and the remains of the wooden piles of the old Redcastle yair [fish trap].[41] It is thought possible that these piles may also have been part of a wooden causeway connecting the crannog to the shore.[42]

Due to its importance as a wintering area for wildfowl and wading birds, most of the Beauly Firth and its shoreline was designated as a Site of Special Scientific Interest (SSSI) in 1988.[43] The boundary of the SSSI specifically includes all of Redcastle pier. It was also included in the designations in March 1999 of the Inner Moray Firth, both as a Special Protection Area (SPA) and as a Ramsar site, with an ecosystem of intertidal flats, saltmarsh and sand dunes supporting a winter peak of over 26,000 waterfowl. [The Convention on Wetlands, signed in Ramsar, Iran, in 1971 is an intergovernmental treaty for international action and co-operation on conservation and use of wetlands.] More recently, in March 2005, the sub-tidal sandbanks in the Beauly Firth were designated as a Special Area of Conservation (SAC). There are currently two proposals to environmentally protect the area further. The first of these is to designate much of the area around Redcastle as a conservation area. The second is to assign the entire Moray Firth as a Nationally Important Marine Area (NIMA), due to its population of breeding bottlenose dolphins, its wintering marine waterfowl and some underwater geological features known as 'mermaids' tables'.

NOTES

[1] See Chapter 1, note 18.

[2] See Chapter 1, note 25.

[3] See Chapter 1, note 3.

[4] See Chapter 1, note 40.

[5] See Chapter 1, note 30.

[6] Killearnan parish hearth tax rolls are contained in the 'Cromartie Papers belonging to Her Grace the Duchess of Sutherland and Countess of Cromartie', Vol XVIII (1692). They are held at NAS GD305/1/164/271.

[7] See Chapter 1, note 108.

[8] The document entitled 'Rentall of the Estate of Readcastle for Crop 1710' is held at NAS CS96/1/94/1. It details the rentals (in victual and/or Scots money) payable by the farmers and other rent payers of Killearnan and Kilmuir parishes to the Redcastle estate in 1710. It also names many of the farmers and businessmen, one of the earliest documents to do so.

[9] See Chapter 1, note 108.

[10] See Chapter 1, note 22.

[11] Eighteenth-century taxation Survey Books are lodged in the NAS under the E326 series. Ross-shire lists are contained in: Window Tax (E326/1/108–110); Commutation Tax (E326/2/45); Inhabited House Tax (E326/3/54); Male Servants Tax (E326/5/1–27); Female Servants Tax (E326/6/2–26); Carriage Tax (E326/8/1–19); Horse Tax (E326/9/2–33); Farm Horse Tax (E326/10/4, 12); and Dog Tax (E326/11/2). A useful guide to window and other property-based taxes is given in Gibson, J, Medlycott, M and Mills, D, 'Land and Window Tax Assessments' (2004).

[12] See Chapter 1, note 108.

[13] The construction and repair of the Parliamentary and Military roads in the Highlands is recorded in the 'Reports of the Commissioners for Highland Roads and Bridges', Vols I–III (1802–63) held at HCA CRC2/1/2.

[14] The earliest road map of the Redcastle area is that of Taylor, G and Skinner, A, 'A Plan of the Cross roads in the Shires of Ross and Cromarty' (1775) held at HCA D87. Other eighteenth-century maps that show local roads are: Walpoole's 'New Map of the Counties of Orkney, Caithness, Sutherland and Ross and Cromarty' in the 'New and Complete British Traveller' (1784); Ainslie, J and Faden, W, 'Scotland, drawn from a

series of angles and astronomical observations' (1789); Urquhart, D, 'Sketch of the Black Isle in the North Highlands of Scotland' (1794); and Lieut Campbell, 'A new and correct map of Scotland or North Britain with all the Post and Military Roads, etc.' (1794). I am indebted to Alasdair Cameron of Wellhouse for access to a copy of the Urquhart map.

[15] Two nineteenth-century maps of 'Ross and Cromarty Shires' were surveyed by John Thomson in 1820 and 1830. The latter was published in his 'Atlas of Scotland' (1832). The 'Map of Scotland' was published by Lewis, S *circa* 1841 and is available online at www.archivemaps.com. These maps show that the roads that are still to be found around Redcastle today were in existence by the early nineteenth century. The direct route between Redcastle and Scuddel Ferry is shown on Brown, P, 'Reduced Plan of the Survey of the Commons of Milbuy, Cromarty, Etc.' (1816) available at NAS RHP4045. At one time thought to be an ancient route, this is more probably part of an eighteenth-century drove road.

[16] See Chapter 1, note 120.

[17] The construction and repair of the Parliamentary and District roads in the Black Isle (District 7 of Ross-shire) is recorded in 'The Sederunt Book for Redcastle District of Roads under the Commutation Act 1807', Vols 1–3 (1807–66) held at HCA CRC2/10/1.

[18] See Chapter 1, note 108.

[19] See Chapter 1, note 132.

[20] See Chapter 1, note 84.

[21] See Chapter 4, note 31.

[22] The minutes of the Black Isle District Committee (1890–1930) are available at HCA CRC7/1/1–3.

[23] The minutes of the Road Board of Ross and Cromarty County Council (1890–1930) are archived at HCA CRC3/7/1–5.

[24] Killearnan Parish Council was formed in 1890 under the Local Government (Scotland) Act (1889). The original minutes have not survived but those for 1910–30 are archived at HCA CRC6/7/1c.

[25] The evidence of crofters Finlay Mackay of Drynie Park and Kenneth Davidson of Knockbain given in October 1883 to the HM Commissioners of Inquiry into the 'Condition of The Crofters and Cottars in the Highlands and Islands of Scotland' (Napier Commission) is recorded in Vol IV (1885). The fixing of the first Fair Rents in Killearnan parish is recorded in the Report of the Crofters Commission for the year 1887–88, Appendix A, Table 4, HMSO (1889).

[26] The 'Landlord Return' of the Redcastle estate to the Napier Commission Inquiry in 1883 is held at NAS AF/50/6/2.

[27] See Chapter 1, note 140.

[28] See Chapter 3, note 20.

[29] British telephone directories (1880–1984) are searchable by subscription at www.ancestry.co.uk.

[30] See Chapter 4, note 31.

[31] See note 24.

[32] The minutes of Avoch District Council are contained in three minutes books and three files of loose papers at HCA: D275/A1a (1930–37 Delegated Duties); D275/A2a (1931–61 Statutory Duties); D275/A3a (1938–56 Delegated Duties); D275/A1b (1957–61 All Duties); D275/A1c (1963–68 All Duties); D275/A1d (1969–75 All Duties).

[33] Poor Fund allocations to individual residents of Killearnan parish are detailed in 'The General Register of the Poor – Killearnan (1865–1924)' which is available at HCA CRC6/7/2. There is a '100-year rule' on access to data for individuals.

[34] The Jack Holmes Planning Group report was entitled 'The Moray Firth – a Plan for Growth in a Sub-Region of the Scottish Highlands' and was presented to the Highlands and Islands Development Board in March 1968. This was followed by a Special Report to HIDB by Ormiston, J H, 'Moray Firth – an Agricultural Study' (1973). Two maps showing proposals to develop housing in the area between Redcastle and Tore and to route the A9 through Redcastle are on pages 80 and 100.

[35] The activities of Highlands and Islands Enterprise (HIE) are described on its website: www.hie.co.uk. It was previously constituted with nine Local Enterprise Companies (LEC), but since 2007 these have been disbanded and replaced with three main regional offices. The Black Isle previously fell under the ambit of Ross and Cromarty Enterprise (RACE) and is now administered by the Inverness and East Grampian office.

[36] Killearnan Community Council was inaugurated in October 1977. I am indebted to the current chairman, Mr John Mackintosh, for access to copies of its minutes and newsletters.

[37] The diverse activities of the Highland Council are described on its website: www.highland.gov.uk.

[38] See Chapter 4, note 31.

[39] See Chapter 1, note 120.

[40] The report for Historic Scotland entitled 'Coastal Assessment Survey of Inner Moray Firth' was undertaken by the University of Edinburgh Centre for Field Archaeology. The section covering Redcastle is contained in Vol 1 (September 1998), pages 37–42. The Redcastle quarry and its associated pier are classified by RCAHMS as an 'industrial site' and as a 'military installation (rifle range)' of built heritage and archaeological interest.

[41] The list of statutory buildings designated by Historic Scotland in Killearnan parish can be searched online at Historic Scotland's website: www.historic-scotland.gov.uk. They can also be accessed via www.rcahms.gov.uk using the 'Pastmap' and 'Canmore' facilities.

[42] See Chapter 1, note 7.

[43] Environmental SSSI, SPA, Ramsar and SCA designations for the Beauly Firth and Inner Moray Firth are available from Scottish Natural Heritage (SNH) at www.snh.gov.uk and www.jncc.gov.uk.

Chapter 6

PEOPLE AND PLACES

6.1 Early Maps

A map of 'Ross in the 12th century' is appended as an inset to Bain's[1] *History of the Ancient Province of Ross*. It is a sketch map with place names known from the twelfth century, and shows 'Tarrudale' and 'Gargasoun' but not Etherdouer (Redcastle), which was not founded until the late twelfth century. The fourteenth-century 'Gough' map of Britain shows in the 'Conntaty de Roffe' [County of Ross], an unnamed settlement on the northern shore of what appears to be the Beauly Firth. This may, therefore, represent the first mapping of Redcastle.[2]

The first detailed mapping of Scotland was carried out by the Scottish cartographer Timothy Pont in the late sixteenth century.[3] Unfortunately, there is no known copy of his map of the 'Ard-meanach' [Black Isle], although his notes, from which the map would have derived, have survived. Redcastle is named as 'Castel Riwy ... [with] St Andrews chappell whair ther is a faire about Lammes'. The text also describes other locations and their relation to Redcastle; for example, 'half a myl from the castell is Kirewran with a paroch kirk ... 2 myl thence Achachroisk with manie ancient monuments betuix ... a myl from Castel-Ruy is Culcowye'. [The word 'riwy' or 'ruy' does not appear in Old Scots and is perhaps an anglicised version of the Gaelic word *ruadh*, meaning reddish.]

The earliest map that names Redcastle (actually 'Redcasst') seems to be Gerhard Mercator's 'Scotiae Regnum' map of 1595. Unfortunately, it locates the castle at the head of the Cromarty Firth, whilst 'Bewlye Abbey' is placed on the north shore of the Beauly Firth where Redcastle should be.[4] This error is repeated by John Speed in his 'Kingdom of Scotland' map of 1610. Robert Gordon's (1636–52) manuscript map of 'Part of Ros' may show Redcastle, but the area around the Beauly Firth has been overdrawn at least twice and an illegible name, though located correctly on one of the overlapping redrawings, appears to be stroked out.

The first correct naming and placement of Redcastle (actually 'Red Ca') seems to be on the 'Scotia Australis' map of 1618.[5] This map is based on John Speed's survey and was engraved by Solomon Rogiers. The well-known cartographer, Jean Blaeu, published his 'Theatrum Orbis Terrarum Sive Atlas Novus' in 1654. This remarkable atlas contains numerous maps of Scotland based on original surveys carried out by Timothy Pont and Robert Gordon. Three of them show Redcastle (actually 'Reedcastell'): the 'Scotia Regnum'; the 'Extima Scotiae' (Figure 41); and the 'Moravia Scotiae Provincia'. The former is unusual in misplacing Redcastle between 'Kessach' (nowadays North Kessock) and 'Munlochy', whilst the other two maps place it correctly. The Blaeu maps are also interesting in showing 'Hiltoun' (a short distance inland from Corgrain Point) and 'Cultow' or 'Cultowy' (nowadays Tarradale). These are also named on Gerard van Keulen's 1727–34 'Afteckening van de Noord Oost hock van Schotland', which does not name Redcastle but has a small drawing of it. The name of 'Cultow' is repeated on Herman Moll's 1745 map of 'The Shires of Ross and Cromartie', but it is named 'Taradle' on George Wade's 'Plan of the Murray Firth and Cromarty Firth' of 1730.

Figure 41: A portion of the 1654 Blaeu 'Extima Scotia' map, showing Reedcastell (reproduced by permission of the Trustees of the National Library of Scotland)

The first published maps to locate and name Killearnan were Joseph Avery's 1725–30 'Plan of the Murray Firth', drawn up for the York Building Company, and his 1727 'Plan containing Lochness, Lochoych, Lochlochey and all the rivers and strips of water that runs in and set out from the same'. [The York Building Company was contracted by Parliament to manage to estates that were forfeited after the first Jacobite rebellion of 1715.] These maps spell Killearnan as 'Killurning'. Exactly the same spelling is found on the Wade (1730) map. John Ainslie's map of 1785 is of interest in marking two places whose names are not found on other maps: 'Girnal' (near Taradale) and 'Knocknaguy' (at the location of Hilltown of Redcastle, near Corgrain Point).[6]

After the Jacobite rebellion of 1745–46, James Alexander Grante produced a *Carte ou sont traces toutes les differentes routes, que S A R Charles Edward Prince de Galles, a suivies dans la Grande Bretagne*. It was published in 1747, and shows the routes traversed by the Jacobite army and the sites of the major battles. Furthermore, it marks 'Red Castle' as the only feature on the Black Isle,[7] somewhat remarkably as the Mackenzies of Redcastle played no part in the rebellion. In the aftermath of the Battle of Culloden, General Watson, the Quartermaster General of Scotland, was appointed to oversee a survey of Scotland and produce a set of military maps that would help the army to quell any future uprising quickly. William Roy was commissioned in 1747 to commence the survey, and in 1749 he was contracted to extend his survey to all of North Scotland. The survey was completed in 1755, and the maps were deposited in the King's Library where they remained confidential until it was deemed, around the turn of the nineteenth century, that peace had prevailed and there was a need to improve the economy of the Highlands.

Figure 42: A portion of the 1750 Roy map, showing Red Castle
(© The British Library Board. All Rights Reserved)

Roy's maps were drawn at a scale of 1,000 yards to 1 inch, and most are extraordinarily detailed.[8] However, the map covering the Killearnan area (Figure 42) is disappointing, because it marks only 'Redcastle', 'Kirk of Redcastle', Spital (spelled 'Spittle') and Tarradale (spelled 'Tarradle'). Strangely, Kilcoy castle is not shown, although Tore and Kinkell castles are. A road from the Kessock Ferry to Redcastle is shown, but it appears to terminate at Redcastle. The positioning of Redcastle and Tarradale are accurate; however, Spital is placed near the southern edge of the current Spital Wood, at a point considerably north of the area now known as Spital Shore. What appear to be villages are shown at four locations: Spital Wood; Kirk of Redcastle; about half a mile east of Redcastle (probably Hilltown, which was located on the lower slopes of Gallow Hill); and about one mile north of Redcastle (probably Burntown, which was located between Chapelton and Parkton). There is no evidence of a village around Redcastle itself, where only the castle is shown.

This is something of a mystery. Seventeenth-century records indicate that the term 'Miltown' was used to refer to the whole area around Redcastle (rather than any specific hamlet), but by the mid-eighteenth century the existence of 'Milton of Redcastle' is well documented – for example, in the Killearnan parish kirk session minutes. A possible explanation is that before *circa* 1750 most of the population of Redcastle lived to the west and north of Redcastle, where their houses would not be in view from the castle. This possibility is supported by Bishop Forbes' diary[9] of his visit to Redcastle in 1762, in which he wrote a description of the view from the top of the castle which refers to two mills on the Redcastle burn but fails to mention any 'village'. This is corroborated by other documentary evidence, which also suggests that the Redcastle mill may have been located at the mouth of the Redcastle burn during and before the eighteenth century (where it could be accessed by boat), but that the village of 'Milltown (or Milton) of Redcastle' was not built at its present location until the late-eighteenth or early nineteenth century.

Many of the eighteenth-century maps show roads crossing the Black Isle. For example, George Wade's 1730 'Plan of the Murray Firth and Cromarty Firth' (which is probably the most accurate of the early maps) shows a road from Kessock Ferry through Redcastle (and onwards to Scuddel Ferry over the Conon river) taking a more inland route than the present shoreside road. This route is also the one shown in the Roy (1750) map. Conversely, Herman Moll's 1745 map of 'The Shires of Ross and Cromartie' shows a road from Kessock Ferry to Dingwall using a route similar to the present A9 and A835. The earliest known detailed road map of the area is the 'Plan of the Cross Roads in the Shires of Ross and Cromartie' drawn by Taylor and Skinner[10] in 1775 (Figure 37, page 264). It shows that the road from Kessock Ferry to

Dingwall, via Scuddel Ferry, crossed a road from Fortrose to Beauly (using a route similar to the present A832) at a point between Linnie and Parkton (rather than at Tore, where they currently cross). From this crossroads, a branch road to Redcastle took a route following the Redcastle burn to the north-west of Gallow Hill via Parkton and Chapelton.

Other maps also show this five-way intersection, which must have been important at that time – for example, Ainslie and Faden's 1789 map of 'Scotland, drawn from a series of angles and astronomical observations' and Lieut Campbell's 1794 map of the 'Post and Military Roads of Scotland'. Urquhart's 1794 map entitled 'Sketch of the Black Isle in the North Highlands of Scotland' (which was drawn to accompany an agricultural survey of Northern Scotland) also shows five roads intersecting at this point. Even the much later Lewis's 'Map of Scotland', published *circa* 1841, shows the intersection, indicating that these roads were in existence well into the mid-nineteenth century. The roads led (anticlockwise) north-west to Scuddel Ferry, west to Beauly, south to Redcastle, south-east to Kessock Ferry and east to Fortrose. Traces of parts of the Scuddel Ferry, Redcastle and Fortrose roads can still be found. Redcastle could also be accessed from the west, using a road that branched off the Beauly to Fortrose road near Tarradale and passed by the Killearnan parish church. This route continued (as it still does today) through Redcastle and along the north shore of the Beauly Firth to Kessock Ferry.

These early road maps probably showed only the routes that could be traversed by horses and carriages. Many other minor tracks and bridleways would have existed and older routes would have fallen into disuse; for example the road (originally thought to be of eleventh-century construction, but now considered more probably to be a late-eighteenth-century drove route) that led directly from Redcastle to Scuddel Ferry. Sections of this road are still visible north of Blairdhu and through Spital Wood, and its route is shown on some later eighteenth- and early nineteenth-century maps and charts – for example, on the 'New Map of the Counties of Orkney, Cathness [sic], Sutherland, Ross and Cromarty' published in 1784 in Walpoole's 'New and Complete British Traveller', and on Brown's 'Reduced Plan of the Survey of the Commons of Milbuy, Cromarty, etc.' of 1816.[11] Surprisingly, the remains of this road are not recorded as a historic monument by the RCAHMS.

The most detailed and reliable mapping of Scotland in the early nineteenth century was undertaken by John Thomson.[12] His map of the 'Southern Part of Ross and Cromarty Shires' was based on surveys by John Craig and was originally published in 1826. It names Killearnan, Red Castle, Kilcoy Castle, Allanrick (Allanglach), Aranfely (Arpafeelie) and shows the Redcastle pier, somewhat exaggerated, as well as the principal roads in the area laid out very much as they are today. Subsequently, Thomson incorporated this map (as map XXV) into his comprehensive 'Atlas of Scotland', published in 1832. The atlas also contains an index and an interesting historical introduction to earlier geography and mapping of the counties of Scotland. Another important map of the early nineteenth century is the Redcastle estate plan surveyed by Edward Sang and Sons of Kirkcaldy.[13] This map (Figure 8, page 75) was drawn up for Patrick Grant's trustees prior to the sale of the estate.

The resultant map, completed in 1825, is extraordinarily detailed. As well as all the major features of the area, such as the castle, the parish church, the school, the quarry and the pier, it shows the locations of all the estate houses and the division of the fields. There is also a tabulation of the persons occupying each house and field. Another interesting feature of the plan is the large number of crofts and associated buildings at the south-western corner of Spital Wood. This village, called 'Whitewells Maillers' in the plan, had also been shown on Roy's map of 1750 (Figure 42, page 292) and must have been a centre of a considerable population in the eighteenth and early nineteenth centuries. Twenty crofts are drawn on the 1825 estate plan between Spital Wood and Spital Shore.

A common crofting name in the Spital and Garguston area in the early nineteenth century was Logan. In a document written in about 1980 by William Logan (who was born in Muir of Ord in 1906 and lived in Canada), there is a reference to an ancient, abandoned and overgrown graveyard which he recalls visiting with his father in about 1916.[14] He describes the site as less than a mile from Redcastle and near to Tarradale quarry. As he would have been only ten years old at the time, these distances must be taken as very approximate, but a location around the site of the old Spital village seems most likely. He also recollects having to 'fight our way through a tangle of thorns and bushes until we stumbled on the ancient weatherworn headstones of red sandstone ... much sunk into the ground and measured roughly six inches thick, eighteen inches wide and stood somewhat less than two feet above the earth. The Logan names were barely decipherable'. There seems to be no other record of this graveyard.

Unlike the 1750 Roy map, the 1825 estate plan shows the rows of houses at Milton of Redcastle, suggesting that Milton of Redcastle estate village was initially built during the late-eighteenth century or the early nineteenth century. The plan also indicates the existence of houses immediately to the north of the Redcastle quarry and to the west of the parochial school. This land was part of the church glebe and the houses, probably known as 'Croftmore', would have been occupied by the farm workers who tended the glebe. Croftmore is a name that appears in early sasines, but it does not appear in any later documents, suggesting that the buildings there were demolished soon after 1825 (probably after Milton of Redcastle and Quarry of Redcastle were fully built). Today, this area is farmland and there is no visible trace of past habitation.

Other details on the 1825 plan are of interest. For example, Blairdhu farmhouse was located a little to the south-east of its present site, and Garguston farmhouse appears to be located substantially to the west of its present location. Similarly, the farm now known as Fettes was not on its present site, but a little to the east and named 'Drimmore' (sometimes 'Drummore'), whilst the area of woodland that still stands to the south-west of Fettes House was named 'Willan Bush'. Newton of Redcastle, however, was located at its present site and was comprised of several more houses than nowadays. The plan is also noteworthy in showing the locations of Burntown and Hiltown. Burntown lay about half a kilometre north of Chapelton, midway between Chapelton and Parkton, whilst Hiltown was about half a kilometre inland from Corgrain Point. Another point of interest is the spelling of two of the geographic features: Corgrain is spelled 'Corry Grain', whilst Gallow Hill is spelled 'Gallows Hill'. The latter may be a simple typographical error, but it is a commonly held belief that Gallow Hill was the site of a medieval gallows. However, there does not appear to be any evidence to verify this assertion and this plan seems to be the only document to use the term 'gallows'.

6.2   The Ordnance Survey

The Ordnance Survey commenced the task of large-scale mapping of Britain in 1840, but it was not until 1872 that Capt Coddington of the Royal Engineers was commissioned to survey the Black Isle area. Two 1:10,000 (*circa* 6 inch:1 mile) sheets published in 1880 cover the majority of the Redcastle area, whilst a set of fifteen sheets of the higher scale 1:2,500 (*circa* 25 inch:1 mile) map published in 1881 cover Killearnan parish.[15] They are known as the First Edition or 'County Series' maps (Figure 43). Features such as houses or fields are numbered on the higher scale sheets, and an accompanying reference index[16] gives a brief description of each (for example, 'house with garden' or 'arable field', etc.). The set of higher-scale sheets is also accompanied by a name book[17] which explains the origin and provenance of all the place names used on the sheets. Together, the maps, index and name book provide an extraordinarily detailed insight into both the topography and life of the area in 1872. The information contained in the name book was gleaned by the surveyors from local literate people, such as the minister, schoolteacher and parish registrar. Three entries are of some interest in terms of the folklore of the period. Firstly, the Redcastle crannog (Figure 2, page 20), named as a cairn, is recorded as 'supposed by some of the inhabitants of the surrounding district to have been erected to mark the grave of some Danish warrior of note who had fallen in battle somewhere near Redcastle'. It is now known not to be a burial cairn but a true marine crannog.

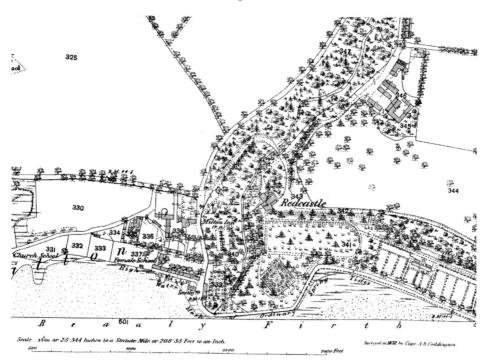

Figure 43: A portion of the 1872 first series Ordnance Survey map, showing Milton of Redcastle, Redcastle Mains, Redcastle and its Gardens (reproduced by permission of the Trustees of the National Library of Scotland)

Secondly, the pier at Quarry of Redcastle is recorded in the name book as 'supposed to have been partially constructed by Oliver Cromwell and used for shipping stone from quarries in the vicinity'. This is probably only partially true, as the original pier that Cromwell's Covenanters had used to land troops in 1649 was probably a little to the west of the pier that had been constructed in 1725 to ship stone for Inverness harbour, and that had been greatly extended by Thomas Telford in 1804 to ship stone for the Caledonian Canal. The pier is named on the 1:10,000 (*circa* 6 inch:1 mile) map as a 'Volunteers' Rifle Range' and marks the locations of the marker's butt and target stance. The principal users of the range were originally the 4th (Knockbain) Company Ross-shire Volunteers.[18] They were formed in 1860, but were consolidated with the other Ross-shire Companies in 1880 to form the 1st Battalion Ross-shire Rifle Volunteers, with headquarters in Dingwall. In 1881, they became part of the Seaforth Highlanders.

Thirdly, Corgrain Point is described as a conspicuous point of land about one mile east of Redcastle and 'at this point timber is shipped and coals. Some is landed for the use of adjoining properties. A short distance to the east is a pier which has at one time been used for this purpose but is now in a very bad state of repair'. The remains of the pier at Corgrain Point are still visible (Figure 10, page 82), and a coal depot – which no longer exists – is marked at the east entrance to Redcastle on the 1:2,500 (*circa* 25 inch:1 mile) Ordnance Survey map of 1872. The pier to the east of Corgrain Point was at Lettoch and its remains are also still detectable.

The Milton Inn had a sign board and is described as a small public house, one storey high and thatched, with office-houses attached. The other houses of Milton of Redcastle are described in the name book as 'for the most part, one storey high and chiefly thatched and only in a middling state of repair'. They are not individually identified on the first edition Ordnance Survey map, but they were the premises of the village tradesmen, some of which are now category B listed buildings,[19] including the smithy, the mill (also known to have been used subsequently as a weaving shed and as a joiner's shop), the West Lodge at the entrance to Redcastle, and two cottages – named Inver (now Ashgrove) and Rosemount.

The latter was the site of the last village shop, the original having been in what is now the rear garden of Rosemount. Interestingly, the mill was not located on the Redcastle burn but some twenty metres to the west. There was a mill pond (behind the Gardener's Cottage), with a sluice gate to carry water along a lade to the wheel when required. The existence of a dam at the mill pond is recorded in the reference index,[20] but there is no evidence of it today. In 1981, Historic Scotland categorised the mill as 'Milton Old Factory' and referred to the building as 'a probable weaving shed, now a joiner's shop'. Valuation Roll[21] entries suggest that the mill may have ceased operation around 1872, and it is possible that it was converted into a weaving shed then. The building is described as 'a two storey, seven bay, symmetrical range facing SW with a centre door, wide windows, those at ground floor having relieving arches, and a bull's eye vent in the SE gable'. Today, a large millstone (Figure 44) is included as a feature in the small garden laid out within some of the old mill walls, but there is no evidence of the architectural features described in the listed building report of 1981.

The water flowing in the Redcastle burn was controlled by a sluice gate at the outflow of the large mill pond between Greenhill House and Parkton. There was also a pipeline, some of which is still visible, which diverted water into a channel which fed water to Redcastle Mains and powered the water mill there. The channel runs alongside the estate road leading from Chapelton to Redcastle Mains, and the water wheel can still be seen in the farm buildings.

Redcastle's water supply came from a spring west of the castle and close to the Redcastle burn. The spring water was fed to a small underground pump room where there was a manual ram. Garguston farmhouse was served by a similar pump house that was located close to the westernmost of four crofts at Garguston Shore. It was part of that crofter's lease to work the hand pump periodically to fill the farm's water tank. The site of the pump house is marked as a well on the first edition 1:2,500 (*circa* 25 inch:1 mile) map, and its remains can still be seen today.

Figure 44: The millstone at Milton of Redcastle (2008)

Rather strangely, Blairdhu Farm is named on the 1:2,500 (*circa* 25 inch:1 mile) map as 'Blackmuir'. This is only occasion on which this version of the name appears in any documentation of the Redcastle area. It seems likely to be a mistakenly anglicised translation of the Gaelic *Blar Dhu*.

The maps also show two crofts remaining in the village of Spital Wood (also known as Braes of Garguston). There must have been a rapid decline in the number of crofts and the population in this village after 1825, when Patrick Grant's estate map[22] (Figure 8, page 75) showed twenty crofts there. By the turn of the century, only one cottage (named as 'Spittal Croft') remained occupied. The 1:2,500 (*circa* 25 inch:1 mile) map shows that it was located about midway along the south-eastern edge of the wood roughly due north of Garguston Farm.

It had a garden and there was a pond alongside. The other croft on the map is located at the eastern corner of Spital Wood, but it appears to already have become ruinous by the turn of the century.

Revisions of the Ordnance Survey maps of 1872 were published in 1907 by the Ordnance Survey at scales of 1:10,000 (*circa* 6 inch:1 mile) and 1:2,500 (*circa* 25 inch:1 mile).[23] They are known as the Second Edition maps. They show both rows of houses in Milton of Redcastle, as well as the smithy. However, all the buildings that lay between Rivulet Cottage and the West Lodge at the entrance to Redcastle were no longer in existence. They had presumably fallen into disrepair as the population declined and had been demolished around the turn of the century. They had included the Milton Inn and the original general merchant's shop. The inn had closed some years earlier (about 1875–80) and the shop had moved to the house now known as Rosemount. It is not known for how long there had been a shop in Redcastle, but its existence in the early nineteenth century is recorded in an advertisement published by the *Inverness Journal*[24] on 11 April 1828. It is headed 'An Excellent Situation To Let', and provides a brief description of its location and fittings:

> A shop in the centre of the village of Milton, Redcastle, with a cellar and store room of great length. It is furnished with shelves, counter and writing desk etc. and admirably calculated for a merchant. Furnished or unfurnished lodging, with a kitchen, can also be had; and possession may be obtained at Whitsunday next. Apply to Donald Noble, Redcastle.

All four houses, plus the old Free Church school, are shown in Quarry of Redcastle, as are the tracks of the old narrow gauge railway that emerged from the Redcastle quarry and led out to the end of the pier. An undated photograph, published on page 11 of Margaret Oag's book,[25] also clearly shows the five buildings viewed from the end of Redcastle pier. The Free Church school appears to be fully roofed, suggesting that the photograph dates from the late-nineteenth or early twentieth century. It seems to be the only photographic record of Quarry of Redcastle from this period.

It is not recorded when the railway track along the Redcastle pier was dismantled. The Caledonian Canal Commissioners were expected to remove it after the quarry was no longer required for construction of the canal (*circa* 1820), but this may not have been done until the extensive repairs to the canal (in 1843–47) were completed, or perhaps even later. Close to the point at which the railway exited from the quarry, the maps show a large building surrounded by an arc of four smaller buildings. These are not shown on the earlier (1872) maps, but it seems likely that these would have been the remains of offices, store or tool sheds and crane platforms left behind after the closure of the quarry *circa* 1875. In that area today, a substantial amount of dressed stone is still visible in the undergrowth.

Redcastle and its immediate environs are split between six sheets of the 1:2,500 (*circa* 25 inch:1 mile) second edition map. They show interesting detail of the area. For example, a well is shown in the Redcastle quarry. Fresh spring water still flows from the quarry face into the basin of the quarry, which now holds a small pond at the western end (not shown on the map). This well was used by the residents of Quarry of Redcastle as a source of fresh water until piped mains water arrived in 1959. An old iron pipe, still visible below the outflow, is probably the pipe which took water to the manse. Another source of fresh water was the Grey Well (Figure 31, page 230), which is located on the north side of the road linking Milton of Redcastle to Killearnan parish church. The trough is dated 1844, and is marked as a 'trough' on the 1907 map but as a 'well' on the 1872 map.[26] Until the 1950s, this was the nearest source of drinking water to Killearnan School. There is also an old well opposite Rivulet Cottage, which feeds into a stonewalled ditch that still channels the fresh spring water along the north side of the service road into Quarry of Redcastle, then under the road to dissipate into the Beauly Firth at a point opposite the remains of the old Free Church school. Even in summer, these sources do not normally dry up – nor do they freeze in winter.

Another feature of the 1907 second edition 1:2,500 (*circa* 25 inch:1 mile) map is the diagonal path that runs from Blairdhu Farm through Spital Wood. This is the line of an old road north (now thought to be the remains of an old drove road) from Redcastle to the River Conon at Scuddel Ferry. Surprisingly, it appears only on a few early maps,[27] although some earth and stone work can still be seen in Spital Wood. Like the earlier 1872 map, the 1907 map also shows Spital Croft, the last remaining croft in the area south of Spital Wood (Braes of Garguston). A little to the north of it, in Spital Wood close to the line of the Black Isle railway line, there was a sawmill that had not been marked on the 1872 map.

The 1907 second edition Ordnance Survey maps were used for the Land Utilisation Survey carried out in 1930–38 by schoolchildren and students, supervised by geography teachers across the whole of the UK. The project was led by Professor Dudley Stamp of the London School of Economics, who published the detailed findings in 1948 under the title *The Land of Britain – its Use and Misuse*, and collated the data onto hand-coloured 1 inch:1 mile (1:63,360) maps.[28] The Redcastle area (Figure 45) was surveyed by the Drumsmittal School in January–June 1932, and every field is marked on the individual sheets of the 1:10,000 (*circa* 6 inch:1 mile) map using seven classes of land use: forest and woodland, marked F/coloured dark green; meadowland, M/light green; arable land, A/brown; heath and moorland, H/yellow; gardens, G/purple; unproductive land, W/red; water, W/blue. Predictably, the fields of the Redcastle area are predominantly marked as arable (A), with only the large field to the east of the castle and three of the fields at Garguston Shore being marked as meadowland (M). Surveyors were also requested to classify forests and woodlands as high forest, coppice, scrub/newly planted, or cut-down; and to further indicate whether they were coniferous, deciduous or mixed. The Gallow Hill woodlands are shown to be predominantly high forest/mixed, cut-down/coniferous or heathland, with some newly planted (1928–30) coniferous areas.

Figure 45: The Killearnan portion of the 1932 Land Utilisation Survey map
(© Audrey N Clark)

No Third Edition 1:10,000 (*circa* 6 inch:1 mile) or 1:2,500 (*circa* 25 inch:1 mile) survey was carried out by the Ordnance Survey in Ross-shire, so all mid-twentieth-century larger-scale maps of the area are based on revisions of the previous second edition maps of 1907 (which themselves were revisions of the 1872 survey). This is unfortunate, because although several were published,[29] it means that there are no totally reliable detailed maps of Redcastle from this period. Like the earlier large-scale first and second editions, the 1:63,360 (1 inch:1 mile) Ordnance Survey map of 1929[30] confusingly uses the name 'Milton' to cover the whole area around the Killearnan parish church and the hamlet of Quarry of Redcastle, whilst the name 'Redcastle' covers the castle itself and the village of Milton of Redcastle. The detail of the map is also remarkably inaccurate. For example, at Quarry of Redcastle only three buildings are shown, which is surprising, as all four houses were in occupation and, although it was by then in poor condition, the Free Church school was still a substantial building. This map also shows the two rows of houses in Milton of Redcastle, as well as the mill and the Gardener's Cottage but, surprisingly, the West Lodge is not shown. At Garguston Shore, there are four croft buildings shown, although only one was in occupation; and at Chapelton two buildings are shown, although all three (and the smiddy) were still in occupation. In spite of its inaccuracies, however, this map appears to be the only Ordnance Survey map to show the location of the windmill that was built in 1928 to pump water to the Killearnan manse from the spring in the Redcastle quarry.

A larger scale 1:25,000 (*circa* 2.5 inch:1 mile) map of the so-called 'Provisional Edition' was published in 1950. Sheet 28/54 covers the Redcastle area. Features of interest include the remaining croft at Spital Wood (Braes of Garguston) being shown as a ruin, and the mile posts at Milton of Redcastle, Corgrain Point and Garguston cottages still being in place. Also of interest is that this map does not show the house built in 1941 above Parkton Farm, presumably because this was not regarded as a sufficiently major revision. The subsequent 'provisional edition' 1:25,000 sheet NH55 of 1961 shows the Parkton house, as well as two houses (Reay Cottage and Reay House) remaining at Chapelton.

Two 1:10,000 (*circa* 6 inch:1 mile) revisions, NH54SE and NH55SE, were published in 1959 and 1972. The 1959 sheet shows only the mile posts at Milton of Redcastle and Corgrain Point, whereas the 1972 sheet shows none. It is not known when, or why, they were removed. This map also shows all five buildings at Quarry of Redcastle, whereas the 1972 sheet shows only three. Sheet 27 of the 1929 series 1:63,360 (*circa* 1 inch:1 mile) map[31] had also shown only three houses. This confusion simply indicates that the detail on these revised maps needs to be viewed with care, because different Ordnance Survey surveyors will have put different interpretations on features that required revision. The 1959 sheet is also of interest, in that it is the first that does not show Corgrain Cottage, which had served as the 'East Lodge' to Redcastle and had last been occupied in 1930. This map is also the first to name the Redcastle crannog (Figure 2, page 20); all previous maps refer to it as a 'cairn'. A revision of the second edition 1:2,500 (*circa* 25 inch:1 mile) map of 1907 was published in 1971 as sheet 5649–5749. It is probably the most reliable map of the period, and was the map used by Highland Council Planning Department until the Ordnance Survey introduced digital online mapping.

In 1992–94, the Ordnance Survey published metric revisions of the 1:10,000 NH54NE and NH55SE maps that had been first published in 1959. These maps are of interest in being the first to name 'Carron Cottage' at

Chapelton and for their misspelling of 'Rivulett Cottage', but many of the geographic features shown on the previous large-scale maps are absent – for example, the old track through Spital Wood, the last croft in Spital (Braes of Garguston) and the water channel that drove the turbine of the saw mill at Redcastle Mains.[32]

Redcastle is shown on sheet 26 of the 1995 Ordnance Survey 'Landranger' 1:50,000 (2 cm:1 km) series of maps. As in the maps of the early twentieth century, the term 'Milton' is used as a generic name to cover Killearnan, Quarry of Redcastle and Milton of Redcastle. Redcastle itself is named, along with Newton, Greenhill House and the farmhouses at Garguston, Blairdhu, Fettes and Parkton. This map can now be accessed online through 'getamap' on the Ordnance Survey website.[33] Sheet 432 (Black Isle) of the 2002 Ordnance Survey 'Explorer' 1:25,000 (4 cm:1 km) map also names the Killearnan manse (although neither the old nor the new manses are used any longer for that purpose), the quarry (disused), the pier, the crannog, Redcastle Mains and Chapelton. It also contains a remarkable error in not showing the new bypass of the A832 around Garguston Farm. Instead, the road is shown to follow the line of the old road that ran between Garguston farmhouse and the farm outbuildings, a road that has been closed off since the 1980s!

Interestingly, the Black Isle Explorer map also details the positions of six of the original (1836) Redcastle quarry milestones. There is one on the A832, 450 metres to the east of Ryefield, one at the eastern end of Avoch village, another on the B9161 close to Knockbain House (Figure 38, page 265) and three on the unclassified road between Tore and Croftnacreich (one near the new cemetery at Tore, one close to Allanglach and one opposite the old Artafallie post office). They all remain in place, although the stones on the A832 and at Allanglach no longer stand vertical. They are all triangular in section and feature an arrowhead somewhat crudely chiselled out of the top surface, but there are no signs of any mileages, which presumably were painted on the sides. Most of the stones now have a small metal pin inserted into the small hole on the top face where, in the past, a metal plate (perhaps of cast iron) would have been attached. The stone close to the new Tore cemetery has a chiselled recess into which such a plate would have fitted. This map also indicates the positions of two of the metal mile posts that were placed in 1892 along the shore road from Redcastle to North Kessock (one in Milton of Redcastle and one near Coul Point). Nowadays, neither post is in place.

The most up-to-date large-scale maps of the area can now be obtained through the Ordnance Survey 'Landplan' facility.[34] This allows maps of any selected area at any scale to be downloaded from data at 1:10,000 (10 cm:1 km) digitally derived in 2004. However, the printout of the Redcastle area contains a surprising number of inaccuracies and omissions. For example, as in the

1992–94 revision, it: mispells 'Rivulett Cottage'; refers to the house now known as Killearnan Brae as 'The Manse'; marks the position of the well at Rivulett Cottage, but records neither the Grey Well nor the well in the Redcastle quarry; misplaces Quarry House; and shows the houses in Milton of Redcastle out of scale.

Digital images of Ordnance Survey maps are now licensed for specialist purposes; for example, a map showing the current boundaries of Redcastle, Kilcoy and Tarradale estates together with Garguston Farm is available through the 'Who owns Scotland' website. More worryingly, the Scottish Environmental Protection Agency has published an 'Indicative River and Coastal Flood Map' that shows where the coastline of Scotland would be if there was a ten-metre rise in sea level as a result of global warming. All of the houses in Quarry of Redcastle and some in Milton of Redcastle would be underwater! (The houses of Quarry of Redcastle and the lower row of houses in Milton of Redcastle are built on the five-metre contour line.) Satellite images of the area are now also available, notably through the websites of Google Maps and Microsoft Virtual Earth.[35] At the present time, the resolution of the latter seems to be superior. Aerial photographs of the Redcastle area are also available on the internet.[36]

6.3   Murders and Other Crimes

Many old Scottish castles form the settings for ancient legends and mysterious folklore. In the case of Redcastle, part of the folklore is that a man was buried alive there as a medieval human sacrifice.[37] There is also a legend that in the late seventeenth century a large number of the cattle on the Black Isle fell ill with a strange disease that ended in madness and death. The proprietors of the Redcastle and Kilcoy estates (who were Colin Mackenzie [4th of Redcastle] and Roderick Mackenzie [4th of Kilcoy] in the latter part of the seventeenth century) offered a large sum of money as a reward to anyone who could find a cure. An old warlock said that he could do it if he was provided with a human sacrifice. The proprietors agreed to his proposal and an old tramp who frequented Linnie was lured into a barn at Parkton, where he was tied up by the warlock and disembowelled alive. His heart, liver, kidneys and pancreas were reduced to powder and administered to the cattle. Before the tramp died, he is said to have uttered a curse: 'Let the day never come when the family of Redcastle shall be without a female idiot, or the family of Kilcoy be without a fool.'

An extraordinary facet of this event is that it had been predicted in a Gaelic poem by Kenneth MacKenzie, the Brahan Seer (Coinneach Odhar Fiosaiche), who was born in the early seventeenth century. A translation of some of the (Gaelic) stanzas that he wrote is as follows:[38]

When the girls of Kilcoy house cry out
'The cup of our murders is flowing over'...
During forty years or more
And his coat shall be many curses...
He shall then be thrown empty and sorrowful
Like an old besom behind the door...
And the lairds as poor as the sparrows
And curses in the shedding of blood.

It is not recorded whether the cure worked (or if the curse is now revoked), but it is certainly true that the fortunes of the Mackenzie families in both Kilcoy and Redcastle were to decline quickly thereafter. Kilcoy became unoccupied from *circa* 1780 and was a ruin by the middle of the nineteenth century, although the Inverness Field Club reported that slates were still falling off the roof in 1862. Similarly, the Mackenzie owners of Redcastle were destined to become bankrupt and their castle judicially sold by the end of the eighteenth century.

Being a rural area with a relatively small population turnover, the incidence of serious crime in the parish of Killearnan over the centuries is low. Nevertheless, there are notable exceptions, some of which are well documented through court papers and proceedings. Others are less well recorded and may be subject to a degree of fantasy. For example, according to a report of the Inverness Field Club, Kenneth MacKenzie, a sheriff of Inverness and an uncle of Mackenzie of Kilcoy, was murdered in Kilcoy Castle by a freebooter called 'Black Calder'. Kenneth is supposed to be buried under the original flagstone floor of Killearnan parish church, and his ghost is said to have haunted Kilcoy Castle. However, no date is attributed to the event and no corroborating evidence seems to have been recorded.[39]

Another ill-documented case of murder in Redcastle is described in the preface to the 'Killearnan Collection of Gaelic Poetry' compiled by Rev. Aeneas Macdonald.[40] The murdered man is said to have been Archibald MacDonald, born about 1750 and clerk to the factor of Clanranald of South Uist. Archibald was also a Gaelic poet and is said to have been murdered at Redcastle on an unspecified date whilst on his way to Inverness to publish his poems. He is supposedly buried in Killearnan graveyard, but no surviving records have been discovered to verify the story. [The Mackenzie and Ranald clans were long-term enemies, so it would have been dangerous for a Ranald to pass through Mackenzie country, even in the late-eighteenth century.]

A murder which is well documented[41] occurred on 25 October 1748. The Killearnan parish kirk session minutes of 31 October state that 'Farquhar Murchison was inhumanly murdered in the fields betwixt Blairdow and Pecks the 25th inst by his wife, Elizabeth MacKenzie ... and by his servant Kenneth

MacDonald, as appeared by the precognition taken by the Sheriff, the 26th inst'. Farquhar was a tacksman in Newtown was an elder and member of the kirk session. After the murder, Kenneth MacDonald had fled to Glen Strathfarrar, where he had attempted to hire a guide to take him over the 'Corriarrock' [sic] to Fort William (a somewhat circuitous route), where he intended to enlist in the military. However, he was arrested in Glen Strathfarrar and was incarcerated with Elizabeth MacKenzie in Dingwall Tolbooth. A warrant for their transmission to Inverness Tolbooth to await trial at the ensuing circuit court was issued in Inverness on 16 March 1749.

They appeared before the High Court of Judiciary in Inverness on 6 April 1749, but the trial was postponed by a petition from Kenneth and Jane Murchison (whose relationship to Farquhar Murchison is not stated), who requested that the trial should be held in Edinburgh because it was 'thought proper to try them before the supreme court of judiciary and to ordain the Sheriff of Ross to take a full precognition of all the facts and circumstances relating to said barbarous murder'. This petition was granted, but it was not carried out because Kenneth MacDonald and Elizabeth MacKenzie were finally tried by the Inverness Circuit Court on 17 October 1749.

At the trial, a petition was made on behalf of Elizabeth 'craving banishment and transportation'. This was accepted and the Court intimated that they would announce her sentence on the next day. Kenneth MacDonald denied the charge of murder, whereupon the prosecution advocate presented numerous witnesses to the event. Many could not speak English, and Euan Baillie of Abriachan was appointed as 'sworn interpreter'. Alexander MacIntyre, also a servant of Farquhar Murchison, told of 'criminal correspondence suspect' between the two accused. Margaret MacKenzie of Kilcoy described the accused as 'in company at the deceased's house'. Isobel MacKenzie of Tarradale claimed that the two were 'in company together' on the evening of the murder and that she had seen Kenneth MacDonald with a long pointed knife. John MacLennan of Pecks had seen Kenneth MacDonald and Farquhar Murchison 'grapple' at the roadside. Janet MacGillandrish of Kilcoy had been in Farquhar's house when he had been brought home wounded, and she had been told by him that the wound was inflicted by Kenneth MacDonald. The Court was then informed that a search for Kenneth had been made but he could not be found. However, Dugald MacDonald of Strathfarrar described how he had spoken with Kenneth at 10 a.m. the next day, and that he had 'a blooded knife and blood-stained shirt'. James MacKenzie, the Redcastle doctor who had attended Farquhar that evening, stated that he had suffered 'a mortal knife wound close to his heart', and that Farquhar had said that he 'had now got what he was promised by Kenneth'. In the face of such overwhelming evidence, Kenneth offered no defence and the jury 'all in one voice' found him guilty.

Next day, Elizabeth and Kenneth were both sentenced. Kenneth was 'to be hanged [on 29 December 1749] by the neck by the hands of the common hangman upon a gibbet until he be dead and his moveable goods and gear to be … [gathered] and inbrought for His Majesty's use which is pronounced for Doom'. The sentence was carried out on the Barron Muir of Inverness, close by the Edinburgh Road, where a gallows was permanently erected until 1812.

Elizabeth was 'banished to one of His Majesty's plantations in America never to return to Scotland during all the days of her life'. The Court also ordered her:

> …upon the first mercat day thereafter to be whipt in Inverness by the hands of the common hangman, receiving double the number of strypes as usual upon her naked back at each of the many places and at the accustomed time of day and thereafter to be incarcerated in said Tolbooth therein to remain till she is delivered and transported from the port of Inverness in the manner before settled on.

Unfortunately, there seems to be no record of where Elizabeth was taken or of the means by which she got there.[42] It is possible that she was pardoned or died in jail awaiting her transportation.

A case of serious assault that has become known as 'The Wild Women of Redcastle' occurred on 29 March 1816. Having discovered in a field at Braes of Garguston about ten bushels of smuggled malt, John Proudfoot, an Officer of the Excise, decided to go to William Leitch's house in Garguston to procure a horse and cart so that he could remove the sacks of malt. He succeeded in obtaining a cart but he had to yoke his own horse, leaving his saddle and bridle at Leitch's house. On arriving back at the site of the malt, he found himself surrounded by a mob of women and girls, who told him that they would not allow him to carry off the sacks. They then pelted him with stones, forcibly unyoked his horse and destroyed the cart and harness. Proudfoot engaged a man by the name of Noble to fetch his horse and, in the meantime, ripped up the sacks with his knife to scatter the malt.

With his horse retrieved, he went to William MacFarquhar's house in Spital, followed by the women, who continued to throw stones at him. In Spital, he was able to borrow a saddle and bridle so that he could return to William Leitch's house to retrieve his own. On arriving there, he was again confronted by the mob of women and in the ensuing fracas he struck one girl with his stick 'in order to intimidate the rest'. That action provoked the girl to raise 'a cry of murder', whereupon 'four or five women and some men' turned on him. He retreated through the stable to the house but was caught, bound with ropes, dragged by his heels across a midden, thrown into a dirty pool and again pelted with stones. Only when two men came to his assistance did the mob reluctantly disperse. In John Proudfoot's statement of the event, he claims that he was 'very much bruised and injured by the violence he had experienced and on reaching Inverness he was bled and attended by a surgeon for ten days'.

Five women (Janet Young, Margaret Cunninghame, Jane Munro, Ann Fraser and Margaret MacLennan) and three men (John MacLean, Donald Campbell and Alexander Simpson), all from Braes of Garguston, were held chiefly responsible and brought to trial.[43] They were sentenced to twelve months detention in Dingwall Tolbooth for 'assaulting, maltreating, wounding and deforcing an Officer of the Revenue'. It is not recorded what became of the malt!

It seems that the activities of excisemen were not welcomed in Killearnan in the early nineteenth century, because another similar case arose in 1823. Two crofters of Spital Wood village, John Fraser and his son Donald, were accused of 'assaulting, beating, wounding, deforcing and obstructing' Peter Grassie and other (unnamed) Officers of Excise. They were tried on 18 April 1823 in the Circuit Court of Judiciary (High Court) in Inverness.[44] Donald was found not guilty and John, who could speak no English and required a sworn interpreter, was found 'guilty in terms of his own confession'. This meant that no witness statements needed to be presented. Two persons (Colin MacKenzie and his wife, Catherine Aird) had been cited as witnesses. They had initially refused to obey the citation and a warrant had been issued for their detention in Inverness jail until the trial. However, because John pleaded guilty, Colin and Catherine's statements were not required and, in consequence, the precise nature of John's offence is not recorded. He was sentenced to imprisonment for two months in Dingwall Tolbooth, so presumably his offences were not as serious as those of the 'Wild Women of Redcastle'.

It is worthy of note that illicit distilling was still taking place in the late nineteenth century. An article in The Scotsman[45] on 10 March 1885 describes how 'the Beauly preventative staff, while searching in Redcastle wood, discovered a smuggler's bothy, and mashing and fermenting tuns, which they destroyed'. However, it appears on this occasion that the guilty party was not discovered.

Another of the crofters of Spital Wood village was involved in court proceedings in 1824. John Campbell had taken out a loan of £14 with the Inverness branch of the British Linen Bank in December 1823. However, he failed to keep up the repayments, and a letter of horning was issued on 12 June 1824. This seems to have been ineffective, so the manager of the bank further petitioned against him[46] in the Sheriff Court on 16 September 1824. He was ordered to be detained in Inverness Tolbooth until he made payments or was 'otherwise liberated by course of law'. Presumably this action had the desired effect, because there appears to have been no subsequent court action against John Campbell.

Another well-documented[47] murder took place in 1835. John Adam, a quarryman, was accused of murdering his wife, Jean (or Jane) Brechin, at Kilcoy by striking her twice on the head with a stone and hiding her body under turf and stones in the ruins of an old hut. The body was discovered about two weeks later on 10 April 1835, but initially it could not be identified, so a 'murder' notice was posted (Figure 46). It describes her body as 'bearing such marks of violence as leave no doubt she was cruelly murdered' and provides many details of the body features and a particularly interesting description of her clothing.

A plan drawn up by G Campbell Smith of Banff and dated 9 May 1835 indicates that the body had been quickly identified. It is entitled 'Sketch of the Site of Ground about the House in which the Dead Body of Jane Brechin was found on 10 April 1835'. John Adam was subsequently arrested. At his trial, Adam denied that Jean was his wife and claimed never to have seen her before. However, it transpired that he had bigamously married her in Montrose on 8 March 1835, three weeks before the murder. When he was arrested, Adam was in possession of £75, money that allegedly was part of a sum of £113 that had been the proceeds from the sale of Jean's shop in Montrose. Hugh MacKay, the Killearnan parish schoolmaster, featured as a witness at the trial in Inverness High Court in September 1835. (Strangely, he was recorded as residing in the cottage known as 'Prescaultin' or 'Hazel Bush', next to Blairdhu Farm, not in the 'handsome and commodious' new schoolhouse reported by the *Inverness Journal* of 16 April 1830.)

John Adam was found guilty and sentenced to hanging by the public executioner. The sentence was carried out in front of a large crowd at the Longman on 10 October 1835. Before his burial in Inverness jail, John Adam's head was examined by a 'phrenologist', who declared 'his conscientiousness to be deficient, but his secretiveness and amativeness to be strong'. John Adam's body has subsequently been reburied and now lies under the new police headquarters in Perth Road, Inverness.

Until 1812, executions in Inverness were carried out at the gibbet on Barron Muir, near Edinburgh Road. The hanging of John Adam, 'the Mulbuie murderer' as he became known, was the last public hanging to take place in Inverness, although one subsequent execution, that of Joseph Hume of Lhanbryde in March 1908, took place in Porterfield prison. There is a plaque in the car park of the new police headquarters, which commemorates John Adam's burial. It reads:

MURDER!

WHEREAS the Body of a FEMALE was found about 8 o'clock in the morning of yesterday—FRIDAY—the 10th instant, in the ruins of a Hut within the new Plantation on the heights of Kilcoy, bearing such marks of violence as leave no doubt she was cruelly murdered.

APPEARANCE OF THE BODY.

The BODY is apparently that of a married woman about forty years of age; 5 feet 7 inches high, stout in figure; dark brown hair, mixed with some grey hairs, long at the back of the head, cut short over the forehead; wore a false front or curls of dark brown hair; coarse flat features, thick lips, small nose marked by small pox; had a scar from the centre of the forehead downwards across the nose, and left cheek, 4½ inches in length, apparently occasioned by small pox, or a burn.

DRESS.

The DRESS was a black silk velvet bonnet, lined with black silk persian, trimmed with black silk ribbons; a net cap; a black figured bobbin net vail; a mantle of claret coloured cloth, bound with black satin; a check verona handkerchief; a small crimson merino shawl with a light border; a purple or puce worsted gown, (lindsey woolsey or winchey of home manufacture,) trimmed with velvet; a puce figured silk band; a light blue petticoat, and an under dark blue petticoat, both home made woollen stuff, a pair of coarse blue worsted stockings, white in the toes; cloth selvage garters; shoes such as usually sold in Shops, mended under the toes and heels: a cotton shift, marked on the breast with the letters I. B.: a coarse flannel jacket: a pair of drab jean stays; a pocket made of printed cotton. tied with a piece of blue striped tape, and containing four-pence of copper, and small pill box marked " J. Mac kenzie, Chemist and Druggist, Forres," the last word scored through, wore a plain marriage ring marked " Gold," on the inside, on the 3d finger of the left hand; and gloves of green kid.

PLACE WHERE FOUND.

The PLACE where the body was found, is at the top of the Millbuie on the heights of Kilcoy, in the Parish of Killiernan or Redcastle, County of Ross, and between 200 and 300 yards in a straight line eastwards from the House of Alexander Macdonald, Changekeeper, which stands close to the Parliamentary Road leading over the Millbuie.

The Public are earnestly requested to communicate to the Procurator Fiscal of Ross, Dingwall, any circumstances which may lead to the discovery of the name and usual residence of the deceased, and of the person or persons by whom she has been murdered.

The body lies in the Town House of Dingwall, and will be kept uninterred, until Wednesday the 15th instant: to afford an opportunity of identifying it.

DINGWALL, 11th April, 1835.

Inverness: Printed by R. Carruthers.

Figure 46: Notice of the 1835 murder of Jane Brechin by John Adam (The National Archives of Scotland, JC26/1835/126)

It is believed that the earthly remains of John Adam, the last person to die by public execution in Inverness, lie buried beneath this site as required by statute in the year of his death, 1835. The Lord is merciful and gracious. Psalm 103v8. January, AD 2000.

On 14 September 1878, the *Inverness Advertiser*[48] reported that Andrew Granger, the tenant farmer at Fettes, had been tried for murder, having been accused at the Grant Arms Hotel in Grantown of 'wickedly and feloniously attacking and assaulting the now deceased James Fraser, then one of the police constables of the County of Elgin stationed at Grantown and did with a knife cut or stab said James Fraser one or more times, in one or more places, in his stomach or belly whereby he was mortally injured and in consequence thereof died on 19 July'. In his defence, Granger recalled being drunk before leaving Inverness by train, having allegedly been given drugged whisky in Muir of Ord. Then he had drunk more whisky in Forres, which he claimed must also have been had. In consequence, he had no recollection of what happened in Grantown. The outcome was that he was found not guilty of murder but guilty of culpable homicide, the jury believing the act to have been committed while he was labouring under 'delirium tremens'. He was sentenced to five years' penal servitude.

The last murder to be committed in Killearnan took place in 1890. Originally from Tomintoul, Jane Bain was the nineteen-year-old mother of an illegitimate child, registered at birth on 13 August 1888 as James Robert Bain but whose father was John MacLeod, a merchant in Barbaraville, near Cromarty. Jane and her sister, Isabella, had left Barbaraville because they had fallen out with their mother and had been living with their aunt, Ann Docherty (recorded as Dougharty in the 1881 and 1891 censuses) at Braes of Kilcoy, who was helping to look after James. Ann had asked for 10/- per month to look after James, but neither Isabella nor Jane had regular work so could not pay. On 13 January 1890, Jane drowned James by holding him down in a pool of water and hid his body under a tree in Muillans Wood on the 'west side of the road leading from Dingwall to Tore, 360 paces due south of the house of Donald Fowler, crofter at Newton of Ferintosh'. Initially, Jane told her aunt that she had put James in the poor house in Inverness, but next day she confessed and asked that the policeman from Conon be called. James' body was recovered and a post mortem confirmed death by forcible drowning.

A precognition was held on 5 May 1890, at which James was described as 'a well nourished male of about 18 months old', and the indictment was recorded as 'you did throw James Robert MacLeod, your illegitimate son, into a pool of water, and did kick him on the head, and did drown and murder him'. At her trial,[49] held in the High Court at Inverness on 8 May 1890, Jane pleaded not guilty to murder on the grounds of insanity, not being responsible for her actions at the time, and claiming that her mother had been the cause of her actions, having declared that 'she would be glad to hear that Jane had put the child in a hole'. Jane was found guilty of culpable homicide, but the jury unanimously recommended mercy and she was sentenced to seven years' penal servitude. Her initial arrest and subsequent trial are reported in the *Scottish Highlander*[50] of 6 February and 15 May 1890 respectively. Jane served her sentence in Perth prison, being recorded there as a twenty-year-old prisoner in the 1891 census.

6.4 Early Population Enumerations

With a few exceptions, such as those who appeared in High or Session Courts or those who were compeared to appear in front of their presbytery or kirk session, ordinary people in Scotland are rarely named in any documentation until the advent of the Old Parish Registers. The Presbytery of Dingwall minutes[51] date from 1649 (although they do not name any Killearnan resident) and those of the Presbytery of Chanonry[52] date from 1707. The first 'ordinary' residents of Redcastle (that is, other than the heritors or the minister) with the dubious distinction of being named by the Presbytery were Lachlan Mackenzie and Isobel Fraser, who were reported as living together in adultery in 1718. The kirk session minutes[53] and the records of births and marriages[54] (not deaths) for Killearnan parish both commence in 1744. Thus, prior to the middle of the eighteenth century, there is very little information on the resident population of Redcastle.

At the time of the Union of the Scottish and English Parliaments in 1707, it was estimated that the population of Scotland was a little over one million. Ten years earlier, it would undoubtedly have been higher, because Scotland suffered years of harvest failures and famine during 1696–99 which took a heavy toll. Although neither an enumeration nor a census, the list of the rentals[55] payable to Redcastle estate in 1710 contains the names of many of the farmers and other rent payers of that period. They include: William, Kenneth and John Glass; John, Kenneth (miller) and Murdo Mackenzie; Thomas and Donald MacLennan; Roderick and John Bayne; Alexander and Donald Junor; Alexander (shoemaker) and Donald McCahie; Donald and John McIver; John Keil; Kenneth Noble; Donald Buy; Alexander Bizel (smith); Donald MacInurich; John Mathesone; Roderick Tuach; John Anderson (taylor); William MacInlaylor; Thomas Ross; Donald Munro (smith); John Kolly (crofter); Kenneth McForgan; David Duncan; John Clark; William Gow; Andrew Mitchell; and Donald MacAndrew.

The first enumeration to establish the population of Scotland with some degree of accuracy was carried out in 1755 by the Rev. Dr Alexander Webster, who also requested (on behalf of the Chancellor of the Exchequer) parish ministers to submit information on the numbers and age range of people in their parishes.[56] The Scottish population is recorded as 1,265,300, of whom 400,652 were under eighteen years and 125,899 were over fifty-six. The significance of these ages is related to the estimation of the numbers of 'fighting men' (defined as eighteen to fifty-six years old) that could potentially be available in times of war. The Killearnan population was recorded as 945, of whom only 189 (twenty per cent) were potentially fighting men.

The ministers were also requested to supply information on their income and the numbers of protestants and papists in their parishes. In Killearnan, there were no known papists and the total emolument of the minister was assessed at £49-5-10½d sterling, comprising £2-1/- as the value of the glebe, £36-7-6½d in victuals and £10 16/- in stipend money.

The next enumeration was carried out in 1791 by Sir John Sinclair, when, as part of the collection of data for the Old (First) Statistical Account,[57] Rev. David Denoon (I) estimated the population of Killearnan to be 1,147. Within this total, there were sixty-one farmers, twenty-one weavers, fourteen shoemakers, fourteen tailors, nine carpenters and wheelwrights, eight masons, seven smiths and five millers. The number of residents on the Poor Roll was thirty-five, and the number of itinerant poor had decreased substantially due to a local agent of the 'Inverness Hemp Manufactory' who distributed hemp and paid up to 6d per day for spun sailcloth and pack-sheeting.

This enumeration was followed in 1798 by a census of all male inhabitants between the ages of fifteen and sixty years residing in the parish.[58] This information had been requested of Lord Seaforth, Lord Lieutenant of Ross, by Henry Dundas, Home Secretary, as a precursor to the formation of a local volunteer corps. This corps was to form part of a nationwide defence system to protect the country against possible invasion by France. It is not clear who undertook the count, dated 3 March 1798, but it was probably Rev. David Denoon (II), the parish minister who had succeeded his father in 1792.

It records that Killearnan parish was populated by 262 men of fighting age (twenty-three per cent of the 1791 population) and also had available fourteen horses fit for carts or wagons, six draught oxen and 203 small horses or garrons. The name, occupation and place of residence of each man is listed, therefore this enumeration provides the earliest detailed statistical documentation of the population of the parish. The 262 men were categorised as follows: the two estate proprietors (Charles Mackenzie of Kilcoy and James Grant of Redcastle) and the moderator (Rev. David Denoon) collectively employing twenty-five male servants; fifty-eight tenant farmers with fifty-seven sons, farm labourers and male servants; twenty-nine mealers (also known as maillers or cottars); eighty-eight tradesmen and other artisans; and two schoolteachers.

The locations of the tenants and the numbers at each location provide an indication of the agricultural and economic makeup of the Redcastle area, for example: at Spittal there were three tenants; Garguston (one); Braes (four); Pecks (one); Blairdoo [sic] (one); Newton (two); Barntown (two); Chappeltown (three); Burntown (two); Dam Park (three); Milntown (two); Corrigrain (one). Similarly, maillers were recorded at Spittal (four); Killearnan (one); Braes (one); Blairdoo (one); Dam Park (one) and Corrigrain (one). The numbers of the tradesmen in the Redcastle area are also revealing; for example, there were eight weavers, all located at Spital, whilst at Milntown there were four masons, four wrights, three blacksmiths, three millers, two gardeners, a tailor and a boatman.

After the 1791 enumeration carried out by Sir John Sinclair, the government undertook further estimations of the population each ten years. The Killearnan population is shown to have grown throughout the first half of the nineteenth century, for example, reaching 1,371 in 1821 and 1,479 in 1831. In the Killearnan chapter of the New (Second) Statistical Account of Scotland,[59] written in 1837–38 by Rev. John Kennedy, it is estimated that there were 324 families in the parish living in 293 houses. The working-age male population comprised fifteen farmers, 119 cottars, sixty-four labourers, 155 agricultural workers, sixty tradesmen, six blacksmiths, five masons, seven carpenters, one wheelwright, six sawers, two millers, six innkeepers, sixteen shoemakers, two shopkeepers, eight tailors, seventeen weavers and one auctioneer. In addition, fifty-two females were permanently employed as servants, whilst others spun flax or wool and gained day work in the fields as required.

6.5 National Population Censuses (1841–61)

The early enumerations were only headcounts, and it was not until 1841 that the first (UK) national census to name all individuals and record their ages, residences and occupations was taken.[60] For the purposes of the 1841 census, the parish was divided into three districts. District 1 contained the western communities stretching northwards from Spital Shore to Kilcoy, Wellhouse, Drynie Park and Cairnurenan. District 2 contained the coastal communities stretching from Lettoch and Croftnacreich westwards to Milton of Redcastle and Quarry of Redcastle. District 3 contained the eastern farming communities of Drumnamarg, Tore, Muckernish and Tore Wood. The total population of the parish was 1,644 (of which 909 were female), the most heavily populated areas being the crofting communities of Tore Wood (140), Cairnurenan (117) and Drumnamarg (ninety-two).

The 1841 census provides the first 'official' recognition of Quarry of Red-castle (Figure 36, page 251) as a separate community, and although individual houses are not named or numbered, it lists eighty-six people within twenty-four households as being resident in the hamlet. The population of 'Milltown' of Redcastle, on the other hand, was only seventy-one (in seventeen house-holds). Thus Quarry of Redcastle was more populous than Milton of Redcastle at that time, but their occupational profiles were entirely different. The residents of Quarry of Redcastle were predominantly in manual labouring occupations, there being seven stone masons and quarriers (all living in the same house), seven carpenters, six agricultural labourers, four widows, three women of 'independent means', two plasterers, a tailor, and a house servant, the remainder being nineteen wives and thirty-six scholars and young children. On the other hand, many of the residents of Milton of Redcastle were younger skilled tradesmen, craftsmen, professionals and business entrepreneurs. They included the schoolmaster (Alexander MacKenzie), a merchant (the shopkeeper, Hugh Chisholm), the miller (James Ross), a farmer (Angus Urquhart), two tailors (Roderick MacGregor and John MacDonald) and two blacksmiths (Alexander and John Fraser). Unfortunately, the business of Alexander Fraser and Co., Contractors, Undertakers and General Dealers, which had existed in the village since at least 1804, was declared bankrupt in September 1844[61] and discharged of its debts in January 1845.

Notably, the 1841 census records no innkeeper, although the Milton Inn was certainly in existence, being run by the farmer Angus Urquhart. Many small local inns at that time were little more than a room in a farmhouse, where the farmer served ale that he had brewed from his own grain crop. Angus Urquhart had succeeded his father (also Angus), who is recorded as a farmer at Milton of Redcastle in the late eighteenth century, and at Blairdhu in the early nineteenth century. Both are buried in Killearnan churchyard, where Angus (snr), who died in January 1831, is recorded on a flat stone and Angus (jnr), who died in May 1868, is recorded on a plaque set into the west wall. There was an ancient alehouse at Newton which was first recorded in 1533, when James V granted 'the keeping of the Reidcastell … with the mill and alehouse' to Robert Innes of Innermarky.[62] Thereafter, the alehouse features in sixteenth- and seventeenth-century charters[63] and in eighteenth-century sasines[64] of Redcastle estate. Unfortunately, the 1841 census does not separately record any houses under the name of Newton, but there is a publican (Alexander MacDonald) recorded at Cairnuirnain, which appears to be the name used in the 1841 census to describe all of the area north of Fettes (other than Kilcoy and Braes of Kilcoy). This may suggest that the inn at Newton was still in existence in 1841.

Some individuals of note recorded in the 1841 census include Donald

Noble, the kirk officer (for which he received a salary of £1 per year), and Lewis MacKenzie, who was an elder of the parish church but who would become a stalwart of the Free Church. A freak fatal accident was reported under the headline 'Melancholy Accident' in the *Inverness Journal* on 1 May 1835. The article describes how 'a fine young boy of the name of Noble, about 11 years of age, while incautiously attempting to turn the wheel of a water mill at Redcastle fell into the dam, and by the impetus given the wheel was crushed to death'. It is not known whether the boy was the son of Donald Noble or where the accident occurred. It could have been at Parkton or Redcastle Mains, both of which had water-driven mill wheels. The remains of the mechanism can still be seen on the side of one of the barns at Parkton. The water trough, through which the wheel turned, is deep and steep-sided, indicating that the wheel was large and would readily trap anyone in the trough. At Redcastle Mains, both the channel that took water from the Redcastle burn and the water wheel still exist. The wheel is located within one of the farm buildings, and although it no longer turns, it is complete and water still flows through the deep trough.

Another individual person of note was a three-year-old child, William George Dick, who had been born in Contin but had moved to Parkton, where his parents, William and Janet Dick, had become the tenant farmers. William (jnr) was destined to become Redcastle's best known entrepreneur, being one of the original partners to form Macrae and Dick.[65] The formation of the new partnership was announced in the *Inverness Courier*[66] on 18 July 1878 (Figure 47).

Roderick Macrae had already built his 'postmaster and horse hirer' business in Beauly and, for an investment of £1,500, took on William Dick as his partner in order to expand into Inverness. The business featured in the *Inverness Courier* of 7 December 1882, when a particularly severe snowstorm hit the town, during which:

> The streets of Inverness were blocked by the snowfall and rendered not passable. Early pedestrians had considerable difficulty in threading their way along to their places of business, and it was not until Mr Dick of the firm of Macrae and Dick, horse-hirers, kindly sent out a large snow-plough with four horses, to clear the streets, that traffic could be engaged in without serious inconvenience.

By 1890, the partners had also expanded into tourism, offering excursions from Inverness to local sites of historic and geological interest in horse-drawn coaches. The company is now one of Scotland's largest motor dealerships and its headquarters remain in Inverness. William Dick died in December 1910 and is buried in Killearnan parish churchyard, where he is recorded on the tombstone shared with his parents and sister as 'Job and Post Master, Inverness'.

NEW POSTING ESTABLISHMENTS IN INVERNESS.

SPECIAL ANNOUNCEMENT.

RODERICK MACRAE, POSTMASTER and HORSE HIRER, BEAULY, being frequently asked by several Gentlemen in INVERNESS to Open a BRANCH ESTABLISHMENT there, he now begs leave to inform his numerous Friends, Noblemen, Gentlemen, Commercial Travellers, and the General Public, that in order to carry this out efficiently, he has assumed as Partner in the Inverness business Mr WM. G. DICK, Redcastle, who is already well known, and he hopes that, under his management, all those favouring them with their patronage will have every reason to be satisfied.

___

With reference to the above,

MESSRS MACRAE & DICK are now prepared to execute Orders for POSTING and HIRING in all its branches in a style hitherto unknown in Inverness. They have secured the Stable and Yard adjoining the City of Glasgow Bank, lately occupied by Mr Macdonald, of the Station Hotel; also, the Stable and Yard of the Glenalbyn Hotel, so that Orders given at either Yard will have prompt and careful attention.

First-class Open and Close Carriages, Landaus, Waggonettes, T Carts, Phaetons, Dog-carts, Gigs, &c.

NEW HEARSE AND MOURNING CARRIAGES.

RIDING HORSES FOR LADIES AND GENTLEMEN.

Lorries kept, and all kinds of Carting performed.

LUGGAGE AND GOODS SENT TO SHOOTING QUARTERS.

Edward's Court, Academy Street,
Glenalbyn Yard, Young Street,
Inverness. June 1878.

Figure 47: Announcement of the partnership of Macrae and Dick, from the Inverness Courier, *18 July 1878 (© The British Library Board. All Rights Reserved)*

Two of the widows recorded in the 1841 census of Quarry of Redcastle (Anne MacLeod and Janet Thomson) are also recorded in the Killearnan parish church Poor Roll[67] for 1841–42. Anne received 4/- per week and Janet received

11/- per week. Anne and her mother had lived in the hamlet for some time. They are recorded as 'widow MacLeod' and 'widow MacLeod's mother' in the Poor Roll as early as 1829, when, after a particularly bad harvest, Colin Mackenzie of Kilcoy sent 'five bolls of meal to the poor of the parish'. The MacLeods received two pecks (about eighteen pounds or eight kilos) from the distribution. It is notable that most of the parishioners named in the Poor Rolls (of which there were forty to fifty per year) were living in the more populated crofting areas on the higher ground to the east and north of the parish. As befits its wealthier inhabitants (and younger age profile), no residents of Milton of Redcastle feature in the early Poor Rolls.

At the castle, which had recently been purchased by Col Hugh Baillie MP, only four people were in residence. They were masons and a carpenter, who would have been carrying out the extensive alterations and refurbishments commissioned from William Burn in 1840 (Figure 11, page 86). The 1841 census also provides the first opportunity to identify other hamlets in the area and the occupations of their residents. For example, Robert Trotter was the tenant farmer at Garguston. His descendants were destined to purchase the farm and remain there into the twentieth century. At Garguston Shore, there were four crofts with eighteen people in residence, and at the hamlet of Chapelton there were three houses whose residents were a cartwright (Hugh Fraser), a blacksmith (James Robertson) and some agricultural labourers. The 1841 Poor Roll includes 'widow Fraser' of Chapelton, presumably Hugh's mother. She received 4/- per week in 1841, but this was raised to 12/6d in 1843.

In the mid to late 1800s, the term 'agricultural labourer' (abbreviated to 'Ag Lab' in the censuses) referred to a number of occupations – for example, ploughmen, cattlemen and general farm workers (sometimes called outdoor workers). There were essentially two types. Those who 'lived in' were usually hired for six months of the year. They were paid their keep (bothy accommodation and food) plus a lump sum at the end of their term of engagement. Most of these were young and unmarried. The second type was the 'day labourer', who had his own cottage and received a much higher proportion of his wages in cash. Marriage for them was a practical possibility, and the wife might also obtain some employment in the fields (for example, weeding or harvesting). However, income was unreliable, as they were laid off in the winter and during spells of bad weather. This meant that they often had to rely on poor relief to pay their rent, bring up a family or care for elderly parents.

Cottars (or maillers) were provided with the security of a rent-free cottage, but they were tied to the farm and had to work whatever hours were required for very little pay. Some had a garden, for which they usually paid rent. There were numerous agricultural workers with cottar status in Redcastle – for example, there are references to 'Whitewells Maillers' (also recorded as 'Spital Maillers', the original name for the village at Spital Wood)[68] and 'Milntown Maillers' at Redcastle.[69]

Crofters had lifetime tenure on their cottage and land, but they had to pay rent. Their land was generally less productive than that of the farms, but nevertheless three to four acres could normally sustain a family. They were not required to work on the farm and could earn additional income through other activities, such as fishing or hand loom weaving. In Killearnan, most of the crofting land was on the higher ground of the Millbuie in the eastern and northern parts of the parish around Croftcrunie, Tore, Cairnurenan and Drynie Park.

The daughters (and some sons) of farm workers were commonly expected to work in domestic service. This could variously be at the heritors' mansions (where they might live in) or in the houses of farmers, tradesmen and other professionals. To obtain such employment, it was essential to have a good reference either from the schoolteacher or the minister. However, it was insecure employment, as they could be dismissed without a reference at the whim of their mistress or employer. In the censuses, they were sometimes recorded as FS (female servant) or MS (male servant). Without employment in domestic service, girls had to undertake 'domestic duties' at home until they were married.

As in 1841, the 1851 census[70] divided the parish into three districts. However, the boundaries were not the same as in 1841, so direct comparisons are not always possible. The eastern District 3 was similar to that of 1841, but now included Croftnacreich and Lettoch. District 1 was now defined by the shoreline eastwards from Spital Shore through Quarry of Redcastle and Milton of Redcastle to Corgrain Point, and District 2 was now confined to all the northern crofting and farming areas around Kilcoy, Wellhouse, Drynie Park and Cairnurenan. The total population of the parish had dropped to 1,383 (fifty-five per cent female), comprising 308 households living in 261 houses.

The northern District 2 was notable for the large increase in crofts of four to six acres that were recorded – for example, eighteen in Kilcoy and thirteen in Drynie Park. This may have been partially due to migration from those areas of the Highlands most affected by the potato famine of 1848, but would also have been because higher ground was being cleared for crofting, as had been described by Rev. John Kennedy in the New (Second) Statistical Account. The evidence of large numbers of crofts in the Drynie Park area is still visible from the number of small fields and the ruins of cottages that can be seen today north and east of Spital Wood. Heaps of field clearage stones, ploughed up over many years, still lie in some field corners. Also, there are examples of 'consumption' walls between the fields, so called because they are wider than normal dry stone walls and were constructed in this way in order to 'consume' the ploughed-up field stones.

The 1851 census names the hamlet of Quarry of Redcastle as 'Quarry Street', and records seventy-nine residents from twenty-one households living in eleven houses. There is no evidence that the original L-shaped quarry workers' bothy was still in occupation, the eleven houses being contained within four separate buildings numbered from west to east: 1–4 in the building now known as Quarry House (housing twenty-seven residents); 5 and 6 in the building now known as Quarry Cottage (thirteen residents); 7 and 8 in the now demolished Garden Cottage (seven residents); and 9–11 in the building now known as Pier Cottage (thirty-two residents). Quarry House and Pier Cottage were overcrowded by any modern standards! [NB There is no record of Garden Cottage ever being known by this name, but it has been adopted here for identification purposes and in recognition of its reputation for having a fine garden.]

Within the decade since 1841, there had been substantial change in the professions of the residents of Quarry of Redcastle, there now being only five carpenters and sawmillers, five agricultural workers and four quarriers. One of the agricultural workers was William MacKenzie, the husband of Catherine Logan, who had been subjected to four years of compearing by the Free Church over the birth of their illegitimate son, John, in 1846. They lived in No. 5 (Quarry Cottage). Another family of MacKenzies lived in No. 6 (Quarry Cottage). They were Donald, who was a shepherd, his wife Margaret, fourteen-year-old Catherine and eleven-year-old John. Catherine's marriage to James MacGregor from Kessock is recorded in the Killearnan Old Parish Registers for December 1854. She was the last person from Redcastle to be recorded in the Old Parish Registers before statutory civil registration of births, deaths and marriages was introduced in Scotland in 1855.

The population of Milton of Redcastle, named as 'Village of Redcastle' in the 1851 census, had grown to ninety-four. Thus it had overtaken Quarry of Redcastle as the main centre of population in Redcastle, a numerical advantage that it retains to this day. As in 1841, Milton of Redcastle seemed to attract the more affluent residents of the area. Roderick MacGregor, the tailor, and the Fraser family of blacksmiths were still resident, although Alexander Fraser had been declared bankrupt in 1844. Amongst those who had moved into the village were: William Deedman (shopkeeper); Alexander MacKenzie (Free Church schoolmaster); Duncan McKay (miller); George Ross (carpenter and ironmonger); Andrew Mackintosh (carpenter); Lewis MacKenzie (meal-monger); and John Macrae (shoemaker). According to *The Scotsman* of 18 November 1846, John Macrae's business affairs were due to be examined at the Dingwall Sheriff's Office on 18 December 1846, but he seems to have averted bankruptcy as he continued in business in Milton of Redcastle until the 1880s. One occupant of Mains of Redcastle (or 'Redcastle Square', as it is called in the 1851 census) was a fifty-six-year-old farm servant named John Falconer. He was involved in a fatal accident on his way home from Inverness in 1853. The *Inverness Advertiser* of 14 June reports that on the shore road below Coulmore he was 'overpowered by drowsiness or giddiness' due to the excessive heat of the day, unconsciously fell in front of his cart and expired a few minutes afterwards. He had probably suffered a stroke.

The 1851 census was the first to identify the parish schoolhouse. This was located (where it still is) just north of the Redcastle quarry on the by-road leading to Blairdhu Farm. It was occupied by Rev. Hugh Skinner, the head-master of the parish school (and also the 1851 Census Enumerator for the parish). He appealed to the Commissioners of Supply against the rental valuation of the schoolteacher's house in September 1855, but he failed to appear at the hearing and, in consequence, lost his appeal. Two further points of interest are focused on the Robertson family in Newton (also known as 'Fettes Crossroads'). The first is the recording of a sewing school mistress, Helen Robertson. The second is the recording of Margaret Robertson as a postmistress. The local newspapers[71] in the period 1820–40 abound with advertisements tendering postal routes within northern Scotland, and also contain numerous articles about improvements taking place in postal services throughout the area. Unfortunately, no records of the sub-post office that was located at Newton seem to have survived, thus its date of opening is not known. It is likely to have opened shortly after the introduction of the penny post in 1840, but as Margaret would have been a sub-postmistress, and therefore not an employee of the post office, the British Postal Archives have no records of the parish's first post office.

The 1861 census of Killearnan parish[72] usefully provides a summary of the physical geography of each district, of which there were four. District 1 was essentially the same as in 1851, covering the western shore of the parish from Spital Shore to Corgrain Point and inland to Garguston, Newtown and Parkton. It therefore included Milton of Redcastle, which is described as 'a small village with a few houses', and Quarry of Redcastle, which is described as 'a row of ten houses' (actually there were only four buildings which provided eleven separate residences). The hinterland 'consists of nearly all large farms. The soil is very fertile, well cultivated, and produces excellent crops of wheat, oats, barley and turnips'.

District 2 covered the area east of Corgrain Point and included Coulmore, Lettoch and Croftnacreich. It is described as 'elevated and generally level, the soil light and not well cultivated. It is occupied by crofters. The south part is descending with a steep and well wooded declivity. Coulmore farm is very extensive, well cultivated and produces excellent crops'.

District 3 covered the north-western area and included Wellhouse, Drynie Park and Kilcoy. It is 'of a hilly description, descending with a gradual decline to the south. The soil is light and dry and is generally occupied by crofters with the exception of 2 or 3 farms. Kilcoy Mains is a very extensive farm, highly cultivated and produces most excellent crops'.

District 4 covered Tore, Drumnamarg and Muckernich. Much of the description in the census book is illegible, but it states that 'the soil in the greatest part ... produces generally light crops with the exception of Tore Mains ... which produces excellent crops of wheat, oats and barley'.

The 1861 census records that there were fourteen dwellings (twenty-four households) in Milton of Redcastle, and the population had grown to ninety-nine, the highest that would ever be recorded in any census. As in the previous censuses, there was a high proportion of businessmen and skilled tradesmen, many of whom were incomers from more distant parts of Scotland. They included: John Swan, a boot and shoemaker from Raasay; William Smith, a blacksmith from Banff, who had taken over from the Frasers at the smithy; John Cameron, a stone quarrier from Argyll (many stonemasons were itinerant); and James Elder, a meal miller from Resolis who had been the successful applicant when the lease of the mill was advertised in the *Inverness Advertiser* on 5 May 1858. The Free Church school in Quarry of Redcastle also had a new head teacher, Donald MacIntosh, who lived in No. 1 house at Milton of Redcastle.

The Ross family was still selling ironmongery but appears also to have diversified into drapery, and, despite the arrival of John Swan, John Macrae was still running his shoemaking business. The inn (and its farm) was still in the hands of Angus Urquhart and his family, although he would soon be declared bankrupt. The notice of a meeting of his creditors was placed in the *Inverness Advertiser* on 16 November 1861, and the inn would soon be taken over by Alexander Campbell. Andrew Mackintosh was still a successful carpenter employing four men, but his son, Alexander, is not recorded in the 1861 census. He had been convicted for the theft of £1-3/- in June 1859. He pleaded guilty and was sentenced to imprisonment for fourteen days and to the Reformatory School of Inverness for three years. The incident is recorded in the *Inverness Advertiser* of 2 August 1859 and concludes, 'we have no doubt, if he attends to Mr Craster's instructions, he will become a better member of society'.

William Smith, the new blacksmith, also became a victim of bankruptcy. He had taken the lease of the smithy in 1858 in response to an advertisement that appeared in the *Inverness Advertiser* of 4 May 1858. It offered 'the well-known smithies of Chapelton and Millton of Redcastle. Also carpenters shop at Chapelton. Offers for the same to be sent to Mr Alison, Redcastle'. However, in June 1863 the Caledonian Banking Co., to whom he owed £108-3-10d, lodged a petition for sequestration of his estate.[73] A notice to other creditors was placed in the *Edinburgh Gazette* [no. 342] and a creditors' meeting was held in Robertson's Hotel, Dingwall, on 1 July 1863. William's total debt was assessed at £176-17-4½d and his assets at £79-14-9½d. Those assets included £35-18/- from the value of the tools and stock in the smiddy, and only £5-10/- from the value of the contents of his house (which comprised two tables, four chairs, bed and bedding, fire tongs, kitchen dresser, crockery, cooking utensils, and attic beds and bedding). The balance of his assets were unpaid accounts due to him from, among others, Col [Hugh] Baillie of Redcastle, Robert Trotter of Garguston, Angus Cameron of Wellhouse, William Dick of Parkton, Alexander Campbell of Redcastle Inn, James McKenzie Alison of Greenhill, George MacLennan of Spital Shore and Rev. William MacKay of Killearnan manse. William was discharged of his debts in December 1863 and his (ordinary) creditors received 1/6d per £1.

The blacksmith business in Redcastle was succeeded by Donald Robertson and in Chapelton by James Robertson. Both of their descendants were destined to remain at those businesses well into the twentieth century. Strangely, none of the businesses in Milton of Redcastle are recorded in Slater's Directory[74] of 1860, but the 1867 edition lists: Duncan MacLennan, the miller; Donald Robertson, the blacksmith; Alexander Campbell, the innkeeper; both ministers (Rev. William MacKay of the Established Church and Rev. Donald Kennedy of the Free Church); and six of the farmers of the Redcastle estate (Duncan Cameron of Wellhouse, James Dallas of Blairdhu, William Dick of Parkton, Mrs (Catherine) Trotter of Garguston, George Tuach MacKenzie of Whitewells and Mrs (Ann) Wilson of Fettes, whose husband, Alexander, was a JP. He died in November 1865 and is buried in Killearnan graveyard. George Tuach Mackenzie had recently taken over at Whitewells as a result of a fire in 1866 which had destroyed the year's crop, valued at £171-9-8d, but uninsured. William Ross, the tenant, had unsuccessfully petitioned against Henry James Baillie (who inherited Redcastle in 1866) for a suspension of a half year's rent (£32-10/-) on the basis that it had been the proprietor's responsibility to insure the crop.[75]

In contrast to the continuing increase in the population of Milton of Redcastle, the population of Quarry of Redcastle had reduced to fifty-four people within nineteen households in eleven dwellings within the hamlet. Four of the residents were classified as paupers, three being widows and the other being a 'registered lunatic' who was financially assisted by the Free Church Paupers' Fund,[76] receiving £2 per week. There had also been a considerable turnover of residents, with only three people remaining since the 1841 census. These were Kenneth MacDonald and James Kennedy (both quarriers) and Janet Kennedy (the widowed mother of James Kennedy). There is no record in the Killearnan Old Parish Registers of James Kennedy's birth, but he was a fourteen-year-old in the 1841 census and is recorded as living in Quarry of Redcastle in every subsequent census up to 1891. He died in 1896 and seems to have lived his entire adult life in the hamlet.

Kenneth MacDonald and his wife, Margaret, had a large family. Their gravestone in Killearnan parish church graveyard records two sons (Alexander and John) who died in infancy in 1831 and 1835. In the 1841 census, they are recorded as having four children (Anne [fifteen], Christina [seven], Margaret [four] and Alexander [one]). In the 1851 census, three children are recorded (Margaret [fifteen], Alexander [eleven] and Kenneth [nine]). The 1861 census shows Alexander as a quarrier aged twenty-one, and another child, Mary Ann, at eight months old. This census again records Christina, now aged twenty-eight, and Mary Ann as Christina's daughter. Margaret died three years later in 1864, and although Kenneth is recorded in the 1871 census, he died in June of that year at the age of sixty-five. He (like James Kennedy) was a quarrier who seems to have lived his entire adult life in the hamlet of Quarry of Redcastle.

The three houses at Redcastle Mains farm, referred to as 'Redcastle Square' in the early censuses, were generally occupied by the head gamekeeper (Murdo MacKenzie in 1861) and other estate workers. The head gardener (Thomas Fraser in 1861) lived near the eastern entrance to the estate at Corgrain Cottage. It is noticeable that in all the early censuses the castle is occupied only by a few housemaids or workmen. Col Hugh Baillie was an MP who lived mainly in London and seems only rarely to have visited Redcastle. The estate manager and clerk at the time was James McKenzie Alison, who lived at Greenhill House and is recorded in the 1861 census as a wood merchant. His complex business affairs would soon lead him into financial trouble.

6.6 Fearchair-a-Ghunna

Farquhar MacLennan (or Fearchair-a-Ghunna, as he would become known) was a vagrant who resided much of his life in and around Redcastle. He originated from Strathconon, where he is said to have been born in 1784, although there does not seem to be a record of his birth in the Old Parish Registers of either Urray or Contin. His parents were crofters, but they were also involved in the distilling and smuggling of illicit whisky.

Farquhar had an 'aberration of intellect', but it is not clear whether this was due to a mental illness or to an incident in his youth. In one version, Farquhar is said to have been sent by his father to Strathpeffer to purchase barley seed. He returned with the seed after midnight and proceeded to sow it. However, the poultry had eaten it before anyone arose in the morning and the severe chastisement given to Farquhar by his father is said to have 'injuriously affected his naturally feeble mind'. In another version, Farquhar is said to have been employed as a herdsman at Croftrunie in Killearnan; however, he fell asleep and the cattle strayed into a cornfield. Allegedly, his employer hit him on the head with a spade, a blow from which he is said never to have completely recovered.[77]

Farquhar seems to have left Strathconon in 1809 after his brother, Tom, was accidentally killed in a confrontation with excisemen during which his father was apprehended for illicit distilling and smuggling. He was employed by farmers in the Black Isle to clear fields of stones and he learned to blast large stones with gunpowder, which seems to have become his favourite pastime. During his wanderings from farm to farm, he dressed in old rags, chains and feathers and carried a sack of assorted articles which he collected and traded in Inverness. Amongst his possessions were several old pistols and a sword. However, his prize possession was a remarkable musket with six barrels, which was so heavy that it required a rest. He aimed mainly at crows, ducks and rabbits, but seems rarely to have hit anything. Hence he became known by the nickname of 'Fearchair-a-Ghunna', or 'Farquhar of the Gun'.

From time to time, Farquhar lived in an outhouse at the Killearnan parish church manse in Redcastle. He did not seem well disposed to Rev. John Macrae, the parish minister at the time, whose congregation Farquhar observed 'didn't outnumber the toes of my left foot'. (This was not an exaggeration. After the Disruption of 1843, the Established Church of Scotland in Killearnan had only five communicant members, one of whom was Rev. MacRae himself.) One day, Rev. Macrae's dog met a horrid death from eating bread containing pins. The minister blamed Farquhar, and ordered him to be evicted and his possessions thrown into the sea. Farquhar then set up home in an old hut near Tarradale, which he called 'The Garrison'. He is recorded in each of the three censuses for 1841–61 at Muir of Tarradale and is variously described as 'idiot', 'fatuous pauper' and 'pauper and havling'.

Despite being a simpleton, Farquhar had high self-regard. This probably stems from his well-to-do roots, being related to the famous dancing and piping MacLennan family. His sister, Catherine, married Murdoch MacLennan, a well-known bagpiper. He is also said to have been quick-witted in Gaelic, the only language he spoke. He was well-known for his recitation of a long Gaelic prayer but, despite this, he would attend the Rev. John Kennedy's English-language sermons at the Free Church because his perceived equals were there, believing that only common people attended Gaelic-language sermons. With the same stubbornness, he would not accept money from the Parochial Poor Fund.

When he fell ill at the age of eighty-four, he refused medication, but he was ultimately taken to Inverness Northern Infirmary, where he died on 21 September 1868. His death certificate states his age as seventy-eight, and is in the name of Beaton, which may have been his mother's maiden name. Another explanation is that the Inverness Registrar did not know Farquhar's surname, and gave him the same name as the previous person in the register (James Beaton). The cause of death is recorded as 'debility unknown'. It is said that he had asked for his body to be taken to Strathconon, but he is buried in an unmarked grave in the Tomnahurich cemetery in Inverness. The money he saved from selling scrap is supposedly buried, but the hoard has never been found.

At one time, an oil painting of Farquhar, set in a gold-gilt frame, hung in the Clachuile Inn near Fairburn at the head of Strathconon in Urray parish. However, this inn closed in 1918, and the present location of the painting is not known. A photograph of Farquhar is held in the Highland Photographic Archive in Inverness and can also be viewed on the Am Baile website.[78]

6.7   National Population Censuses (1871–1901)

The 1871 census[79] divides the parish into more or less the same four districts as in 1861, the only significant change to District 1 being the inclusion of Wellhouse and Linnie. The census enumerator was now James Smith, a shoemaker who lived in Milton of Redcastle, whilst the previous incumbent, Rev. Hugh Skinner, the parish schoolmaster, had become the parish registrar.

Quarry of Redcastle is recorded with only eight separate dwellings, in which fifty residents lived in nineteen households. The numbers assigned to the houses were reversed from the previous censuses: Nos. 1–3 were now in Pier Cottage; No. 4 was Garden Cottage; No. 5 was Quarry Cottage; and Nos. 6–8 were in Quarry House. Although this new (east to west) system of numbering was to remain for the next 100 years, a reminder of the previous (west to east) numbering system can still be seen in Pier Cottage, where the number 11 is painted on the stone lintel above the eastern doorway.

With the quarry no longer in use, eight agricultural workers now resided in Quarry of Redcastle. Four of these were unmarried females, one being Elspet MacKenzie, who was still living with her parents and her two illegitimate daughters. However, five long-serving ex-quarriers still remained there. Kenneth MacDonald was now sixty-six years old and had worked in the quarry all his life. His wife, Margaret, had died in 1864 and he was now living with his daughters, Ann and Christina, both of whom would remain in the hamlet until the turn of the century. The Free Church Paupers' Roll for 1868 had recorded Kenneth as a sixty-two-year-old widower receiving 5/5d per week from the General Register of the Poor.[80]

Another of the ex-quarriers, Hugh MacLeod, and his wife Janet, had lived in the hamlet and had raised their family there since before 1851. By 1871, they were also in need of financial support from the Paupers' Fund and received £1-2/- per week. Hugh was now aged sixty-three and had suffered paralysis. In 1874, he was offered a place in the Black Isle Combination Poor House (which was in Fortrose), but he declined in favour of engaging a Mrs MacKenzie to care for him at 1/6d per week. He died in 1888.

In Scotland, the administration of poor relief was transferred under the Poor Law Amendment Act (1845) from the parish church to a Parochial Board. However, in Killearnan both the Established Church and the Free Church respectively maintained their Poor and Pauper Rolls until 1865, when the General Register of Poor was commenced by the Parochial Board. Even after 1865, both churches continued to record allowances that had been given by the Parochial Board to their poor members and adherents.

James Kennedy, aged forty four, had worked in the quarry since he was fifteen years old in 1842. He had recently married Jane, and they lived in Plei Cottage where James had been brought up by his mother and grandmother, now both deceased. Another Kenneth MacDonald, now aged seventy-four, and Donald Mackenzie, aged forty-one, had both come to the hamlet when the quarry was engaged to supply stone for the reconstruction of the Caledonian Canal. Donald and his wife, Ann, already had a family of four (although their four-year-old daughter, Helen, was to die in 1876). The Kennedy and MacKenzie families were also destined to remain in Quarry of Redcastle until the turn of the century.

As in Quarry of Redcastle, the 1871 census shows a decline in the population of Milton of Redcastle, from ninety-nine in 1861 to eighty-five in 1871. There had also been a considerable turnover of the businesses in the village, the blacksmith now being Donald Robertson, the inn having been taken over by Andrew Campbell (the previous tenant's son), the large carpentry business now being run by Andrew MacIntosh (who employed six men and three boys), and the shop now being a general dealership, owned by Ann MacDonald. Her son, Duncan, is recorded as the 'shop boy'. Other incomers were: Donald Kennedy, a mercantile clerk; John MacDonald, a tailor who employed eight boys; and James Nicol, a farmer from Avoch who was also the tenant of Blairdhu Farm, and who was to become the first person to purchase property in Quarry of Redcastle. Surprisingly, no miller is recorded, although the mill was still in operation. James Elder, the miller, must have been away during the census, because he is recorded in the Valuation Rolls as the mill tenant until 1875.

At Chapelton, James Robertson and Hugh Fraser were still working as the blacksmith and cartwright at the smiddy. They had been there for at least thirty years, having been recorded in the 1841 census. The 1871 census also records (for the first time) the 'square' at Fettes, the farm manager, George Graham, being resident there. It had been built over twenty years previously, but presumably a portion had been converted for residential purposes. In an article published in the *John o'Groats Journal* in 1850,[81] it had been described as 'first-class and in extent unequalled in the north of Scotland, being sixty yards in length, exclusive of front and back wings. The erection of this large building cost, we believe, some figures above £2,000'.

Fettes Farm was previously known as Drimmore (or Drummore), but was renamed after Sir William Fettes, the proprietor of Redcastle in 1826–36. Drummore is named in late eighteenth- and early nineteenth-century manu-scripts,[82] which record Colin McKenzie as a 'farmer in Redcastle' whose parents farmed at Wellhouse and who erected their son's tombstone in 1818 in Killearnan churchyard. (There is also a 1791 gravestone in Killearnan church-yard, which records James Noble as a previous farmer there.) Prior to 1869, Fettes Farm had been tenanted by George and Alexander Wilson and by George Baillie. The tenancy was advertised in *The Scotsman* on 17 June 1869 as:

...at present in the occupation of the Proprietor, and consisting of about 360 acres. The lands are in high condition and the buildings and fences in good repair. The dwelling-house, which is distant about four miles from the Beauly station on the Highland Railway, is commodious and the situation is, in point of climate and access by roads, most desirable. The tenant's entry will be at Martinmas first, and the conditions of let and a plan of the farm will be communicated to inquirers by Dr Mackenzie, at Eileannach, Inverness; or Messrs Horne, Horne and Lyell WS, 39 Castle Street, Edinburgh. George Graham, the grieve upon the farm, will point out the boundaries, and give such further information as may be required on the spot. Sealed offers, addressed to the Right Hon Henry James Baillie, the Proprietor, at Redcastle, by Inverness, will be received until the 1st July next; but the highest or any offer may not be accepted.

The offer made by Andrew Granger was accepted. Ten years later, he would be committed for murder.

At Redcastle, the Mains 'square' was occupied by Charles Logan, the grieve, and John Stuart, a forester. The West Lodge was occupied by a carpenter, Angus Cameron. The head gardener, Thomas Fraser, had relocated from Corgrain Cottage to the Gardener's Cottage at Milton of Redcastle. Greenhill House was still occupied by James McKenzie Alison, but he is recorded as a shipowner and his son, Alexander, had become the estate clerk. Previously, James had variously self-styled himself as a wood merchant, commission agent and shipowner. However, on 11 March 1879, the Caledonian Banking Co. petitioned for the sequestration of his estate on account of a debt due to them of £2,033-6/-, and creditor notices were published in the *Edinburgh Gazette* (no. 8982) and the *London Gazette* (no. 24694).[83] On 18 April 1879, the *Inverness Advertiser* recorded that he had undergone an initial examination of his complex financial affairs, at which his assets had been assessed at £1,438 and his liabilities at £2,909. He had been involved in loss-making ventures involving the transportation of manure and coal with two schooners (the *Active* and the *Enterprise*) that were mortgaged (together with two houses in Inverness) to the Caledonian Bank. It also transpired that he was already carrying losses from previous farming interests at Lettoch and Artafeelie, for which he had repaid his debtors at 10/- in the £1. His liabilities were finally assessed at £4,121-9-7d and his assets at £1,391-2/-, including fifteen tons of coal lying at Kessock valued at £12. He was discharged of his debts in February 1881 and the thirty-four listed (ordinary) creditors, mainly businesses in Newcastle, Edinburgh, Inverness and Beauly, each received a dividend of 3/8d per £1. James McKenzie Alison relocated to Wellbank, Urray, where he died on 9 May 1894, aged seventy-two.

Many of the residents of Milton of Redcastle in 1871 were also recorded in the 1881 census,[84] although the Milton name is not used in this census. These included: Thomas Fraser, the gardener; Ann MacDonald, the general merchant; John MacDonald, the tailor (now employing only two boy apprentices); John Macrae, the shoemaker; and Donald Robertson, the blacksmith. Amongst the new residents were William Bailey, a gamekeeper who lived in Corgrain Cottage, and Thomas Laing, described as a rural messenger, who was destined to remain as the village 'letter carrier' well into the twentieth century. It is notable that no innkeeper is recorded. Indeed, no innkeeper would again be recorded in the village, suggesting that the Milton Inn was no longer in existence after *circa* 1880. This trend is also discernable from the Valuation Rolls of the period. In 1855–67, most of the properties in Milton of Redcastle had been recorded as being in private (leasehold) ownership. However, it appears that these owners did not remain after their nineteen-year leaseholds had expired. This may have been due to a change of policy on behalf of Henry James Baillie, but it is more likely that the dwindling population of Redcastle could no longer sustain profitable businesses and they had relocated to the larger and growing population bases in Inverness and Dingwall. Although the Milton Inn was the first casualty, the mill and the smiddy also closed around this time, resulting in all the dwelling houses reverting in ownership. To this day, the houses of the lower row in Milton of Redcastle remain the property of the Redcastle estate.

Although he had now purchased Quarry House, James Nicol, the farmer, is recorded as a resident of Rivulet Cottage – the 1881 census being the first to specifically name this cottage, located between Quarry of Redcastle and Milton of Redcastle. James and his wife, Lillias, who had lived in Milton of Redcastle and farmed at Blairdhu since 1870, had made the purchase of Quarry House in 1880. A later sasine extract shows that the Nicols assigned the house to their niece, Lily Jane Bisset, in 1884. She was a dressmaker who also lived in Milton of Redcastle, and was one of several skilled tradespersons who began to occupy the houses of Quarry of Redcastle after Redcastle quarry closed and agricultural practices became less labour-intensive. Others included: Kenneth Cameron, the grocer from Milton of Redcastle; Alexander Edward, a retired merchant; and his daughter, Mary, a schoolteacher at Killearnan Public School. Mary's marriage to Duncan Grant of Nuneaton in 1905 is recorded in the Killearnan parish church Proclamation Register.[85]

The 1881 census[86] uses the name 'Hamlet of Quarry' to refer to Quarry of Redcastle. The population had further decreased to thirty-nine, and the three remaining working-age ex-quarriers (Donald MacKenzie, Hugh MacLeod and James Kennedy) had all become general labourers, albeit Hugh was now retired, suffered paralysis and was registered as a pauper. The number of families had also decreased, to fifteen, and these occupied only seven houses. Notably, no house was given the number 1. In earlier censuses, this house had been the easternmost part of Pier Cottage. It had presumably fallen into disuse. To this day, its ground and upper floor fireplaces are still visible on the eastern gable of the cottage.

Another resident of note was Margaret MacLennan. Her mother, Ann MacLennan, had been recorded in the 1841 census as being of 'independent means'. They were both living in Quarry of Redcastle in 1851, when Margaret was also recorded in this way. However, in the 1881 census she becomes a 'retired lady's maid', and in the 1891 census a 'retired dressmaker'. Not only was her means of earning a living something of a mystery, but she also seemed economical with her age, variously understating it for census purposes as forty-one in 1851, forty-nine in 1861, fifty-nine in 1871, sixty-eight in 1881 and seventy-five in 1891!

With both the Free Church school and the SSPCK female school now closed, the only school in the area was the Killearnan Public School. The new headmaster, James Davidson, had also become the parish registrar. As part of his duties in relation to the census, he was requested to provide information on the numbers of Gaelic speakers in the parish. He is recorded as having made no return, but it was later estimated that of the parish's 1,049 population, 558 spoke Gaelic.

James Davidson's assistant teacher, John Tuach, lived in the cottage next to the church where his father, George, was a crofter. There is a photograph of

Killearnan parish church (taken by Urquhart of Dingwall) which also shows this cottage (known later as Manse Cottage or Manse Park) in Margaret Oag's book.[87] At Newton, the postmistress was now Catherine Robertson, the daughter of Margaret Robertson, the previous postmistress who had been there since 1851. She was obviously kept busy by increasing volumes of post as her sister, Isabella, had now become the sub-postmistress. Hugh Fraser, the cartwright, and James Robertson, the blacksmith, were still resident at Chapelton, and Robert Trotter remained as the farmer at Garguston. At Greenhill House, there was a new estate manager, John MacLennan, in residence, whilst at Parkton Farm, Robert Chisholm had taken over from William Dick (snr). William had died in 1863 and his wife, Janet, had died in 1870, when the farm had been taken over by the children. On 23 July 1878, the *Inverness Advertiser* reported that at the Redcastle Inn, William Dick (jnr) had been presented with a gold watch on leaving the village to commence business as a partner in the firm of Macrae and Dick, postmasters. One of his sisters also received a gold watch, but it is not specified whether this was Catherine or Mary.

There was also change at Fettes Farm as a consequence of the imprisonment of Andrew Granger for murder in 1878. The *Inverness Advertiser* of 25 March 1879 records that the 'fine arable farm of Fettes, on the Redcastle estate, has been secured [on a nineteen-year lease] by Mr Duncan Cameron, Union Street, Inverness, at, we believe, a considerable reduction upon the former rent'. Duncan Cameron was a merchant in Inverness, and he sublet the farm to William Asher. Almost ten years later, in February 1888, Duncan Cameron wanted to quit the farm. In an attempt to do so, he took out an action for £1,000 damages against James Baillie, Henry Baillie's heir, claiming that Henry Baillie had failed to implement his obligations with regard to the lease. At the hearing, reported in *The Scotsman* of 24 February 1888, the judge found against Duncan Cameron on the basis that he had 'an absolutely good lease ... [and that] there was no danger of his eviction ... [and that] having sustained no damage ... there could be no claim'.

Not satisfied by this outcome, Duncan Cameron raised a further action against James Baillie in the Court of Session in July 1888. This action was based on a memorandum to the original nineteen-year lease that had been signed by the late Henry Baillie's factor, but not by Duncan himself. It allowed the rent to be paid in bills rather than in cash, a modification that Duncan Cameron claimed was, in effect, a second lease which had caused him to be 'in a state of uncertainty' and therefore that 'the doctrine of grassum' should apply [a grassum is a sum of money paid or promised by a tenant when his lease is renewed]. The *Scottish Highlander* of 5 July 1888 records that this action was also lost by Duncan Cameron on three counts:

(i) That it was 'an abuse of language to say that there were two leases', the memorandum being deemed to be in the tenant's favour as it allowed him longer to pay.

(ii) That to consider himself in a state of uncertainty because of the change of proprietorship of Redcastle estate was 'extravagant'.

(iii) That to challenge the lease on the doctrine of grassum was 'simply ridiculous, and would be laughed out of Court'.

Three years later, James Baillie sued Duncan Cameron for £1,516-7/- in rent arrears plus costs. Duncan Cameron claimed that new rent arrangements had come into effect in 1879 and offered to settle on that basis. However, he was unable to establish his claim, and a report in *The Scotsman* of 13 July 1891 indicates that he also lost that action. Duncan Cameron did not have a happy experience with the business of farming!

The census of 1891[88] refers to the hamlet of Quarry of Redcastle as the 'Village of Quarry' and records a continuing decline in population. Only twenty-five residents from thirteen families remained. These included the seventy-eight-year-old Margaret MacLennan, who had lived on 'independent means' since 1851, and James Kennedy, the quarrier who had been born in the hamlet in 1827. Neither would survive into the twentieth century. Also still there were Ann MacKenzie (now widowed) and Elspet MacKenzie (with her two daughters). Both had lived in the hamlet for at least thirty years since 1861. Confusingly, Ann's daughter Johanna was living with Elspet. Donald and Ann MacKenzie's gravestone stands in Killearnan parish graveyard. It records their dates of death, but the spaces for their ages are left blank. It also records that they had lost two sons in infancy and a daughter, Helen, aged ten in 1876 (she is recorded in the 1871 census).

The Free Church affiliation was still strong, even if the number of communicants was declining. Lily Bisset (who owned Quarry House and is described as a thirty-year-old dressmaker in the 1891 census) had been appointed 'Collector' for the District of Quarry, and she must have excelled at the job. For the year 1891–92, she raised a total of £13-13-6d from Quarry of Redcastle residents, almost a fifth of the church's total for the year. Johanna MacKenzie (who is described in the 1891 census as a 'retired housekeeper') and Lillias Nicol (Lily Bisset's aunt, who lived with her in Quarry House) were major contributors. Lily married Alexander Jack, a farmer from Avoch, in 1895. Their proclamation is recorded in the Killearnan parish church register for 1894. They were destined to return to Quarry House when they retired in 1915. Lily's aunt, Lillias Nicol, died in Quarry House in 1900. She left a legacy of £10 to the moderator and congregation of Killearnan Free Church.

Another person still living in Quarry of Redcastle in 1891 was Ann Dingwall. She remained the only resident of Quarry of Redcastle recorded as a communicant member of Killearnan parish church. She was partially disabled by a bad knee, and in 1884 she applied for support from the Killearnan General Poor Relief Fund. She was awarded 1/6d per week, increased in 1899 to 2/3d per week and supplemented from time to time for thatch repairs and the purchase of flannel and shoes (5/- in 1888, and 10/- in 1896 and 1898). Somewhat surprisingly, she was also awarded £1-6/- from the Free Church Paupers' Fund as a contribution to the repair of the thatch on the western end of Pier Cottage, a part of that house which was later to be called Sunny Croft. Presumably, with the number of paupers in the parish declining (only one is recorded in the hamlet in the 1891 census) the Parochial Board had broadened its remit from providing cash handouts for the poor to that of a 'community fund'. The one pauper was Elizabeth Logan, who lived with Ann Dingwall in Pier Cottage. She, too, is recorded as being awarded £1-6/- in 1890, 10/- of which was for the purchase of flannel, presumably for petticoats and blankets. Surprisingly, Manse Park (which was more commonly known locally as Manse Cottage) is included as part of the 'Village of Quarry'. It was the cottage next to the church that had been occupied by George and John Tuach in 1881. It was now occupied by a domestic servant and a visitor, so perhaps the Tuachs were out of the area on census night or they no longer lived there.

At Milton of Redcastle, the population had declined to forty-two, living in thirteen family groups within twelve houses. Thomas Fraser, who had served as head gardener at Redcastle for fifty-two years, had retired at the age of eighty. He died, aged eighty-eight, in June 1896 and is buried in Killearnan churchyard. In her book *Fragments of Auld Lang Syne*, Phillipa Russell[89] describes Thomas Fraser as 'the "philosopher of the garden" … a quaint and interesting character … his shrewd wisdom and grasp of mind being most unusual … who used seaweed as manure'. He was succeeded by his son, Hugh. The estate gamekeeper, who lived in Corgrain Cottage, had now become James Grant. He had previously worked in Elgin and had successfully applied for the post through an advertisement that had been placed in the *Inverness Courier* of 2 May 1890. It stated: 'Gamekeeper – wanted at the term. First-class man to take charge of moor and low-ground shooting. Must understand "driving". Best references as to character. Apply No. 903 Courier Office.' There were seventeen applicants from as far afield as Staffordshire, Perth, Sutherland and Caithness.[90]

Of the artisans, only Donald Robertson, the blacksmith, remained in the village. John Macrae, the shoemaker who had practised in the village since 1860, had been replaced by John MacLeod. James Nicol's family had moved from Rivulet Cottage into Quarry House, and a carpenter named William MacIntosh was now resident there. Also at Rivulet Cottage was the other

William MacIntosh, who had been appointed as headmaster of Killearnan Public School in 1889 but is recorded as an 'elementary schoolteacher'. He was destined to remain in the village until the 1930s, gaining much fame in later life as a bone-setter.

A feature of the 1891 census is the mispelling of common words by the census enumerator, Thomas Laing, the Redcastle letter carrier. He consistently records the words 'schoolar', 'masson' and 'villiage' in the census entries. Another feature is the number of railway navvies that are recorded as lodgers in the area. They were constructing the Muir of Ord to Fortrose branch of the Highland Railway, which opened on 2 February 1894. The line was thirteen and a half miles long and was constructed at a cost of £57,000. There were four intermediate stations at Redcastle, Allangrange, Munlochy and Avoch.

Although numbers of Gaelic speakers had been requested from parish Registrars in 1881, the 1891 census was the first to record Gaelic-speaking individuals. Remarkably, every adult resident of Quarry of Redcastle is recorded as dual English- and Gaelic-speaking. In Milton of Redcastle, twenty-eight of the forty-two residents were dual-speaking and one (Isabella Young, a ninety-one-year-old pauper) spoke only Gaelic. Some others in the area also claimed to speak only Gaelic, for example: William Noble and his sister Mary, who were crofters in Spital Shore; Ann Fraser and her husband Alexander, who was a shepherd in Spital Wood (Braes of Garguston); and William MacDonald, who was a general labourer in Chapelton.

No minister of the Established Church of Scotland is recorded in the 1891 census of Killearnan, because the newly appointed Rev. Aeneas Macdonald was living at Tarradale, awaiting the completion of his new manse. As usual, none of the Baillie family were resident at Redcastle over census night, only a housekeeper, Catherine MacLennan, being recorded. She must have been lonely in such a large house. The other estate residences were occupied variously by the estate manager, John MacLennan (at Greenhill House), the Chisholm family of farm workers (at the Redcastle Mains) and the game-keeper, James Grant (at Corgrain Cottage).

The 1901 census[91] is the latest currently available due to the '100-year rule'. As in most of the previous censuses, the parish was subdivided into four districts, of which No. 1 covered the area bounded by Spital Shore in the west, Wellhouse in the north-west, Parkton in the north-east, and Corgrain Point in the east. The district contained sixty-five inhabited and five uninhabited houses, one of which was in Quarry of Redcastle and four were in Milton of Redcastle. The population of the district was 287, of whom 137 spoke both English and Gaelic, and two spoke only Gaelic (William and Catherine MacDonald of Chapelton).

For the only time since 1841, the 1901 census recorded that the population of Quarry of Redcastle had increased since the previous census, from twenty-five to thirty-two. However, this was because two large families had moved into the hamlet. They were a shepherd, Donald Beaton, with his wife Jessie and six children, and a wood carter, William Duncan, with his wife Margaret and five children. The Beatons were very short-term, being resident only in 1900–01. Quarry Cottage comprised a two-storey main house with a single storey 'but and ben' attached to its eastern elevation. The leasehold of the main house, Quarry Cottage (west), was purchased from Redcastle estate by John MacKenzie in 1899. He was the son, born in 1877, of Donald and Ann MacKenzie, the quarrier and his wife, who had lived there since the 1850s. John had become a policeman serving with the Chinese Marine Customs in Peking. The sasine extract describes the property as '12 poles 15 yards, bounded on the west by old footpath from Redcastle quarry to public road near Killearnan church and on the north by service road through the village of Quarry'. John purchased the family home after his parents died, presumably in order to retire there, but he never returned. Another sasine records that James Robertson, the blacksmith at Chapelton, purchased his house and smithy from Redcastle estate in August 1901. Clearly, James Baillie was prepared to sell off surplus estate properties at this time; however, it is noteworthy that most of the sales were of the leaseholds and the ownership of all the properties would revert to the Redcastle estate by the middle of the twentieth century.

Figure 48: Mackenzie, General Merchants, shop at Milton of Redcastle circa 1900
(reproduced from an original by permission of Carolynn Thompson)

The population of Milton of Redcastle had further declined from forty-two to thirty-four. Only Donald Robertson, the blacksmith, and Thomas Laing, the letter carrier, remained in the village from 1891. Hugh Fraser, the head gardener at Redcastle, also remained in the Gardener's Cottage (but, for census purposes, this house was not considered to be within the village). Amongst the new arrivals in the village were the new district registrar, William Fraser, who was the son of Hugh Fraser, the carpenter who had lived and worked in Chapelton since the 1850s. Also new were Mary Mackenzie and her widowed mother, Elizabeth, who had taken over the shop as 'general merchants' (Figure 48). At Rivulet Cottage, William MacIntosh, the carpenter, was still resident, whereas William MacIntosh, the head teacher at the Killearnan Public School (and the previous parish registrar), had relocated to the schoolhouse. His assistant teacher was his niece, Isabella Grigor, who also lodged in the schoolhouse. She was a temporary monitor until Annie MacIntosh began work in November 1901.

At the seven farms in the district, only three farmers remained from 1891. One of these was the County Councillor, Parish Councillor and Chairman of the School Board, Robert Trotter (jnr). His father (and mother after his father's death) had been the tenant farmers there since the 1820s, and had been credited[92] with the farm's 'highly improved and fertile condition' and with having 'spared neither time nor expense in bringing it to that state'. Robert had purchased the farm in June 1899, but sadly his ownership was short-lived as he died in August 1901, and the farm was sold to Alexander Ogilvie Stewart Spence in May 1902. The Black Isle District Committee[93] recorded Robert's passing and referred to him as 'possessed of great practical knowledge and urbanity of disposition'. His death certificate was the last to be issued by William Fraser as parish registrar, and records him as a 'farmer and landed proprietor'. (The previous certificate is also interesting. It is that of an unknown man who had been drowned and whose body had been found on the sea shore around Lettoch.) Robert Trotter's tombstone is located against the eastern wall of Killearnan churchyard. He was the third generation of the Trotter family to farm in the area. His parents (and their eight children) are commemorated on a plaque attached to the western wall at the opposite end of the churchyard, and his grandfather (John) is buried below the plaque (Figure 49).

Other farmers recorded in the 1901 census were William Campbell at Blairdhu, and Donald MacLean, who had farmed at Parkton since the 1880s. Fettes Farm had now been taken over by Donald MacDonald, and another Donald MacDonald was now the farm manager at Redcastle Mains, where he was resident. Greenhill House was occupied only by James Fraser, a forester, and his sister, Grace, a housekeeper. Actually, the census reverses their roles, describing Grace as the forester and James as the housekeeper!

Figure 49: Plaque in Killearnan parish church graveyard in memory of Robert Trotter of Garguston, 1785–1850

Corgrain Cottage was still occupied by the gamekeeper, James Grant, and his family, and the associated bothy was occupied by two woodcutters. Other entries of note included Finlay MacDonald, described as a 'station agent', and various other railway workers around Newton (named Railway Crossing in this census) and Redcastle Station. Another was William Meikle at Fettes, who is described as a 'free-stone quarry foreman', presumably of either Tarradale quarry or the Kilcoy quarry near Tore, as Redcastle quarry had been closed twenty-five years previously. Rev. Aeneas Macdonald was now resident in the manse. He was a widower who lived with his two young sons, his mother-in-law and his sister-in-law. He was not happy with the accommodation or its water supply, and his complaints would frustrate the heritors for many years to come.

Crofters and shepherds were recorded at Drynie Park, Wellhouse, Garguston Shore and Spital Shore. At Spital Wood (named 'Spittal Croft' in the census book), Donald MacKay, a sheep dealer, was living with his wife, Flora, his eighty-four-year-old mother, Janet, and two lodging shepherds. This was the only house in the old village of Spital Wood (Garguston Braes) that was still occupied, there having been twenty crofts shown in the village on Patrick Grant's 1825 plan of the Redcastle estate.

The house had been previously occupied since at least 1851 by Alexander and Ann Mackenzie. Alexander had variously been described in the censuses as a crofter, farmer of eight to twelve acres, and crofter and quarryman; the house had variously been named as 'Spittal Wood', 'Spital Farm House' and 'Spittal Croft'. The progressive decline of the village is well documented in the successive censuses. For example: in 1891, a shepherd, Alexander Fraser, together with his wife Ann and six children, were recorded in 'Spital Wood'; in 1871, two cottages in 'Spittle Side' were occupied respectively by Ann McKenzie and the family of John and Ann Campbell; and in 1861, three cottages in 'Spittal' were occupied respectively by John and Ann Campbell, Murdoch and Ann McKenzie, and Roderick and Ann Logan. Unfortunately, it is not possible to identify the village specifically in the 1851 census, as the crofts seem to be included partly in 'Spittlewood' and partly in the farms at Whitewells and Wellhouse; whereas in the 1841 census, there are entries under 'Granthill' and 'Juniperfield', as well as 'Wood of Spittal', Whitewells and Wellhouse.

6.8   The Inland Revenue 'New Domesday' Evaluation

No detailed census data from 1911 is yet available. However, in the period 1910–15 the Inland Revenue carried out a valuation of every house in the UK, on a parish-by-parish basis (Scotland was surveyed in 1911–12). It is sometimes referred to as the 'New Domesday' survey. The boundaries of every property are marked out and numbered on copies of the relevant 1:2,500 (*circa* 25 inch:1 mile) second edition Ordnance Survey maps[94] and the data is fully documented in associated field books.[95] The survey therefore provides an accurate and revealing picture of the ownership, occupants, condition and value of every house in the UK at that time.

Milton of Redcastle comprised eleven buildings: the smithy; the mill; five houses in the southern (lower) row nearest the sea; and four houses in the northern (upper) row. The ownership of all the buildings had reverted to the Redcastle estate, the previous leaseholds having expired before 1900. The mill was used as a workshop, but its roof was sagging and it was generally dilapidated. The smithy was slated and the attached house was thatched and occupied by Donald Robertson. The easternmost house of the lower row (which would become No. 1 Milton) was in fair repair and occupied by Donald Ross, who was a labourer. To the west of this house was a block of four houses. They were all single storey, thatched and variously in poor to good repair. In the upper row, the unnamed westernmost house was in dilapidated condition and occupied by the elderly Williamina McIntosh. To the east of this house were three houses, all thatched with attic bedrooms. The house that would become Inver (later Corrie Cottage) and Ashgrove were in fair repair and were occupied respectively by John Allan, a roadman, and Thomas Laing, the postman. The easternmost house of the upper row (which would become Rosemount) is described as a 'thatched shop, house, store and gardens' (Figure 48, page 336). It was occupied by Mary Mackenzie, merchant, and the gardens included the entire field on which the inn and the general merchant's shop had been previously located.

The businesses run by Mary Mackenzie and Donald Robertson are the only two listed in Slater's Directory for 1911.[96] Mary Mackenzie's parents had taken over the village shop from Alexander Edward in about 1895. She was the sister of Sandy 'Kinkell' Mackenzie, a larger-than-life character who made his fortune in gold mining in South Africa. When he returned in 1929, he purchased Easter Kinkell House and became known for his tweed suit (which the locals called 'corned beef tartan') and his gold nugget tiepin.[97]

Rivulet Cottage was occupied by David Christie. The accommodation consisted of: sitting room, bedroom, parlour, kitchen, scullery, pantry and WC on the ground floor; and three bedrooms, two boxrooms and servant's bedroom on the first floor. The steading comprised a cart shed, byre and barn with two storerooms. The whole property was in good repair and included the two fields on either side of the service road to Quarry of Redcastle.

Quarry House in Quarry of Redcastle was owned in its entirety by Lily and Alexander Jack. However, they had not yet retired from their farm at Munlochy and the house was still subdivided into three, the tenants being three spinsters: Jane Tuach, Catherine Forbes (and her father, George, an estate worker) and Isabella Gray. The house is described as being in poor repair, with its slated roof sagging and requiring extensive repairs. Quarry Cottage was two houses. Both were thatched with clay floors and in poor repair. The western two-storey house was owned by John MacKenzie, but it was unoccupied and unfurnished. The smaller eastern 'but and ben' was owned by the Redcastle estate and was occupied by John Matheson, a seventy-five-year-old ex-quarrier. Garden Cottage was also thatched and owned by the Redcastle estate. It was in fair condition and occupied by John Chisholm, who had cottar status. Pier Cottage was two houses, the western house being called Sunny Croft. It had been bought by Alexander MacLeod and was slated and in good repair. He lived in one room and sublet the other two rooms to Alexander MacLennan, a stone mason, and Alexander Cook, a labourer. Pier Cottage (east) was owned by William MacLennan, who had purchased it in 1902. The tenant was William Duncan, the wood carter (now described as a contractor) whose large family had helped to swell the population of the hamlet in the 1901 census. The house was thatched and in good repair.

The school at Quarry of Redcastle was unoccupied, but the Free Church still held the lease from the Redcastle estate. It was slated but in poor condition. The Inland Revenue field book states its dimensions as: 'frontage thirty-six; depth twenty; height thirteen'. The units of measurement are not stated but are feet, corresponding with the remnants of the stone walls that are still visible. The piece of land on which the Free Church school was built, and which had been the subject of a feu dispute in 1883, was still leased by the Free Church but rented to David Christie of Rivulet Cottage. It is described as 'a garden without buildings', so presumably was still cultivated.

Redcastle Mains Farm (Figure 50) is named Home Farm in the field books and included the 'grieve's house' (with byres, sheds, stables, barns, cattle fold, looseboxes, dairy and granary), the 'ploughman's house' (with barn, hay loft, granary and water-powered sawmill) and the 'steading' (with office and bedroom).

Other buildings at the Mains had been included in the survey of Redcastle itself, as they were used exclusively by the proprietor, James Baillie – for example, as wash houses and garages (See Chapter 1, page 102. Greenhill House was occupied, at a yearly rent of £15, by Rev. Charles Matheson, the retired minister of the United Free Church of Killearnan. The other farms included: Parkton (sixteen acres, occupied by Donald MacLean at a yearly rent of £125); Fettes (373 acres, owned and occupied by Donald MacDonald, with a seventeen-horsepower Allan engine operating a generator in the steading at 'Cattle Mains'); Garguston (358 acres, owned and occupied by A O Stewart Spence); and Blairdhu (114 acres, occupied by Alexander MacLean and owned by Donald MacDonald of Fettes).

Figure 50: Redcastle Mains (2004)

Although Corgrain Cottage (and its bothy) is shown on the associated map, it is not recorded in the field books. This suggests that it was vacant in 1911 and missed by the Inland Revenue officers, because it is recorded in the Valuation Rolls as being occupied up to 1930, latterly by a gamekeeper, Donald McDonnell. In 1901, the cottage and its associated bothy had been occupied by a gamekeeper, a woodcutter and a saw miller. In the nineteenth century, it had been a residence for either the head gardener or the gamekeeper, and had on occasion been referred to as the 'East Lodge'.

Killearnan parish church is described as stone, lime and slated with nave, two transepts, choir, vestry, and heating chamber. The glebe was nine acres and contained two barns (one wooden and the other corrugated iron) as well as stone and slated offices (now the house known as Finlaggan). The manse was occupied by Rev. Aeneas Macdonald. It is described as built in 1892 with: a study, drawing and dining rooms, anteroom, parish room, kitchen, scullery, wine cellar and WC on the ground floor; five bedrooms, nursery, boudoir, bathroom and WC on the first floor; and a servant's bedroom in the attic. There was also a coal cellar, wash house, milk house and store in an external building close to the Milton of Redcastle–Garguston road. This outhouse is still in use today.

Killearnan Public School (Figure 32, page 232) contained three classrooms and two cloakrooms, and the schoolhouse contained a sitting room, kitchen, closet and three bedrooms upstairs. However, there was no water supply and therefore only an earth closet in an outbuilding. Sourcing a proper water supply was to become an ongoing issue over the next fifty years.

At Chapelton, there was a row of three cottages, one with a carpenter's workshop and one with a smithy. They were in fair repair, with thatched roofs and attic bedrooms. The smithy in the centre of the row was owned by James Robertson and unoccupied, although Angus Campbell was a tenant in the attached cottage. The carpenter's workshop at the eastern end was owned and occupied by John Fraser. It also had a 'stirk house and byre', but this was in very poor condition [a stirk is a young bullock or heifer]. The other house (at the western end of the row) was owned by Donald MacLean of Parkton Farm and occupied by George Mackay.

There were three croft houses remaining at Spital Shore, all owned by the Redcastle estate. They were variously in poor, fair and good repair, two of them being thatched, whilst the other (in good repair) was slated. The occupants in 1911 were James Robertson, the blacksmith who owned the smithy at Chapelton, and crofters John Gollan and Robert Chisholm, the latter two being given 'tenant meliorations' in the valuation, as they had built their houses and supplied the materials. As these crofts had been there at least since 1800, presumably this refers to the renovation of these houses. At Garguston Shore, there was one croft owned by A O Stewart Spence of Garguston Farm and occupied by James Mackintosh. The house is not described, but in 1921 it was reported as being unfit for human habitation. Today, it is still a working croft. The associated map also shows three other buildings in Garguston Shore, each with its own well, one to the west and two to the east of the occupied croft, but these had become ruinous and unoccupied by 1911.

6.9   Register of Electors

Prior to 1832, only significant landowners were entitled to vote. The (First) Reform Act of 1832 raised the number of the Scottish electorate from *circa* 4,500 to *circa* 65,000, although those who lived in rural areas were largely unaffected. Partly as a consequence of the 'Chartist' movement, the (Second) Reform Act of 1867 doubled the electorate by giving the vote to ratepaying males, owners of small urban properties, tenants and lodgers paying more than £10 per year. The (Third) Reform Act of 1884 further extended the vote, especially in rural areas, to include all adult male householders (such as crofters) but failed to enfranchise all males by excluding various groups, such as living-in servants and those in receipt of poor relief. Only when the

Representation of the People Act came into effect in 1918 did all males become eligible to vote.

The earliest Electoral Roll for Ross-shire that has survived is for 1913–14.[98] At that time, as only male house owners and tenants were eligible to vote, the roll records only twelve residents of Redcastle. They were: John Allan, roadman residing in Inver Cottage; John Chisholm, cottar in Garden Cottage; William Chisholm, ex-quarrier in Quarry Cottage (west); Alexander Cook, described as a 'residenter' in Milton of Redcastle; Donald Grant, crofter living in Rivulet Cottage; Thomas Laing, postman in Ashgrove (although he died in 1913); Donald MacDonald, road surfaceman in Milton; Alexander MacKenzie, retired farmer; John MacKenzie, owner of Quarry Cottage (west), who lived in China; Donald Robertson, blacksmith and parish registrar in the smiddy at Milton of Redcastle; Donald Ross, labourer residing in No. 1 Milton; and Walter Ross, carpenter in Milton of Redcastle.

Five of the employees of the Redcastle estate were also eligible to vote. They were: Angus Cameron, lodge keeper; Hugh Fraser, head gardener, Donald MacDonald, grieve; Donald McDonell, gamekeeper; and John MacKintosh, porter. Other notable residents listed in the Electoral Roll of 1913–14 were: William MacIntosh, school headteacher, resident in the schoolhouse; John Fraser, carpenter at Chapelton; James Mackintosh, crofter at Garguston Shore and parish church sexton; and all four of the local farmers, A O Stewart Spence of Garguston, Donald MacDonald of Fettes, John Munro of Blairdhu and Donald MacLean of Parkton.

Women of property over the age of thirty were also given the vote under the Representation of the People Act (1918). However, it was not until 1928 that all women over twenty-one were given the same voting entitlement as men. Unfortunately, the next surviving Electoral Roll for Ross-shire seems to be for 1947–48.

6.10 World War One

There are surprisingly few references to World War One in any of the contemporaneous records of Redcastle. Even the local newspapers carried only minimal information on the progress of the war, although the *Ross-shire Journal*[99] did emphasise the magnitude of the losses by reporting the deaths and injuries suffered by the local regiments on a weekly basis. Many of these articles, generally on page 5, published photographs supplied by the relatives of those killed. On 11 February 1915, Col A F Mackenzie of the Seaforth Highlanders addressed a meeting in Killearnan School on the Volunteer Training Corps scheme. The meeting resolved to establish a corps in Killearnan and a committee was formed. Several of the local Redcastle figureheads were included: Rev. Alexander MacDonald (convenor); Donald McDonell (secretary and treasurer); William MacIntosh (commandant); and A O Stewart Spence. Each of the twenty members paid a minimum fee of 1/- (although many paid more according to their means) to undertake rifle training on the Redcastle pier twice per week. The last entry in the corps' accounts was made in February 1917, after which it seems to have disbanded. William Macintosh presented the corps with gold medals for presentation to the best rifleman in 1915–16 and 1916–17. Donald McDonell was the winner in 1916–17, and the medal remains to this day in the possession of his descendants.[100]

The Killearnan Parish Council[101] recorded in November 1915 that it had organised a meeting in the school to publicise Lord Derby's Recruiting Scheme, and that certain named individuals had been selected to attend (presumably as potential recruits). The County Road Board[102] recorded that a 'Lights on Vehicles (Scotland) Order' had been issued in February 1916, and would apply to all roads within a six-mile strip round the coast. It applied to all traffic, including 'hand vehicles', which required a white light at the front and a red light at the rear. The Black Isle District Committee recorded in June 1917 that it had arranged for 'Food Economy Cooking Lessons' to be given at the local schools. The Killearnan Public School log book[103] makes only one reference, in July 1915, when at the end of the school year 'the scholars unanimously decided to give the usual prize money to War Relief Schemes'.

The population of Milton of Redcastle declined during World War One. Donald Robertson, the blacksmith, Mary Mackenzie, the shopkeeper, Hugh Fraser, the head gardener, and Margaret MacLennan were the only survivors. Thomas Laing had died in July 1913. His gravestone is in Killearnan graveyard. He had been the village postman since 1876, when three days per week he had walked to the post office at Newton crossroads to collect the post that had been delivered by the Royal Mail coaches[104] (on their way to and from Inverness and Dingwall/Tain) each evening around 4.30 p.m. He then walked to North Kessock via Tore to deliver and collect post, returning along the coast road, a total distance of about fourteen miles. No doubt he saw many unusual happenings during his travels to and from North Kessock, but surely none stranger than that encountered by his predecessor in 1856. The *Inverness Courier* of 8 August, under the headline of 'A Shower of Frogs', described the event as follows:

The post-runner between Redcastle and Kessock, when passing Artafelie, on Sunday last, was suddenly enveloped in what appeared to be a shower of frogs. They fell fast upon his hat and shoulders, and dozens of them found an easy resting place in his coat pockets. The air was quite darkened with them for about 30 yards by 14 or 15 yards, and the road was so densely covered with the dingy little creatures, that it was impossible to walk without treading on them. They were about the size of a bee, and were quite lively when they found themselves on the road.

Initially, people collected their letters from Thomas Laing's house in Milton of Redcastle. House deliveries commenced in 1886, but in practice those houses that were some distance from main routes had their letters left at convenient places where they could be readily picked up. There is a recess in the wall at the junction where the service road to Quarry of Redcastle meets the Milton of Redcastle–Garguston road. It was presumably a place where letters and other deliveries could be left for the residents of Quarry of Redcastle. After the opening of the Black Isle Railway in 1894, the post office moved from the Newton crossroads to Redcastle Station, and a post box was installed in the Redcastle estate wall, opposite the shop at Milton of Redcastle. The train delivered mail at the station at 11.10 a.m. and collected outgoing mail at 6.30 a.m. and 4.27 p.m. Only in 1910, three years before his death, was Thomas Laing issued with a bicycle. (By 1918, the railway timetable showed that trains departed from Redcastle Station for Muir of Ord at 8.00 a.m., 1.25 p.m. and 5.20 p.m., and for Fortrose at 10.02 a.m., 3.32 p.m. and 6.12 p.m.)

In Quarry of Redcastle, Lily and Alexander Jack retired to Quarry House during World War One. One of their previous tenants, widow Catherine Forbes, moved into the house in Milton of Redcastle that had previously been occupied by John Allan, the roadman, who had died during World War One. Catherine died in October 1936, and is buried with her husband, who had died in May 1890, in Killearnan churchyard. Both parts of Quarry Cottage had been empty prior to the war but William Chisholm, an ex-quarrier, became John MacKenzie's tenant in 1915. He had become a roadman and was also the precentor of Killearnan parish church. His wife, Anne, gave birth to a daughter, Margaret Henrietta, in 1916. Garden Cottage continued to be occupied by Redcastle estate workers, one of whom was John Chisholm and his wife Isabella. Their daughter and granddaughters were also destined to live in that house. Until 1920, Sunny Croft was occupied by its owner, Alexander MacLeod. Thereafter it was occupied by Margaret MacDonald, who was William Chisholm's widowed sister. In 1915, she gave birth to a son, Thomas John Chisholm MacDonald, who was baptised six months later in the parish church.[105] The baptism record does not record the father, because John MacDonald of the 12th Battalion Royal Scots is one of the twenty-four names on the Killearnan war memorial which stands outside the former Free Church at the Newton crossroads. Two other MacDonalds who died in World War

One are recorded on tombstones in Killearnan churchyard. They are Lieut Roddie MacDonald, who died, aged twenty, of wounds in France in April 1917, and Corporal Duncan MacDonald of the Machine Gun Corps, who died, aged twenty-five, in France in July 1918. He was the son of Donald and Ann MacDonald, who lived in the Redcastle West Lodge until 1931.

In his book *Inverness, Highland Town to Millennium City*, Norman Newton[106] writes that 'not everybody was in a hurry to serve the colours. Especially in rural areas, many men sought exemption from military service because of the nature of their work'. This was evident from the many advertisements placed in the local press by the Ross-shire Recruiting Committee and the various regiments, such as the Cameron Highlanders and the Seaforths. However, there was no reluctance to join up by the Noble family who lived in Manse Cottage (or Manse Park). In consequence, they had to endure by far the greatest suffering to befall a Killearnan family during World War One. The parents, William and Catherine, had five sons, the first born having died at seven weeks of age in 1893.

If that was not sufficient tragedy, the *Ross-shire Journal* of 12 May 1916 published a full-page commemorative feature on the anniversary of the Battle of Aubers Ridge, at which the Easter Ross (No. 1) and Black Isle (No. 2) Companies of the 4th Seaforths were in the front line and suffered heavy losses. It describes the full horror of the battle and records the Roll of Honour. Included is the following passage:

Noble, Private James, 1789, son of Mr and Mrs Noble, Manse Cottage, Killearnan, was omitted from the original casualty list, but subsequently reported missing, and later on reported presumed to be dead. His brother, 2319, Pte D [Donald] Noble, was wounded on the same day. Another brother, Corpl. A [Alexander] Noble, 1st Camerons, was killed on October 5th 1914, while a fourth brother, Private R [Roderick] Noble, is serving with the 15th H.L.I [Highland Light Infantry].

A poignant gravestone in Killearnan graveyard (Figure 51) confirms that Alexander, a twenty-one-year-old Cameron Highlander, was killed in October 1914, and James, a seventeen-year-old Seaforth Highlander, was killed in May 1915. It records that Roderick had also been killed (on 1 August 1917, aged twenty-two). All three are inscribed on the war memorial at Newton crossroads, and the website of the Commonwealth War Graves Commission[107] records that Alexander's grave is at the Vendresse cemetery and James's is at Le Touret, whilst Roderick has no grave but is recorded on the Menin Gate in Ypres.

Figure 51: The grave of the Noble family of Manse Cottage, showing the deaths of three sons in World War One

Another son of Redcastle whose name is on the Killearnan war memorial is Second Lieut Duncan MacLean of the Otago Regiment, New Zealand Forces, who was killed on the Western Front on 3 March 1918, aged thirty-five. Duncan was the youngest son of Donald MacLean of Parkton Farm. He had immigrated to New Zealand in 1906, and had set up a successful agricultural business there. He had come to Europe at the outbreak of World War One with the 1st New Zealand Expeditionary Force, and had fought at Gallipoli and Passchendale, for which he earned the D C M. The *Ross-shire Journal* of 12 April 1918 carries a photograph of him, and quotes from a letter sent by his chaplain to his parents:

> He was accorded a full military funeral with firing party and band and battalion present this afternoon. His body is laid in a quiet little churchyard [at Hondeghem] far behind the firing line. The place will be marked by a cross

with his name. I am sure you must have been proud of him, for he was a son that any father and mother might well have been proud of. In this great cause he did what he could. He served his King and country with every ounce of his strength. Will you please accept through me the sympathy of the battalion in the day of your heavy affliction.

Duncan is commemorated on the family tombstone in Killearnan churchyard.

A tragic accident involving three men is reported in the *Ross-shire Journal* of 29 August 1919. They were: Dr MacDonald, a military medical officer who had been relieving Dr Brodie, the County Medical Officer of Health; Mr Grant from Burton-on-Trent, who had been the late Lord Burton's Secretary; and his brother Lieut Grant of the Artillery. The Grant brothers were visiting their parents, who lived at Rivulet Cottage, their father being a retired Redcastle gardener. The men had set off from Redcastle into the Firth to shoot seals, but their boat was overturned in a squall. The incident had been seen from the shore (according to one account,[108] from the manse nursery window) but no other boat had been available and all three were drowned.

Although it is not recorded in the school log book, the children of Redcastle were treated to a 'Peace Day' party at the end of World War One. According to a report in the *Ross-shire Journal* of 8 August 1919, 'they met at the school at noon and marched to a field at Redcastle waving flags enthusiastically to the strains of bagpipes and drums'. There were races and games, with prizes totalling £8-10/-. A celebratory supper and dance for fifty servicemen who returned to Killearnan after World War One is recorded in the *Ross-shire Journal* of 13 February 1920. It was held 'by the kind permission of Baroness Burton' in the garage at Redcastle, and the catering was provided by Mr and Mrs Macdonald of the Station Hotel in Muir of Ord. Mr A O Stewart Spence of Garguston presided and was accompanied by other local dignitaries (although, strangely, none from Redcastle). After dinner, 'the ladies joined the company for an excellent dance, the music for which was provided by Miss Macleod, Drumsmittal, piano; Mr James Kemp, Munlochy, violin; and Piper Alex Maclennan, Strathpeffer'.

After the end of World War One, there was much consideration of the erection of memorials to those who had died. 'Thistle Day' was held throughout Scotland on 24 June 1922 for the raising of funds for the Scottish National War Memorial. It is recorded in the Killearnan Parish Council minutes of 21 July 1922 that the parish collected £20-2/-. On Saturday 31 March 1923, at 2.00 p.m., the Killearnan war memorial at Newton crossroads outside the Free Church was ceremonially unveiled by Col A F MacKenzie (Figure 52).

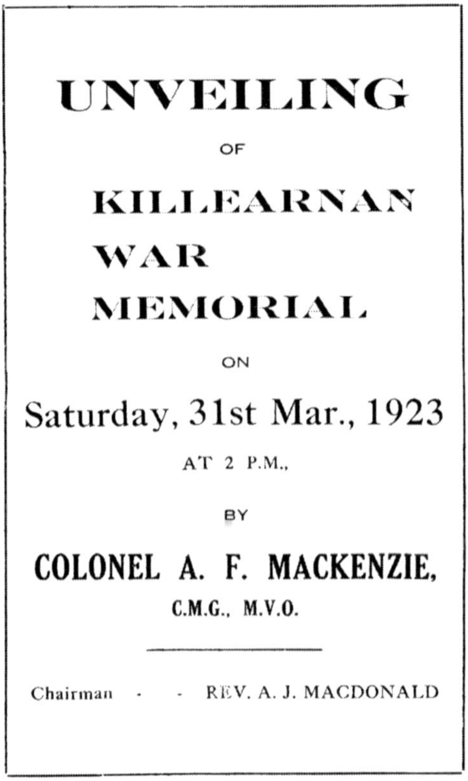

UNVEILING

OF

KILLEARNAN

WAR

MEMORIAL

ON

Saturday, 31st Mar., 1923

AT 2 P.M.,

BY

COLONEL A. F. MACKENZIE,

C.M.G., M.V.O.

Chairman - - REV. A. J. MACDONALD

Figure 52: Programme of the 1923 unveiling ceremony of the Killearnan war memorial at Newton crossroads (reproduced with permission from the collection of the late Frances [Ada] McDonell)

6.11 Redcastle between the Wars

All three of the privately owned houses of the hamlet of Quarry of Redcastle changed ownership in the period from 1923 to 1931. In 1925, Pier Cottage (east) was purchased by Christina and Margaret MacAndrew, where they remained until 1960. The western part of Pier Cottage, called Sunny Croft, was also continuously owner-occupied. Having been occupied by Margaret MacDonald since 1920, the leasehold was purchased in 1935 by Duncan MacBeth, who was a roadman. The MacBeths remained until 1955. The eastern single-storey 'but and ben' part of Quarry Cottage was still owned by Redcastle estate. It had been used as a bothy for itinerant estate workers since the turn of the century, and appears to have continued to be used for that purpose up to 1940. The two-storey Quarry Cottage (west) was occupied by William Chisholm, the roadman and parish church precentor, who had been the tenant since 1915. William purchased it from John MacKenzie in 1923 and lived there with his wife, Annie, until 1935, after which it lay empty until 1941. Garden Cottage was owned by the Redcastle estate, and the lease was taken over in the early 1930s by Margaret Chisholm (Annie's sister). Margaret married Thomas MacDonald, a chauffeur at the Kinlochewe Hotel, who returned home each weekend. The MacDonalds called their house 'The Quarry House', but this does not seem to have been adopted as a formal postal address.

Although Lily and Alexander Jack owned all of Quarry House, they leased the western single-storey portion in 1924 to Murdo MacGregor. Then, on the death of the Jacks in 1931, the house was sold to the Rev. Duncan and Mary Grant. There was a servitude right of way along the front of Quarry House (an extension of the service road through the hamlet) to allow access to the estate land to the west; however, this was waived in 1932. The Grants undertook major renovations that were carried out by a labourer, Alexander Ross, who lived onsite. Unfortunately, the Grants did not live to enjoy their refurbishments, since both had died by 1935. Their young daughter was brought up by the Rev. Dr Lewis Sutherland and his wife, Jean. They used Quarry House as a summer retreat until 1954, when they purchased it.

At Milton of Redcastle, all the houses were owned by the Redcastle estate, with the exception of Inver. It had been purchased by George Forbes, who named it and lived there until 1957. By 1930, the shop had been taken over from Mary Mackenzie by John MacDonald. His son, Ian, was destined to succeed him. By 1920, the westernmost house of the upper row at Milton of Redcastle had become ruinous. Its last occupant had been the ninety-two-year-old Williamina McIntosh, who died in April 1917. She was the daughter of Andrew McIntosh, the carpenter who had run his business in Milton of Redcastle since the early nineteenth century, and who had died in February 1880. Both are buried in Killearnan churchyard. Throughout the inter-war years, the house next to the shop (which was to become Corrie Cottage) continued to be occupied by the family of Thomas Laing, the postman who had died in 1913. The lower row of houses (which would become Nos. 1–4 Milton) were occupied by a succession of tenants, many of whom were short term, but amongst the longer term tenants were Margaret MacLennan, who had lived there since 1910, and Walter Ross, the carpenter, both of whom were occupants of these houses until the 1940s.

Three generations of the Robertson family occupied the smithy and its associated house at Milton of Redcastle. Donald Robertson, who was the son of a blacksmith, had come to Redcastle to take over the smithy in 1865. He died in December 1898, and the business was carried on by his son, Donald, until March 1947, when he died at the age of eighty-eight. His son, also

Donald, continued to live in the smithy house until the 1950s, but the smithy became a store and the building was demolished in the mid-1960s. Only some remnants of its walls are now visible.

William MacIntosh, the carpenter and contractor whose business was in Muir of Ord, died in 1911 and is buried in Killearnan churchyard, where his gravestone records that 'few shall ever him transcend, as husband, parent, brother, master, friend'. Thereafter, Rivulet Cottage was used from time to time by retired Redcastle estate workers. For example, in 1920 Duncan Grant, a retired gardener, was in residence. His two sons had been drowned in a boating accident whilst visiting him in 1919. In August 1929, it was made available to William MacIntosh, the retired head teacher of the Killearnan school. He was known locally for his skill as a bone-setter and herbal therapist, who was visited by people from all over the Black Isle to have broken bones and various ailments treated. It is said that HRH Edward, Prince of Wales, also visited him during a private visit to Redcastle in 1931. William MacIntosh died in August 1936, whereupon the cottage became occupied by Capt Duncan Boyd, a retired Merchant Navy captain who was a recluse and remained there until 1951, when he died. Greenhill House also had several occupants in the inter-war years. In 1920, it was rented to Mrs Lizzie Gilroy, who was the widow of George Gilroy, a successful Edinburgh builder. She died in 1933, and the house was then rented by Lieut-Col Frederick Graham-Bissell until 1939, when Redcastle was taken over for military purposes and Baroness Burton relocated to Greenhill House.

By 1911, there had been only one remaining croft at Garguston Shore, the other being recorded in the Valuation Rolls as 'ruinous'. It had been in the Mackintosh family since the nineteenth century, and was currently worked by James Mackintosh, who had renovated the croft house in the 1920s. During the latter years of Rev. Aeneas Macdonald's tenure at Killearnan parish church (1890–1932), James had also been the parish church sexton and the tenant of the church glebe. He died in November 1937 and is buried in Killearnan churchyard. His son, Hugh, took over the tenancy of both the croft and the church glebe until he died in March 1973. Hugh's son, John, still works the croft and is the current Chairman of the Killearnan Community Council.

The four houses at Chapelton underwent considerable change after World War One. Both John Fraser, the carpenter, and James Robertson, the blacksmith, had wound up their businesses by 1925, and the workshops had been incorporated into the houses. They became occupied by a succession of different residents, for example, Madeline MacKay, Elizabeth MacDonald and Catherine MacLennan, who were all widows. One of the houses (subsequently known as Reay Cottage) was generally kept empty, as it was reserved for the use of Lady Burton's chauffeur when she was in residence at the castle (and, after World War Two, in Greenhill House).

Consolidation of the farms began to occur during the inter-war years. At the end of World War One, Garguston was owned by A O Stewart Spence, who also rented Whitewells. Both Fettes and Blairdhu were owned by Donald MacDonald, although Blairdhu was rented by Alexander MacLean. Parkton was owned by Donald MacLean, but both he and his wife, Anne, died in 1922. They are both buried in the family lair in Killearnan churchyard. The leasehold of the farm was taken over by their daughter, Annie. By 1921, Garguston had been sold to Ralph Stewart MacWilliam, and William Morrison had become the tenant of Blairdhu. A succession of farm managers and grieves were appointed to Redcastle Mains. They variously lived at the Mains, Greenhill House or at the other estate farms. The houses at Redcastle Mains were also occupied by estate workers, one of whom, Donald McDonnell, the gamekeeper, had moved in 1930 from Corgrain Cottage (and may have been its last occupant) to the 'Old Office'. Although he died in 1955, his family would remain in residence there until 1957.

It is interesting to note that by the end of World War One, James Baillie had sold the leaseholds of most of the larger local farms. He had also sold the two larger farms in the east of the estate, Lettoch and Coulmore. This is reflected in the annual valuation of the estate during the inter-war years. For example, in 1925 the remaining properties owned by the estate were valued[109] at £903-9-9d, representing only thirteen per cent of the total valuation of Killearnan parish. Fifty years earlier, in 1875, before any of the major properties had been sold, the Redcastle estate had accounted for fifty-nine per cent of the total valuation of the parish.

In 1932, an agricultural census was carried out by the Department of Agriculture in every parish in Scotland.[110] The data form a remarkable snapshot of the cultivated parts of Killearnan. There were a total of eighty-nine individual holdings (of which seventy-five were rented), providing employment for ninety-three persons (seventy-three male). There were 4,112 acres in cultivation, and 1,633 acres of rough grazings. Of the cultivated areas, the coverage was:

- Barley – 140 acres.
- Oats – 1,077 acres.
- Potatoes – 83 acres.
- Turnips/swedes – 560 acres.
- Rye grass – 2,017 acres.
- Permanent grass – 215 acres.
- Other crops (for example, peas/beans/carrots) – 11 acres.
- Fruit – ½ acre.

Of livestock, there were:

- 160 horses (127 working, 12 trap/saddle ponies).
- 1,262 cows (278 in milk, 99 with calf, 13 bulls in service).
- 1,902 sheep (790 ewes, 36 rams in service).
- 58 pigs (12 sows in milk, 1 boar in service).
- 3,616 poultry (3,220 hens, 318 ducks, 15 geese, 63 turkeys).

6.12 World War Two

Access to the Black Isle (and much of the rest of northern Scotland) was restricted during World War Two. Local residents were required to carry a 'Permit to Enter' and a 'Certificate of Residence in a Protected Area', which were issued by the police and had to be shown at the sentry points in Beauly and at the Kessock Ferry in order to gain access to the area. For example, John Fraser, the head gardener at Redcastle, carried Certificate number CR16258, issued on 9 March 1940 by Sgt D MacRae of Beauly. This certificate, together with his National Registration Identity Card and his National Insurance Card, is still in the possession of his family.[111]

As in other parts of the country, Redcastle's schoolchildren were required to carry gas masks to school. Food and clothes rationing were in force and every household was issued with ration and clothing coupon books, although allowances could be augmented by growing vegetables, keeping hens, catching rabbits and reknitting clothes from old wool. 'Knitting for Britain' was a common slogan amongst women, and many men joined the Home Guard. Because of the military presence, letters and telephone calls were censored.

Redcastle was requisitioned by the War Office for military purposes in 1939. Initially, it was used as a barracks by the 67th Light Infantry, but later it was taken over by the RAF, who used the estate grounds to store munitions. Bombs were transported by rail to Redcastle station and were loaded on lorries for the short trip down to the castle. The official capacity of Redcastle was 5,000 tons,[112] and it is said that 1,000-pound bombs lined the castle drive. A long tunnel-shaped building that still stands close by the eastern drive into the castle from Corgrain Point was constructed to store high explosives, such as gelignite (Figure 53). Photographs from that period show up to sixty men in residence.

In May 1939, the Killearnan kirk session was approached by John Graham, the school head teacher, requesting the use of the church at Redcastle Station as a temporary reception for children who might be evacuated in the event of war. There is no further record of this in the kirk session minutes, but some children from Glasgow were boarded out at Linnie and Tore. After the war, some of them were employed in the gardens at Redcastle and remained in the area until the mid-1950s. It is also recorded in the kirk session minutes that Rev. George Ballingall requested six months' leave 'to undertake work among the Forces of the Crown'. However, he seems never to have been called to undertake chaplaincy duties in the forces.

Figure 53: World War Two bomb store at Redcastle (2006)

Many of the families who had been tenants and occupiers of the estate-owned houses of Milton of Redcastle after World War One, remained there during and after World War Two. They included John MacDonald (who had taken over from Mary Mackenzie at the village shop), Donald Robertson (the blacksmith), Henrietta and Annie Laing (respectively, the widow of the second marriage and the daughter of Thomas Laing, the postman), Walter Ross (the carpenter) and Margaret MacLennan. The only house that was in private ownership was Inver, and it remained with the Ross family until 1960.

At Chapelton, two of the widows, Madeline MacKay and Elizabeth MacDonald, remained in occupation during World War Two. At various times they were joined by new temporary residents, one of whom was William Fraser, the estate head gamekeeper, who would move to Quarry Cottage in 1941. Two other long-term residents were Capt Duncan Boyd at Rivulet Cottage, and Catherine Noble at Manse Park (or Manse Cottage). She died in October 1950, and the house was taken over by William Thomson.

Donald MacDonald of Fettes Farm died in January 1941. He had lived in

Fettes since 1899, when his father had purchased the farm. He had also been a representative of Killearnan parish on many public bodies, including Killearnan School Board, Killearnan Parish Council and Black Isle District Committee. His family presented his family bible to the parish church, and the kirk session recorded that he had 'won the esteem of all who value goodness of life and the practice of righteousness'. An obelisk in Killearnan churchyard marks the family grave in which lie Donald, his father (Kenneth), his mother (Jessie) and other members of the family. In 1936, Donald had sold the leasehold of the farm back to the Redcastle estate, and it was advertised for rent in *The Scotsman* of 27 January 1937:

> To Let, with entry at Whitsunday (28th May) 1937, the well-known Farm of Fettes in the parish of Killearnan, extending to approximately 355 acres of first-class arable land. The farm is situated about half a mile from Redcastle Station. It is in a high state of cultivation and has for many years been in the occupation of the proprietor, Mr Donald MacDonald, who has sold the farm. The farmhouse is commodious, with every convenience, and there is an excellent steading. The boundaries will be pointed out by Mr D C McDonell, Overseer, Redcastle.

James and Kenneth Riggs were the successful applicants. Later that year, Annie MacLean of Parkton also died and this farm was also leased to the Riggs. Annie is commemorated on the family gravestone in Killearnan churchyard. The house that stands above Parkton Farm was built in 1941 and initially housed farm workers. In 1950, some of the Parkton Farm buildings were converted to a farmhouse, which was occupied by the grieve.

In 1941, the Redcastle estate head gamekeeper, William Fraser, and his wife, Eliza, moved into Quarry Cottage (west), which they named 'Tigh na Mara'. Eliza became the local Registrar of Births, Marriages and Deaths in 1945 and used the front room as her office. They had a son (who died in childhood) and four daughters, one of whom was a schoolteacher in North Kessock and was one of the last occupants of the Killearnan schoolhouse. She recalled once as a young girl seeing the local 'ghost', a black-clad female, whilst returning home at night along the shore road from Kessock Ferry to Redcastle. (Strangely, there are stories[113] of other nocturnal supernatural events along this road.) The occupant of the eastern 'but and ben' part of Quarry Cottage at that time was William ('Beel') MacAndrew, the brother of Christina and Margaret MacAndrew of Pier Cottage (east).

Somewhat surprisingly, it was not until February 1950 that it was proposed to inscribe 'the names of the fallen in the recent war' on the war memorial at Newton crossroads (Figure 54). The plaque, which contains six names, was unveiled in January 1951. One of these was James Gregor Riggs, the son of the Riggs family who were the tenant farmers at Fettes and Parkton. He was a RNVR commando attached to the Special Z Unit on HMS President, and died in action in Singapore aged twenty-one on 5 November 1944. He is buried at Kranji cemetery.[114]

Figure 54: The Killearnan war memorial at Newton crossroads (2008)

6.13 Post-war Redcastle

In 1947, Garguston Farm was purchased from Robert MacWilliam by William Wylie Martin. The 1947–48 register of the electors for Killearnan (or the 'Civilian Residence Register', as it was called) contains the names of 411 voters.[115] Of these, twenty-four were resident at Fettes Farm, twenty-two at Garguston Farm/Garguston Shore and eight at Redcastle Mains – showing that the three local farms were still major local employers (there were also a further three residents of Garguston Farm on the Services Register). In contrast, there were only sixteen voters at Milton of Redcastle (twenty-four in Redcastle itself; the Gardener's Cottage and the West Lodge are included), nine at Quarry of Redcastle and seven at Chapelton. These numbers had changed little by 1959–60, when 404 voters were registered in Killearnan, of whom twenty were resident at Fettes, eighteen at Garguston, fifteen at Milton of Redcastle and seven at Quarry of Redcastle. With Redcastle empty, Greenhill House now had eight resident voters, including Baroness Burton and her husband, William Melles.

It is of interest to note that the ten most common surnames in the electoral register at this time were: Mackenzie (9.6% of the entries), MacKay (5.4%), MacDonald (5.2%), Macleod (4.5%), Urquhart (4.2%), Fraser and Ross (3.0% each) and McRae, Mackintosh and Maclennan (2.2% each). These can be compared to the surnames on the list[116] of 263 men between the ages of fifteen and sixty years compiled in 1798, in which the ten most numerous were: Mackenzie (8.7%), MacDonald (8.0%), Noble (7.6%), McRae (5.3%), Young (4.9%), Fraser (4.2%), Maclennan (3.8%), Mackintosh and McIver (3.0% each) and MacKay (2.7%). Thus, over the 150 years following the end of the eighteenth century, surnames that have become more common include Mackenzie, MacKay, Macleod, Urquhart and Ross. Many previously common surnames in the parish that have substantially declined include Bisset, Fraser, Glass, Logan, MacDonald, MacFarquhar, McIver, MacKay, Mackintosh, Maclennan, McRae, Noble and Young.

An insight into the post-war improvements that were rapidly overtaking the parish can be found in the Killearnan chapter of the Third Statistical Account of Scotland,[117] written by Rev. George Ballingall in 1955. There had been continued mechanisation and consolidation of the farms by absorbing the old crofts. Tractors were now much more common than horses, with the consequence that the blacksmiths at Chapelton and Milton of Redcastle were no longer in business (the only smithy still working was at Tore). The main crops were now oats, potatoes, turnips and barley in a six-year rotation cycle with grass. The fattening of beef cattle had supplanted dairy cattle, as milk was now delivered in bottles. Commuting to work or school in Muir of Ord,

Beauly or Dingwall was now common. Mains electricity had arrived in 1952, and the telephone box at Milton of Redcastle was installed in 1953. Of the local businesses, only Ian MacDonald's shop at Milton of Redcastle was still open, and it was in competition with motor vans that were 'very convenient to country people as they deliver butcher meat, bread and groceries to their doors'.

Referring to housing conditions, Rev. Ballingall remarks that 'the old single or double-burner paraffin lamps are hardly ever seen now, as most houses have an electricity supply', and that 'there are only two or three houses left with roofs of straw thatch'. One of these was Garden Cottage at Quarry of Redcastle. He also remarks that 'the old-fashioned but-and-ben with small windows and a water supply consisting of an outside pipe or well are becoming fewer and fewer, although there are still too many lacking a proper water supply'. This was a further reference to Quarry of Redcastle. Both Quarry House and Quarry Cottage (named Tigh na Mara at the time) had wells in their front gardens, but water from these was used only for washing. The steps down to the well at Quarry House are still visible. There is also a well in the back garden. For cooking and drinking, water was carried from the spring in the quarry. Mains water did not become available in the hamlet until 1959, apparently as a consequence of a drought in the summer of 1955 during which all the wells dried up (with the exception of the spring close to the Redcastle burn, which had supplied water to the castle).

The confusion arising from the lack of numbering or naming of the houses of Redcastle began to be resolved in the later years of the twentieth century, when, for the first time, Milton of Redcastle and Chapelton were separately identified in the Valuation Rolls for 1955–56. (Quarry of Redcastle had always been separately identified and until 1955 had included Chapelton.) In Milton of Redcastle, the houses of the lower row became individually identified (from east to west) as 'Smithy House No. 1 Milton', and Nos. 2, 3 and 4 Milton. Smithy House was occupied by Donald and Margaret MacKenzie, and No. 4 Milton by Donald MacLean, a forester. Nos. 2 and 3 Milton were being rebuilt in 1955–56, and were described as 'under construction'. This was not popular amongst the owners of the houses of the upper row, because the old cottages of the lower row had been single-storey. Now they were to be two storeys high and would block out the view of Redcastle Bay.

By 1969, Milton No. 4 had become uninhabited and some of the remains of its walls are still visible today. In the upper row, the westernmost house was named Inver (later renamed Ashgrove) and remained in the ownership of George Forbes, whilst the shop (later named Rosemount) had become owned by Ian MacDonald. The middle house (later named Corrie Cottage) was still occupied by Annie and Thomas Laing. Thomas, in his father's footsteps, was also a postman. He was a tall, upright man, who had served in the Guards and was well known as the local football referee. Before World War Two, some occupants of the castle used to refer to the two rows of houses in Milton of Redcastle (Figure 55) as 'Regent Street' and 'Oxford Street', but the local residents referred to the upper row as 'Princes Street' and the lower row as 'Poverty Row', reflecting their respective private and estate ownership!

Figure 55: Milton of Redcastle, with 'Regent Street' on the left and 'Oxford Street' on the right (2006)

In the years after World War Two, Redcastle Mains acted as the local social centre where concerts and film shows were held. In 1955–56, the Redcastle farm manager resided at Rivulet Cottage, and there were foresters in the Gardener's Cottage and in the 'Old Office' at Redcastle Mains. For the rest of the century, they and the West Lodge would generally be occupied either by estate staff or rented out. One person who was a local notoriety was Miss Augusta Mary Bruce, who lived at Redcastle Mains. She was the daughter of Thomas Charles Bruce MP, and had been one of Baroness Burton's ten bridesmaids in 1894. She was regularly to be seen travelling around the area in her pony and trap. She died aged seventy-eight in December 1949, and her trap is still garaged at Redcastle Mains.

Another well-known personality was Donald McDonell, who had lived in the 'Old Office' since 1930, and had risen from gamekeeper and forester to estate manager. His wife was a nanny to the Baillie family and his daughter,

Frances (always known as Ada), had been born in the castle, attended Killearnan Public School (fourth from the right in the top row of pupils in Figure 30, page 226) and became the Baroness's personal secretary. Donald died in October 1955 at the age of eighty-three, and Ada later moved to the Dochfour estate, where, in retirement, she was engaged in archiving the Baillie family papers. She died in April 2007.

The two easternmost cottages at Chapelton, one of which had been the smithy, became named 'Tigh na Fhuaran' and 'Springwell Cottage'. However, by 1969 they were never again to be occupied and were demolished in 1972. Only some remnants of the walls are now visible. The other two houses at Chapelton had become named 'Reay House' and 'Reay Cottage' (which, until 1962, was reserved for Baroness Burton's chauffeur). By 1967, Reay Cottage was occupied by Ronald and Margaret MacKenzie, but it too was demolished after they relocated in 1972 to the Smithy House (No. 1 Milton of Redcastle). Reay House is now named 'Corran Cottage' and is the only remaining house in Chapelton.

Rev. Dr Lewis Sutherland and his wife, Jean, purchased Quarry House in 1954 and converted it into a single dwelling house. However, Dr Sutherland died whilst on holiday in Redcastle in July of that year, and in 1963 Jean sold the house to Clotilde Buchanan (known as 'Cloey'). Cloey was the daughter of Col Arthur Buchanan OBE, the Coalition Unionist MP for Coatbridge from 1918 to 1922 and a descendant of the Buchanan whisky family.[118] There is a portrait of Cloey, painted by her friend Elizabeth Cameron of Allangrange in 1951. She lived in Quarry House for almost fifty years, helping to create Black Isle Frozen Foods Ltd at Allangrange, until she died in May 2005. The subsequent sales particulars described the house as 'a delightful family house situated in a truly idyllic position ... in the charming rural hamlet of Redcastle'.

By the mid-1950s, the condition of the other houses at Quarry of Redcastle was deteriorating. In 1955, William Fraser retired as head gamekeeper (Figure 56), and the family vacated Tigh na Mara (Quarry Cottage). His assistant (Jack Fraser, no relation) took over the lease. In 1956, the thatched roof of Garden Cottage (No. 3 Quarry Cottages) collapsed, and by 1960 it was described in the Valuation Rolls as 'ruinous'. It was purchased and totally demolished in preparation for a new house, but this was never built. Some of the stone was probably used to build garden walls in the neighbouring properties. Similarly, Sunny Croft (Pier Cottage) had fallen into disuse, and by 1965 was described in the Valuation Rolls as 'uninhabitable'.

Figure 56: The Fraser family at Quarry of Redcastle circa 1950 (reproduced from an original with permission from Lilian Campbell)

With no further need for the 'Quarry Cottages', Redcastle estate sold the freeholds in 1977–78 to private purchasers, who carried out major renovations and modernisations that radically changed the character of the hamlet from a 'working village' into the row of three secluded residences that now remain. In his postscript to the Third Statistical Account of Scotland[119] written in 1982, D P Willis observed that 'croft houses and cottages are now occupied by newcomers to the area ... who travel to work outwith the parish'. This was certainly true of the new residents of the hamlet of Quarry of Redcastle. The Kessock Bridge was opened in 1982, halving the road distance from Redcastle to Inverness.

The almost derelict bothy of Quarry Cottage (east) and the two-storey house Tigh na Mara (referred to as Nos. 4 and 5 Quarry Cottages) were linked internally, thus creating the single property now known as Quarry Cottage. The author of this book and his wife are the current owners. Pier Cottage (east) and Sunny Croft (referred to as Nos. 1 and 2 Quarry Cottages) were also linked internally, thus creating a single property that was then named 'Larchtree House'. In 1983, it was resold and renamed Pier Cottage, reflecting its position at the base of the Redcastle pier. The new owner, Kitty MacDuff-Duncan, gained some local fame for hand-rearing a young heron (known as 'Herbie'). For seven years, Herbie could be seen every morning standing on the road outside one of the houses, patiently waiting to be fed with fresh fish or, more usually, tinned sardines. He (it was always assumed that Herbie was male) was last seen in 2003. In 1997, Pier Cottage was purchased by its present owners and until 2004 was offered for holiday lettings. Among the many visitors who rented it during 1999–2003 were members of the Chisholm family from Australia. Alice Chisholm, almost eighty years old, was the daughter of Ann Noble and had lived in Quarry Cottage as a young girl in the 1920s.

On the Redcastle estate, Greenhill House, the West Lodge and the Gardener's Cottage remain in good condition and are leased. One house at Redcastle Mains is now named Clocktower Cottage (although the clock is not working), and the others have either become stores or offices of the Redcastle Farming Partnership. The farm buildings at Parkton are becoming derelict but are used for storage, whilst the surrounds, like the old greenhouse area below Redcastle gardens, are used for pheasant-rearing. The locations of the mill pond, sluice gate and water wheel at Parkton are still clearly visible.

The twentieth century witnessed a huge reduction in the population of Redcastle, reflected in the decline of the Killearnan population, reaching 500 in 1971. The consequence was that several houses became unoccupied or ruinous, including: Corgrain Cottage; the Redcastle Smithy; No. 4 cottage of the lower row at Milton of Redcastle; the (unnamed) westernmost house of the upper row at Milton of Redcastle; Garden Cottage at Quarry of Redcastle; and three cottages at Chapelton. Two currently unoccupied houses that could still be renovated are the schoolteacher's house and the new farmhouse at Parkton, built during World War Two to house landworkers.

However, the story of Redcastle's buildings during the twentieth century is not one of complete decline. Some new buildings were built in the latter half of the century. In 1955, six houses were built by Ross and Cromarty County Council at Garguston Shore Road. They are numbered 3 to 8, because numbers 1 and 2 were never built. The original thatched Manse Park (or Manse Cottage) was demolished in 1970, and the private house now known as Woodlands was built on the site – although a little to the east, to allow improved access into the manse steading, which was converted to the house now known as Finlaggan in 1985. The new manse, built in 1986 after the old manse was sold to its present owners, is now named Killearnan Brae, and the old manse is named Killearnan House. The new parish church hall was opened in 1993, and the three most recent private houses to be built are Peediequoy (at Newton crossroads), Killearnan Lodge (west of the parish church) and The Shore House (at Garguston Shore, close by the pump-house that once pumped water to Garguston Farm), completed in 2008.

The consequence of these developments is that the population of the civil parish of Killearnan is now growing again. In the 1981 census, the population was recorded as 559, and in 2001 it was 602.[120] It is hard to imagine that 160 years previously, in 1841, the population had peaked at 1,644. In July 2008, there were only twenty-one residences listed in the IV6 7SQ postcode area[121] and the resident population was around forty. In the 1841 census, 157 residents were recorded!

NOTES

[1] See Chapter 1, note 3.

[2] The original map of '14th century Britain' is known as the 'Gough' map. It was purchased by Richard Gough in 1774 and is now part of the Bodleian Library (Oxford) collection. The Scottish section is reproduced in Hume-Brown, H, 'Early Travellers in Scotland' (1891). Both this map and the twelfth-century map published in Bain (see Chapter 1, note 3) can be viewed at www.ambaile.org.uk.

[3] The surviving sixteenth-century maps of Timothy Pont have been fully researched and indexed by the NLS and can be viewed at www.nls.uk/pont. The map of the Ardmeanach has not survived, although those of Easter Ross (map G20), Inverness and the Great Glen (map 5) and Moray and Nairn (map 8) have survived.

[4] Early maps on which Redcastle is marked incorrectly include those of: Mercator, G, 'Scotiae Regnum' (1595); Speed, J, 'The Kingdom of Scotland' (1610); and Gordon, R, 'Part of Ross' (1636–52).

[5] The earliest map to place Redcastle correctly is 'Scotia Australis' (1618), engraved by Solomon Rogiers after a survey by John Speed. This map can be viewed at www.vintage-graphics.com. The remarkable maps of Jean Blaeu, originally published in 'Theatrum Orbis Terrarum Sive Atlas Novus, pars quinta' (1654), have been published by the NLS as the 'Blaeu Atlas of Scotland' (2006). Redcastle is located correctly on map 35 'Extima Scotiae' and map 36 'Moravia Scotiae Provincia', but incorrectly on map 2 'Scotia Regnum'.

[6] Eighteenth-century maps that locate Redcastle include: Avery, J, 'Plan of the Murray Firth' (1725–30) and 'Plan containing Lochness, Lochoych, Lochlochey and all the rivers and strips of water that runs in and set out from the same' (1727); Keulen, G van, 'Afteckening de Noord Oost hock van Schotland' (1727–34); Wade, G, 'Plan of Murray Firth and Cromarty Firth' (1730); Moll, H, 'The Shires of Ross and Cromartie' (1745); Ainslie, J, 'A Chart of part of the North of Scotland' (1785). These maps can all be viewed at www.chartingthenation.lib.ed.ac.uk or at www.nls.uk/maps. Avery's 'Plan of the Murray Firth' (1725–30) was prepared for the York Building Company, the role of which after the 1715 Jacobite rebellion is reviewed in Millar, A H (ed.), 'A Selection of the Scottish Forfeited Estates Papers 1715; 1745' in *Scottish Hist. Soc.*, Vol LVII, pages xxxiii–xxxviii (1909).

[7] After the Battle of Culloden, James Alexander Grante produced a map entitled *Carte ou sont traces toutes les differentes routes, que S A R Charles Edward Prince de Galles, a suivies dans la Grande Bretagne*. It was published in 1747 and marks 'Red Castle' as the only feature on the Black Isle.

[8] High-resolution digital images of the Roy, W, 'Military Survey of Scotland (1747–55)' can be viewed at www.nls.uk/maps/roy, and also at HCRL using the website of the Scran Trust, www.scran.ac.uk. Redcastle and the surrounding area is located on maps 26/2a and 2d.

[9] See Chapter 1, note 58.

[10] See Chapter 5, note 14.

[11] See Chapter 5, note 15.

[12] See Chapter 5, note 15.

[13] See Chapter 1, note 125.

[14] The extract from a document by William Logan of Canada was provided to the author in a private communication from Mr John MacDonald of Kilmuir.

[15] The First Edition (or 'County Series') Ordnance Survey of Scotland Ross and Cromarty maps (surveyed 1872–73) were published in 1880–81. Two sheets (XCIX and C) of the 1:10,000 (*circa* 6 inch:1 mile) map cover the Redcastle area. Fourteen sheets (LXXXVIII 13 and 16; XCIX 3, 4, 7, 8 and 12; and C 1, 5, 6, 7, 9, 10 and 11) of the 1:2,500 (*circa* 25 inch:1 mile) map cover Killearnan parish, of which XCIX 8 and 12, and C 5 and 9 cover the Redcastle area. The complete set is available for view at the NLS Map Library, Edinburgh. Only the 1:10,000 maps can be viewed at HCA in Inverness. These are also available online at www.british-history.ac.uk and www.old-maps.co.uk.

[16] The Ordnance Survey of Scotland, Parish of Killearnan reference index book to the 1:2,500 First Edition sheets (surveyed 1872–73) is available in the NLS Map Library, Edinburgh.

[17] See Chapter 4, note 2.

[18] A brief history of the Ross-shire Rifle Volunteers is given in Fairrie, Lieut-Col A, 'Cuidich 'n Righ, A History of the Queen's Own Highlanders (Seaforth and Camerons)', page 39 (1983).

[19] See Chapter 5, note 41.

[20] See note 16.

[21] See Chapter 4, note 31.

[22] See Chapter 1, note 125.

[23] The Ordnance Survey of Scotland second edition maps (surveyed in 1904) are revisions of the original 1872 survey. They were published in 1905–07. As in the First Edition, two sheets of the 1:10,000 (*circa* 6 inch:1 mile) map and fourteen sheets of the 1:2,500 (*circa* 25 inch:1 mile) map cover Killearnan parish (see note 15 for sheet identification numbers). They are available for view at the NLS Map Library, Edinburgh or at HCA. The 1:10,000 maps are also available online at www.british-history.ac.uk and www.old-maps.co.uk.

[24] See Chapter 1, note 120.

[25] See Chapter 2, note 40.

[26] See notes 23 and 15.

[27] See Chapter 5, notes 14 and 15.

[28] The UK-wide Land Utilisation Survey was carried out in 1930–38 under the leadership of Professor Dudley Stamp of the London School of Economics. The Redcastle area was surveyed by the Drumsmittal School in January–June 1932. The survey was published in 1948 (with later editions in 1950 and 1962) under the title of 'The Land of Britain – its Use and Misuse' and the data was transferred onto hand-coloured 1 inch:1 mile (1:63,360) maps. The maps are available at www.visionofbritain.org.uk/maps.

[29] The principal larger-scale Ordnance Survey maps of the Redcastle area published in the mid-twentieth century are: the Provisional Edition 1:25,000 (circa 2.5 inch:1 mile) sheets 28/54 (1950) and NH55 (1961); the 1:25,000 sheet NH54NE (1959 and 1972); and the 1:2,500 (circa 25 inch:1 mile) sheet NH 5649–5749 (1971). Metric revisions of previous NH54 and NH55 sheets were later published at a scale of 10 cm:1 km (1·10,000). They are known as NH54NE (1994) and NH55SE (1992).

[30] There was no 'Third Edition' survey of Ross and Cromarty undertaken by the Ordnance Survey of Scotland. The 1 inch:1 mile map that covers the Redcastle area is Sheet 27 (1929).

[31] See note 30.

[32] See note 29.

[33] The current Ordnance Survey maps of the area are the 1:50,000 'Landranger' sheet 26 (revised 1995) and the 1:25,000 'Explorer' sheet No. 432 (revised 2002). Digital images of these maps are available online using the 'getamap' facility at www.ordnancesurvey.co.uk and at www.multimap.com, although the latter cannot generate the Redcastle area at high definition. The Landplan facility is available to registered businesses through subscription and printouts can be obtained at OS-approved outlets, such as HMSO offices.

[34] See note 33.

[35] Satellite images of the Redcastle area can be downloaded from various sources, including Virtual Earth from http://local.live.com and http://maps.live.com, Google Maps from http://maps.google.co.uk and the Ordnance Survey from http://www1.getmapping.com. At present, the sharpest image of the Redcastle area at high resolution is from Virtual Earth.

[36] For example, aerial photographs of the western portion of Killearnan are downloadable from www.garywilliamson.co.uk and www.flickr.com/photos/upnorth.

[37] The reference to the medieval human sacrifice in Redcastle is given in Grant, I F, 'Highland Folk Ways', page 5 (2003).

[38] The story of the seventeenth-century sacrifice of a tramp at Redcastle is told by the editor (Alexander Mackenzie) in 'The Celtic Magazine', Vol 2, pages 92–3 and 261–3 (1872) and in Mackenzie, A, 'The Prophecies of the Brahan Seer', pages 57–9 (1970).

[39] The alleged murder of Kenneth MacKenzie by the Black Calder at Kilcoy is described in 'Kilcoy Castle', Trans. Inverness Sci. Soc. and Field Club, 2, 238–240 (1882).

[40] Rev. Aeneas Macdonald's 'Killearnan Collection of Gaelic Poetry' forms parts 132–135 of the Carmichael-Watson Collection deposited in the University of Edinburgh Library. The story of the murder of Archibald MacDonald is told in the introduction to song no. 94. Some other miscellaneous poems and letters of Gaelic interest collected by Rev. Macdonald of Killearnan are held in NLS MS3781–4.

[41] The warrant of transmission for trial against Elizabeth MacKenzie is at HCA L/INV/HC14/12/2. The transcripts of the trial of Kenneth MacDonald and Elizabeth MacKenzie in 1749 are contained in the North Circuit Books Nos. 10 and 11 (NAS JC11/13 and 14). The warrant of commitment and death sentence against Kenneth MacDonald is recorded at HCA L/INV/HC12/5.

[42] The banishment of Elizabeth Mackenzie is listed in Dobson, D, 'Directory of Scots banished to the American Plantations 1650–1775' (1984), but no information on the ship or place of embarkation is given. The banishment is also recorded in 'The Scots Magazine', Vol 11, page 509 (1749).

[43] The warrant of commitment and trial papers relating to the sentence of imprisonment of the 'Wild Women of Redcastle' in 1816 are held at HCA L/INV/HC/9/38 and HCA L/INV/HC/10/33.

[44] The transcript of the trial of John and Donald Fraser is available in the 'Solemn Database' at NAS JC11/67, pp24r. Other process papers are available at HCA L/INV/HC/9/49/5.

[45] See Chapter 1, note 140.

[46] Papers referring to the horning of John Campbell of Spital, Redcastle by the British Linen Bank in 1823–4 are held in HCA L/INV/SC/17/13.

[47] The murder notice and other papers relating to the murder of Jean Brechin and the trial of John Adam (1835) are collected at NAS JC26/1835/126 and NAS AD14/35/19. I am indebted to Alasdair Cameron of Wellhouse for sight of the 'Sketch of the Site of Ground about the House in which the Dead Body of Jane Brechin was found on the 10th April 1835', which is not contained in the NAS papers. The execution is recorded in Young, A F, 'The Encyclopaedia of Scottish Executions, 1750–1963', page 111 (1998).

[48] See Chapter 1, note 120.

[49] The precognition papers relating to the murder of James McLeod by his mother, Jane Bain, are held in the records of the Crown Office at NAS AD14/90/18, and the trial and case papers are held in the papers of the High Court of Judiciary (1890) at NAS JC 11/113 (pages 43–5); JC15/1 (pages 186–7); and JC26/1890/213.

[50] See Chapter 1, note 120.

[51] See Chapter 2, note 16.

[52] See Chapter 2, note 17.

[53] See Chapter 2, note 24.

[54] See Chapter 2, note 25.

[55] See Chapter 5, note 8.

[56] The first census of the population of Scotland is recorded in Webster, Rev. A, 'An Account of the Ecclesiastical Benefices, the Patrons of Several Parishes and the Number of People in Scotland' (1755) and is available at NLS MS89 and NLS

AdvMS35.1.9. The original documentation for Killearnan parish has not survived, but the transcribed data is given on pages 72 and 188 of NLS MS89.

[57] See Chapter 1, note 105.

[58] The list of all male inhabitants residing in the parish of Killearnan between the ages of fifteen and sixty years was prepared (probably by Rev. David Denoon) for the Earl of Seaforth, Lord Lieut of Ross, and is held at NAS GD46/6/45(12). It is dated 3 March 1798 and was requested by the Home Secretary as a preliminary to the creation of the Ross-shire Volunteers. It contains the names, places of residence and occupations of 263 men.

[59] See Chapter 1, note 132.

[60] The handwritten pages of the Enumeration Books of the National Decennial Censuses for Killearnan parish (1841–1901) have been transferred to microfilm and can be viewed at HCRL. They have also been scanned electronically and can be accessed through the subscription service at www.scotlandspeople.gov.uk.

[61] The Court of Session papers recording the bankruptcy of Alexander Fraser and Co. of Milton of Redcastle in January 1845 are held at NAS CS280/31/14.

[62] See Chapter 1, note 14.

[63] See Chapter 1, note 30.

[64] See Chapter 1, notes 144 and 152.

[65] A brief biography of William Dick (1838–1910), who was brought up at Parkton, and a history of Macrae and Dick (founded 1878) can be found at www.macraeanddick.co.uk/history.

[66] See Chapter 1, note 120.

[67] See Chapter 2, note 65.

[68] See Chapter 1, note 125.

[69] See Chapter 1, note 112.

[70] See note 60.

[71] See Chapter 1, note 120.

[72] See note 60.

[73] The sequestration and bankruptcy papers (1863) of William Smith, blacksmith in Redcastle, are contained in NAS CS318/8/366. They contain a detailed inventory of his assets, creditors and debtors.

[74] Listings of Killearnan businesses and other commercial enterprises are given in Slater, I, 'Royal National Commercial Directory and Topography of Scotland', pages 1452–55 (1867). The 1860 edition does not list any Killearnan businesses.

[75] The fire at Whitewells Farm in 1866 and the unsuccessful claim for suspension of rent by the tenant, William Ross, against Henry James Baillie of Redcastle is documented at NAS CS275/29/109.

[76] See Chapter 2, note 55.

[77] The life of Farquhar MacLennan is described in 'Fearchair-a-Ghunna, The Ross-shire Wanderer' (1995, reprinted in 2004). The original version of this monograph was published in 'Varia Celtica' under the title of 'Fearchair-a-Ghunna, The Ross-shire Wanderer: his Life and Sayings' by the Author of 'The Maid of Fairburn etc.' (1881), held in AUSLA SB089a1. A 1908 version is also held in the Queen Mother Library of

Aberdeen University. Farquhar's family tree is charted in MacDonald, M A, 'By the Banks of the Ness – Tales of Inverness and District', page 92 (1982). A photograph of Farquhar can be seen at www.ambaile.org.uk. The original photograph is part of the Cook collection in the Highland Photographic Archive, Inverness.

[78] See Chapter 1, note 4.

[79] See note 60.

[80] See Chapter 5, note 33.

[81] See Chapter 1, note 135.

[82] See Chapter 1, note 112.

[83] Details of the sequestration and bankruptcy in 1879–81 of the complex business affairs of James McKenzie Alison of Greenhill (ship owner, commission agent and previously factor of Redcastle estate) are given in NAS CS318/25/7.

[84] See note 60.

[85] The Killearnan Parish Church Marriage Proclamation Register (1890–1935) is available digitally at NAS CH2/918/3.

[86] See note 60.

[87] See Chapter 2, note 40.

[88] See note 60.

[89] See Chapter 1, note 141.

[90] A collection of the seventeen applications, with references and testimonials, for the post of gamekeeper at Redcastle estate, advertised in the *Inverness Courier* on 2 May 1890, is held at NAS GD176/2475. James Grant of Elgin was the successful candidate.

[91] See note 60.

[92] See Chapter 1, note 135.

[93] See Chapter 5, note 22.

[94] See Chapter 1, note 160.

[95] See Chapter 1, note 161.

[96] The Killearnan entries in Slater's Directory, Ross and Cromarty can be found on page 1262 (1911).

[97] The life of Sandy 'Kinkell' Mackenzie and his parents (who ran the shop in Milton of Redcastle) is described in an article entitled 'My Coat is all Wool' by Frances Macleod, published in the Clan Mackenzie Magazine (2008).

[98] A useful introductory account and listings of surviving early electoral registers is given in Gibson, J, 'Electoral Registers and Burgess Rolls 1832–1948' (2008). The earliest surviving Register of Electors for Ross and Cromarty covers 1913–14 and is available at HCA C309. Names are listed alphabetically. Registers from 1946 onwards are available at NLS.

[99] See Chapter 1, note 120.

[100] See Chapter 1, note 162.

[101] See Chapter 5, note 24.

[102] See Chapter 5, note 23.

[103] See Chapter 3, note 20.

[104] See note 74.

[105] The Killearnan Parish Church Baptismal Register (1903–37) is available digitally at NAS CH2/918/3.

[106] Newton, N.S., 'Inverness, Highland Town to Millennium City', page 91 (2003).

[107] The names of men from Killearnan parish killed whilst serving in the military during World War One and World War Two are recorded on the Killearnan War Memorial at Newton (Fettes) crossroads. Most are also recorded by the Commonwealth War Graves Commission on the searchable website www.cwgc.org. Several are also recorded on graves in the Killearnan parish church graveyard (see Chapter 2, note 11).

[108] See Chapter 2, note 40.

[109] See Chapter 4, note 31.

[110] The agricultural survey of Killearnan parish carried out in 1932 by the Department of Agriculture is held at NAS AF40/21/39. For the eighty-nine individual holdings, it contains aggregated data on the total acreage of each crop, the numbers of livestock, and the numbers of persons employed.

[111] See Chapter 1, note 166.

[112] The use of the Redcastle estate as an ammunition dump is described in www.ww2inthehighlands.co.uk, a website developed by Cauldeen Primary School in Inverness.

[113] See Chapter 1, note 15.

[114] See note 107.

[115] See note 98.

[116] See note 58.

[117] See Chapter 1, note 167.

[118] The career of Col Arthur Buchanan MP is recorded in 'Who's Who of British Members of Parliament, Vol III (1919–45)' published by Stenton and Lees (1979).

[119] See Chapter 1, note 167.

[120] The population of Killearnan civil parish in the 2001 census is recorded at www.scrol.gov.uk.

[121] The twenty-one house names and addresses within the postcode area IV6 7SQ can be viewed at www.royalmail.com.

Index

A

B

Blaeu, Jean, 291, 364

Blairdhu, 15, 68–70, 96, 98, 101, 146–7, 149, 187, 190, 250, 257–8, 268, 270–1, 273, 279, 294, 296, 299, 301, 304, 306, 310, 315–6, 322, 324, 328, 331, 337, 341, 344, 353

Blundell, Rev. Odo, 20, 110, 246

Bois, Andrew de, 25

Bolster, Rev. Richard, 193, 196–8

Bosco, Andro de, 24, 112, 127, 255

Braes of Garguston, 15

Brahan Seer, 305, 366

British Library, 7

Brown, Rev. Susan, 197–200

Bruce, Augusta, 107, 360

Bruce, Robert the, 26, 85, 112

Buchanan, Clotilde, 279, 361

Burgh of Barony, 34, 65, 78, 114

Burn, William, 86–7, 108, 122, 252, 319

Burntown, 15, 68–70, 147, 149, 151, 257–8, 261–2, 293, 296, 315

Burton Property Trust, 109

Burton, Baroness, 102, 104–5, 107, 124, 230, 280–1, 349, 352, 358, 360, 361

Burton, Lord, 99, 192, 279, 349

Butter, Patrick, 213, 215, 232

C

Cairnurenan, 315–6, 320

Caledonian Canal, 70–2, 81, 176, **237–44**, 245, 247–8, 250, 252–4, 262, 297, 300, 328

Caledonian Canal Commissioners, 82, **237–8**, 240, 242–4, 248, 253

Cameron, Duncan, 271, 324, 332–3

Cameron, Elizabeth, 361

Cameron, Mary, 229

Cameron, Rev. Alexander, 103, 181–2, 227

Cameron, Rev. Hector, 194–5

Campbell, Alexander, 174, 323–4

Campbell, Andrew, 328

Campbell, Rev. Patrick, 177

Campbell's Farewell to Redcastle, 177, 203

Carmichael, Rev. Dan, 199–200

Carn Dubh, 20, 246

Carn Glas, 18–19, 110

Carn Irenan, 19, 65, 125, 201

Carron Cottage, 303, 361

censuses, 84, 95, 101, 173, 178, 215, 246–7, 249–50, 269–70, 274, **315–25**, **327–339**, 340–41, 364, 367–8, 370

cess, 120, 257–8, 260

Chanonry, 29, 113, 177, 234, 263

Chapelton, 15, 23, 68–9, 98, 101, 111, 126, 137, 146–9, 151, 154, 236, 257–9, 264, 275–6, 278, 280–2, 286, 293–4, 296, 298, 303–4, 315, 319, 323–4, 328, 332, 335–7, 343–4, 352, 355, 358–9, 361, 363

Charles I, 31

Charles II, 31, 33–4, 144

chicken pox, 224

Christmas day, 73, 85, 223

Church of Scotland, 98, 132, 139–40, 154, 169–71, 176–8, 182–3, 189, 191, 197, 202–3, 206, 209, 227, 269, 326, 328, 335

Clachnaharry, 237–42, 246, 248, 253

Clocktower Cottage, 363

Commissioners for Highland Roads and Bridges, **261–8**, 287

Commissioners of Supply, 68, 74, 93–4, 120, 123, 155, 207, 221, **257–61**, 262, 268–9, 271, 322

communion season, 157–8, 203, 223, 237

communion tokens, 158, 171, 203

communion vessels, 157, 192, 197

Compulsory Officer, 222, 224

Constantinople (Istanbul), 57–9, 118

COPAC, 8

Corbet, John, 213, 215

Corgrain, 13, 15, 68, 78, 81, 257–8, 296, 315

O

Old Bailey, 52–3
Old Parish Registers, 38, 42, 146–8, 178, 202, 236, 241, 246, 313, 321, 325
Old Pretender, 138, 151
Ordnance Survey, 101, 123, 187, 215, 229, 234, 250, 252, 272, 284, **296–305**, 340, 365–6
Ormond, 26–7
Oyer and Terminer, 52, 118

P

Papal Bull, 24, 126
Parkton, 15, 68, 92, 98, 104, 106, 258, 264, 268, 270, 276, 293–4, 296, 298, 303–5, 317, 322, 324, 332, 335, 337, 341, 343–4, 348, 353, 356–7, 363, 368
patronage, 126, 134, 163, 169, 179
Pecks, 15, 68–9, 154, 306–7, 315
Peel, Sir Robert, 87, 268
Pier Cottage, 247, 276, 321, 327–8, 331, 334, 341, 350, 356, 361–2
piracy, 55
Pitlundie, 41, 115
poll tax, 254, 257, 284
Pont, Timothy, 290–1, 364
post office, 191, 282, 304, 322, 345–6
potato famine, **268–9**, 320
Presbytery of Chanonry, **132–46**, 150–1, 153–6, 159, 161–70, 176–7, 183–7, 189, 191, 193–8, 201–4, 206–9, 211–3, 215, 261, 313
Presbytery of Dingwall, 129, 132–4, 142, 191, 201, 206, 313
Presbytery visitation, 140–2, 144, 146, 160–1, 165–6, 196, 207, 210
Prescaltin, 176, 250, 258, 310
Prince Charles Edward Stuart, 148, 154, 202, 292
Privy Council, 29, 113, 142, 205
Proudfoot, John, 309
Ptolemy, Claudius, 22, 111

Q

Quarry Cottage, 7, 101, 221, 224, 245, 247, 281, 321, 327, 336, 341, 344, 346, 350, 355–6, 359, 361–2
Quarry House, 96, 247, 279, 305, 321, 327, 330, 333–4, 340, 346, 351, 359, 361
Quarry of Redcastle, 7, 14–5, 78, 82–3, 96, 98, 172–4, 176, 178, 180, 182, 187, 216, 218, 221, 241, 244–5, 247, 249–51, 271, 276, 278–9, 280, 284, 286, 295, 297, 300–5, 315–6, 318, 320–5, 327–8, 331, 333, 335–6, 340, 341, 346, 350, 358–9, 361–3

R

RAF, 354
Ramsar site, 286, 289
Ramsden, Rev. Iain, 200
RCAHMS, 7, 10, 18–9, 35, 104, 109–11, 122, 124, 204, 286, 289, 294
Reay Cottage, 303, 352, 361
Reay House, 303, 361
Redcastle bay, 66, 219, 359
Redcastle burn, 72, 104, 106, 109, 126, 276, 286, 293–4, 298, 317, 359
Redcastle church, 193–7
Redcastle crannog, 20–1, 65, 110, 125, 286, 296, 303
Redcastle Farming Partnership, 363
Redcastle inn, 171, 174, 298, 300, 316, 324, 330, 332
Redcastle Mains, 15, 60, 68, 70, 92, 98, 102, 109, 178, 182, 270, 276, 279, 286, 298, 304, 317, 322, 325, 329, 335, 337, 341–2, 353, 358, 360, 363
Redcastle market, 68, 79–80, 122
Redcastle mill, 41, 69, 71, 256, 286, 293, 298–9, 317, 340
Redcastle pier, 74, 98, 172, 234–6, 238–41, 244–6, 248, 250, 252, 286, 294–5, 300, 345, 363

Lightning Source UK Ltd.
Milton Keynes UK
28 August 2009

143162UK00002B/25/P